ALSO BY JOAN NATHAN

Quiches, Kugels, and Couscous

Joan Nathan's Jewish Holiday Cookbook (revised)

The New American Cooking

The Foods of Israel Today

Jewish Cooking in America, Expanded Edition

The Jewish Holiday Baker

Jewish Cooking in America

The Jewish Holiday Kitchen

The Children's Jewish Holiday Kitchen

An American Folklife Cookbook

The Flavor of Jerusalem (with Judy Stacey Goldman)

King Solomon's Table

King Solomon's
TABLE

A Culinary Exploration of Jewish Cooking
from Around the World

Joan Nathan

Photographs by Gabriela Herman

ALFRED A. KNOPF   NEW YORK   2017

THIS IS A BORZOI BOOK
PUBLISHED BY ALFRED A. KNOPF

All rights reserved. Published in the United States by Alfred A. Knopf,
a division of Penguin Random House LLC, New York,
and in Canada by Appetite by Random House, a division of
Penguin Random House Canada Limited, Toronto.

www.aaknopf.com

Library of Congress Cataloging-in-Publication Data
Names: Nathan, Joan.
Title: King Solomon's table : a culinary exploration of Jewish cooking from
around the world / Joan Nathan ; photographs by Gabriela Herman.
Description: First edition. | New York : Alfred A. Knopf, [2017] |
Includes bibliographical references and index.
Identifiers: LCCN 2016047294 (print) | LCCN 2016047838 (ebook) |
ISBN 9780385351140 (hardcover : alk. paper) | ISBN 9780385351157 (eBook)
Subjects: LCSH: Jewish cooking. | LCGFT: Cookbooks.
Classification: LCC TX724 .N375 2017 (print) | LCC TX724 (ebook) |
DDC 641.5/676—dc23
LC record available at https://lccn.loc.gov/2016047294

All photographs are copyright © by Gabriela Herman,
with the exception of photographs on page 7 by Allan Gerson
and on page xvi from the Yale Babylonian Collection
Jacket photo by Gabriela Herman
Jacket design by Kelly Blair

Manufactured in China
Published April 5, 2017
Second Printing, July 2017

To Allan

When the woman saw that the tree was good for eating and a delight to the eyes, and that the tree was desirable as a source of wisdom, she took of its fruit and ate. She also gave some to her husband, and he ate.

—Genesis 3:6

Contents

Foreword

I met Joan in 1987, on a gastronomic tour of the Republic of Georgia and the Soviet Union. What struck me from the first day was that Joan was utterly tireless. She was always making connections everywhere we went: asking restaurant owners about the origins of the dishes they were serving, striking up conversations with the Tbilisi farmers selling their jewel-red pomegranates, finding out which vegetables were in season in the markets, and learning where cooks' families had come from. She had an inexhaustible interest in food and the people who were creating it, and she innately understood the importance of taste and our cultural roots. It has been nearly thirty years now since we met, and I know now more than ever that Joan is an unstoppable force.

Over the last four decades, Joan has become the most important preservationist of Jewish food traditions, researching and honoring the rich heritage that has connected people for millennia. I still marvel at her devotion, which is so evident in this book: A meticulous historian and intrepid anthropologist, Joan follows the threads of Jewish food culture across centuries and continents, tracing the surprising and delicious ways they cross and weave. Just as important, she is a clear-voiced storyteller and food writer who takes us on little journeys that bring each dish to life, whether it is a favorite spinach salad with walnuts and cilantro she first tasted on that trip of ours to Georgia, a comforting spiced Moroccan vegetable soup used to break the fast of Yom Kippur, or Sri Lankan breakfast buns with a cinnamon-laced onion confit, adapted from a bun Joan found at a roadside stand in Sri Lanka that reminded her of the homey taste of Jewish sweet onion rolls. This is what makes *King Solomon's Table* so important, and such a pleasure to read: Joan celebrates both the diversity and unexpected commonalities of these foods from around the world. And she shows us how simple, beautiful, and real food can bring us all together, around the table and across the globe, forming the heart of our communities.

—ALICE WATERS

Introduction

"So King Solomon exceeded all the kings of the earth in riches and in wisdom. And all the earth sought the presence of Solomon, to hear his wisdom, which God had put in his heart. And they brought every man his present, vessels of silver, and vessels of gold, and raiment, and armor, and spices, horses, and mules, a rate year by year."

—1 Kings 10:23–25

Setting King Solomon's Table: A Brief History of Jewish Food

The beautiful walls of the Paradesi Synagogue in Kochi, Kerala, are adorned with the history of the Jews in India. On a recent trip there, I read an inscription suggesting that Jewish traders might have reached India from Judea, crossing the Indian Ocean during the reign of King Solomon. *Of course,* I thought, since, as scholars have told us, until the eleventh century C.E., 90 percent of Jews lived in the Middle East and used the Arabian Sea and the Indian Ocean as their major highways for trade. It is a long journey, of thousands of miles, so the evidence of their seafaring prowess is there for all to see.

I became fascinated with this arduous journey and what spurred people of that distant era to make it. Unable to jump into a time machine, I did the next best thing: I visited Chendamangalam, a tiny village about twenty miles north of Kochi, resplendent with coconut, mango, and cinnamon trees and cardamom and pepper vines. As I walked toward the bank of the nearby Periyar River, which flows into the Arabian Sea, I imagined ancient Hebrew adventurers and traders arriving on the shores and marveling at the lushness of the terrain.

Although there is little evidence as to the exact date, Jewish traders may have traveled to this area in search of spices, precious stones, timber, and ivory tusks as early as the tenth century B.C.E, around the time that the Bible tells us that King Solomon was seeking jewels and other precious treasures to build his temple.

Little is known about King Solomon—and some scholars even doubt his existence—but his story offers an image of a ruler presiding over a diversity of cultures, an abundance of food, and reaching beyond his borders to feed his kingdom. In the biblical account, Solomon was a large exporter of wheat and olive oil, which he bartered to the Phoenician king Hiram in return for timber and the use of skilled workmen. Solomon is said to have ruled for forty years, amassing enormous wealth. With a ravenous appetite for all aspects of life, he had seven hundred wives (among them a daughter of the pharaoh) and three-hundred-some mistresses. The biblical book of Kings tells us that some of his wives came from Egypt, Moab, Ammon, Edom (present-day Jordan), Sidon (present-day Lebanon), and Anatolia (present day Turkey)—the lands near and surrounding Judea in ancient Israel. These women likely would have brought pomegranates, dates, olives, and a variety of other foods and methods for preparing them; a different spice here, a different ingredient there; salting, drying, and pickling the fish, fruits, and vegetables to preserve them. According to tradition, the twelve tribes of Israel brought even more variety to the land—each tribe tithed the king and his family with jewels, minerals, exotic materials, and new foods and spices for one month a year. Our mythology of Solomon and his reign overflows with a table full of foods from the then-known world.

As I traveled many parts of the globe, tracking the legends of Solomon and his court and looking for more information about his era, I sought to discover what makes Jewish cooking unique. It is unlike the cuisines of empires, influenced by the cultures they vanquish, or national cuisines that have a homeland or stable center with defined boundaries. As a wandering people Jews have influenced many different local cuisines as they carried their foods to new lands: via Jewish trade routes; while fleeing prejudice in search of safer lands; or while migrating in search of new opportunities. Yet regional and global influences on the food Jews ate remained circumscribed by allegiance (no matter how strict) to the laws of *kashrut* (see page xxvii) and by the rituals for Passover and other holidays. These traditions have held Jews together for more than two thousand years as they have journeyed throughout the world. How amazing it is—sometimes it even takes my breath away—when, gathered around the Passover table, we think that Jews are sitting around similar tables across the world, eating symbolic foods absorbed from culinary traditions developed over thousands of years.

In *King Solomon's Table,* I will trace, through recipes and stories, the journey of many of these dishes. Take the macaroon: with roots in the Fertile Crescent (present-day southern Iraq and the surrounding regions), almonds, sugar, rosewater, and sometimes eggs were blended together, along with cardamom, a local touch. The cookie then journeyed wherever Jews went, picking up flavors along the way. Or think about chicken *paprikash*, a dish made with peppers that came from South America to Hungary, via Jews who were often the middlemen selling sweet and hot paprika. Of course, all Hungarians now recognize *paprikash* as their own, but the Hungarian Jewish version is unique in that it does not use sour cream or bacon in the sauce.

Now consider the cheesecake: originating in ancient Rome or perhaps earlier, a Jewish version with ricotta is popular today at Christmas all over Italy (see page 335) and an earlier gruel recipe traveled from Italy to Romania with the introduction of cornmeal from the New World. It returned to the Americas as *malai*, a delicious breakfast cheese pudding (see page 47), while yet another version became our "New York" cheesecake, first with farmer's cheese in central Europe, then cottage cheese, and finally the American processed sour cream and Philadelphia cream cheese that is found today in cheesecakes all over the world. The cake has subsequently returned to Europe, as I learned when I tasted a version made by a Japanese chef in France who replaced the traditional graham cracker crust with one made from the more regional speculoos cookies (see page 338).

Sometimes, a spark of familiarity comes from a dish that has traveled, as Jewish dishes have done, from Iraq to the Ukraine to China. The art of making *kreplach*—the Jewish wonton—was learned from the Chinese and perhaps the Khazars, many of whom supposedly converted to Judaism. It subsequently became an iconic dish to break the fast of Yom Kippur and for Purim, integrated into Jewish cuisine in Poland before Jews ever thought of crossing the Atlantic to the United States. Similarly, at a recent birthday party, I was delighted to hear three people talk about stuffed cabbage—one from Argentina, whose parents came from Poland, where he insisted it was *golishkes;* another from Hungary, who called it *toltolott kaoszta;* and a third from Austria, who named it *holishkes.* Here we see the same ancient concept of meat wrapped in cabbage—but the meat used for stuffing and the sauces vary ever so much depending on the regional path and the linguistic variants of the Jews who are eating it.

But let's not get ahead of ourselves. Let's go all the way back to the Babylonians to get at the roots of these traditions.

Babylonian Roots of Jewish Food

To truly delve deep into the roots of Jewish food, I had to look at an ancient text from Babylon, a cosmopolitan city even in the second millennium B.C.E., before the concept of one God was known.

These earliest known "cookbooks" contain forty-four recipes inscribed in cuneiform in the Akkadian language on three clay tablets from about 1700 B.C.E. They are preserved at the Babylonian Collection in the Sterling Memorial Library at Yale University.

One fall day, I met with Ulla Kasten, an archaeologist and the associate curator of the collection. I was thrilled to cradle one of the beautiful tablets in my hand. It felt cool and smooth to my touch; the complex writing looked impossible to comprehend.

I had read about the tablets in *The Oldest Cuisine in the World,* a fascinating book by Jean Bottéro, so I knew they included recipes for stews (even borscht!), vegetables, breads, and barley, giving us clues to diet in the Fertile Crescent. Although these recipes list extravagant ingredients and elaborate preparations for large feasts for kings and gods, ingredients like lentils, chickpeas, sesame seeds, dill, cumin, coriander, and nigella

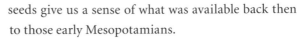

seeds give us a sense of what was available back then to those early Mesopotamians.

Ulla ushered me into a small classroom with a map on one wall and a blackboard. "There was no writing before the beginning of the fourth millennium," she said in a slight Danish accent. "As long as people lived in small villages (and the numbers were few) they could either remember or keep track of everything on their fingers, how many sheep they had, how many goats . . . but as villages grew bigger into towns and cities they could no longer keep track. So writing was invented for practical purposes."

She then showed me a copy of a map dating back to the third or second millennium B.C.E., when people were sailing on the oceans and leading caravans of camels on what we now call the Silk Road, traveling from Anatolia and the Levant all the way to Xinjiang in northwestern China. Describing to me the extent of trade in ancient times, she had me gazing at examples of bronze pots with intricate designs from Persia and almost identical pots made of porcelain found in China. Clearly, merchants were learning from one another, bartering sesame seeds, cinnamon, ginger, and turmeric and whatever else they could transport. Chicken, for example, was domesticated in about 1400 B.C.E. from several species native to Southeast Asia, mostly for egg production and cockfighting (hens were eaten when they were too old to lay eggs and cocks when they were too old to participate in cockfights). Rice, which originated independently both in China and India, came later to parts of Mesopotamia and Persia. Sugarcane slowly made its way westward from its beginnings in India, Southeast Asia, and Indonesia, reaching Mesopotamia with traders by the seventh century B.C.E.

Meanwhile, two hundred years or so after this period and around three hundred years before the birth of Solomon, in about 1400 B.C.E., seven hundred miles south of Babylon in the cosmopolitan city of Ur, the Bible tells us there lived a shepherd named Abram (later to be called Abraham), an early adherent of monotheism. Heeding the word of God, he gathered his wife, brother, nephew, and servants, along with cows, goats, and probably provisions like dried chickpeas and sesame seeds, and left his native city, setting out for Canaan, later described as a land of milk and honey (actually date jam). The book of Deuteronomy also tells us that Canaan flowed with figs, dates, olives, grapes, pomegranates, barley, and wheat. And here Abraham and Sarah used what they learned and brought with them from Babylonia, integrating these ingredients and skills into the foods of their new home.

Later, their grandsons and their descendants would add more foods from Egypt, such as fava beans, melons, cucumbers, leeks, dill, and onions, into their cooking. They might have learned from the Egyptians how to make bread from beer yeast, the art of force-feeding geese for foie gras, and other ways of treating food. Thanks to hieroglyphics, archaeological digs, and the Bible, we have records of how, during the Jews' sojourn in Egypt, these foods were integrated into the Jewish way of life before the Exodus (if it happened) and subsequently brought back with them to the land of Israel.

Later, when King Solomon's Temple was destroyed in 586 B.C.E. by Nebuchadnezzar's army—now we are within recorded history—thousands of Jews (as many as fifteen thousand by some accounts) were exiled through present-day Syria and Lebanon to Iraq, as described in the books of Jeremiah and Lamentations.

Food and Daily Life in Biblical Israel

I love to daydream about Jerusalem inside its walls during the biblical period, a small town by our standards. Whenever I am in Jerusalem, I make sure to sit at a coffee shop in the old city, eating a fresh soft *bagelah,* a floppy roll with a hole, dipping it into spices—salt, cumin, sesame seeds, and perhaps a little *za'atar.*

Daily life in ancient Israel was not much different from other parts of the Middle East. Just as Jews are today, the early Hebrews were divided into many different sects with different dietary concerns. There was a great discrepancy between the foods consumed by the wealthy and by the poor.

As in other places around the Mediterranean where bread, wine, and olive oil were the main staples of the diet, the wealthy could eat a varied diet while the poor ate mostly gruels made out of barley. A passage in Samuel describes how someone brought David and his troops "wheat, barley, flour, parched grain [*freekeh*], honey, curds, a flock, and cheese" as provisions to eat. Archaeological and other evidence (as well as the biblical accounts) suggests that people in that region also ate watermelons and pomegranates, as well as wild greens like dandelion, purslane, wild celery, *akouba* (wild artichoke), and *khubeiza* (wild mallow) that they grew or bought in the bustling marketplace. Combined with domesticated vegetables like leeks, scallions (green onions), onions, and garlic, the greens were often engulfed in dough, enclosed in triangles, and baked into pocket bread. Later, the breads were sweetened with bee honey, figs, or date jam. At Qumran, near the Dead Sea, I saw an ancient date-honey press, similar to an ancient wine press but smaller. Additionally, beginning in the early Canaanite period, pickled or cured olives were used as food, while the oil necessary for cooking was made from olives and grapes, which were big industries in the ancient world.

Stews, sometimes made from goat, lamb, or beef, with chickpeas, fava beans, and lentils—think of Esau's stew—and infused with local herbs like dill, were most often simmered in wide iron pots hung over embers; later they were set on top of taboun ovens where bread was made slapped on the walls inside. In later eras the meat stews would become the Sabbath stews of the Jews, with the custom of first boiling the meat, then adding the vegetables and beans as in a Libyan stew (see page 272). On special occasions, like the spring feast that would eventually become Passover, the meat was roasted. Fish such as tilapia came from Lake Tiberias, and people also ate grouper, mullet, and sea bream from the Mediterranean.

In Jerusalem, Jewish life eventually centered around the Second Temple. But in 70 C.E., this life was destroyed when a Jewish revolt against Rome failed and the temple was destroyed. According to the first-century Roman Jewish historian Titus Flavius Josephus, an estimated one million Jewish people died, while countless others were taken to Rome in captivity. (Today this number is thought to be greatly exaggerated, but it does reflect the severity of the calamity as perceived by a contemporary witness.) Even before the exile, Jewish cooks, like everyone, carried recipes in their heads for salting, pickling, and drying. As they moved to modern-day Egypt, Libya, Greece, Rome, Sicily, Spain, Italy, and France, they brought with them old traditions and adapted to new ones.

In later periods, as the dietary laws and the prayers for the sanctity over bread and wine were added to Jewish meals, these customs spread to Jewish life the world over.

Back to Babylon

Until the tenth century C.E., Babylon (and later Baghdad)—with its industry, commerce, and rabbinical scholarship—was the intellectual center of the Middle East, home to great Jewish thinkers. Here the Babylonian Talmud was gradually compiled between the third and sixth centuries C.E.

History makes clear that Babylon was also a center for great food. In the bustling marketplaces, much like those of the Middle East today, one could find turmeric, cinnamon, and fenugreek coming from the far reaches of the then-known world. At home, cooks would make *sikbaja*, fried and pickled fish which would become *escabeche* (see page 218) in Spain; sweet and sour meat dishes like *mahshi*, sometimes accompanied by beets (see page 280), or *keftes* infused with tamarind, pomegranate, and date syrups (see page 287); and, as previously mentioned, macaroons with cardamom. All of these dishes originated in this fertile valley between the Tigris and Euphrates Rivers. Another indigenous custom, as I mention earlier, was domesticated chicken. It was no coincidence, then, that *t'beet*, a chicken, nestled in rice with spices, cooked overnight in the oven (see page 249), became the Sabbath main dish of the Babylonian Jews. Whenever I get a whiff of these spices, I am reminded of the Indian *biryani* from which the dish probably originated.

From the eighth century, a unique group of Jewish merchants and traders, known as the Radhanites, emerged. These merchants were first described by Ibn Khoradadbeh, the Director of Post and Police, in his book *Masalik Wal-Marmalik* (Roads and Kingdoms), around 870 C.E. The word "Radhanite" comes from the Persian, *rad* meaning "path" and *dan,* "someone who knows." Together the word means "someone who knows the way."

These Radhanites brought a revolutionary international trade network to Mesopotamia and beyond, with major trading routes beginning in Narbonne (an important port at the time), near the Rhône Valley of France, and winding all the way through Baghdad before ending in the silk routes of India, Russia, and China. (This was five hundred years before Marco Polo even traveled to the Orient.) The Radhanites traded products like papyrus, spices, textiles, wine, fenugreek, nigella seeds, and olive oil.

The Slow Exodus to Europe

In the first centuries of the common era, through merchants and the marching armies of the Persians, Greeks, and the Arab Caliphates, vegetables like green peas were already grown in Egypt, while chard, beets, and rhubarb—used as a vegetable—came from Persia to the Mediterranean and ancient Israel, and also traveled in the opposite direction up to Ukraine and other places in the surrounding area. In a sense, *many* cuisines, not just Jewish cuisine, were already becoming mashups.

In the seventh century, when the Omayyad Caliphate moved into Sefarad, as Spain was called in the Bible, they quickly dominated the south of the country. The Omayyads allowed Jews who lived there to remain and to practice their religion. Population numbers are very difficult to determine during these early times, and scholars vary greatly in their speculations, but we do know that the first few centuries of Islamic rule were widely considered a so-called Golden Age in Spain, as Jews and Muslims settled first in Andalusia and later in the north. For them all, Spain—with its terrain and Mediterranean diet—was both comfortable and familiar, and those who lived here thereafter became known as Sephardic Jews, speaking a Spanish Hebraic language called Ladino.

When I wandered around the warrens of the once-Jewish quarters in Seville and Gerona, I smelled a stew similar to *hamim,* called *adafina* in Morocco, a familiar Sephardic Sabbath dish. As Ladino developed, so too did Jewish food in Spain, as Mesopotamian dishes like *keftes* took on Ladino names like *albondigas* and added new ingredients. So many eggplant dishes existed that a Catalonian song listed seven different variations. I have tasted Jewish forms of *pastel*, a hand-held pastry stuffed with meat or eggplant, all around the world—*rodanchos*, stuffed with pumpkin in Greece; *sambousak*, stuffed with chickpeas from Iraq (see page 75); *empanadillas*, stuffed with tongue, pine nuts, and raisins from New Mexico, and, of course, called *empanadas* all over Latin America. It is an emblematic food of the Sephardic Jews. It morphed into blintzes (see my *Jewish Cook-*

ing in America) in Eastern Europe, and *palascinta* in Hungary (see my *Jewish Holiday Cookbook*). Sponge cakes, called *pan d'Espagna* (see page 343), with eggs separated and the whites beaten to stiff peaks, a technique learned in Spain, would go from the Iberian Peninsula to the far reaches of the earth, when the approximately 235,000 Jews were expelled from Spain in 1492. Until the beginning of the fourteenth century, the majority of Jewish food was from Sefarad and based on Mediterranean ingredients like olive oil. Muslim and Jewish food not only influenced Spain, but from Spain spread through the whole modern world.

The Rise of Ashkenazic Food

When I tasted smoked beef (what we call corned beef; see page 298) in Strasbourg, France, I thought of the Jews from about 1000 c.e., settling in tiny villages in Ashkenaz, the name Jews gave to Alsace-Lorraine, the valley between the Rhine River and the Vosges Mountains and spilling over to southern Germany. When they were emancipated in the nineteenth century and allowed to settle in cities, a new exodus of Jews from Poland, Romania, and Russia joined them. Early on, they developed a local cuisine that included Germanic-sounding dishes like kugels (puddings made out of leftover bread or noodles with fruit), *knödel, knepfle* (matzo balls; see page 139), and *gehackte leber* (chopped liver; see page 78). Flatbreads of the south were replaced by hearth breads such as the later *barches*, a braided bread that today we call challah (see page 147).

From Troyes to southern Germany, with its northerly climate, Ashkenazic food was born. No longer would Jewish food be uniquely Mediterranean: Olive oil was swapped for goose and chicken fat, goat cheese became cow cheese, and horseradish was used instead of romaine, arugula, or other "bitter herbs" at the Passover Seder. Today, what most people think of as "Jewish" food came from Ashkenaz, though in fact these foods were predated by those of the Mediterranean.

In Germany and Alsace-Lorraine, stews with cabbage and corned beef, like *choucroute alsacienne,* were eaten for the Sabbath, as was pot-au-feu, which could cook passively in a public oven or on a nail hanging over the fireplace.

While Hebrew remained the language of prayer, these Jews also developed a Judeo-German dialect known as Yiddish, transcribed into Hebrew characters. Ashkenazic Jews trace their linguistic ancestry to this and other medieval Franco-German communities and their descendants in Europe.

It was during this period that the famous Talmudic scholar Rabbi Shlomo Yitzchaki, known more commonly as Rashi, was active. Rashi's home in the wine-growing Champagne region became one of the most important centers of Jewish life in Europe. Eventually he also founded a yeshiva (what today we might call a boarding school). His students helped tend his vineyards in order to study with him in the evenings. Rashi's writing gives us a sense of the vitality of the Jewish communities in eleventh-century northern France, and his commentaries on the Talmud and the Torah are fascinating glimpses into the cooking of northern France during this period.

Rashi was a thinker who knew both religion and agriculture. He condemned, for example, the force-feeding of geese to produce foie gras and excessive amounts of goose fat, which was essential to Jewish cooking in those days and would be developed to a high art in Alsace-Lorraine and Hungary. "Israel will one day pay the price for these geese . . . for having made these beasts suffer while fattening them," he wrote.

While Rashi would have eaten salted herring as an everyday dish, Jews in the south would have eaten salted cod. We know from his writings that Jews, like others at the time, ate vegetables like cabbage, cucumbers, asparagus, radishes, turnips, and squash in soups and stews. We also know that almonds were a big part of the diet in France and Spain. Pressed almonds, for instance, were made into a milky substance to drink, and it was used in sauces during the medieval period as almond and soy milk are today.

During this time, many Jews were suppliers of spices and other foods to the royal court and to Catholic religious institutions. They were involved in agriculture and were vintners; the wine for Mass was often bought from Jews. I have often wondered if the expulsion of the Jews from France in the fourteenth century was the reason that for the next few centuries, French cuisine contained few, if any, spices.

A Turning Point: Genizah and Maimonides

He who saved me from the desert and the frightful experiences in it will save me while on sea.
—Excerpts of the last letter to Moses Maimonides from his brother David, twelfth century,
Cairo Genizah Collection, Cambridge University Library, Cambridge, UK

On my journey in search of Jewish food, my travels took me to Great Britain, where I visited Dr. Ben Outhwaite, the head of the Genizah Research Unit at Cambridge University. Although scholars knew of the existence of the Genizah collection of ancient documents, it was Rabbi Solomon Schechter who gained access to the Ben Ezra Synagogue in Fustat (Old Cairo) at the end of the nineteenth century. (A *genizah,* coming from the Hebrew word for "to hide," is, in the most basic sense, a storage area in a synagogue used to archive religious documents.) The Cairo Genizah housed the most extraordinary collection found so far; parchment and papyrus fragments from the Middle Ages that could not be thrown away because the word of God was written on them.

This "sacred trash," which included mundane documents such as bills of lading, lively letters, and even shopping lists, sheds light on everyday life in the period from the tenth to the end of the nineteenth centuries, with most of the material coming from the tenth to the thirteenth centuries, when the Jewish community of Fustat was at its height. It is clear from the documents that active trading was going on by land and sea throughout the Indian Ocean between Aden in Yemen, Bangalore in India, Fustat, and Ceylon (present-day Sri Lanka and a way station to China), with cardamom, turmeric, and other spices tucked inside baskets of rice as hidden gifts from one merchant to another.

From the Cairo Genizah we learn other interesting tidbits. For example, we know from a letter that wheat was sent to Yemenite Jews in Aden—a land where it was either scarce or still nonexistent—to make the Sabbath bread.

David Maimonides, the brother of Moses, wrote one of the letters housed in the Genizah, indicating that he corresponded with his brother while on his travels. Born in Cordoba sometime in the 1130s, Moses and his family soon left Spain because they faced the dire choice imposed by the then *calif*: convert to Islam, die, or leave. They first moved to Fez, then to Jerusalem, and finally settled in Fustat, where Maimonides pursued his writing. He was essentially supported by David, whose death in a shipwreck on a journey to Ceylon devastated Maimonides for years. Eventually, what began as a secondary interest in science and the physical world became his means of income, as this brilliant thinker became a physician and doctor to the court of the great Sultan Saladin, looking after his harem.

From Maimonides's writing we see that in the tenth century the center of commerce and culture shifted west, away from Baghdad, first to Egypt, then to other centers like Spain and France, to towns like Toledo and Lunel, where great thinkers lived before the Ottoman Empire was founded in 1299.

We also learn much about Jewish food. At a time before the printing press, and when women's wisdom still did not fall into the realm of written texts, recipes were handed down by word of mouth. This is one reason why the writings of Maimonides are so important. As a doctor, he wrote about the healing properties of food and spices to cure diseases and to balance the humors, or bodily fluids, that were then considered the four major elements of the human body. (The humors are black bile, yellow bile, phlegm, and blood.) The ancients believed that in order for a person to be healthy, all of the humors must be in balance. The idea of chicken soup (see page 132) as the "Jewish penicillin" owes a great deal to Maimonides, who wrote in *On the Causes of Symptoms* that it be used as a cure for whatever might ail you. You will see quotes from Maimonides and the documents of the Genizah scattered throughout this book.

Centers of Jewish commerce and learning sprang up in the more western countries as Jews moved easily to cities in Greece, Spain, Italy, and France. "The fruit of the lively traffic was the great blossoming of trade, with a world market stretching from China and India, Iraq and Egypt, to Morocco and Spain," wrote Abraham Joshua Heschel in his biography *Maimonides*. "Pilgrimages and journeys for study were frequent."

The Old World Expanding

Whenever I sit down to a meal, I play a little game with myself. I ask myself which ingredients are from the New World and which from the Old World. Columbus and the conquistadores sent tomatoes, beans, chocolate, corn, peppers, potatoes, sweet potatoes, and other foods back to Europe, where they eventually prospered and became integrated into Old World cooking, before they returned to the Americas transformed.

Ships sailed from the New World to Lisbon and were welcomed by companies like the House of Mendes, a famous Jewish merchant family that made their reputation, and their fortune, as early importers of black pepper from the East. During the Inquisition, the family was driven out of Spain—first to Portugal, then to Amsterdam and Venice, ending finally in Istanbul where Doña Gracia Mendes entered the city like a queen with all of her entourage. Through their extensive network, the Mendes family and others helped distribute the new products throughout the Mediterranean world. Within a generation, these transplanted Jews became known, erroneously, as Turkish traders or *marchands portugais*, who were the first to have recipes for *sauce portugais*, which of course was tomato sauce.

I can just imagine the "Turkish" merchants in Italy, telling growers that corn, which became known as *il gran turco* or the Turkish grain, would taste better than semolina or millet in their polenta, gruels, and other foods or telling farmers that potatoes and corn should be grown for their animals and were good boiled for human consumption as well. These traders likely encouraged middlemen to convince farmers in the fertile Danube Valley of Romania to replace their traditional crops of millet and semolina with corn. Once established, corn replaced the older grains in *mamaliga* (see *Jewish Cooking in America*), the national dish of Romania.

So, by word of mouth, the traders, now settled in port cities around the Mediterranean—Livorno, Venice, Naples, and Constantinople, to name a few—integrated the new ingredients into the Sephardic dishes they brought from Spain. Gradually favorites like Jewish eggplant bits (see page 62) and *caponata* (see page 60) would be embellished with peppers and tomatoes. Cooks would use a thin dough called *mallawa* in Yemen and Iraq, laminated with butter—a technique common in India—and filled with eggplant, cheese, or spinach and cheese early on, which became known as *borek* in the Ottoman world and *bureka* in Israel. As the Ottomans made forays into Europe, this thin dough eventually gave rise to croissants and other layered crescent-shaped pastries.

As the Catholic Church started gaining power in Europe, Jews in Spain and elsewhere often lived in mortal danger, realizing that they had to go into exile, convert, or be killed. Suspicion was everywhere. Telltale signs of Jewishness were not eating pork, preparing an overnight beef stew to eat on Saturday, or showing a preference for such dishes as eggplant or almond macaroons.

As Jews started to seek safe haven outside France, Germany, and Spain, King Casimir III invited them to settle in Poland in 1334. For at least five hundred years, they remained there and in the neighboring countries that are now Romania and Hungary, and eventually in the Pale of Settlement, meaning Belarus, Latvia, Lithuania, and the Ukraine.

By the sixteenth century, the great majority of Jews who lived in Eastern Europe (an estimated 60,000 by 1550) had arrived there from the West, and brought their various foods with them. The Jewish Sabbath stew of *cholent* (see page 277), which in Spain included rice, chickpeas, or fava beans, now incorporated potatoes, lima beans, or kidney beans from the New World. And their common pot-au-feu would often include potatoes, sweet potatoes, and carrots; it came to be called *tsimmes*, meaning a "big fuss" in Yiddish. *Tsimmes* would be regionalized; in parts of Poland near Krakow, a vegetarian version with carrots, sugar, and sweet potatoes was popular (see my *Jewish Holiday Kitchen*) and another version that used beets, sweet potatoes, and meat is associated with Vilnius (see my *Jewish Cooking in America*).

Throughout these centuries Jews were traveling regionally and all over the world. Take Ukraine: In the mid-eighteenth century this breadbasket of the former Soviet Union was home to about 300,000 Jews. Some of the Ukrainian Jews' ancestors were traders with the Greeks along the Black Sea during the Greek Empire, while others may have come from the semi-nomadic Khazars. Others came from Spain at the time of the Inquisition, and still others from Europe during the frequent expulsions in the following centuries. Of course, we cannot forget that of the six million Jews killed during the Holocaust in Europe, 900,000 were from the Ukraine, one third of the Jewish population of that country. This meant that 900,000 family traditions were annihilated, including 900,000 foodways in one country alone. Today, around 60,000 Jews remain in the Ukraine, though many more have recently immigrated to Israel and other countries.

As the rise of the Industrial Age gave birth to factories, great inventions began to change the world. Coal- and wood-burning stoves rapidly outdated open-hearth cookery, the steam engine took the place of the horse and buggy, ready-made clothing eliminated handmade dress, and refrigeration and later freezing replaced endless salting, smoking, and preserving.

But life was still hard for most Jews in Eastern Europe: Pogroms (organized massacres of the Jewish community), forced military conscription, lack of civil rights, periodic expulsions from towns and villages, and displacements due to industrialization all made things difficult.

Word soon spread about the so-called promised lands in France, the United States, Canada, and other countries that sought to increase their population and workforce. Many of the two and a half million Eastern European Jews were tempted by the rumor that life was so good in America that they could "eat challah every day." Companies enticed them with free passage, land, and, most important, jobs. France took in more than 100,000 Jews in the nineteenth century, many of whom were employed in the garment trade or were bakers, wine dealers, or owners of appetizing stores. The rubber industry in the Amazon drew Jews from northern Morocco, and the Baron De Hirsch Fund brought many from Eastern Europe to Argentina. If Jews were not allowed into America or Canada because of the quota system, they went south to Argentina, Brazil, Colombia, and other places in South and Central America.

A World of New Cooking

The United States gave nearly two and a half million Jewish immigrants great opportunities in the food business. The butchers, bakers, and pushcart peddlers of herring and pickles soon became small-scale independent grocers, wine merchants, and wholesale meat, produce, and fruit providers, performing the same work many of their fathers and forefathers had been doing in Europe. Names like Lender's Bagels, Sara Lee, Beigel's, and Levy's Rye Bread all tell the tale. Not only did these immigrants go into the business of food, but they also adapted their recipes to the new environment.

By the time I was growing up, in the 1950s and '60s, processed food and TV dinners were at their height; using them meant you were really American. Advertising geniuses, attempting to appeal to the Jewish public who were keen for more "American" ingredients to create more "American" dishes, pushed their products into traditional foods like kugels, now made from packaged noodles and canned goods such as Dole pineapple or Ocean Spray cranberries. I am happy to say that a new generation of cooks is removing these processed foods from their recipes, trying to make the dishes taste more authentic and true to their origins.

Until 1965, the year I graduated from college, immigrants to the United States came mainly from countries like France, Germany, Hungary, Italy, Poland, and the Soviet Union. Since three-fourths of the Jews were from Eastern European backgrounds, "Jewish" food reflected this immigration in homes and delis in America. The Immigration and Naturalization Act of that year eliminated the rigid quota system and created a large influx of newcomers, many of them from Latin America. With the breakup of the Soviet Union in the late 1980s, immigrants from countries like Azerbaijan, Lithuania, and Uzbekistan have enhanced our taste buds. At the same time, travel abroad thanks to credit cards, cheaper airlines, and organizations like the Peace Corps and other international programs gave young Americans a chance to experience the cultures and cuisines of faraway lands. In home kitchens, the food processor and other gadgets have encouraged American cooks, who were never very good with mortars and pestles, to make hummus and pesto until the two became so ubiquitous that they are now packaged everywhere. This thirst for the new has only increased over these years.

Today, foods like hummus, eggplant salads, pomegranate syrup, and stuffed savory and sweet pastries such as *burekas* or knishes are found frozen and in restaurants all over. You can learn how to make them on TV, from an ever-growing number of cookbooks, and from the ever-present Internet blogs, magazines, and YouTube. And of course, we all still crave the new: In Hong Kong, a Canadian Jewish chef named Matt Abersol makes brisket in his yakitori restaurant Yardbird; in Buenos Aires, Tomás Kalika makes pastrami at Mishiguene, one of the city's hippest restaurants; and in Rio de Janeiro, David Hertz, the head of Gastromotiva, is building a food education network for the poor.

In Israel, the early Zionists tried to re-create the food of Eastern Europe, but gradually, as generations passed, Israeli food has come to mean a great mix from all over the Middle East and the world. When I visit Israel today, I see how dynamic the food has become, a mashup of global flavors. There, amid lush vineyards, refurbished grain mills, and cheese boutiques, you'll find a new generation of Israelis channeling their passion, energy, and creativity toward eating and drinking. After World War II in Israel it was considered not politically correct to think about the pleasure of eating. Israel was a socialist state and even if people thought about food, there were more important things. Then, little by little, Israelis—like Americans—started traveling and learning about their own foods and the foods of other cultures. During the two intifadas, at a time when they were particularly isolated, many chefs began to look into their own families' backgrounds to better understand their personal and national cuisines. Since then, they have been taking their own culinary experiments on the road and showcasing them all over the world. Formerly simple family dishes such as the Yemenite *kubbanah*, an ancient buttery laminated dough that bakes in the oven all night (see page 156) and North African *shakshuka* (see page 16), a simple dish with tomatoes and eggs, are now found on restaurant menus around the world.

Because of Israel's climate and the technical expertise of Israeli agronomists, the country has become a source of great ingredients such as cherry tomatoes, avocados originally brought there from South America, even kiwis grown from fruit from New Zealand. Farmed sea bream and sturgeon in Galilee produce some of the best caviar in the world. Israeli food is now being recognized in restaurants around the globe, as is the Diaspora food of the Jews. Perhaps it's because so many young people are discouraged by politics, or maybe it's part of the worldwide rediscovery of sustainable foodways. Whatever the reasons, cooks are reaching back in history, even to the Bible, for inspiration: Persian pomegranate molasses, Iraqi date jam, Indian mango pickle (called *amba*), Syrian tamarind paste, and, of course, ancient chickpeas, are now part of our diet. How lucky we all are to have a global cornucopia at the ready, with any spice or sauce just a few clicks of the fingertip away.

My favorite way to picture Jewish food is as that beloved Jewish staple, the bagel. A mass of flour, water, salt, and yeast is combined to form a dough; and so too Jewish cuisine has been created, using ingredients and techniques local to its people. As the dough is rolled and stretched, so the people, and their cuisine, begin to spread. New ideas, new foods, and new recipes are picked up along the way. Eventually, the rope is tapered at the end; the recipes and techniques at one end seem quite different from the other. But then, with a twist of a wrist and a pinch of the fingers, the beginning and the end of the rope are united—the cuisine goes back to its roots, simultaneously incorporating the new tricks learned along the way and enriching other cuisines.

Today, the terms "modern" and "Jewish cooking" are now often found side by side. It is my hope that you will use these dishes to grace your holiday and everyday tables without even traveling. How fortunate we are that every day the old and the new come together, and we may partake of the foods that appeared on King Solomon's table so many years ago.

The Jewish Dietary Laws

Years ago I had the privilege of covering a banquet celebrating the three-thousand-year history of Jerusalem for the *New York Times*. One of the chefs was the late Jean-Louis Palladin, who wanted to cook kosher foie gras. The liver—the source of foie gras—is filled with so much blood that observant Jews must broil it to extract the prohibited blood before eating. Jean-Louis, having been told the rules, thought he had figured out a way of searing the outside, then using the tender inside for a dish. Since that method does not rid the organ of all the blood, the supervising rabbi, observing what Jean-Louis was doing, threw out about forty pounds of this fresh foie gras and Jean-Louis, much to his dismay, had to start over. The chef asked the good rabbi how many years the dietary laws had been in effect, and he replied, "Three thousand." The chef retorted, "Isn't it time to change them?"

There is something soothing about continuity in Judaism. Several generations after Abraham, our traditions recount, Moses led the Hebrews from slavery in Egypt to freedom, traveling through the desert to Mount Sinai, where, as the Bible describes, they received the Ten Commandments. The laws of *kashrut*, eventually written in the books of Leviticus and Deuteronomy, were transmitted by word of mouth and united Jews in their many diasporas throughout history. These laws were later expanded in the Talmud and codified and elaborated on by rabbis and scholars throughout history.

Jews in different times and places have had differences in understandings of the dietary laws, and many Jews have adhered to them to varying degrees of strictness, in and outside of their homes. But those who are observant of the laws of *kashrut* are permitted to eat meat only from an animal that has cloven hooves and chews its cud. They may eat the meat of cows, sheep, and goats, even giraffes, but must avoid the meat of rabbits, horses, dogs, cats, and—of course—pigs. Edible fowl include turkeys, chickens, geese, and ducks but not birds of prey. In addition, *kashrut*-observing Jews may eat only fish having both fins and scales, thus excluding all shellfish as well as bottom-feeders like catfish and monkfish.

The Bible specifies that no blood be eaten from an animal. The rabbis of the Talmud expanded upon this basis to create the ritual laws of how meat was to be slaughtered in everyday life. A *shochet*, a ritual slaughterer, makes a quick stroke across the throat with a knife that is perfectly smooth and very sharp, so that the animal does not suffer. After the kill the *shochet* ensures that the animal was healthy by examining the lungs and meat for certain types of lesions, cuts, and bruises. Since the Torah—unlike the more ancient cuneiform tablet recipes—absolutely prohibits the consumption of blood, which represents life, the meat must go through a process called *melichah,* in which it is soaked, salted, and then washed again to ensure that no blood remains. The hindquarters cannot be used unless certain nerves and blood vessels are excised. For the same reason, eggs must be inspected to make sure they do not contain blood spots.

Pareve (neutral) food such as fish, eggs, vegetables, fruits, nuts, and grains may be eaten with either milk or meat. *Milchig* (dairy or dairy products) must be cooked and eaten separately from *fleishig* (meat) dishes, because three times in Exodus and Deuteronomy the Hebrew Bible states that a kid cannot be cooked in its mother's milk. The rabbis understood the biblical cooking of a kid in its mother's milk as a blanket prohibition against cooking, eating, or deriving benefit from milk and meat products together. This separation has been gradual. In northern France during the eleventh century (the time of the Talmudic commentator Rashi), for example, the separation specified that milk and meat be eaten from separate spoons but not separate plates, as they are today. Some Jews today maintain two entire kitchens—two dishwashers, stoves, and refrigerators, as well as two sets of pots, utensils, and dishes that are used exclusively for either milk or meat dishes.

In ritually observant homes, no cooking is permitted on the Sabbath, the day of rest. This rule inspired robust stews such as *cholent* (see page 277) and kugels (see page 182) that could be prepared in advance and allowed to simmer for a long time over a low flame or in a warm oven all night long.

The present laws of *kashrut* as formulated by the rabbis of the Talmud (mid first millennium) were observed by most Jews until the emergence of the Reform movement in Germany; they continue to shape, to some extent, the culinary practice of many contemporary Jews.

> I have taken all practical measures to ensure that the recipes contained herein fulfill the requirements of *kashrut* and have provided *pareve* substitutes for butter where necessary, but within the many observant communities there are different views on the dietary laws. Accordingly, although rabbinic authorities have been consulted in the preparation of this text, the ultimate responsibility for ascertaining the conformity with *kashrut* of any particular recipes rests with the reader.

King Solomon's Table

Pantry

De Seminibus Hoc (Seeds to Have on Hand): Poppy seed, rue seed, rue berries, laurel berries, anise seed, celery seed, fennel seed, lovage seed, rocket seed, coriander seed, cumin, dill, parsley seed, caraway seed, sesame.

De Siccis Hoc (Herbs to Have on Hand): Laser root, mint, catnip, sage, cypress, origany, juniper, shallots, *bacas timmi,* coriander, Spanish chamomile, citron, parsnips, ascalonian shallots, bull rush roots, dill, fleabane, Cyprian rush, garlic, legumes, marjoram, *innula silphium,* cardamom.
—Apicius, *De re Coquinaria* (Cookery and Dining in Imperial Rome), first century C.E.

When I was a child, my mother's pantry consisted of several white painted wooden cupboards in a separate room adjacent to the kitchen. My own pantry today is more contemporary, with drawers in my kitchen instead of in a side room. The drawers beneath my cooktop are packed with oils, vinegars, and spices, while the drawers to the side contain grains and legumes. A few steps away, beneath my hunter-green marble baking center, I keep my flours, chocolates, and other items for breads and desserts. Garlic and dried herbs grown in my garden hang from nearby beams so I can pick them when needed. Perishable items such as cheese, sauces, and other condiments for cooking live in the refrigerator.

I buy some things in bulk, like basmati rice, good-quality chocolate, and yeast, that I store in the freezer. Doing this saves a little money and allows me to always have my essentials on hand.

My so-called pantry is a diverse microcosm of the world where I have lived for my entire adult life. It includes jars of preserved lemons that I learned to make years ago, before they were trendy, from a woman from Fez who lived in Washington, D.C.; *zhug,* a hot sauce that I first tasted at a Yemenite home in Jerusalem, returning to watch how to make it; *harissa,* a red hot sauce from North Africa; chickpeas from the Middle East; basmati rice from India; roasted sesame seeds from Korea; and my latest sweet obsession, Hungarian apricot jam made from fruit leathers to fill pastries and cookies.

As I travel to many parts of the world, interviewing home cooks and eating their delicious food, the stories, secrets, and techniques that I discover stay with me, resonating in my kitchen every day.

Spices

> What is to be borne in mind about spices: Of coriander, that which is fresh, green in color, dry. Of cumin and caraway and the like. Of cinnamon, that which is rough, thick, tightly coiled, with a penetrating aroma, burning to the tongue . . . Of pepper, what is fresh, not old. Of ginger, that which is *maghrus,* "implanted." He will clean all the spices extremely well and grind them fine.
> —*A Baghdad Cookery Book: The Book of Dishes* (*Kitab al-Tabikh*), thirteenth century

I have lots of spices in my kitchen, but I rarely buy them from a grocery store. Part of the fun of traveling is bringing fresh spices home to remind you of your journeys. I don't recommend putting them in the freezer; rather, keep them well-sealed in a dark, cool location with minimal humidity—they can last many years if properly stored. What is important is to determine if they still have a pungent aroma and flavor, as that is what fades over time. They do not literally go bad unless they are kept in humidity and develop mold, or become somehow contaminated. With this in mind, be careful to buy only enough spices for about six months so that they'll stay as fresh as possible. Ground spices will fade more quickly, while whole spices like cinnamon sticks, nutmeg, and cloves can stay pungent for many years. However, you don't have to travel to be adventurous in the kitchen. Go to ethnic and specialty stores in your own town before you order online; you'll be very happy with what you find. Here are some of my favorites.

ALLSPICE was brought from its Jamaican homeland to England, where it was called pimento because the explorers who found it thought they had discovered a giant peppercorn. It became known as "all spice," as this berry of a Caribbean tree has the flavor of cinnamon, nutmeg, and cloves. The British brought it to the Middle East, where it is called English pepper. It is found in many rice dishes and stuffed vegetables there instead of, and sometimes in addition to, cinnamon, nutmeg, and cloves. Because I lived for several years in Jerusalem, this familiar spice always reminds me of my second home.

BAHARAT is a spice blend of the lucky number seven, one of the mystical numbers in Judaism; the name comes from *bahar,* a general term for spices in both Arabic and Hebrew. Every cook in the Middle East has his or her special blend of salt, pepper, cinnamon, cumin, paprika, turmeric, nutmeg, allspice, cardamom, ginger, and/or coriander. To ensure freshness, I make my own in small batches. In deference to the cooks whose recipes I've learned and adapted, each time I mention *baharat,* I note their particular combination.

This is my go-to version, which I occasionally vary depending on its use. You can also purchase very good blends at spice markets or specialty stores—I'm always fascinated by how this one mixture varies depending on which market, in which city, in which country, I'm visiting.

½ teaspoon Hungarian sweet paprika
½ teaspoon freshly ground black pepper
½ teaspoon cayenne or hot paprika, or to taste
1 teaspoon ground cumin
½ teaspoon ground cinnamon
1 teaspoon ground turmeric
1 teaspoon salt
½ teaspoon ground nutmeg
¼ teaspoon ground allspice
¼ teaspoon ground coriander

1. Stir all ingredients together in a small bowl. Store in an airtight container at room temperature for up to 6 months.

CARDAMOM is found in Indian curries, but in faraway Sweden it is also common to find the sweet and pungent seeds ground into a powder and mixed into breads and pastries. I love it in scones with its cousin, ginger (see my *New American Cooking*) or in a delicious almond with cardamom and ginger Passover cake from Iran (see page 343). I prefer to peel whole cardamom pods and freshly grind the seeds whenever I need the powder in baked goods. For stews or curries, I'll often grind up the seeds as well as the outer pods, which will disintegrate when cooked. Once, while riding an elephant in southern India, I passed hundreds of cardamom bushes.

CINNAMON is a confusing spice, especially in America, where it is more common to find cassia than "true" Ceylon cinnamon. Cassia (*Cinnamomum cassia*), of the same genus as Ceylon cinnamon, is more robust and spicy and used more readily in main course stews than the delicate, nuanced cinnamon (*Cinnamomum zeylanicum*) native to Ceylon (modern-day Sri Lanka) and India and best used for desserts. Ceylon, cassia, and at least twenty more varieties come from the inner bark of different types of trees in the genus *Cinnamomum*, a type of evergreen in the laurel family. Today, Ceylon cinnamon is known mostly for research linking cinnamon to reducing cholesterol and blood sugar levels, as well as stimulating cognitive functions, particularly in Alzheimer's patients, and helps to prevent coughing. I love to add Ceylon cinnamon to my coffee and desserts, but prefer the oomph of Vietnamese or Indonesian cassia in savory dishes like tomato sauce (see page 173).

CINNAMON SUGAR is something I like to keep on hand to sprinkle on all sorts of breakfast treats and baked goods. The sweetly scented sugar is excellent on matzo *brei* (see page 19), *Csúsztatott Palacsinta*—Hungarian Apple Pancakes (page 32), or Orange-Almond *Mandelbrot* (page 318). To make cinnamon sugar, stir together 1 cup of sugar with 1 to 2 tablespoons cinnamon (preferably Ceylon). It keeps in an airtight container for months.

CUBEB is a peppery spice that has hints of allspice in its flavoring. The cubeb berry was used in recipes found written on the cuneiform tablets from 1700 B.C.E. and remained popular until allspice, with a similar flavor profile, was discovered in the New World in the early sixteenth century, eventually replacing it. Today, cubeb is again being found in spice stores; it is used as a flavoring for tobacco and gin and is also a favorite of chefs who are always looking for the next new flavor.

CUMIN, the dried fruit of a plant in the parsley family, is one of the most beloved spices in the Middle East and Spain. Bukharan Jews from Uzbekistan make a delicious *plov* with cumin seeds, meat, and carrots (see page 282); Jews in Kochi, India, season their spicy chicken with cumin and coriander (see page 259); and it is a secret ingredient in my hummus (see page 51). I have a friend who sprinkles it on everything—salad dressing, chicken, and vegetables—because the spice makes her feel that she can stay at home and still cross the Mediterranean. On a recent trip to Morocco, I learned the breakfast custom of dipping a hard-boiled egg first in cumin, then in salt. When I last had breakfast in Alice Waters's kitchen, she had mixed cumin and sea salt in a tiny ceramic bowl and we sprinkled it on our poached eggs over sautéed greens. Now I use Alice's cumin salt to dip my eggs . . . much easier!

> Abaye taught: Now that you have said that an omen is significant, each person should become accustomed to eating at the beginning of the year gourds, fenugreek, leeks, beets, and dates.
>
> —Babylonian Talmud, Horayot 12a

FENUGREEK, a plant in the Fabaceae (legume) family, is known as *hilbeh* in Hebrew, *shanbalileh* in Persian (although this is just the word for fenugreek leaves), and *methi* in India. The seeds, leaves, and even sprouted seeds are used in cooking, each part of the plant imparting a different flavor to a dish. It is a sign of fertility in places like Yemen and recommended for Rosh Hashanah because the Talmud says that its Aramaic name (*rubia*) is similar to the wish *sheh-yirbu* (may our merits increase).

Fenugreek seeds are commonly found in Indian curries or, in the United States, as a flavoring in artificial maple syrup. With a sweet scent but bitter flavor, the seeds have been used since ancient times as a cure-all for any number of ailments, from gout to a lackluster male sex drive. While some health benefits are up for debate, the seeds are proven to help new mothers increase their milk supply.

GINGER, a root native to India and China, is one of my favorite spices and is the first spice I turn to when feeling sick. I love it fresh, candied, and dried. Today, much of the world's supply of ginger is grown in Jamaica (think ginger beer!). If using fresh ginger, I store it in the freezer.

NIGELLA SATIVA is said to be a spice so ancient that the seeds were used in the tombs of ancient Egypt. Nigella seeds are sometimes confused with a variety of totally different spices, such as black sesame seeds or black caraway. To make matters more confusing, these seeds are known by different names around the world. In India they are called *kalonji,* translated as "onion seeds," while in Russia they are called *chernushka,* a diminutive of the word *chernyy,* meaning "black." In Iraq they are called *habbat soda,* which means "black seeds"; and in Israel and the neighboring countries, they are *habbat Baraka,* meaning "blessed seeds." Whatever you call them, familiarize yourself with nigella seeds.

These tiny black seeds come from the *Nigella sativa* plant, native to the Middle East and India and a member of the Ranunculaceae family, which includes delphinium and clematis. Archaeological finds of nigella seeds date back to prehistoric times, from 1900 B.C.E. in the Middle Kingdom of Egypt. Their unique flavor is slightly bitter and a little peppery—they're the black specks found on Armenian string cheese. I love to sprinkle them on a number of dishes like *burekas,* the melt-in-your-mouth pocket pastries filled with spinach and feta (see page 23) or Ethiopian *dabo,* a Sabbath bread (see page 151). I also mix them with fennel, poppy, and sesame seeds as a topping on my traditional six-braided challah (see page 147).

You will love nigella seeds, but they have a very intense flavor, so use them sparingly.

PEPPERCORNS are wonderful to have on hand. Rather than use preground pepper, whose flavor quickly diminishes, I prefer to freshly grind whole peppercorns in a pepper mill. I use preground pepper for big soups and stews where I need a large quantity of seasoning.

POPPY SEEDS, with their nutty, earthy flavor and crunchy texture, are sprinkled on bialys, *pletzel* (see page 161), and challah (see page 147) and are used in a filling for baked goods (see page 313). They are used in Central Europe, especially Hungary and Poland, as well as the Middle East and India. I buy them in bulk because I use them so often.

Whether sprinkled on pasta or softened in milk as a filling for *hamantashen,* they are delicious.

SEA SALT is another favorite. Even with all the trendy salts like Maldon salt on the market today, I still stick to a good coarse *fleur de sel,* sea salt, or "kosher" salt—all salt is kosher. Whenever I go to France, I stock up on it from the grocery store Monoprix, where, in the basement, you can buy all kinds of *fleur de sel* in bulk. I use it when cooking and try to sprinkle it on dishes whenever I can. When baking, however, I prefer a finer-grained salt. None of these salts are iodized; iodized salt was produced when people lacked iodine in their diets.

SESAME, the oldest seasoning and oil known to mankind, originally came from China to Assyria and India at least four thousand years ago. Soaked, cooked, and ground, sesame paste—called tahina—is a must in hummus (see page 51) and key to Tahina Cookies (page 304). Roasted sesame seeds are sprinkled on top of breads, bagels, and *bagela* (Middle Eastern soft bagels). Ground, they are a key ingredient in halvah, a candy found throughout the Middle East and eastern Europe (see page 302). I often buy whole roasted sesame seeds in bulk at Asian and Middle Eastern grocery stores.

SUMAC has today become another trendy spice. It is known as *summaq* in Arabic and *sumak* in modern Hebrew (both from the Aramaic *summaqa*). I grew up fearful of using the husk of these tiny berries because I was told they were poisonous. Although the white-berried variety is like poison ivy, with the blister-inducing chemical urushiol, the red-berried sumac is safe to handle and its dried and ground berries have a tasty, lemony flavor. It is often found sprinkled on rice in Iran and grilled meat and kebab in Iraq; mixed with *za'atar* as a spice mixture in Israel, Jordan, and all the Levant; or just sprinkled by itself on fish, on salads, or wherever and everywhere you can imagine.

A member of the Anacardiaceae family, sumac grows all over the Middle East as well as Africa and North America. Look for the red berries, but avoid the white. If you're lucky enough to forage for fresh sumac berries, have fun drying and grinding them yourself.

TURMERIC is another ancient spice receiving renewed interest today, due in part to its purported health benefits, from aiding in weight loss to acting as an anti-inflammatory. More recently, it is even being studied for its usefulness in fighting cancer. Often used as a "poor man's saffron," turmeric adds a golden hue and slight bitterness to anything it touches.

VANILLA SUGAR is a mixture I love for baking or making ice cream. I like to bury a vanilla bean, native to Madagascar, in a bowl of sugar. If a recipe calls for sugar and vanilla extract, I will just substitute this vanilla-scented sugar and eliminate the vanilla extract altogether. I love its delicate flavor and perfumy aroma. When I run out of the sugar, I use a sharp knife and extract the beans for ice cream or a cream sauce.

ZA'ATAR is something I pick up whenever I am in the Middle East. It is the name for both the herb and the spice blend. *Za'atar* the herb is a wild oregano, *Origanum syriacum,* whose flavor is a cross between Greek oregano and thyme. The spice blend includes sesame seeds, salt, and sometimes sumac and is good to waken the brain. I prefer versions with a bit of sumac in them and I often make my own. Since the herb *za'atar* is a relative of the thyme and oregano family, you can use oregano from your own garden to make the blend, picking the herb just before it blooms, drying it, and then mixing it with the other herbs and, if you like, sour salt (citric acid), called lemon *duzi* in Iraq.

yield: about ¾ cup *za'atar*

¼ cup dried oregano, thyme, or a combination
2 tablespoons dried sumac
¼ cup roasted sesame seeds
Salt to taste

1. Pick any stems or twigs from the dried oregano and thyme, then rub the leaves between your fingers into a bowl. Add the sumac, sesame seeds, and salt to taste. Store in an airtight container for up to 9 months.

Other Pantry Items

APRICOT JAM is so easy to make from dried apricots. Called *mishmish* in Hebrew and Arabic, apricots have one of the shortest seasons of all fruit. In Arabic there is the term *bil-mishmish,* meaning that you must hurry to do something or you will lose the opportunity. To preserve the bounty of apricots, most are made into jams. One type is made with fresh apricots, cooked down for a long time, while another, made from the dry fruit, is thicker and easier to use in fillings for *hamantashen* (see page 311) and other cookies and cakes, courtesy of the Austro-Hungarian Empire. I prefer this thick jam, also called *lekvar*—just be sure to use the dried apricots with sulfur added, because this helps preserve the flavor and bright orange color.

yield: 2 cups

2 cups (about 1 pound/450 grams) dried apricots
¼ cup (0.11 pound/50 grams) sugar
Zest of 1 lemon

1. Mix the apricots, sugar, lemon zest, and 2 cups water in a saucepan set over medium-high heat. Bring to a simmer, lower the heat, and cook uncovered, stirring occasionally, until the apricots soften and absorb most of the water, about 30 minutes. Stir constantly at the end of cooking to avoid scorching.

2. Purée the mixture in a food processor. Store in an airtight container in the refrigerator for up to 1 week or freeze for up to 6 months.

Note You can substitute dried plums for the apricot to make prune *lekvar*. When using as a filling, it is a good idea to microwave the jam for about 15 seconds so that it spreads more easily.

CHICKPEAS, also known as garbanzo beans, are one of the oldest protein sources known to mankind. Found in Mesopotamia at least 8,500 years ago, they spread throughout the Middle East and, since the 1970s, throughout the world in packaged hummus.

After years of cooking with chickpeas, I have concluded that despite the temptation to use canned chickpeas, the flavor is much better using dried Turkish, Bulgarian, or Israeli chickpeas found in Middle Eastern stores. My favorite trick is to buy dried chickpeas and, immediately upon returning home, soak them overnight in cold water to cover by about 6 inches, cook some, and then drain and freeze the rest in 2-cup batches in individual sandwich-size plastic bags. Whenever I need them for hummus (see page 51), falafel (see page 66), or for the many chickpea soups and stews (see pages 124, 277) I make, I just take them out of the freezer. When substituting canned beans, figure 1 cup of dried chickpeas equals 2 cups of cooked or canned; if you use canned chickpeas, rinse them in water before using.

HARISSA, North African red hot sauce, has developed a big following. One sign of the popularity of North African food is the fact that this hot sauce is now prepared and sold in open-air markets and grocery stores throughout the United States and France. In Tunisia, Morocco, and Algeria, recipes vary slightly from village to village. I use it in *shakshuka* (see page 16), fish *b'stilla* (see page 242), and Tunisian *brik* (see page 21), and add it to whatever dish I am making that needs a bit of punch.

yield: about 1 cup

1 ounce (28 grams) fresh hot red chili peppers, such as tiny hot peppers from New Mexico or cayenne peppers (about 18)

½ cup (120 ml) extra-virgin olive oil, plus more as needed

7 to 8 cloves garlic, peeled

½ teaspoon ground cumin

½ teaspoon ground coriander

1 teaspoon coarse salt, or to taste

1. Cut the stems from the peppers, remove half the seeds, and soak the peppers in warm water until soft, then drain and squeeze out any excess water. Grind the peppers as North African Jews do, in a meat grinder, or simply pulse in a food processor with ¼ cup (60 ml) of the olive oil, the garlic cloves, cumin, coriander, and salt. The consis-

tency should be that of a thick purée, and the color bright red. Place in a jar, pour the remaining olive oil over the *harissa*, cover, and refrigerate.

2. Let sit for a few days before using, until the *harissa* becomes less opaque. Use sparingly, as it is very hot.

   Note I love Pereg Gourmet's prepared *harissa* too, although it is not always easy to find.

LENTILS, another source of protein, also come from the East and have been around at least since biblical times, when Jacob served Esau an earth-colored (*edom*) lentil stew (see page 129) to fool his brother. I like lentils in soups and salads and make sure to always have the French Puy variety in my pantry. In general, the black, green, or brown lentils hold their shape when cooked, but the yellow, red, or orange varieties get very soft.

PRESERVED LEMONS are a wonderful addition to your pantry. Use smooth, thin-skinned lemons, such as the Meyer variety. Sometimes I even throw in a few kumquats when they are in season. For color and flavor, I also put a fresh bay leaf in the jar.

People always ask me how I use my preserved lemons. I throw a whole (deseeded) lemon into my hummus (see page 51) and add a little of its preserving juice for an extra punch. Or, I dice the rind and add it to salads or salad dressings. I love to scatter pieces over fish (see page 239) and stuff chickens with a whole lemon (see page 266)—after the chicken is roasted, I dice the lemon to use as a condiment.

> **yield: 8 preserved lemons**
>
> About 16 lemons
> About ½ cup coarse kosher salt
> 2 tablespoons olive oil
> 4 fresh bay leaves (optional)

1. Cut off the very ends of 8 of the lemons. Slice each one lengthwise into quarters, cutting to but not through the opposite end. Gently open half the lemon over a bowl and sprinkle a tablespoon of salt into it, then open the other half and add another tablespoon, using 2 tablespoons total per lemon.

2. Put the cut lemons in a large jar—it's fine if you have to pack them in, as they will shrink. Extract the juice from the remaining lemons and completely cover the cut ones in the jar with the juice. Slip in the bay leaves, if using. Let sit for a day, lightly covered with a towel.

3. The next day, pour a thin film of olive oil over the lemons and their juice. This will help keep them sealed while they preserve. Cover the jar tightly and put in the refrigerator or store at room temperature, allowing to cure for 3 to 4 weeks. They will last for at least a year.

SCHMALTZ, or at least what I call schmaltz, is something that I only use for matzo balls, kasha lasagne with a confit of onions (see page 178), matzo muffins (see page 183), *farfl* (see page 185), and an occasional batch of chopped liver (see page 78). I refrigerate my chicken soup, skim the fat off from the top, and put it in a jar to store in the freezer. Voilà! Simplified schmaltz.

ZHUG, or Yemenite green hot sauce, has been an addiction of mine since the first time I tasted it, many years ago in Jerusalem. I use it on falafel (see page 66) and as an everyday green hot sauce.

yield: about 1½ cups

4 fresh green Serrano or jalapeño peppers (about 4 ounces/113 grams),
stems removed and seeds removed, but reserved

1 whole head garlic, peeled

½ bunch fresh cilantro, well rinsed and dried

½ bunch fresh parsley, well rinsed and dried

1 teaspoon ground cumin

Seeds from 2 green cardamom pods

1 teaspoon salt, or to taste

¼ to ½ cup (60 ml to 120 ml) olive oil, plus additional to cover

1. Put the peppers with the garlic, cilantro, parsley, cumin, cardamom seeds, and salt to taste in the bowl of a food processor. Begin blending and gradually add ¼ cup (60 ml) of the olive oil. Purée to a smooth paste. Taste and adjust for seasonings, adding some or all of the pepper seeds if you want more heat.

2. Transfer the contents to a sterilized glass jar, cover with additional olive oil, and seal so the jar is airtight. The *zhug* will keep for several months in the refrigerator, and the flavor will only become better with age.

A Note on Equipment

People sometimes ask what tools to use in the kitchen. I think every cook should treat herself or himself to a food processor and a standing mixer, to help slice, grind, knead, whip, and beat. I also use a spice grinder or mortar and pestle. A good set of knives, most importantly a sharp paring and chef's knife, is essential. A good pepper grinder, a salt box, lots of wooden spoons, a few whisks, a bench scraper, and a good rolling pin are also musts. And don't forget: Your hands are the most important tool of all!

Morning

Azerbaijani *Kukusa* with Swiss Chard and Herbs

Smoky *Shakshuka* with Tomatoes, Peppers, and Eggplant

Matzo *Brei*

Chilaquiles, Mexican "Matzo" *Brei*

Tunisian *Brik* with a Fried Egg

Spinach-Feta *Burekas*

New Old-Fashioned Bagels

Rickshaw Rebbetzin's *Thatte Idli,* Indian Steamed Rice Dumplings
with Nuts and Raisins

Csúsztatott Palacsinta, Hungarian Apple Pancakes

Shtritzlach, Toronto Blueberry Buns

Siberian *Chremsel,* Matzo Pancake Casserole

Delkelekh, Cheese Danish Pastries

Sri Lankan Breakfast Buns with Onion Confit

Arkansas *Schnecken* with Pecans

Chocolate Babka

Malai, Romanian Cornmeal Ricotta Breakfast Pudding

Putterkuchen, Butter Crumble Cake

Azerbaijani *Kukusa* with Swiss Chard and Herbs

I thought it fitting to start the book with this easy and delicious herb-infused frittata, a living vestige of an early dish from ancient Persia and Babylonia. It shows not only the wanderings of the Jewish people, but also their good taste.

During the early Middle Ages, when Babylon was the rabbinic center that sent rabbis with their families and family recipes to the south of France, a common dish used by cooks of the region was *kuku,* an egg dish served warm or at room temperature. Found in southern French Jewish cookbooks today, the dish has wandered down to Morocco and back again to France, where it is served cold as an appetizer at weddings and other happy events and warm for breakfasts, lunch, or dinner.

This particular *kuku* morphed into *kukusa* (pronounced "kyu-kyusa") on the Silk Road and serves as a perfect example of a wandering comfort food. This recipe is from Stanley Yunayev, the father of the chef at Chateau de Capitaine, a restaurant in Sheepshead Bay, Brooklyn, who comes from the city of Quba, where in one neighborhood called Red Village the population has been almost entirely Jewish for more than fifteen hundred years. The first Azerbaijani Jews, so the story goes, were mostly mountain people, coming from Babylon sometime between 500 and 700 c.e. or maybe even earlier. No one seems to know. I hought to be one of the lost tribes of Israel, the Azerbaijanis are some of the last Jews to migrate to New York.

---

yield: 6 to 8 servings

3 tablespoons olive oil

2 large sweet onions, sliced very thin

About ½ cup clipped chives

3 scallions, diced

About 8 ounces (226 grams) fresh Swiss chard or spinach, trimmed of stems and chopped

3 cloves garlic, minced

1 bunch cilantro, finely chopped

½ bunch dill, snipped

Salt and freshly ground black pepper to taste

1 teaspoon ground turmeric

8 to 10 large eggs

Handful of arugula or other bitter greens or herbs

½ cup (50 grams) walnuts, coarsely ground

1. Heat the olive oil in a 12-inch nonstick pan set over medium heat. Add the onions, chives, and scallions and sauté until golden, about 15 to 20 minutes.

2. When the onion mixture is golden, add the Swiss chard or spinach, garlic, cilantro, dill, salt and pepper to taste, and turmeric and cook for about 10 minutes over low heat, until any liquid released from the spinach and herbs is evaporated.

3. Whisk the eggs in a mixing bowl, then carefully incorporate the eggs into the vegetables and herbs in the frying pan, using a rubber spoon to smooth the surface. Cook covered, over low heat, for about 10 minutes, or until the eggs are set. The color should be deep green, almost black. Uncover and bring to the table in the frying pan with a handful of arugula on top and sprinkle with the walnuts. You can also serve this cut up at room temperature as an appetizer or snack.

Note In Azerbaijan, the many variations of this dish include vegetables ranging from asparagus to eggplant to squash. In the summer, try experimenting with the bounty of fresh herbs that are available near you. I have made this dish with kale, bok choy, lovage, fennel fronds, and arugula and served it sprinkled with feta as well as the nuts. Just keep the ratios about the same, and you're sure to have a delicious dish.

Smoky *Shakshuka* with Tomatoes, Peppers, and Eggplant

yield: 8 servings

As I walked along the Duke of Gloucester Street in Colonial Williamsburg, Virginia, I thought about one of my favorite characters in Jewish history, a physician named Dr. John de Sequeyra. The only Jewish resident of eighteenth-century Williamsburg, he lived as a boarder in several clapboard houses, some of which are open to the public. Born to a notable Portuguese Jewish family in London in 1712, de Sequeyra came to Williamsburg in 1745 and was the first visiting physician at that city's "Public Hospital," the country's first public facility for the care of the mentally ill, where he worked until his death in 1795.

A bachelor, the doctor came to the Americas in his early thirties. Little is known of his life, except for some ephemera—for example, de Sequeyra's portrait at the Winterthur Museum in Delaware, commissioned by a devoted patient. On the back, among other things, is written, "He [de Sequeyra] first introduced into Williamsburg the custom of eating tomatoes, until then considered more of a flower than a vegetable."

None other than Thomas Jefferson acknowledged Sequeyra as the person who introduced and encouraged people in Virginia not to fear but to cultivate and eat the tomato, a member of the sometimes poisonous nightshade family.

On that same trip, I ate brunch nearby at the Gabriel Archer Tavern at the Williamsburg Winery and was surprised to see *shakshuka* with pork chorizo on the menu along with shrimp and grits and French toast with local blueberry wine syrup, all prepared by Chef Ika Zaken, who came there from Israel.

Everybody who knows me knows that I love *shakshuka*. Its name comes from an Arabic and Hebrew word meaning "all mixed up." According to many friends from North Africa, this dish was always made when women were busy . . . with a lover . . . and then made a quick meal for their husbands. *Shakshuka* was born in Ottoman North Africa in the mid-sixteenth century, after Hernán Cortés, who first encountered tomatoes in Mexico in 1519 (they are originally from the Andes and spread as seeds), introduced the tomato to the Old World.

I make it often for brunch, sometimes letting guests poach their own eggs in the tomato and pepper sauce and seasoning it with feta cheese, Greek yogurt, cilantro, parsley, and, when a little spice is needed, *harissa* (see page 10).

After I tasted Ika's rendition of *shakshuka,* I traded in all my other recipes. His is full of flavor, with grilled peppers, eggplant, and smoked paprika to give it some kick. Try it—you won't be disappointed.

———————

1. Preheat the oven to 450 degrees and line a jelly roll pan with parchment paper. Cook the peppers and the eggplant, pricking them first with a fork, turning occasionally with tongs, until slightly soft and blackened, about 20 minutes. You can also grill the vegetables, turning every 5 to 7 minutes, until they are charred and soft, about 20 minutes. Do not cook them until they are completely soft, though, as they will finish cooking in the *shakshuka*. Set aside to cool in a plastic bag for about a half hour, then remove the stem and seeds, peel, cut the peppers roughly into ½-inch squares, and just chop the eggplant.

2. Heat the oil in a wide, heavy-bottomed pot over medium-high heat. Add the peppers and fry until warmed through, about 3 minutes, then add the chorizo, if using, and garlic and cook for 6 to 7 minutes, stirring occasionally. Add the tomatoes and simmer, uncovered, over medium-low heat for 30 minutes, stirring occasionally, or until the juices are reduced.

3. When the mixture is thickened, add the smoked paprika, salt, pepper, sugar, eggplant, and all but 3 tablespoons of the cilantro. Stir to combine. Adjust seasonings to taste, especially the sugar, and add a little water if the mixture is too thick.

4. With the back of a large spoon, make 8 shallow wells in the *shakshuka*. Gently crack the eggs into the wells, cover the pot, and poach over medium-low heat for about 5 to 10 minutes, until the egg whites are set. Serve sprinkled with the remaining cilantro and, if you like, some Bulgarian feta cheese.

Note I love to make a big batch of *shakshuka* for brunch and often double or even quadruple the recipe. I often prepare the *shakshuka* (minus the poached eggs) ahead of time, freezing it up to a month in advance. A day before brunch, I let the *shakshuka* thaw in the refrigerator. Then, when I want to eat the tomatoey sauce, I simply reheat it in a large pot and set a few small nonstick skillets on the stove. Willing guests can then ladle a little sauce into the skillets, crack in an egg, cover, and poach their own eggs to order. Or for a smaller crowd, I poach all the eggs at once in a large pot. Either way, it is always a crowd pleaser and the star of the show. Just be sure to have mimosas or Bloody Marys nearby!

4 red bell peppers

1 medium eggplant (about 1 pound/453 grams)

2 tablespoons olive oil

3 lamb, beef, or chicken chorizo (about 9 ounces/255 grams), sliced in rounds (optional)

5 cloves garlic, chopped

12 medium tomatoes (6 pounds or about 2¾ kilos) chopped, or 28 ounces (794 grams) canned tomatoes, roughly chopped

1 tablespoon smoked Spanish paprika

2 teaspoons salt, or to taste

½ teaspoon freshly ground black pepper, or to taste

1 tablespoon sugar, or to taste

1 bunch cilantro, chopped

8 large eggs

Crumbled Bulgarian feta cheese, for garnish (optional)

Matzo *Brei*

Once I had the privilege of hosting Sheila Lukins, the author of *The Silver Palate Cookbook,* who has since sadly passed away, at our Passover Seder. The next day, Sheila wanted to have a matzo *brei* cook-off with my brother-in-law Sam Gerson. If you're not familiar with matzo *brei*—meaning "fried matzo"—you just need to know that there is really no recipe for this Passover breakfast fare, mentioned in the Talmud as "crumbled or pulverized bread made into an omelet or pancake."

Sam made a savory variety with Parmesan cheese, the technique learned from his mother, Peshka, who did this in Zamosc, Poland, where matzo *brei* was a time-honored breakfast dish. (She would have shaken her head at the Parmesan cheese.) He carefully broke a few matzos in pieces, then soaked them in water, drained them, covered the matzo with beaten egg, added some cheese, and then fried it.

Sheila, on the other hand, broke up her matzo, put it in water, drained it, then mixed hers with milk and fried it with eggs in little pancake shapes, serving them with cinnamon sugar or a dollop of jam and sour cream. Of course, as I remember the cook-off, it was a tie ... but Sam insists he won. Each time I make what Sheila called "morning-after matzo *brei,*" I remember our time together fondly.

---

yield: about 12 matzo *brei*, or 6 servings

4 pieces unsalted matzo

6 large eggs

3 tablespoons milk

Salt and freshly ground black pepper to taste

3 tablespoons unsalted butter

Cinnamon sugar for sprinkling (optional)

Sour cream or Greek yogurt and jam for serving (optional)

---

1. Break the matzo into large pieces and put them in a bowl. Pour 2 cups (470 ml) of warm water over the matzo and let it soak for 2 to 3 minutes. Drain.

2. Beat the eggs with the milk, salt, and pepper, then stir in the drained matzo. Melt the butter in a nonstick skillet over medium-low heat. Spoon about 2 tablespoons of the mixture onto the frying pan, making small pancakes. Cook 2 to 3 minutes, then flip and cook until lightly browned.

3. Serve with cinnamon sugar and, if you like, dollops of sour cream or Greek yogurt and jam.

Note Although it's not traditional, I like to serve these matzo *brei* with smoked salmon and avocado. Alternatively, I sometimes add a diced unpeeled apple, in which case I add a little cinnamon sugar too.

Chilaquiles, Mexican "Matzo" Brei

When Jonathan Gold, the first and only food journalist to win the Pulitzer Prize, and star of the documentary *City of Gold,* wants a Jewish fix, he recalls the deli days of his Los Angeles childhood. "I grew up in the most Reform family possible," Jonathan, now the *Los Angeles Times* restaurant critic, told me. "My dad's idea of being Jewish was taking us to Jewish delis. He felt more Jewish there than he did in *shul.* Sundays were deli day at Junior's or Canter's."

When asked what he made his family for breakfast the day I spoke with him, he answered in a fashion that seemed to sum up everything about a Jewish foodie in Southern California: "*Chilaquiles,* basically eggs with leftover corn tortilla chips stirred with a little salsa and finished off with Mexican sour cream and a sprinkling of chopped herbs. We call it Mexican matzo *brei.*"

It's a nifty way to use up stale corn tortillas and the salsa sitting in the refrigerator. You can make this dish all year long for breakfast, lunch, or dinner and, if you like, as I do, substitute fried matzo (page 154) for the corn tortillas during Passover.

yield: 4 servings

Peanut oil for frying

8 corn tortillas or 4 matzos, broken into wedges of quarters or eighths

1 medium white onion, diced

Large pinch of salt

4 large eggs, lightly beaten

1 cup prepared salsa of choice

About ½ cup crumbled *cotija* cheese or shredded cheddar cheese

A few dollops of *crema* or sour cream

Sliced avocado

4 chopped scallions

4 tablespoons chopped cilantro

---

1. Warm a thin film of oil in a large nonstick skillet over medium-high heat, then add the tortilla wedges or matzo pieces and fry, turning occasionally with tongs, until just crisp, but not so crisp as a tortilla chip, about 1 to 2 minutes per side. Do this in batches if necessary, removing the fried tortillas or matzos to drain on a paper towel–lined baking sheet. This can be done a few hours in advance.

2. Drain all but 2 tablespoons of the oil out of the pan (reserving the oil for another use if you like), then, over medium heat, sauté the onion with a pinch of salt until translucent, about 5 to 10 minutes. Pour in the eggs with another pinch of salt and scramble until almost set, about 3 to 4 minutes. Add the fried tortillas or matzos back to the pan, then pour in about ½ to 1 cup of the salsa, carefully stirring a few minutes until the salsa is hot and the tortillas or matzos just begin to soften.

3. Serve in the pan or on a platter, sprinkled with the *cotija* or cheddar cheese, dollops of *crema* or sour cream, slices of avocado, and chopped scallions and cilantro.

Tunisian *Brik* with a Fried Egg

On my first trip to Morocco, I watched the royal baker in Rabat making *warqa*, the indigenous Moroccan pastry for *b'stilla* (see page 242). The woman—*warqa* bakers are typically women—took pieces of the wet dough made of very high-gluten flour and water and splashed it onto a hot griddle, until the splotches came together into a thin, crispy dough, also called *brik*. As she made them, one by one, she stacked the finished *warqa* on top of one another.

One day, while filming some recipe how-tos, I noticed that the crew was hungry. Luckily, I had a package of *brik* leaves, similar in size to large Indian *dosa*, stashed away in my refrigerator!

I took out a large, thin square sheet of dough, broke an egg inside it, and quickly folded it into a triangle before slipping it into the bubbling oil. Four minutes later, we were rewarded with the best fried egg you could imagine, especially when we dabbed my homemade *harissa* (see page 10) over the whole crispy, gooey concoction.

Brik are a perfect breakfast or brunch dish, with only one catch—they are best consumed fresh out of the oil, and thus someone (perhaps you) has to be stuck at the fryer. Take comfort in the promise of a perfectly fried egg—super-soft and fluffy white with a runny yolk that turns into a sauce the second you crack into the crispy *brik*.

---

yield: 4 *brik*

1 package *brik* leaves (see note)

4 large eggs

Peanut or vegetable oil for frying

Harissa for dipping (see page 10)

Salt and freshly ground pepper to taste

---

1. Heat at least 3 inches of oil in a wok or large pot until the oil reaches about 375 degrees. Line two baking sheets with paper towels. Remove the *brik* leaves from the packaging and cover with a damp towel (this prevents them from drying out).

2. Put one leaf on your work surface with one of the points facing down (so that the leaf looks like a diamond instead of a square). Working quickly, crack an egg into the center, fold the bottom corner of the leaf up to the top, and gently slide into the hot oil. Fry for 1 to 2 minutes, or until golden on the bottom, then flip over with tongs and fry a few minutes more until golden brown all over. Remove from the oil and drain on the prepared baking sheets. Repeat until all the eggs are used up, tightly wrapping any remaining *brik* leaves and freezing for up to 6 months.

3. The *brik* are best served soon after they come out of the oil, but may be kept warm in a 300-degree oven for up to 10 minutes. Serve with *harissa* and salt and pepper to taste.

Note Machine-made Tunisian and Algerian *brik*, similar to *warqa* and often called *feuilles de brik*, are found in Middle Eastern markets, many supermarkets, or online.

Spinach-Feta *Burekas*

yield: 30 *burekas*

My madeleine is a buttery pocket pastry filled with Bulgarian feta cheese and spinach, called *buricchi* by Jews from Italy, *bureka* by Jews in Israel, and *borek* by Ottomans and Jews of Balkanian origin. Traditionally, they are Sabbath morning breakfast fare accompanied by *huevos haminados,* hard-boiled eggs that have been cooked for hours and hours (see page 81).

Borek are one of the crowning jewels of the legacy of the Ottoman Empire, probably coming there as the laminated pastry *paratha* from India, through Yemen as *malouach,* serving all over the Gulf and Egypt as a base for a delectable breakfast *umm ali,* going another way to Spain and then from there to Florence as *burrichi,* and eventually gracing France as puff pastry and, of course, yeasted as the splendid croissant.

Until recently I hadn't tasted a homemade *bureka* since the early 1970s, when I was foreign press attaché to the late Teddy Kollek, the legendary mayor of Jerusalem. In those days, every Friday morning like clockwork, a Moroccan named Simantov would enter the municipal office building with a tray held from a handle above carrying Turkish coffee spiked with cardamom pods—called in Arabic "hell"—and these crispy, hot-from-the-oven triangular buns. Each bite was heavenly and I looked forward to this end-of-the-week treat.

A few years ago, Mike Solomonov, the James Beard Award–winning chef of Zahav in Philadelphia, made *borek* for a chefs' brunch at my home in Washington. I carefully followed his lead, working softened butter into the dough made with a little oil, vinegar, flour, and soda water. Treating it like croissant dough, I turned it several times and left it to rest in the refrigerator overnight.

The next day, as I rolled out the dough, I tried to make rectangular ones like Mike's, but these were not like the crispy buns I longed for, so I formed mine into triangles and started crimping the edges. Ashley Aditi, a culinary graduate and an intern from a Turkish Jewish family in Tel Aviv, told me to treat the dough gently and not to press the edges down. "You want a little of the filling to ooze out and you'll see all the layers that you have made from the dough," she said. I did as I was told, following the advice learned from Ashley's grandmother, whose family had been making it for generations in the Ottoman Empire, and perhaps before.

I replaced half the cheese with spinach in the filling, then brushed an egg wash on top and sprinkled each pastry with sesame and black nigella seeds. Most I put straight into the freezer, but I cooked a few, just to taste. When I pulled them out of the oven, I waited a few minutes and took a bite. They were just as I remembered. I gave one to my husband, Allan, whom I met in Jerusalem, where he was working for the Justice Ministry near my office. As he bit into his, he recalled the same taste memory of Friday mornings, something I had never known that we shared before.

Now these homemade *burekas,* worth every single calorie, are our Friday morning breakfast treat. You may be intimidated to make your own dough (and if that is the case, I permit you to cheat with a good-quality frozen puff pastry that will not be as thin as the homemade dough), but do give it a try. The dough is very forgiving, and it does not have to be perfect—a few cracks in the edges will still yield delicious results.

———————

1. **to make the dough** Mix 2½ cups (340 grams) of the flour and the teaspoon of salt together in the bowl of a standing mixer with the paddle attachment. With the mixer running on low, add the oil, vinegar, and enough soda water until the dough holds together but is still tacky and shaggy—it won't be smooth and glossy. Remove from the bowl and knead a few times on a floured surface, just to bring the dough together, then cover and let rest for 30 minutes.

2. Line a small baking sheet or tray with parchment paper. Divide the dough in half, heavily cover the counter with flour, and roll one piece into a rough square, about 12 by 12 inches. Using your hands, shape half of the butter into another square about 6 by 6 inches. Put the square of butter in the center of the dough, then fold the dough over the butter to completely enclose the butter. Gently roll the dough back into a square, about 12 by 12 inches, to distribute the butter throughout the dough.

3. Repeat with the remaining dough and butter. Fold the dough pieces in half, wrap well with plastic wrap, and lay on the prepared sheet. Refrigerate for 30 minutes.

4. Remove the dough from the refrigerator and let it sit at room temperature for about 15 minutes. Gently press one piece of the dough. If the butter is malleable and does not pierce through the dough, it is ready to roll. If not, let it sit out a few more minutes (this process is called "tempering" the dough).

5. Tapping the dough gently but firmly with a rolling pin, roll the dough into a rectangle, about 10 by 12 inches. Fold the dough into thirds like a letter, then fold in half from top to bottom. Roll into a square of about 6 by 6 inches. Repeat with the other piece of dough. Rewrap both pieces of dough in the plastic wrap, put back on the sheet, and refrigerate for another 30 minutes.

6. Repeat this folding, rolling, and refrigerating process two more times, then refrigerate the wrapped dough overnight. You may also freeze the dough, wrapped well in plastic and stored in a freezer bag, for up to 6 months. Simply defrost overnight in the refrigerator and proceed with the recipe.

7. **to make the filling** First, taste your feta. If it is very salty, you will not need to add salt to the filling. If it is only a little salty, then you should add about ½ teaspoon of salt, or to taste.

DOUGH

2½ to 3 cups (340 to 405 grams) unbleached all-purpose flour, plus more for rolling

1 teaspoon sea salt

1 tablespoon vegetable oil

1 tablespoon distilled white vinegar

¾ to 1 cup (165 to 225 ml) soda water

1½ cups (3 sticks/339 grams) unsalted butter, at room temperature, divided

Spinach and feta filling (recipe below)

1 large egg

1 tablespoon nigella seeds (optional)

1 tablespoon roasted sesame seeds

SPINACH AND FETA FILLING

1 pound (453 grams) feta cheese, drained and patted dry

2 large eggs

15 ounces (425 grams) blanched and squeezed, chopped spinach, fresh or frozen (thawed, drained, and squeezed well if frozen)

Freshly ground black pepper to taste

Salt to taste

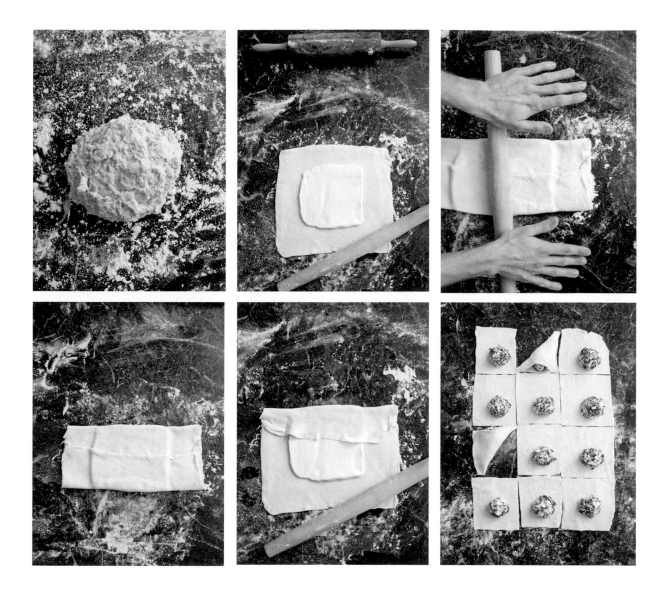

8. Pulse the feta and eggs in the bowl of a food processor fitted with a steel blade until blended but not puréed. Remove to a medium bowl and then stir in the spinach, pepper, and salt as needed.

9. Preheat the oven to 375 degrees, space the two racks in the middle of the oven, and line two baking sheets with parchment paper.

10. Remove the dough from the refrigerator and temper the dough as you did before. Roll one of the pieces into a rectangle about ¼ inch thick. Cut the rectangle lengthwise into 3 strips, then make 4 cuts across to yield 15 squares that are 4 by 4 inches.

11. Put a heaping tablespoon of filling in the center of each square of dough. Then fold each square over the filling from corner to corner, into a triangle. Gently press the corners together, but don't seal the edges closed; you want

to see the buttery layers once the *burekas* are baked. Put each pastry onto the prepared baking sheets. Repeat with the other piece of dough.

12. Break the egg into a small bowl and beat with a teaspoon of water. Brush the tops with the egg wash and sprinkle with the nigella and sesame seeds.

13. Bake for about 15 to 20 minutes or until golden.

Note I often make tiny *burekas* to serve at parties or with cocktails. First roll one of the dough pieces into a rectangle about 15 inches by 20 inches; then cut into 5 strips lengthwise and 6 strips widthwise, yielding 30 squares. Fill each square with a heaping ½ teaspoon of filling and proceed with the recipe.

I also freeze them unbaked so they can be ready at a moment's notice. Fill the pastries and put them on parchment-lined baking sheets, freeze until solid, then transfer to an airtight container or bag. They keep frozen for up to 6 months. When ready to bake, preheat the oven to 375 degrees, put them frozen on the prepared baking sheets, and proceed from the egg-wash step. Of course, they take a few more minutes to bake from frozen, but are still just as delicious! If you have leftover filling, use it for frittatas or a filling for omelets.

New Old-Fashioned Bagels

In Northern California, East Coast transplants are producing crunchy, chewy, dense bagels on either side of the Bay. In Paris, the French are making bagels thanks to Disneyland's arrival in Europe. And Israel, a bagel desert until forty years ago because of the lack of water, now has bagels everywhere.

Right near where I live in Washington, D.C., Mark Furstenberg and his avid young bakers at Bread Furst are making a Montreal-style bagel—thinner and smaller, but with salt and less sweetness. This "new" type of bagel is what bagels used to be like. The water may not be New York's, but I argue that the bagels are just as good, and maybe even better.

After years of bagel baking and watching the wonderful evolution taking place today, I believe that you have to use high-gluten baking flour, and that after the dough rises, you should let the formed bagels rest in the refrigerator as long as possible to allow the flavor to really develop. I now boil my bagels in a malt syrup solution, which gives them a nice shine and helps the sesame and poppy seeds adhere.

The result: perfectly seasoned, brown, crusty, chewy bagels to serve with smoked salmon or gravlaks (see page 227), red onion, and, of course, a ripe tomato.

---

yield: 12 bagels

1 teaspoon active dry yeast

5 cups (675 grams) high-gluten bread flour, plus more for dusting

2 teaspoons salt, plus more for boiling

1 tablespoon plus 2 heaping tablespoons malt syrup or honey

½ cup (72.5 grams) poppy seeds

½ cup (75 grams) sesame seeds

---

1. Put the yeast in the bowl of a standing mixer with 1⅔ cups (395 ml) lukewarm water. Add the flour, 2 teaspoons of the salt, and the tablespoon of malt syrup or honey and mix on low speed for 5 minutes using the dough hook. The dough will be slightly sticky. Cover the dough and allow to rise at room temperature for about 2 hours.

2. Punch the dough down and turn it onto a floured surface, lightly kneading in up to ½ cup more flour to keep it from sticking if necessary. Shape the dough into a rough rectangle about 1½ inches thick, and about two times longer than it is wide. If you are having trouble forming the dough, stretch it, wait for the gluten to relax, and re-form.

3. Coat a rimmed baking sheet with flour. Cut the dough into 12 pieces. Roll each into an 8- to 10-inch rope, tapering the dough at each end. Circle the dough around your hand, pinching the ends together and rolling under your palm once or twice to seal. Put the bagels on the prepared baking sheet. Cover well with plastic wrap and refrigerate for about 10 hours, or up to 24 hours.

4. Remove the bagels from the refrigerator and heat the oven to 450 degrees. If you have a baking stone or brick you use for baking, put it on a rack near the bottom of the oven; it will retain heat and produce a crisper bagel. Pour

the poppy and sesame seeds into a bowl wider than the bagels and have ready a cooling rack positioned over the sink or another baking sheet (to drain the bagels). Cover a large wide pot of water and bring to a boil; once it reaches the boiling point, toss in about a tablespoon and a half of salt and the remaining 2 heaping tablespoons of malt syrup.

5. Using your hands, carefully add just enough bagels into the boiling pot to cover the surface of the water, making sure that there are no bagels resting on top of one another. Boil for about 3 minutes, then use a spatula or wide slotted spoon to remove the bagels to drain on the cooling rack.

6. Working very quickly, dip the bagels one by one into the poppy and sesame seeds. Arrange the bagels back on the floured baking sheet.

7. Bake on the second-to-lowest shelf of the oven for about 15 to 18 minutes, or until they are golden brown.

Note In Washington, D.C., Frank Ruta, chef at the Grill Room at the Rosewood hotel, experimented with my recipe and added his own topping of sautéed onions that he puts on the bagels in his wood-burning oven before baking. You can also experiment with other seeds besides poppy and sesame, like nigella or caraway seeds, or even rosemary. Go to your favorite Indian or Asian market and come up with your own bagel toppings.

Malt syrup (Eden brand) is available at most grocery stores and online.

The Bagel's Journey from Ancient Egypt to Almost Everywhere

The basic roll-with-a-hole concept is centuries old. No surprise, really, as there's a practical advantage to this design—it's possible to thread such a roll on a stick or a string, facilitating transport. Even the ancient Egyptians had a bagel-like treat.

The evidence suggests that those of ancient Egypt and of the greater Mediterranean came in two types: the soft, sesame-studded variety, called *bagela* in Israel and other parts of the Middle East today, eaten plain or dipped in *za'atar* (see page 9); and a pretzel-like crispy Syrian *ka'ak* (see page 159) flavored much like the *taralli,* a hard, round cracker that has been a snack for centuries in southern Italy. Neither is boiled, a distinguishing characteristic of Polish and American bagels.

Although the boiled and baked bagel was mentioned in the Talmud, the one we know comes from Krakow. The story goes that the Krakow bagel was a product of the 1683 Battle of Vienna. The tale is completely speculative and perhaps even fictitious, but it is a piece of gastronomic lore that has endured throughout the ages. As the story goes, seventeenth-century Poland was the breadbasket of Europe, and King Jan Sobieski was the first king not to confirm the decree of 1496 limiting the production of white bread and *obwarzanek* (bagel-like rolls whose name derives from a word meaning "to parboil") to the Krakow bakers' guild. This meant that Jews could finally bake bread within the confines of the city walls. Furthermore, when Sobieski saved Austria from the Ottoman invaders, a baker supposedly made a roll in the shape of the king's stirrup and called it a *beugel* (the Austrian word for "stirrup").

The bagel has endured through the centuries not only because of its heroic legend, but because it lasted longer than freshly baked bread. Boiling gave the roll an outer sheen and a crunchy, protective crust.

Now here comes some new lore: I heard a theory about the crunch of bagels from a member of the Beigel family, who, until the Holocaust, were for many generations bakers in Krakow and thus, as they baked bagels, took the last name Beigel when Jews got last names in Krakow in about 1821. The theory is that Jewish merchants from Krakow who traveled the countryside to sell their wares in the eighteenth and nineteenth centuries—and possibly earlier—needed to take food with them to keep kosher on the road. According to Jewish law, eating bread at a meal requires a ritual washing of hands and a blessing over the food before eating. But in the countryside, it was difficult because of the risk of contracting typhus from impure water. The Beigel family, aware of this predicament, ingeniously decided to first boil the dough and then bake it, thus putting it in the category of noodles and enabling the merchants to eat without washing. Eventually, though, the *Arukh ha Shulhan* (the Law of the Table), written in 1903, disputed this ruling by saying, "In Talmudic times there was blanched bread, they would blanch the dough in scalding water then bake it in the oven. This is considered true bread, the proper blessing over it is Hamoitzie and the extended Grace-after-meal following it. Nowadays the *igulim* (circular bagels) are as well blanched in scalding water [prior to baking] and are considered true bread." But people liked the shiny texture of the bagel, so the tradition of boiling and baking stuck.

It is unclear when the first bagels made their way to the United States, but seventy bakeries existed on the Lower East Side of New York by 1900. In 1907 the International Beigel Bakers' Union was created and from then on monopolized bagel production in New York City. What is also certain is that immigrants from eastern Europe, with their cravings for the foods of the old country, sparked the New York bagel craze. Today, bagels are almost everywhere . . . in the world.

Rickshaw Rebbetzin's *Thatte Idli,* Indian Steamed Rice Dumplings with Nuts and Raisins

On a sunny day in Kerala, India, my family and I stopped at Ernakulam, the commercial side of the twin cities of Kochi (once called Cochin) and Ernakulam. Our guide walked us through a busy market full of bananas and rice to a curious store called Cochin Blossoms with plants and goldfish in aquariums. We were told that the shop used to be the Hebrew school of the Malabar Jews, whose specific origins are not known. Inside is beautiful Kadavumbagan synagogue, named after a long-gone synagogue in Cranganore where the Jews lived long ago. Until recently all the Jewish merchants from the market nearby came to pray. Now there are only eight people from all Kerala who pray here.

Suddenly, as if by magic, the owner, Elias Josephai—called Babu by everyone—appeared on a rickshaw and, after chatting for a few minutes, invited us to his home. So off we went to a modern building that he built right next to the railroad tracks. He lives on the second floor in an apartment replete with beautiful woodwork and Judaica.

As we entered, his wife, Ofera, was carefully cutting up North American long beans and corn, much tougher and less sweet than ours, to mix with a *masala* (a mixture of spices) and tuck into rice for lunch. As she chopped she told us about her daughter who lives in Israel, and of course we talked recipes. Ofera's food is fiery and vibrant and you can tell she is a master at what she does. She can make delicious food out of seemingly nothing and adds a modern touch to rice and traditional chicken.

A recipe Ofera mentioned particularly intrigued me. Called *thatte* in Malayalam and Tamil for the flat vessel in which *idli* (fermented lentil and rice cakes) are steamed, or known simply as *idli,* these rice dumplings are a delightful breakfast or snack food, especially during Passover if your custom allows you to eat rice or rice products. If not, try them during the rest of the year.

Ofera told me that she invented the dish years ago for her children, using nuts and jaggery, real brown cane sugar from India that is similar to *piloncillo* or *panela,* the Mexican/South American cone-shaped cane sugar. Use your imagination when making the stuffing—feel free to add your favorite ingredients. Ofera usually makes these dumplings from fermented lentil flour.

---

yield: about 8 dumplings

1 cup (55 grams) unsweetened shredded coconut, fresh or dried

8 almonds

8 pistachios

10 to 15 raisins

8 cashews

1 tablespoon grated jaggery, *piloncillo,* or brown sugar

1 teaspoon salt, divided

1 cup (140 grams) white rice flour

1. Pulse the coconut, almonds, pistachios, raisins, cashews, and jaggery or other sugar in the bowl of a food processor fitted with a steel blade. Remove and set aside.

2. Bring 1 cup (235 ml) of water and ½ teaspoon of the salt to a boil in a small saucepan. Stir in the rice flour with the remaining ½ teaspoon salt. Remove from the heat and mix until the water is totally absorbed. Spoon the rice flour mixture into the food processor and pulse until thoroughly mixed and thick.

3. Fill a large sauté pan with about 1 inch of water. Put a bamboo steamer in the pan and line the steamer with a moist paper towel. Bring the water to a boil over medium heat.

4. Fill a small bowl with cold water, then moisten your hands in the water. Scoop up a small, walnut-size clump of the rice flour dough and form into a flat disc, just smaller than your palm. Put about 1 tablespoon of the filling into the center of the disc. Pinch closed, either into a half-moon shape or by folding the sides on top of the filling so they meet in the middle. With wet hands, smooth out the sides. The result will look somewhat like a dumpling. Repeat with remaining dough and filling.

5. Put the dumplings in the steamer, leaving some space between them, as they will expand. Cover and steam for 10 minutes. Remove and serve warm.

Note You can substitute *haroset* (see pages 85–90) during Passover or even chopped trail mix for the filling. If you don't have a bamboo steamer, you can use a regular steamer or anything heatproof with holes in the bottom to set over the simmering water.

Csúsztatott Palacsinta, Hungarian Apple Pancakes

In Hungary, one sign of a good cook is his or her prowess with *palacsinta,* the Hungarian crêpe, blintz, or pastel. I have tasted *palacsinta* alone or stacked in a kind of torte layered with jams, nuts, and chocolate. But Agnes Sanders, a Hungarian immigrant, taught me how to prepare a similar but different dish her mother made in Miskolc, Hungary, during the Stalin period. Since her mother died when Agnes was eighteen, she learned the recipe from her aunt. Now a librarian living in New York City, Agnes calls this "a lazy housewife's cake," because it is foolproof.

This great modern brunch recipe has a meandering history that dates back to the Roman Empire. According to the late George Lang—whose book *The Cuisine of Hungary* is a masterful history lesson—crêpes, *palacsinta,* and blintzes all came to the Austro-Hungarian Empire via Romania from the Roman army two thousand years ago. These pancakes also traveled early on through the Middle East, the other way to Russia, where they became *blinchiki,* or blintzes.

This simple seven-layer cake is made from pancakes that are baked on one side, then literally slid onto a serving plate, one by one, and sprinkled with cinnamon sugar. Having made this several times, I now caramelize and double the amount of apples used in Agnes's original recipe. It can be either a dessert or a brunch dish; it is served with blueberries and raspberries on the side and dotted with Greek yogurt or sour cream.

---

yield: 4 to 6 servings for brunch or 8 servings as a dessert

6 tablespoons (84 grams) unsalted butter, melted and cooled, divided

4 large eggs, separated

2 tablespoons sugar

Grated rind of 1 orange

2 tablespoons orange or apricot juice

⅓ cup (40 grams) unbleached all-purpose flour

Juice of ½ lemon

2 medium Granny Smith or Jonathan apples, cored and sliced very thin

3 tablespoons cinnamon sugar (see page 6) for sprinkling

1 cup (250 grams) Greek yogurt or sour cream

Berries for garnish

1. Mix 4 tablespoons of the butter, egg yolks, sugar, orange rind, and orange or apricot juice in a medium bowl. Then gradually whisk in the flour, making sure to get rid of any lumps.

2. In a separate bowl, beat the egg whites until soft peaks form (either in a standing mixer with the whisk attachment or by hand with a whisk) and fold into the flour mixture. Let sit for a few minutes while you are preparing the apples.

3. Sprinkle the lemon juice over the apples. Put a tablespoon of butter into a 6-inch nonstick pan set over medium heat. Add the apples and caramelize them on both sides, cooking for about 10 minutes total. Put in a small bowl.

4. Wipe out the pan, reheat over medium-low heat, add more butter, and scatter a few tablespoons of the caramelized apple pieces into the pan. Using a ladle, pour about ½ cup of the batter over the apples in the pan. With a circular motion, swirl the pan so the batter completely covers the bottom. If the batter is too thick, you might have to add a bit more juice. Fry the pancakes slowly, but only on one side. This will make about 7 pancakes.

5. Using a spatula, slide each pancake carefully, cooked side down, onto a serving dish. Sprinkle with a little cinnamon sugar, and continue piling until all but one of the pancakes is piled up. Then sprinkle with some more cinnamon sugar and put the last pancake on top, cooked side up. Sprinkle with the remaining cinnamon sugar and serve immediately with Greek yogurt or sour cream and berries.

Note Although it takes just minutes to make these pancakes, you can cook them in advance, freeze, and reheat in the oven at 350 degrees for 30 minutes. Or you can prepare the batter and the apples ahead of time, then fold in the egg whites just before cooking.

Shtritzlach, Toronto Blueberry Buns

yield: 12 blueberry buns

Nearly every person I meet from Toronto describes *shtritzlach,* called blueberry buns in this Canadian city. Some wax nostalgic, while others, like Mitchell Davis, executive vice president of the James Beard Foundation, decry the oblong bun as having a "sweet, flaccid filling."

I discovered that this was one of those recipes that would have been lost but for a few survivors and those that left Poland before the Holocaust.

Although *shtritzlach* means "currant cakes" in Yiddish, blueberries replaced the currants or raisins in summer and that's when the English name stuck. The late Annie Kaplansky ate them in her youth in Rakow, in southwest Poland. When she immigrated to Toronto in the 1920s and opened the Health Bread Bakery, she started making these blueberry pockets, which were a huge hit.

By the time the bakery was sold with the recipe in the 1950s, the buns had become an iconic Toronto Jewish favorite. The new owner, at the renamed Open Window Bakery, used blueberry pie filling, a new popular convenience item. (This could explain why some remember the buns fondly, while others think of them in less pleasant terms.)

When I was testing the blueberry buns, I asked our houseguest Sarah Weiner, founder of the Good Food Awards, to taste them. "My grandma made these but hers were better," she told me. "In her tiny town of Bodzentyn, Poland, where her family owned the flour mill before the war, it was a traditional recipe, made with wild blueberries gathered in the summer." In *The Last Selection: A Child's Journey through the Holocaust,* the author, Goldie Szachter Kalib, also describes these "fresh, oblong blueberry-filled cakes" as popular in Bodzentyn (a thirty-minute drive from Annie Kaplansky's Rakow!). Sometimes they were called merely *yagedes,* Yiddish for "blueberries."

According to Goldie's memoir, the buns, originally served as a breakfast food, especially on the Sabbath, were made with sweet yeast dough brimming with berries. They were clearly an object of nostalgia for Jews who lived in prewar Poland and later came to Toronto. The recipe, like many others, might have been lost because most of the Jewish inhabitants of these small towns in southwest Poland perished in the camps.

Thanks to Annie Kaplansky, Sarah, and Sarah's late grandmother Helen Starkman Fischer, who immigrated to Skokie, Illinois, for rescuing this authentic and delicious pastry that bakes up into golden treats perfect for breakfast or a snack.

1. Mix 2½ cups (310 grams) of the flour, the salt, and ¾ cup (150 grams) of sugar in a mixing bowl, add half the butter, mix well, and as Sarah's grandmother did, make a well in the center. Mix the yeast with ¼ cup of warm water and stir in. Add the 2 whole eggs and the sour cream, mixing well with a spoon. (You can also put everything in a standing mixer.) Then cover with plastic wrap and let sit for about 2 hours until the dough doubles in volume.

2. Using your fingers, blend the remaining ¼ cup of flour and ¼ cup of sugar with the remaining butter and set aside in a bowl.

3. Preheat the oven to 350 degrees and cover two baking sheets with parchment paper.

4. Dust a baking board with flour and roll out the dough to a circle about ⅛ inch thick, adding more flour if the dough sticks. Cut into 12 three-inch rounds and press at least 12 blueberries into each round of dough and sprinkle with a little of the remaining tablespoon of sugar and the candied ginger, if using. Then, cradling the filled circle of dough in one hand, use your second hand to carefully pinch it closed into a 3-by-5-inch oblong shape. Repeat with the remaining dough and blueberries. Put the buns on the baking sheets.

5. Brush the buns with the remaining egg yolk, pat the streusel—the flour-sugar-butter mixture—on top of the buns, and bake for about 25 minutes or until golden—don't worry if some of the juices boil over. That is part of the buns' charm. Serve warm or at room temperature.

2¾ cups (358 grams) all-purpose unbleached flour, divided, plus flour for kneading

½ teaspoon salt

1 cup (200 grams) sugar, divided, plus 1 tablespoon sugar

8 tablespoons (1 stick/ 113 grams) unsalted butter at room temperature, divided

1 tablespoon yeast

2 large eggs plus 1 egg yolk

2 heaping tablespoons sour cream

1½ cups (285 grams) blueberries (about)

2 tablespoons chopped candied ginger (optional)

Siberian *Chremsel,* Matzo Pancake Casserole

yield: about 12 *chremsel*

Tales of how hard life was in Siberia permeated my early married life. My in-laws, Polish Jews, were lucky enough to have been deported to Siberia during World War II as opposed to staying in Poland with the rest of the family, who were carted off to the Belzec concentration camp. I listened to their stories of chopping wood in the brutally cold winters, bribing guards with shirts stitched by Peshka, my mother-in-law, living in a cramped hut, and, most of all, eating the wretched Siberian food. Peshka used to say that even squirrels wouldn't eat the things they were given. When I asked about Passover, she said, "Who thought about Passover? All we wanted was a piece of bread."

I never imagined that anyone would voluntarily live in this vast, distant part of Russia that extends from the Ural Mountains to the Pacific Ocean and north beyond the Arctic Circle. But once when I was giving a talk in Providence, Rhode Island, a woman named Eleanor Elbaum quietly approached me. "Would you like some Passover recipes from a Jewish family in Siberia?" she asked.

"My great-grandparents on both sides came to Siberia after the Crimean War In 1859. My great-great-grandfather was in the army, and when the war ended, the czar permitted him to move to Siberia from Lithuania."

Her father, who was born in Ishim, Siberia, and served in World War I, went into the hotel business. He and her mother, who was born in the old Siberian town of Tomsk, married and lived in Vladivostok, Russia's biggest port on the Pacific side of the country. In 1922, they took a leg of the Trans-Siberian Railway to Harbin, Manchuria, a journey that served as an escape route for Russian Jews after the revolution and remained one during World War II.

Eleanor, who was born in 1932 in Harbin and grew up in Japan, knows about Siberia primarily through the food she ate as a child. "My mother would tell us how she made *piroshki* and *pelmeni,* the Jewish ravioli, and put them outside to freeze. They told me they didn't need a freezer. They had a sort of igloo outside for the food." Because it was practically impossible to buy fresh lemons, her mother would use sour salt when making jams and curing beef. They also ate typical Russian Jewish fare—cucumber and sour cream salad, cabbage rolls stuffed with meat and rice, borscht, kasha, and sauerkraut. "I just remember that whenever we complained about having something too often, like chicken, my father would remind us to feel lucky to eat it," she said. "I tried so many times to get my parents to talk about the past. That generation just wiped out segments of their lives."

Eleanor calls these matzo fritters *chremslach.* I have eaten *chremsel* before, made out of fried potato and matzo meal and stuffed with meat. I've also made a doughnut-like *chremsel* with nuts that I serve for dessert at Passover, a recipe handed down from my German grandmother (see my *Jewish Cooking in America*). First documented in ancient Rome, this type of recipe worked its way to Germany and then to eastern Europe. But I had never seen a casserole of *chremslach,* made from matzo meal and stuffed with blueberry, cranberry, or any other fruit jam, then browned and baked with a little more jam, fresh blueberries or cranberries (it should be a little tart), and honey. It's delicious—and all the more so for the remarkable journey this particular version of the recipe took from present-day Lithuania, to Siberia, across Manchuria to Japan, and then to California, Toronto, and finally to Providence, Rhode Island.

I recommend prepping this dish the night before and baking it before breakfast.

————————

1¼ cups (145 grams) matzo meal

3 large eggs

5 tablespoons honey, divided

Vegetable spray or oil for frying

1 cup blueberry jam, prune *lekvar,* or apricot jam (see page 9), divided

1 cup (190 grams) fresh blueberries or cranberries

1 cup (250 grams) sour cream

1. Bring 1 cup (225 ml) of water to a boil in a saucepan. Put the matzo meal in the water, remove from the heat, and beat it hard, then put it in a food processor equipped with a steel blade and pulse until the dough comes together. Let cool slightly.

2. Beat in or process 1 egg at a time, mixing well to eliminate lumps.

3. Remove to a bowl and mix in 1 tablespoon of the honey. Let rest overnight or a few hours in the refrigerator.

4. Put vegetable spray on your hands and on a board or countertop. Take a tablespoon of dough, pressing it into a large circle while moving from one hand to the other to prevent sticking. Put a heaping teaspoon of the jam in the center of the dough circle. Repeat, making about 12 *chremsel* in all. Then, using a knife to assist with the sticky dough, carefully enclose the jam to make a ball, making sure it is completely sealed. Continue with the rest of the dough. As you finish the *chremsel,* put them on the greased board.

5. Lightly grease a frying pan over medium heat. Add the *chremsel* and fry them, adding more oil if needed. Drain on a paper towel and put in a Pyrex pan large enough to hold them in one layer.

6. Preheat the oven to 325 degrees. Put ½ cup of the jam, the blueberries or cranberries, the remaining 4 tablespoons of honey, and ¼ cup (55 ml) of water in a bowl and mix well. Pour over the *chremsel* and bake in the oven for 20 minutes until warm and bubbly. Serve immediately with sour cream on the side.

Delkelekh, Cheese Danish Pastries

At the end of the nineteenth and beginning of the twentieth centuries, before a wave of Hassidim came to New York from Satmar, Hungary (now Satu Mare, Romania), Hungarian bakers like Mrs. Herbst on Third Avenue and William Greenberg on Madison Avenue dominated baking on the Upper East Side with their Linzer and Dobosh tortes, *schnecken,* and other delicacies—such as what the and other delicacies, such as the so-called Danish Pastry. Originally known as a *delkelekh,* the Yiddish term for a bundle of dough studded with cheese or jam, these traditional Hungarian treats gained their "Danish" name after groups of immigrant bakers decided their wares needed to seem more American.

"When we came home from school the house was redolent with the smell of baking," said Eva Weiss Cooperman, who grew up in the Bronx. "My mother made *delkelekh* every single week. It was a Shabbos breakfast treat." Today the Satmer Hassidim have revived that treat.

———

1. **to make the dough** In the bowl of a standing mixer fitted with the paddle, stir together the yeast and milk. Add the eggs, butter, sour cream, sugar, salt, and flour. Mix until the dough turns into a ball. Transfer to a large bowl, cover with plastic, allow to rest for 30 minutes, then refrigerate overnight.

2. **to make the filling** Mix the farmer cheese, sour cream, sugar, flour, vanilla, egg yolk, and lemon zest in the bowl of the standing mixer. Transfer to a covered container and refrigerate until needed, up to 24 hours.

3. Preheat the oven to 350 degrees and line two baking sheets with parchment paper. Lightly dust a work surface with flour and roll out the dough into a rectangle ⅛ inch thick. Cut into 4-by-4-inch squares. Spoon about a tablespoon of filling into the center of each square. Pick up corners of each square and press points together.

4. Arrange the pastries on baking sheets about 1½ inches apart. Brush with the egg mixture. Bake until golden, about 20 minutes. Allow to cool and serve as is or sprinkled with confectioners' sugar.

Note You can also use your favorite jam in place of the cheese.

yield: about 24 pastries

DOUGH

1 tablespoon active dry yeast

⅓ cup (80 ml) milk, at room temperature

2 large eggs, at room temperature

6 tablespoons (84 grams) unsalted butter, at room temperature

½ cup (125 grams) sour cream

⅓ cup (70 grams) sugar

½ teaspoon salt

3 cups (405 grams) unbleached all-purpose flour, sifted

FILLING

12 ounces (340 grams) farmer cheese

⅓ cup (83 grams) sour cream

⅓ cup (70 grams) sugar

2 tablespoons flour

1 teaspoon vanilla

1 large egg yolk

Finely grated zest of 1 lemon

ASSEMBLY

Flour, for dusting

1 large egg mixed with 1 tablespoon water

Confectioners' sugar (optional)

Sri Lankan Breakfast Buns with Onion Confit

> On my own account I sent with him sixty bags of Ceylon cinnamon, each bag weighing one hundred pounds, which makes a total of twenty spices.
> —The trustee of the merchants in Aden writes to his counterpart in the capital of Egypt in 1130 c.e., document from the Cairo Genizah, Cambridge University Library, Cambridge, UK

On a recent trip to Sri Lanka (formerly Ceylon), I inhaled the heady aroma of cinnamon almost everywhere I went.

I could not seem to escape that scent, and I was glad of it. This was the spice that inspired King Solomon to send explorers to the Indian subcontinent.

Once there was a small Jewish population in Sri Lanka. The writer and traveler Benjamin of Tudela reported that in the twelfth century three thousand Jews lived in Ceylon. Jewish merchants, like David Maimonides (Moses's brother), had an Aden–Ceylon route for spices like cinnamon. Through the years, Ceylon became a place where Jews did business, but they lived on the coast of India, where there were many Jewish communities. They were often in the sesame oil business, and in Ceylon they processed oil from coconuts.

When the Portuguese took over in the sixteenth century, most of the Jewish population left, never to return, and no more than a few Jews remained in the whole country.

Perhaps the best part of my trip was learning about cinnamon and eating a lunch of cinnamon-perfumed dishes at the home of Chaminda de Silva, a cinnamon grower. I watched workers scrape off the outer layer of cinnamon branches four feet long, drying them for three days, until the bark curled into cinnamon sticks lighter and more crumbly than those most of us know in the United States. Some of the sticks are then ground on the property, while the rest are sent to spice companies, mostly in Mexico and South America.

At a roadside stand, I sampled a slightly sweet bun filled with *seeni sambol,* an onion confit relish flavored with ginger, tamarind, and cinnamon. It tasted both foreign and familiar, with the homey quality I remember from Jewish sweet onion rolls.

Back home, hungry for these buns, I emailed the chef at the Bentota Hotel for his recipe. I tinkered with it, enriching the dough with extra sugar and egg, reducing the spiciness but preserving the memory of the cinnamon-laced onion filling.

———

yield: 16 buns

DOUGH

2 teaspoons active dry yeast

1 large egg, lightly beaten

¼ cup (60 ml) milk

4 cups (540 grams) unbleached all-purpose flour, or as needed

2 teaspoons salt

2 tablespoons sugar

4 tablespoons (½ stick/ 56 grams) unsalted butter, at room temperature and cut into small cubes

Nonstick spray or vegetable oil, for greasing

ONION CONFIT

2 tablespoons vegetable oil

2 to 4 fresh or dry curry leaves (can be found in specialty stores or online)

1 pound (450 grams) red onions, peeled and cut into slivers

1 teaspoon crushed red pepper for spicy filling, ½ teaspoon for mild to medium

1 teaspoon salt

1. **make the dough** Using an electric mixer fitted with a dough hook (or working by hand), combine 1 cup water and the yeast. Mix together. Add the egg, milk, 4 cups (540 grams) flour, salt, sugar, and butter. Knead until smooth. Turn into a greased bowl, cover with greased plastic wrap, and let rise until doubled in size, about 2 hours.

2. Divide the dough into 16 balls and let rise for 30 minutes.

3. **meanwhile, make the onion confit** Warm the oil in a large skillet over medium-high heat, then add the curry leaves and onions. Sauté until the onions begin to soften, about 5 minutes, then add the red pepper, salt, sugar, tamarind, ginger, and cinnamon. Continue to sauté until the onions are very soft, about 10 minutes. Remove from heat and set aside.

4. Line a baking sheet with parchment paper. Punch down each ball of dough and press with your fingers to form a circle about 5 inches in diameter. Put a heaping tablespoon of onion filling in the center of the circle, then fold the dough into a ball. Pinch the rounded edges of the dough together and place the bun on the baking sheet. Repeat, placing the buns several inches apart. Brush the tops with the egg yolk mixture, and set aside to rest for about 20 minutes.

5. Heat the oven to 375 degrees. Bake the buns until lightly golden on top and bottom, 12 to 15 minutes; be careful not to overbake or the dough will be dry. Serve warm or at room temperature, for breakfast or a snack.

Note Sri Lankan cinnamon can be found in well-stocked grocery stores, in specialty stores, or online; look for brands labeled Sri Lankan or Ceylonese cinnamon.

1 tablespoon sugar

1 teaspoon tamarind paste

1 teaspoon minced fresh ginger

1 teaspoon ground cinnamon, preferably Sri Lankan

1 large egg yolk beaten with 1 tablespoon water

Arkansas *Schnecken* with Pecans

The rented freezers at Congregation B'nai Israel in Little Rock, Arkansas, are stuffed each April with more than 1,800 latkes, 700 cabbage rolls, 400 kosher beef kebabs, and 700 *schnecken,* all in preparation for the city's annual Jewish Food Festival.

Jewish food fairs in the South date back to just after the Civil War. At that time, the festivals were often fund-raising events, benefiting synagogues or local hospitals—often with oysters. Today, the fund-raisers represent more authentic deli food, serving "start from scratch" Jewish kugels, blintzes, and, of course, *schnecken* that have been regionalized, with pecans replacing the walnuts used in Germany.

Arkansas's Jewish population currently includes roughly two thousand families. According to the Encyclopedia of Arkansas, fourteen towns, like Levy and Altheimer, were founded by or named after early Jewish residents, who often ran the general store and tasted deli food when they went on buying trips to New York.

In Little Rock, Jews first peddled goods brought by riverboats to the outlying community of farmers. Little by little, they became merchants (or, as one Mississippi lady told me, "mercantiles") in stores along the riverbanks, when the river was king, before the advent of the railroad and later the automobile.

The first Jewish settlers came to places like Pine Bluff, lured there by advertisements in Alsatian and southern German newspapers, promising free settlement in Arkansas. They brought dishes like the potato charlotte (which they now call potato "dressing," in Southern fashion).

Leah Selig Elenzweig, the great-granddaughter of an old settler from Pine Bluff, makes her family's muffin-like *schnecken,* a keeper each year at the food festival.

When German and Alsatian cooks brought this recipe to America in the mid-nineteenth century, *schnecken* (from the German for "snail") were made in the South with real brown sugar, not the colored brown sugar we use today. So I use muscovado sugar to maintain the old-fashioned flavor. This particular sticky bun does not ooze with sugar and butter—and is smaller—so you don't have to feel guilty eating it.

---

yield: 12 large *schnecken*

DOUGH

2 teaspoons active dry yeast

1 cup (225 ml) lukewarm milk

4 tablespoons (50 grams) sugar

1 large egg

4 tablespoons (½ stick/ 56 grams) melted unsalted butter

3 to 4 cups (405 to 540 grams) unbleached all-purpose flour, about

1 teaspoon salt

FILLING

8 tablespoons (1 stick/ 113 grams) unsalted butter

1½ cups (215 grams) lightly packed brown sugar

1½ cups (165 grams) toasted pecans, chopped

1 teaspoon cinnamon

1. **to make the dough** Dissolve the yeast in the lukewarm milk with the sugar in the bowl of a mixer equipped with a paddle. Slowly add the egg, the melted butter, 3 cups (405 grams) of the flour, and the salt, mixing continually until a very soft dough forms. Cover and keep in the refrigerator overnight.

2. **to make the filling** The next morning, remove the dough from the refrigerator and melt the remaining stick of butter, then generously brush some of it onto the bottom and sides of 12 muffin tins. Add a half tablespoon of brown sugar and about a tablespoon of chopped pecans to each tin.

3. Sprinkle a board heavily with flour and remove the dough from the bowl, carefully adding enough flour so that the dough will not stick to your hands. Roll the dough out to a rectangle about 12 inches by 14 inches and about ¼ inch thick. Brush enough of the butter over the dough to cover it and then sprinkle with the remaining brown sugar, pecans, and all of the cinnamon, leaving about a half-inch border. Roll up carefully and tightly like a jelly roll.

4. Cut roll into 12 slices and gently nestle into the muffin tins, cut side down. Brush the tops with the remaining melted butter and let rise uncovered for ½ hour.

5. Preheat the oven to 350 degrees and bake for about 25 minutes or until golden. Be careful not to overbake. When the *schnecken* are cool enough to touch, slide a knife around each one and invert them onto a serving platter, scraping any caramelized brown sugar and pecans from the muffin tin on top.

Chocolate Babka

It is probably impossible for many people to hear the word "babka" and not think of the *Seinfeld* episode in which Jerry and Elaine, desperate to bring a chocolate babka to a dinner party, angrily confront another customer at a bakery who gets the last one. They settle for cinnamon, even though Elaine calls it "a lesser babka."

Jerry disagrees.

"Cinnamon takes a backseat to no babka," he says. "Lesser babka? I think not!"

Babka evokes dogmatic opinions. The babka you knew as a child is the babka that you defend passionately as an adult. My husband, Allan, insists that his be dry. Some say fruit has no place in babka; others say it's incomplete without it.

But babka became a Jewish favorite because eastern European cooks found common ground.

"Babka comes from baba, a very tall, delicate yet rich yeast-risen cake eaten in western Russia and eastern Poland," Darra Goldstein, a professor of Russian at Williams College, told me. "A very elaborate babka was eaten at Easter."

The Italians call their version *panettone*, the French *baba au rhum*, and the Viennese and Alsatians *Kugelhopf*. Jews call it *babka*, the diminutive of *baba*, meaning "grandmother," and gave it their own twist when they came to the United States. They often filled the all-purpose sweet dough with chocolate and lots of cinnamon and sugar, making it more like a coffee cake with a streusel topping.

Like many iconic dishes, the babka of memory may not be the tastiest—the dough was kneaded by hand, it was dry, few used butter, the chocolate was not as good as it is today, and the babka was generally not as rich. This is my go-to babka, starting with a lesson with baker Michael London, who learned to make it from the best—the pastry chef at the long-gone Éclair Bakery in New York. I use his recipe as a base with tricks learned through the years.

———

1. Begin making the dough one day before baking the babka. In the bowl of a standing mixer fitted with a paddle attachment, dissolve the yeast in the milk with the ½ cup sugar. Then stir in the eggs, butter, vanilla, and salt, mixing until mostly combined.

2. Switch to the dough hook and gradually add the flour, mixing on low until a soft but not-too-sticky dough forms, about 3 to 5 minutes. You may not need all the flour.

3. Lightly flour your work surface and shape the dough into a thick square. Wrap in plastic and refrigerate overnight, or for 8 to 12 hours.

yield: 2 babkas

DOUGH

1½ tablespoons active dry yeast

¾ cup (180 ml) whole milk

½ cup (100 grams) plus 1 tablespoon sugar

2 large eggs

8 tablespoons (1 stick/ 113 grams) unsalted butter, at room temperature and cut in chunks

1 teaspoon vanilla

¼ teaspoon salt

3 to 4 cups (405 to 540 grams) unbleached all-purpose flour

CHOCOLATE-ALMOND FILLING

6 tablespoons (84 grams) melted unsalted butter, divided

12 ounces finely chopped good-quality bittersweet chocolate, divided

4 ounces almond paste, divided

STREUSEL TOPPING

6 tablespoons (84 grams) unsalted butter, at room temperature

¾ cup (150 grams) sugar

¼ teaspoon salt

½ cup (65 grams) unbleached all-purpose flour

¾ cup almonds, pulsed in a food processor until coarse

4. The next day, remove the dough from the refrigerator and let sit for about 15 minutes before proceeding. Gather together the filling ingredients and grease two 9-by-5-inch loaf pans or one Bundt pan and set aside.

5. Lightly flour your work surface, then divide the dough into two pieces. Roll one piece into a rectangle about 10 by 12 inches and ¼ inch thick. To make the filling: Spread half of the melted butter evenly over the dough, sprinkle on half of the chopped chocolate, and then crumble half of the almond paste over all. Tightly roll the dough lengthwise like a jelly roll, then twist slightly, laying it seam side up in one of the loaf pans or position in half of the Bundt pan. Repeat with the remaining piece of dough, using the rest of the butter, chocolate, and almond paste.

6. If baking in a Bundt pan, put the second filled dough into the other side and pinch together the ends slightly to form a circle. Cover the loaves or Bundt pan with a kitchen towel and let rise until the loaves are almost double in volume, about 1 hour.

7. While the dough is rising, prepare the streusel topping. In the bowl of a standing mixer fitted with a paddle attachment, cream together the butter, sugar, and salt. With your fingers, mix in the flour and the almonds.

8. Preheat the oven to 350 degrees about 20 minutes before you are ready to bake. After the loaves have risen, crumble the streusel mixture evenly over both.

9. Bake the babka loaves for 30 to 40 minutes, or 50 minutes to 1 hour for the babka Bundt, until the bread is slightly hard to the touch. If they seem to be browning too quickly, tent with foil to prevent burning.

10. Cool in the pan(s) on racks for at least 15 minutes, then slide a knife around the edges and remove from the pans.

Malai, Romanian Cornmeal Ricotta Breakfast Pudding

When my husband, Allan, and I visited friends on the Eastern Shore of Maryland one weekend, the hostess told me that she wanted to cook a ricotta cheese cornbread dish for brunch. Taking out a tattered recipe from her mother, the late Millie Schwartz Ludder, she proceeded to make it for us.

Trying to find out the origins of *malai* proved a challenge to me—and it is what makes writing about food constantly fascinating. Cato the Elder, the second-century author of *De Agri Cultura* (On Agriculture), had a similar recipe, which again lets us see the historic connection between Rome and Romania.

My friend's family came to Montreal from Romania when it was part of Ukraine. When I posted a query about this cornmeal pudding on Facebook's Jewish Cooking Group, one member mentioned *malai,* a Romanian cornbread breakfast pudding, while others told me about *alivanka,* a Moldovan cheesecake from the now eastern part of Romania.

After reading some Canadian history, I learned that Clifford Sifton, the minister of the interior in the late nineteenth century, encouraged people from Romania and Ukraine to come settle Saskatchewan by enticing them with free land. This was just before the time of the 1903 Kishinev pogrom in Western Ukraine. Hundreds of thousands of Christians, followed by a great number of Jews, came to Canada during this period, when my friend's family arrived in Montreal, carrying the recipe with them.

---

yield: 6 servings

8 tablespoons (1 stick/
113 grams) unsalted butter,
divided

3 large eggs, divided

⅔ cup (140 grams) sugar,
divided

½ cup (110 ml) milk

½ cup (135 grams) cornmeal

½ cup (65 grams) unbleached
all-purpose flour

Dash of salt

2 teaspoons baking powder

1½ pounds (680 grams) whole
milk ricotta or farmer cheese

Fresh berries or cherries,
to serve

---

1. Preheat the oven to 350 degrees and grease an 8-inch round gratin bowl or similar baking pan with some of the butter.

2. Melt the remaining butter and cool slightly. Put the butter, 1 of the eggs, ⅓ cup of the sugar, and the milk into a medium bowl and mix well. Gradually fold in the cornmeal, flour, salt, and baking powder and mix well.

3. Mix together the ricotta or farmer cheese with the 2 remaining eggs and the remaining ⅓ cup of sugar in another bowl.

4. Spoon half the cornmeal mixture on the bottom of the pan, then pour on all the cheese mixture and finish by spooning and spreading the remaining cornmeal mixture on top.

5. Bake in the oven for 45 minutes to 1 hour, or until golden and set. Serve warm with fresh berries or cherries.

Putterkuchen, Butter Crumble Cake

While en route to Tel Aviv, I once had a seven-hour layover in Brussels. Bob Greenwood, my cousin who has lived there for forty years, picked me up and drove to the culinary center of the city, *le coin gastronomique de Bruxelles,* called the *ventre* (stomach) *de Bruxelles* by the locals.

To my surprise, near the crowded, heavily touristed cobblestone streets are mushroom stores, great fish-fry restaurants, a cheese boutique once owned by Bob's son Jordan, and, around the corner, Jordan's Delicatessen, a deli that at night becomes a tableclothed restaurant.

We met Jordan's partner Jacques Olivier Charles, a Jewish chef from Paris. He was in the midst of starting a brine for his corned beef, which he calls *pickelfleish,* something rarely heard of in Belgium. From a shelf on the wall next to a photo of Elvis Presley and containers of spices, he took out his mother's copy of *La Cuisine de Nos Grand-mères Juives Polonaises* (The Cooking of Our Polish Jewish Grandmothers) and opened to *Piter kuchen,* a recipe he remembered fondly from his childhood.

The name is a Polish corruption of *Butterkuchen,* a German butter cake served mostly for tea, or, in America, for brunch. I asked him why he was making it. "I think about my grandmother who I never knew [she died in a concentration camp]. It is not the taste I am searching for but the memories."

———————

1. In the bowl of a standing mixer fitted with a paddle attachment, dissolve the yeast and 2 tablespoons of sugar in the milk. Let sit for a few minutes, then stir in the the eggs. Add the flour, remaining ½ cup sugar, orange zest, and salt, stirring on low until just combined. With the motor running, drop in the chunks of butter until they are well incorporated. Cover the bowl with a towel and let rise in a warm spot for about an hour. The dough will not double in size.

2. Make the crumble by mixing the flour, sugar, cardamom, cinnamon, and butter with your fingers. Put in a small bowl and refrigerate until ready to bake.

3. Preheat the oven to 350 degrees and grease an 8-inch springform pan or glass pie plate. Spoon the cake batter into the pan, smoothing it down with a spatula, then sprinkle the crumble over the top. Bake for 30 minutes or until the cake is set and golden on the edges. Serve as a coffee cake.

yield: 8 to 10 servings

CAKE

1 tablespoon active dry yeast

2 tablespoons plus ½ cup (100 grams) sugar

⅔ cup (160 ml) milk

2 large eggs

2½ cups (340 grams) unbleached all-purpose flour

Zest of 2 oranges

½ teaspoon salt

12 tablespoons (1½ sticks/169 grams) unsalted butter, at room temperature

CRUMBLE

⅓ cup (40 grams) unbleached all-purpose flour

2 tablespoons sugar

½ teaspoon ground cardamom

½ teaspoon cinnamon

4 tablespoons (½ stick/56 grams) chilled unsalted butter, cut in chunks

Starters

Hummus with Preserved Lemon and Cumin

Bazargan, Bulgur and Tamarind Dip with Nuts

Socca, Chickpea Pancakes with Fennel, Onion, and Rosemary

Caramelized Shallots and Goat Cheese *Tarte Tatin*

Caponata Siciliana di Melanzane alla Giudia, Sicilian Eggplant Caponata
Jewish-Style

Melanzana alla Giudia, Eggplant Jewish-Style

Cilantro Pesto

Scourtins, Buttery Olive Biscuits

Falafel with Cilantro, Tahina Sauce, and *Amba* (Pickled Mango Sauce)

Amba, Pickled Mango Sauce

Carciofi alla Giudia, Fried Artichokes Jewish-Style

Sambousak bel Tawa, Chickpea Pillows with Onions

Sweet and Sour Persian Stuffed Grape Leaves

Chopped Chicken Liver

Huevos Haminados con Spinaci, Long-Cooked Hard-Boiled Eggs with Spinach

Savory Pumpernickel Caraway *Hamantashen* with Caramelized Olive
and Dried Plum Filling

Halleq, Persian *Haroset* with Dates, Apples, Pistachios, and Pomegranate Juice

Ferrara *Haroset* with Chestnuts, Pine Nuts, Pears, and Dried Fruits

Brazilian *Haroset* with Apples, Dates, and Cashews

Maine *Haroset* with Blueberries, Cranberries, and Ginger

Nutless *Haroset* with Apples, Dried Fruit, and Wine

Hummus with Preserved Lemon and Cumin

At mealtime, Boaz said to her [Ruth], "Come over here and partake of the meal, and dip your morsel in the vinegar."

—Ruth 2:14

yield: about 4 cups, or 6 to 8 servings

The use of the word "vinegar" may be misleading in the above mention of hummus, from the book of Ruth, written almost three thousand years ago. Most translations interpret the word *chamootz* to mean "vinegar" (as it does in contemporary Hebrew). However, according to the Israeli author Meir Shalev, the Hebrew letters *chet, mem,* and *zadek* are the root letters of both the words *chamootz* and *chimtza,* which in biblical Hebrew means "chickpeas."

"In biblical Hebrew, there were no vowels, so words were more confusing," Meir told me, and added, "Anyway, if Boaz served his workers pita dipped in vinegar instead of something more substantial like hummus, they wouldn't have been very happy."

Hummus, meaning "chickpea" as well as "chickpea dip" in Arabic and modern Hebrew, is one of the oldest and most beloved dishes known to mankind. Originating in Mesopotamia, it is essential to the cuisine of the Middle East, served for breakfast, lunch, and dinner there for thousands of years. People never seem to tire of eating and discussing this ancient protein-rich paste.

Today, cooks soak and prepare dried chickpeas, often standing over large iron pots for hours until the beans fully soften. Early on, they learned to grind sesame seeds, which came from China to Mesopotamia, into a thick paste called tahina, which was stirred into the softened beans with some olive oil, garlic, a little salt, and pepper. This simple, sacred mix provided poor people their protein for the day, and the arrival of lemons from China added a dash of flavor that perfected this comfort dish of the Fertile Crescent.

In the 1960s, when Americans were traveling throughout the Middle East, they often came back with the taste of garlicky hummus on their breath. And with the advent of the food processor in the early 1970s, it was easy to prepare. In those days, you could only get hummus in mom-and-pop Middle Eastern stores in neighborhoods catering to immigrants, such as Sahadi's in Brooklyn. Today, every grocery store has dozens of varieties.

Because I met my husband in Jerusalem, we requested hummus at our wedding in 1974 and had to give the caterer a recipe for the dip. One guest who had never tasted this before told me my recipe, with its hint of that exotic spice cumin, was so good I could sell it to Zabar's. I didn't heed the call but others did, and now hummus is marketed around the world. Even with all the brands sold today—and some are very good—I prefer to make my own. Try it for yourself; you will see how good it tastes, especially with the preserved lemon and the cumin.

1. If using canned chickpeas, skip the following step.

2. Put the dried chickpeas in a large bowl with cold water to cover and soak overnight. The next day, drain and rinse them, then put them with the baking soda in a large heavy pot with enough cold water to cover by about 3 inches. Bring to a boil, skimming off the scum that accumulates. Simmer, partially covered, for 1 to 1½ hours, or until the chickpeas are soft and the skin begins to separate, adding more water if needed.

3. Drain the chickpeas (dried or canned), reserving about 1½ cups (355 ml) of the cooking liquid or water. In a food processor fitted with a steel blade, process the chickpeas with the tahina, preserved lemon and its liquid, lemon juice, garlic, salt, pepper, cumin, and at least ½ cup (120 ml) of the reserved cooking liquid. If the hummus is too thick, add more reserved cooking liquid or water until you have a creamy paste-like consistency.

4. Heat a frying pan and add 1 tablespoon of the olive oil. Spread the pine nuts in the pan and stir-fry, browning on all sides.

5. To serve, transfer the hummus to a large, flat plate, and, with the back of a spoon, make a slight depression in the center. Drizzle the remaining olive oil and sprinkle pine nuts, paprika or sumac, and parsley or cilantro over the surface.

6. Serve with cut-up raw vegetables or warm pita cut into wedges.

Note Leftover hummus tends to thicken; just add some water to make it the right consistency. After a few days, freeze any uneaten hummus. Otherwise, with no preservatives, the dip will spoil. Baking soda just helps the chickpeas cook faster and breaks them down. And remember to add a little cumin, which is said to prevent gas.

2 cups (400 grams) dried chickpeas (or 4 cups canned or presoaked chickpeas; see page 10)

1 teaspoon baking soda

1 cup (225 ml) tahina

1 whole preserved lemon, seeds removed (see page 11)

3 tablespoons preserved lemon liquid from jar

4 tablespoons fresh lemon juice, or to taste

2 cloves garlic, or to taste

1 teaspoon salt, or to taste

Freshly ground pepper to taste

1 teaspoon ground cumin, or to taste

3 tablespoons extra-virgin olive oil, divided

2 tablespoons pine nuts

Dash of paprika or sumac

2 tablespoons chopped fresh parsley or cilantro

Favism—Why Israelis Make Hummus and Falafel Out of Chickpeas

When Chaim Sheba, an Austrian-born geneticist, came to Israel, he noticed that some soldiers of Mediterranean origins came down with a blood disorder after eating fava beans or even, in some cases, after walking in a field with the fava beans in the springtime and smelling their pollen. This hereditary disorder, which causes people to have abdominal pains and vomiting, resulting from the rapid breakdown of red blood cells, was discovered in 450 B.C.E. by Pythagoras, who warned about this *favism*, the dangers of eating fava beans for some people. Today, thanks to Dr. Sheba and others, we know more about this enzymatic disease. For that reason, Israeli cooks decided to put only chickpeas in their falafel and hummus.

Bazargan, Bulgur and Tamarind Dip with Nuts

Bazargan, Persian for "merchant" or "trader," is the name of the border town known for trading spices between Turkey and Iran, as well as a family name of many merchants. Perhaps the dish, often part of a Syrian Jewish mezze, is named after a merchant family who made a particularly tasty version of it. Whatever the origin, it is simply delicious, with the use of tamarind lending an unusual flair to the flavorful dip. Like the better-known *tabbouleh,* it is made with bulgur. But unlike *tabbouleh, bazargan* is seasoned with fragrant spices and crunchy, toasted walnuts, pine nuts, and pistachios. You can serve it either as a dip or spread in endives or little cups of radicchio so your guests can easily scoop it up with their fingers.

———————

1. Put the bulgur in a mixing bowl with 2 cups (470 ml) hot water. Leave for a half hour or until the bulgur has absorbed the water. Drain off any excess water. Add the onion, garlic, lemon juice, tomato paste, the tamarind paste dissolved in a little warm water, the olive oil, Aleppo or cayenne pepper, cumin, coriander, allspice or cubeb, and salt, mixing well. Drain any excess water and return the bulgur to the bowl. Taste and add a little honey if too tart. If you like, you can make this a day in advance.

2. Just before serving, stir in the walnuts, pine nuts, and pistachio nuts as well as the parsley. Serve as a dip with toasted pita, any kind of sesame cracker, or scooped up in endive or radicchio leaves.

Note *Bazargan* is similar to another Syrian favorite of mine, *mahammar* (see my *New American Cooking*), coming from the Arabic meaning "reddened," which has red peppers, finely chopped in a food processor, thrown in. Why not add one or two here for a more modern and delicious touch?

yield: about 4 cups

1 cup (150 grams) coarse (#2) bulgur

½ small red onion, chopped (about ⅓ cup)

2 cloves garlic, minced

Juice of 1 lemon (about 3 tablespoons)

2 tablespoons tomato paste

1½ tablespoons tamarind concentrate

2 tablespoons olive oil

½ teaspoon Aleppo pepper or cayenne

½ teaspoon ground cumin

1 teaspoon ground coriander

½ teaspoon allspice or cubeb

½ teaspoon salt, or to taste

1 tablespoon honey, or to taste

½ cup (50 grams) chopped and toasted walnuts

½ cup (70 grams) toasted pine nuts

½ cup (62.5 grams) toasted pistachios

1 cup chopped fresh parsley

Pita, sesame crackers, endives, or radicchio, to serve

Socca, Chickpea Pancakes with Fennel, Onion, and Rosemary

Chick-pea flour is appropriate for every woman in the palace.
—Sumerian proverb, circa 2500 B.C.E.

This Sumerian proverb from the time of *The Epic of Gilgamesh,* a story preceding the Old Testament and repeated orally from 2600 B.C.E., tells us how far back the use of chickpea flour goes. When people from the Middle East came to southern Europe about two thousand years later, they brought dried chickpeas, which they ground into flour to be used as a gruel or in pancakes, especially during the winter. Called *socca* in Nice, *cecina* (made of chickpeas) in Tuscany, and *farinata* (made of chickpea flour) in Liguria, these chickpea, crêpe-like, unleavened pancakes are again in vogue in the rest of the world. They were even served recently at a White House state dinner for one hundred African heads of state. What was once food for the masses is now popular for everyone who wants to avoid gluten and live a healthier and more sustainable lifestyle. This vegan and gluten-free dish can be served as an appetizer, for brunch, or as a main dish with a salad.

One thing to note: you need a brick for the oven, which helps keep the temperature high and consistent. Or better yet, use a pizza oven to get a really high temperature and light texture as they have done at Officine Brera in Los Angeles. There you eat the lightest farinata I have had with no embellishments: just chickpea flour, salt, water, and olive oil. Make it either way.

**yield: 1 *socca,*
serving 4 to 6 people**

1 cup (90 grams) chickpea flour

½ teaspoon sea salt

½ teaspoon freshly ground black pepper

½ teaspoon smoked Spanish paprika

1 teaspoon cumin

5 tablespoons olive oil (about)

1 large onion, diced

½ fennel bulb, diced

2 tablespoons fresh rosemary or any other herb

Olives and chard or other colorful leaves for garnish

1. Mix the chickpea flour and 1¼ cups (295 ml) water in a medium bowl. Whisk to get rid of lumps, then stir in the salt, pepper, paprika, and cumin. Cover and let soak in a warm place for at least 4 hours or overnight.

2. In a large nonstick pan, sauté the onion in 1 tablespoon of olive oil and then, after a few minutes, add the fennel and continue to sauté until the onion caramelizes, about 20 minutes. Set the onions aside.

3. Put a brick into the oven and preheat to 500 degrees. Drizzle a few tablespoons or so of olive oil into a 15-inch-diameter pizza pan, large oven-safe frying pan, or a Ligurian *farinata* pan and put on top of the stove until the pan starts to smoke. Remove quickly, and pour in the chickpea batter, swirling with a circular motion to coat the pan as evenly and thinly as possible. It should be thin like a crêpe, and no more than ¼ inch thick. Then cook as is or add the onions and fennel and sprinkle with the rosemary and pepper. Bake for about 10 to 15 minutes, until the top is brown, crisp, and even

starting to burn around the edges. If the top is browning too quickly, lower the heat to 450 degrees. Remove from the oven and slide the *socca* onto a large platter.

4. Serve immediately, tearing off pieces with your fingers.

Note You can add spice combinations like *herbes de Provence*, *za'atar*, or sumac to the pancake, or whatever spices and seasonings you want that go well with chickpeas. In the summer, I like to skip the fennel and rosemary and instead add fresh greens and herbs from my garden. I serve this versatile vegan dish as an appetizer or a main course with a tomato salad (see page 102) on the side or topped with thinly sliced tomatoes from my garden.

Jewish Cooking, Always Trendy

The fear and dread of you shall be upon all the beast of the earth, and upon all the birds of the sky—everything with which the earth is astir—and upon all of the fish of the sea; they are given into your hand, that every creature that lives shall be yours to eat. As with the green grasses, I give you all these.

—Genesis 9:2–3

Don't forget that, according to the Bible, the followers of God were all vegans until after the Flood.

Today, we are often bombarded with the buzzwords "vegan" and "gluten-free." But really, these special diets are easily incorporated into the Jewish dietary laws, and in fact Jewish food has been full of such trends for centuries.

Caramelized Shallots and Goat Cheese *Tarte Tatin*

A person who must pulverize pepper and the like to season food on the Sabbath should crush it with the handle of a knife against the bowl. It is forbidden to use a pestle, for one is grinding. For this reason, it is forbidden for a healthy person to take medication on the Sabbath. This is a decree [enacted] lest one grind herbs. Compare to *Hilchot Sh'vitat Yom Tov* 3:12, which states that one may crush peppers with a mortar and pestle.

—Moses Maimonides, *Mishneh Torah*

One of my favorite desserts is *tarte tatin,* an upside-down apple tart, so I was intrigued by Sophia Young Bapt's converting it into an appetizer using goat cheese and caramelized onions. Sophia, whose mother is American Jewish and father is French Catholic, was born and brought up in France. Now, to connect with her Jewish roots, she is giving cooking classes in France to show young cooks how to make her creative dishes. Here is her rendition of the savory *tarte tatin*.

---

1. **to make the crust** Mix the flour and the salt in a big bowl, then work in the butter with the tips of your fingers until coarse crumbs form. (If preferred, you can use a food processor fitted with a steel blade and pulse the flour, salt, and butter together until coarse crumbs form.)

2. Whisk the vinegar into the egg yolk and pour on top of the flour. While mixing the dough with a fork (or pulsing in the food processor), gradually add ice water, a tablespoon at a time, just until a dough forms, being careful not to overmix. You should use about ¼ to ½ cup water.

3. Form the dough into a thick disc and wrap with plastic. Chill the dough in the refrigerator for at least 30 minutes or up to a few days. You can also freeze the dough for up to 1 month.

4. **to make the *tarte tatin*** Preheat the oven to 400 degrees and butter an 11- or 12-inch tart pan with removable bottom or 10 muffin tins.

5. Peel the shallots, cutting them in two pieces lengthwise if they are large or leaving them whole if they are small.

6. Melt 1 teaspoon of the butter and the oil in a large sauté pan. Then add the shallots, honey, herbs, salt, and pepper to taste and sauté until well caramelized, about 30 minutes. Drizzle in 1 teaspoon of the balsamic vinegar and remove the bay leaves.

7. Prepare the caramel by putting the sugar and 3 teaspoons of water in a small heavy-bottomed saucepan over high heat. The trick is *not* to stir, so the mixture gains color. When the caramel darkens and becomes very fra-

yield: one 11- or 12-inch *tarte* or 10 mini *tartes*

PÂTE BRISÉE
(FRENCH BUTTER PIE CRUST)

2 cups (250 grams) unbleached all-purpose flour

1 teaspoon salt

9 tablespoons (125 grams) cold unsalted butter, cut into cubes

½ teaspoon balsamic vinegar

1 large egg yolk

TARTE TATIN FILLING

2 pounds (907 grams) shallots

2 teaspoons unsalted butter, divided

1 tablespoon extra-virgin olive oil

2 tablespoons honey

2 fresh thyme sprigs

2 fresh or dried bay leaves

Dash of salt

Freshly ground pepper to taste

1 teaspoon plus a few drops of balsamic vinegar

¼ cup (50 grams) sugar

4 ounces (113 grams) fresh goat cheese or feta

grant, remove from the heat and stir in the remaining teaspoon of butter and the drops of balsamic vinegar.

8. Pour the caramel immediately into the prepared tart or muffin tins.

9. Set the shallots with the round side down on top of the caramel, then crumble the cheese on top.

10. Roll out the dough to be a little more than ⅛ inch thick, and cut out in a disc that is ¼ inch larger in diameter than the mold size (or cut enough discs for each individual tart if using a muffin tin). Arrange dough on top of the shallots and tuck the sides down around the edges.

11. Bake for 15 to 20 minutes, or until the crust is golden. Run a knife around the *tarte* or the mini *tartes*, then top with a serving platter, flip, and tap gently to release.

Shallots

The French crusaders found a small purple onion near the coast of Ashkelon, in present-day Israel. They brought it back to France and called them "onions from Ashkelon," which became *échalote* in French and eventually "scallions" and "shallots" in English. Today, scallions and shallots are no longer grown in Israel, but are instead imported from abroad and called *batsal shallot*, or "shallot onion." Some would like to see the original name of *batsal Ashkelon*, "onions from Ashkelon," restored.

The Wandering Eggplant

"Siete Modos de Guisar las Berenjenas" (Seven Ways to Cook Eggplant), a popular Ladino folksong, points to seven ways of cooking eggplant. Some dispute the number, however, and say the song really has thirty-five verses for thirty-five different eggplant recipes. Because eggplant is not only very meaty but very versatile, it can be used in pies, in fritters, and especially in salads and dips.

I feel as if eggplant has been the leitmotif of my culinary career. Throughout my life of eating in homes and restaurants around the world and writing about ethnic foods, eggplant has always been there, calling me to order it from the menu, begging me to request the recipe from the cook. This member of the nightshade family has adapted over place and time, just as I have, and just as the Jewish people have. I love eggplant for its flavor and its parallels to Jewish history—and my own.

Native to India and cultivated in nearby Asia for thousands of years, eggplant traveled along the Silk Road and over the seas in seeds carried in the pockets of Jewish and Arab traders, as early as the eighth century and most likely even long before. When they arrived in places like Italy, France, and Spain, the seeds were planted and flourished. The traders' wives, guided by only vague directions from their husbands, infused the eggplant with familiar spices, creating new dishes with local flavors.

Easily grown in a hot climate, this Zelig of the food world takes on the flavor of the spices in which it is cooked, a quality that has made it a most versatile vegetable in the Mediterranean region.

Historically, because Jews used it in so many dishes, eggplant became known in Europe as the "Jewish fruit" or "apple," and "eggplant eyes" referred to Jewish eyes. The Inquisitors in Spain, according to David Gitlitz's and Linda Davidson's *A Drizzle of Honey*, asked maids if their employers frequently requested eggplant. If they did, they were judged to be Jewish.

Growing up, I scarcely knew eggplant except in eggplant *parmigiana* and the Progresso brand tinned *caponata*. This changed in my twenties when I moved to Jerusalem and was introduced to a whole new world of eggplants—stuffed, boiled, stewed, and pickled—all with exotic spices from Morocco, Turkey, India, and, of course, Israel. Melech Hahatzilim (King of Eggplant), a now defunct Bulgarian restaurant in Ramat Aviv, boasted an entire eggplant menu. Through the years, I have heard many variations of the saying that a woman living in the Middle East should know more than 101 ways to cook eggplant before she is thought worthy of marriage.

When I grew up, there was one type available, even in Jerusalem: the big dark purple, almost black eggplant. Now, through seed catalogues, local farmers and gardeners are growing all kinds: white eggplants, long, narrow Asian ones, the bulbous ones I like so much called *baladiya* (municipal) eggplant, even the tiny green Brazilian ones that when overripe turn bright red.

A quotidian food for many, eggplant also exists in the sacred spaces of Judaism. Each Sabbath, a Moroccan friend makes two types of eggplant as part of the mezze, which begins the Sabbath feast. One type is roasted, with the pulp used as a dip. The other is sautéed, often mixed with tomatoes and other vegetables as a salad. For her, these dishes are a symbol of the *kadosh,* or holiness, of the Sabbath. For me as well, eggplant is more than a food. It represents life and its journeys.

Caponata Siciliana di Melanzane alla Giudia,
Sicilian Eggplant Caponata Jewish-Style

Eggplant shouldn't be sneered at, because it's neither gassy nor hard to digest. It works very well as a side dish and is eaten as a vegetarian main dish too, specially in countries whose inhabitants don't object to its bitter taste. . . . Forty years ago you could hardly find either eggplant or fennel in the markets here in Florence, because they were considered Jewish food and abhorred.

—Pellegrino Artusi, *La Scienza in Cucina e l'Arte di Mangiar Bene*, 1892

yield: 6 to 8 servings

Contrary to the above remarks by Pellegrino Artusi, a well-known gastronome who wrote the authoritative and well-loved book of Italian cooking, few "abhor" fennel or eggplant. It is true, though, that Jews introduced eggplant to Italy, or more precisely Sicily.

Unlike ratatouille and other tomato-eggplant dishes, this *caponata* includes the superior Sicilian pine nuts, raisins and/or currants. It is a delicious appetizer, one that tastes better the day after it is made.

---

1. Heat 2 tablespoons of the oil in a large nonstick frying pan over medium-high heat. Add the onion, garlic, carrot, celery, and 2 tablespoons of water. Cook over medium heat, stirring occasionally, until golden, about 10 minutes.

2. Add the tomatoes and their juices, currants or raisins, sugar (if using), vinegar, and salt and pepper to taste. Stir and cook partially covered over medium heat for 20 to 25 minutes, stirring occasionally.

3. While the vegetables are cooking, heat the remaining oil in a separate large nonstick frying pan set over medium-high heat. Add the eggplant, in batches if necessary, and salt and pepper to taste. Cook uncovered for 15 to 20 minutes, once again stirring occasionally, until the eggplant softens and turns golden. The eggplant will quickly absorb the oil, but do not add more; the oil will release as the eggplant cooks.

4. Add the eggplant, olives, capers, and pine nuts to the pan with the tomato mixture, stir gently to combine, and cook over medium-low heat for 10 minutes. Remove from the heat, add the basil or parsley, and adjust seasoning. Serve cold or at room temperature as an antipasto with crackers, or as a side dish.

Note When making this dish, I taste it and if, at the end, it needs more oomph, I add either lemon juice or a bit of ketchup, depending on what I have on hand. *Caponata* always tastes much better after sitting for at least a few hours or overnight.

Ingredients

½ cup (120 ml) extra-virgin olive oil, divided

1 medium onion, finely chopped

2 cloves garlic, minced

1 medium carrot, finely chopped

1 celery stalk, finely chopped

One 14-ounce (395-gram) can high-quality plum tomatoes, or 2 large tomatoes, chopped and juice reserved

¼ cup (35 grams) currants or golden raisins

1 tablespoon sugar (optional)

2 tablespoons red wine vinegar

Salt and freshly ground black pepper to taste

2 to 3 medium eggplants, unpeeled (about 2½ pounds/1 kilo), cut in 1-inch cubes

¼ cup (40 grams) pitted green olives, chopped

¼ cup (40 grams) pitted black olives, chopped

2 tablespoons capers

⅓ cup (45 grams) pine nuts, toasted, preferably Sicilian

Handful of fresh basil or fresh parsley, chopped

Melanzana alla Giudia, Eggplant Jewish-Style

Eggplant greeted me in Tbilisi, Georgia, in 1987 at the time when the Soviet Union was collapsing. I broke away from my tour group of food writers to attend Sabbath services in the local synagogue. Afterward the rabbi invited me to his home for dinner. There, in a tiny kitchen that tripled as a bedroom and a living room, we ate a lovely Sabbath meal. My favorite dish was a marvelous appetizer that I called "eggplant bits," made from diced pieces of eggplant pulp and its black skin sprinkled with aromatic toasted spices.

In an Italian cooking memoir, I learned that this same old dish was served in Ferrara with melon as a kosher appetizer, instead of the prohibited prosciutto and melon (although *prosciutto di oca*, goose prosciutto or salami, was made famous by the Jews of Mortara, still the center of goose-in-place-of-pork products). As I have always said, Jews are adapters. Still, I prefer this dish alone, rather than with melon—leave the melon for goose prosciutto.

yield: 6 servings as an appetizer

2 pounds (907 grams) long Asian eggplant, unpeeled

1 tablespoon salt

¼ cup (60 ml) olive oil

2 garlic cloves, minced

4 large scallions, chopped

Salt and freshly ground pepper to taste

2 tablespoons chopped parsley

---

1. Cut the eggplants lengthwise into 4 pieces, then cut into ½-inch slices, making sure each piece is covered with the skin. (Use the inside pieces not covered with peel for fritters; see page 209.) Sprinkle the bits with the salt and let sit in a colander over a bowl for 30 minutes. Rinse off the salt and dry.

2. Using a cast-iron skillet if possible, heat about a half inch of olive oil over medium-high heat and sauté the minced garlic, scallions, eggplant bits, pepper, and a little salt, stirring occasionally, for about 10 minutes covered and then uncovered another 10 minutes, until the eggplant is chewy and slightly crisp. Drain on paper towels, then put in a serving bowl.

3. Before serving, adjust the seasonings to taste and sprinkle with the parsley. Serve as a starter with bread or crackers or as a side dish.

Note The Georgian version includes ¼ teaspoon each of ground coriander, cumin, fenugreek, and cayenne pepper added when the eggplant is sautéed.

Cilantro Pesto

Nachum Inlender, the father of my daughter Daniela's wife, Talia, is one of those Israelis living in the San Fernando Valley near Los Angeles who consumes Israeli food whenever he can.

Although he takes pride in his hummus, I prefer what he calls his pesto, made with cilantro, basil, oil, and, of course garlic. It can be used on top of *focaccia bruschetta,* as a dip for vegetables, or just eaten by itself with a spoon. Greek Jews also make a similar spread with parsley, served over tomatoes in the summer.

———————

1. Throw the basil, cilantro, *za'atar,* garlic, salt, and freshly ground pepper into the bowl of a food processor equipped with the steel blade and process until pasty but not totally puréed. Gradually add the olive oil through the tube. Adjust seasonings and serve.

yield: about 1½ cups

2 bunches of basil

1 bunch of cilantro

1 teaspoon *za'atar* (see page 9)

2 to 3 cloves garlic

Salt and freshly ground pepper to taste

1 cup (235 ml) extra-virgin olive oil (about)

Scourtins, Buttery Olive Biscuits

A *scourtin,* an ancient press to mash cured olives, is also the name of a very old biscuit, now served as an appetizer with drinks, a specialty of Nyons, in the south of France, a town that had a Jewish population from at least the thirteenth century and where many Jews fleeing south during World War II took refuge.

I have changed the formula to make these biscuits, prepared from butter and sugar as well as bits of olives left in the press, a bit less sweet and with salt only sprinkled on top. They are delectable served alone or spread with a creamy Provençal cheese and, of course, a glass of wine.

———————

1. In a large bowl or the bowl of an electric mixer, cream the butter and the sugar until the butter is soft and pale yellow. Add the olive oil and mix well. Add the flour and mix gently but thoroughly until the dough is smooth, then add the olives and fennel seed and mix until they are incorporated into the dough.

2. Remove the dough to a lightly floured work surface and mold into a cylinder, about 1 inch in diameter and about 11 inches long. Wrap with waxed or parchment paper and refrigerate for several hours or overnight.

3. When ready to bake, preheat the oven to 350 degrees and line a baking sheet with parchment paper.

4. With a very sharp knife, slice the dough into ¼-inch rounds and put them about ½ inch apart on the prepared baking sheet. Sprinkle with the sea salt.

5. Bake until golden, about 15 to 20 minutes, or until slighly brown around the edges. Remove from the oven and cool on a wire rack.

yield: about 2 dozen *scourtins*

8 tablespoons (1 stick/ 113 grams) unsalted butter, softened

½ cup (65 grams) confectioners' sugar

1 tablespoon extra-virgin olive oil

1¼ cups (163 grams) unbleached all-purpose flour

½ cup cured black Picholine or Moroccan black olives, pitted and coarsely chopped, drained

½ teaspoon fennel seed

1 teaspoon sea salt for sprinkling

Carciofi alla Giudia, Fried Artichokes Jewish-Style

> There is one common feature in the stories about the banquets; the missing item, according to one source, was the artichoke which was the source of pride among the Jews of Rome and still is. Roman aristocracy, during the time of the emperors, and in more recent centuries used to surreptitiously go to the Jewish homes in the "Jewish Street" to eat *carciofi alla giudia.*
>
> —Immanuel Löw and Moses Löw, *Die Flora der Juden,* 1934

yield: 8 servings

I have always loved eating *carciofi alla giudia,* the crisp, flavorful, fried artichokes resembling Baroque golden chrysanthemums, so I was delighted when Paola Modigliani Fano, who makes hundreds of this Roman specialty before Passover, invited me to her home.

"I am Italian Jewish," she said proudly through Iris Carulli, a friend who acted as an interpreter. Although Jews have lived in Rome at least since the second century B.C.E., the Fanos' ancestors came from Spain after the Inquisition in 1492. In 1555, a papal decree created the ghetto, forcing Jews to live there until 1870, the independence of Italy. A few years later, the ghetto walls were torn down, but during World War II the former ghetto, near the Circus Maximus, was used as a place to round up one thousand Jews. At times, as many as five thousand Jews lived in less than an acre, locked in an hour before nightfall and let out in the morning.

Through the centuries, though, the Jewish community survived and welcomed holidays, especially Passover. Since ancient times, artichokes and roast lamb have been two musts on the Roman Jewish Passover table.

To teach me the techniques of transforming an artichoke into a bronze delicacy, she showed me the almost meditative rhythm of cutting and turning the Roman *cimaroli* or *mammole* artichokes, which are smaller than the American Globe variety, without the sharp thorns, and slightly purple in color.

As she tapped the vegetable on the table to loosen its leaves, she talked about the past. "October 16, 1943, when I was four months old, hiding with my family in a village near Rome, was the day the Jews were deported from Rome," she said. "My grandmother was supposed to go back to our house in Rome to pick up some things and bring them back to us. All of a sudden a non-Jewish friend who was eight months pregnant came running to tell her that she had seen something strange happening. 'Old people and young people were being loaded onto lots of trucks,' she said. 'It was terrible.' For this woman, saving our family was more important than saving her pregnancy. She protected our family of five Jews in her house throughout the war. Of almost ten thousand Jews in Rome, only two thousand died in Auschwitz." Paola paused, holding her knife in midair. "If there were eight thousand survivors of the Holocaust, there were eight thousand righteous gentiles that made it happen."

Returning to the present and our happy task, Paola first cooked the artichokes in oil, then, when they were slightly cool, carefully spread out the inner leaves and returned the whole artichokes to the hot oil, letting them sizzle and puff up like dark gold flowers. She told me that when the local Roman artichokes are in season, she cooks hundreds for her family, freezing them after the first fry. She uses one hundred for the two days of Passover and saves the rest for birthdays and family gatherings throughout the year.

"I cook thirty per hour," she said. "While cooking, I think of my grandmother, who taught me this great Passover tradition, passed down to me for generations." Then she paused. "These are ideal conditions and the ideal end for a good *carciofo*." As I bit into the crunchy outside, then tasted the tender heart inside, I savored the moment. I had just eaten a perfect *carciofo alla giudia*.

Since Roman artichokes are picked at their two-week peak during Passover and before chokes have fully developed, I have made some adjustments for the American varieties that came with Italian immigrants. And Paola was right. You will need a sharp paring or bird's beak knife (*coltello da carciofi*), available at specialty stores.

2 tablespoons fine sea salt, or to taste

1 teaspoon freshly ground black pepper, or to taste

2 whole lemons, cut in half

8 American globe artichokes or, if you can get them, Roman

Olive oil for frying

———————

1. Mix the sea salt and black pepper in a small bowl. Fill a large bowl with water, and squeeze in the lemon juice, then drop the squeezed lemon halves into the water. Set both bowls aside.

2. Prepare the artichokes one at a time. Snap off the outer base leaves (technically called bracts) near the stem of the artichoke by hand. Then, holding a small, sharp knife, slice off the hard, dark top of the leaves, leaving the edible bottom, rotating the artichoke in your other hand, parallel to the knife, as you slice, similar to whittling. Continue cutting and rotating until you reach the tender pale yellow/green leaves. Snip off an inch of the thorny top. Then trim the round stem of the artichoke near the heart, peeling off the outer green fiber, leaving about 2 inches of stem, if possible. As each artichoke is completed, put it in the lemon water bowl to prevent oxidization.

3. Fill an electric fryer or deep pot with a thermometer with enough oil to just cover the artichokes and heat to 325 degrees. (I use an electric wok for this.)

4. While the oil is heating, complete the artichoke preparation. Dry an artichoke with a towel, then, holding the artichoke by the stem, tap the flat top against the table to loosen the leaves so that it opens like a flower. Sprinkle the artichoke with the salt and the pepper, rubbing the seasoning into and around the entire vegetable. Set aside and prepare the remaining artichokes.

5. When the oil has reached 325 degrees, add the artichokes in batches of up to 4 at a time so as not to crowd the pot. Lay the artichokes on their side and

cook, turning occasionally with tongs, for about 15 minutes, or until a fork easily pierces the artichoke. The outside should be bronzed.

6. Remove the artichokes from the oil with the tongs, and drain well on a paper towel–lined baking sheet. When they are cool enough to handle, use your fingers to gently open each one. Then, using a spoon—a grapefruit spoon or melon baller—carefully scoop out the choke. You can prepare the artichokes up to this point and freeze or leave out for a few hours until ready to finish.

7. Just before serving, reheat the oil to 350 degrees. Working again in batches, return the artichokes, stem side up this time, to the hot oil for a minute or so, just to crisp. Using tongs, keep the artichokes steady in the hot oil. The leaves will expand, and puff up like a flower. Some leaves may fall off but don't worry. More for the cook to nibble!

8. Drain very well on a paper towel–lined baking sheet, open side down, and then serve immediately in the center of a small plate, with a sprinkle of salt. Eat with your fingers.

Sambousak bel Tawa, Chickpea Pillows with Onions

Linda Dangoor, whom I met in London, is an artist who ran away to Paris, desperately trying to escape her Baghdadi background. Yet she found that in spite of herself, she kept gravitating to family recipes—but always adding new sparks to them. When she returned to London, she wrote a culinary memoir called *Flavours of Babylon: A Family Cookbook.*

These rustic pocket pastries that Linda calls "chickpea pillows"—also known as *sambousak* and *samosa*—date back hundreds, perhaps thousands, of years in her family, and they are a great vegan treat anytime. The only change I have made to her recipe is adding a bit more oil to the dough and giving the non-vegan cook the choice of using butter instead in the dough. Also, I bake rather than fry them.

_____

1. In a food processor fitted with a steel blade, pulse the flour, baking powder, and salt to combine. Add ¼ cup of the oil or butter and ¼ cup ice water, pulsing on and off just until a dough forms. Add additional water as needed, a tablespoon at a time, until the dough forms into a ball, being careful not to overwork the dough. Remove the dough to a large bowl and let rest, covered, for at least 30 minutes.

2. While the dough is resting, warm the remaining oil or butter in a large, non-stick sauté pan set over medium heat. Cook the onions, stirring occasionally, until golden, about 20 minutes.

3. Pulse the chickpeas in the food processor until coarse crumbs form. Add the mashed chickpeas to the onions and stir in the cumin, curry powder, and salt and pepper to taste. Set the filling aside.

4. Preheat the oven to 375 degrees and line a baking sheet with parchment paper.

5. On a lightly floured surface, roll the dough to about ⅛-inch thickness. Using a 3-inch round cookie or biscuit cutter, cut circles out of the dough. Put a heaping teaspoon of filling into the middle of each circle and, using dampened fingers, fold over the dough to make a half circle. Crimp the edges firmly closed and put on the prepared baking sheet. Continue until the dough and filling are used up.

6. Brush the *sambousak* with the egg wash and bake for 20 to 25 minutes, or until golden. Serve warm or at room temperature.

yield: about 24 *sambousak*

3 cups (405 grams) unbleached all-purpose flour

2¼ teaspoons baking powder

1 teaspoon sea salt

¾ cup (180 ml) vegetable oil or 12 tablespoons (1½ sticks/ 169 grams) butter, divided

1 large onion, finely chopped

2 cups (950 grams) cooked chickpeas (from 1 cup/190 grams dried or from one 15-ounce [425-gram] can, drained)

1½ to 2 teaspoons ground cumin

1 heaping tablespoon curry powder

Sea salt and freshly ground pepper to taste

1 large egg yolk lightly beaten with 1 teaspoon water

Sweet and Sour Persian Stuffed Grape Leaves

Walking into Maryam Maddahi's home in Beverly Hills, I heard Persian music and lots of voices. When I was introduced to the sixty gathered family members singing and dancing, I understood why some people have very large houses. The guests, talking mostly in Farsi, nibbled on pistachios, plump dates, nuts, and raisins, signs of welcome in Iran.

Family feasts are routine for this family, as they were for their fellow Iranian Jews in Southern California, who began settling here after the fall of the Shah in 1979. The population here has grown to about forty thousand, with about nine thousand Jews in Iran today.

When I peeked into the kitchen, it was abustle with women relatives, all of whom had brought dishes from home. "When it is your turn, you make your specialties," said Nazy Maddahi, a daughter-in-law. "I assign the other meat and rice dishes to family members."

Although food customs are changing, many first-generation immigrants in Los Angeles still take a full day to shop at grocery stores on Pico Boulevard or the Valley, and then spend another full day cooking, often with old pans brought from Iran.

At Maryam's, the dining table groaned with platters of appetizers, including a display of raw scallions, fresh mint, tarragon, and dill, and her extraordinary grape leaves stuffed with rice and barberries and topped with Iranian golden dried plums and apricots, a recipe she learned long ago from her mother in Tehran.

The taste for sweet and sour in the Jewish palate comes from ancient Persia and Babylonia, where once you used lemon salt for the sour and sugar for the sweet. Grape leaves came two ways, either savory with lemon or, in Iran, sweet like these. Using cabbage, Swiss chard, and beet leaves as an envelope to enclose the rice stuffing originated in Babylon as *mahshi* and spread all over the world. This is a very delicious way to serve stuffed grape leaves as either an appetizer or a side dish.

---

yield: about 70 stuffed grape leaves

1 cup (235 ml) red wine vinegar

1 cup (200 grams) sugar

1½ cups (300 grams) basmati rice

1½ teaspoons salt, divided, plus more to taste

¼ cup (60 ml) grape-seed or vegetable oil

2 onions, finely chopped

1 cup (150 grams) raisins, rinsed and drained

1 cup barberries (100 grams), rinsed and drained (see note)

1 cup (170 grams) dried apricots, finely chopped

1 cup (170 grams) dried Iranian golden plums (see note) or dried plums, pitted and finely chopped

Juice of 2 lemons

One 16-ounce (450-gram) jar grape leaves, drained and put in a bowl of water to cover (see note)

---

1. In a small saucepan, mix the vinegar and the sugar. Bring to a boil, then lower heat and simmer until a thin syrup forms, about 10 minutes. Let cool in pan; the syrup will thicken as it cools.

2. Bring 6 cups (1.41 liters) of water to a boil in a medium saucepan. Add the rice and 1 teaspoon of the salt. Boil uncovered until the rice is al dente, about 10 minutes. Drain and let the rice cool.

3. In a medium skillet over medium-low heat, heat the oil and add the onions. Sauté for about 10 minutes, stirring occasionally, until golden. Add the raisins, barberries, apricots, and dried plums, then sauté for a few minutes, just to warm the fruits through. Then add the rice, lemon juice, and 2 tablespoons of the vinegar syrup. Taste and add more vinegar syrup and salt to taste, just to achieve the desired balance of sweet and sour. Save the remaining syrup.

4. Cover the bottom of a heavy 5-quart pot with a few grape leaves, then add ½ cup of water. On a work surface, put a grape leaf dull side up, and top with a tablespoon of rice mixture close to the stem. Fold over both sides of the leaf, then roll up to close. Place seam side down in the pot, making a single, tightly packed layer before adding more stuffed grape leaves to a second layer.

5. Whisk ¼ cup of water into the reserved syrup and pour over the stuffed grape leaves. Weigh down the leaves with a small heat-proof plate. Cover the pot tightly, bring to a boil, then reduce the heat to low. Simmer until the leaves are tender, about 45 minutes. Serve warm or at room temperature.

Note Barberries, golden dried plums, and grape leaves are sold in Middle Eastern stores and some supermarkets. If you can't find barberries, you can substitute dried cherries or, according to Yotam Ottolenghi and Sami Tamimi's *Jerusalem,* currants soaked in a bit of lemon juice.

Chopped Chicken Liver

"What am I, Your Majesty, chopped liver?" This appetizer doesn't have to be second best. As a rabbi once told me, *gehakte leber* is perhaps the only uniquely Jewish dish.

Chopped liver originated in Alsace-Lorraine, known in the eleventh century as Ashkenaz. There, for the first time, Jews migrating north from the warmer climates of the olive oil–rich Mediterranean learned to use schmaltz—rendered fat from the geese in that part of France. For the Sabbath, they wanted to eat a delicacy made from liver, an organ of the chicken known since ancient times to have so much blood in it that it was thought to contain the soul of man. Before observant Jews could eat liver, the blood had to be removed—because blood symbolizes life—so they put tiny slits in the meat and broiled it to remove the blood before serving. Rendered fat (in this case, chicken fat) lubricated the liver, onions (cooked or raw) sweetened it, and hard-boiled eggs lightened the dish. While French Jews often turned their chopped liver into a kind of pâté (see my book *Quiches, Kugels, and Couscous: My Search for Jewish Cooking in France*), Jews who migrated to eastern Europe enjoyed it in its original chopped form, and that's what they brought to America.

You know a dish is enjoying a renaissance when "mock" or "faux" versions appear. But to me, mock chopped liver, made from mushrooms, green beans, or even lentils, is still second best to the real thing. This version, a favorite at my Hanukkah table or any celebratory meal, is a variation of a delicious chopped liver from Evan Bloom and Leo Beckerman of Wise Sons Deli in San Francisco. (I have added hard-boiled eggs and even more onions.)

Today, when chopped liver is too often made from beef liver with its more pronounced flavor, Wise's chicken liver version, loaded with caramelized onions, is a treat. And please, try it with the schmaltz—it tastes better!

---

yield: about 3 cups chopped liver

5 tablespoons schmaltz or vegetable oil, divided, plus more as needed

1½ pounds (680 grams) yellow onions (about 4), cut in rounds

1 clove garlic, minced

1 pound (453 grams) chicken livers (see note)

2 tablespoons brandy or cognac

2 tablespoons chicken stock

1 fresh or dry bay leaf

¼ teaspoon hot paprika

Leaves from 1 branch of thyme

Salt and freshly ground black pepper to taste

3 large eggs, hard-boiled and peeled

2 tablespoons chopped parsley, or to taste

Pumpernickel rye bread, to serve (see page 164)

---

1. Put 2 tablespoons of schmaltz into a large heavy-bottomed frying pan set over medium heat. Add most of the onions, setting aside about ½ cup to add at the end, and garlic and cover the pan. Once the onions start sizzling, lower the heat and continue cooking, covered, for about 20 minutes, stirring occasionally. Then cook, uncovered and stirring frequently, over medium-high heat for about 20 more minutes, or until the onions are brown and caramelized, and set aside.

2. Meanwhile, rinse the livers and remove the veins with a knife, then pat dry. Warm 2 tablespoons of the schmaltz in a small frying pan set over high heat. Add the livers and sear on all sides, then lower the heat to medium-high and add the brandy or cognac, chicken stock, bay leaf, paprika, thyme, salt, and pepper. Continue cooking, stirring often, for about 3 to 5 minutes, until the livers are just barely pink inside and most of the liquid, but not all, has evaporated. Remove the livers from the heat and discard the bay leaf.

3. Add the livers to the onions and cook for 1 minute, just to warm through. Then, using a hand chopper or a food processor fitted with a steel blade or a knife, finely chop the livers, both the cooked and raw onions, the eggs, parsley, and the remaining tablespoon of schmaltz or more, according to your taste. Adjust the seasonings and serve on dark pumpernickel bread.

Note You can also make this recipe using kashered livers, sold in vacuum-sealed packages. The livers are already broiled, thus removing all blood from them. Follow the directions above but only rinse the livers and pat dry before briefly searing to warm through. Add more schmaltz to your taste, as the livers will be drier than if you use raw livers.

Huevos Haminados con Spinaci, Long-Cooked Hard-Boiled Eggs with Spinach

One of the most ancient symbols of birth, rebirth, and mourning is the incredible egg. Observant Jews eat them for breakfast or lunch on the Sabbath, cooked overnight in their Sabbath stew or boiled in water laced with onions or coffee for flavor and a dark color.

The symbol of the round, smooth egg for rebirth is especially universal in the spring, the time of an abundance of eggs because there is more daylight, and more for hens to eat. "Factory" hens will still lay eggs through the winter because they are kept under artificial lighting and tricked into thinking it is spring and summer because there is more light.

Eggs, a product of the fowl domesticated by the Chinese in about 1400 B.C.E. and then shipped west, are significant in cultures the world over—from ancient Persia to modern India, from small Italian villages to mainstream America. In Jewish communities, the egg is also a symbol of mourning, both personally and communally. When someone in an observant Jewish family dies, the first thing that is traditionally eaten after the funeral is a hard-boiled egg.

As a community, Jews put a roasted egg on the Seder plate as a symbol of life and of mourning for the destruction of the First and Second Temples of Jerusalem. And many Jews have the custom of starting the Passover Seder with eggs, either cooked in salt water or even cooked overnight in sand, a custom still followed today in North Africa.

This recipe for long-cooked eggs with spinach came from the island of Corfu, Greece, to Ancona, Italy, a seaport on the Adriatic coast. I tasted it in Rome, loved it, and it is now a keeper at our Passover Seder. Daisy Dente Modigliani, who shared this recipe with me, hard-boils sixty eggs to serve as the first course of her Passover Seder for both the first and second nights.

This recipe has replaced our simpler family Passover tradition from Poland of serving hard-boiled eggs in salt water, a custom I learned from my mother-in-law when I married my husband many years ago.

---

yield: 12 to 16 servings

12 to 16 large eggs, preferably fresh from a farmers' market

4 tablespoons olive oil

1 large (about 225 grams) red onion, peeled and coarsely chopped (1½ cups)

1 tablespoon sea salt

1 teaspoon freshly ground black pepper

1½ pounds (680 grams) spinach, fresh or frozen (thawed and drained if frozen)

---

1. Put the eggs in a cooking pot and add water to cover by about 2 inches. Then add the olive oil, onions, salt, and pepper. Bring to a boil over medium-high heat, then lower heat and simmer for 30 minutes. Cool and remove the eggs with a slotted spoon. Tap the eggs gently against the counter and peel under cold running water, keeping them as whole as possible.

2. Return the peeled eggs to the pot with the seasoned water and simmer very slowly uncovered for at least 2 hours, or until the water is almost evaporated and the onions almost dissolved. The eggs will become dark and creamy as the cooking water evaporates and they absorb all the flavoring.

3. Remove the eggs carefully to a bowl, rubbing into the cooking liquid any of the cream that forms on the outside. Heat the remaining cooking liquid over medium heat, bring to a simmer, and add the spinach. Cook the spinach until most of the liquid is reduced, stirring occasionally with a wooden spoon, about 30 minutes, or until the spinach is creamy and well cooked. Serve a dollop of spinach with a hard-boiled egg on top as the first part of the Seder meal or as a first course of any meal.

Note To see if the eggs are really boiled, remove one egg from the water and spin it on a flat cutting board. If it twirls in one place, it is hard-boiled. If it wobbles all over the board, it is not cooked yet and the weight isn't distributed evenly. The easiest way of peeling a hot hard-boiled egg is to put it under cold water between your hands and rub it quickly until it cracks, then peel under the running water.

To prepare the symbolic egg for the Passover Seder plate, boil the egg in its shell, dry it, and then light a match underneath to char it.

Savory Pumpernickel Caraway *Hamantashen* with Caramelized Olive and Dried Plum Filling

Purim, taken from the Akkadian word *puru,* meaning "lots," is a very old holiday celebrating the Jewish people's deliverance from Haman's proposed annihilation in the fifth century B.C.E. At Yale's Sterling Library, I saw a clay tablet with a written stamp providing the only existing prototype for the lots cast by Haman—the chief minister of the biblical Persian king Ahasuerus and enemy of the Jews (Esther 3:7)—fixing a date for the impending destruction of the Jews.

During Purim, it is customary to read the Megillah (the book of Esther), dance, drink, and have fun to your heart's content. The most popular treat during the celebration of Queen Esther's saving the Jewish people from wicked Haman are *hamantashen,* triangular cookies filled with dried plums, poppy seeds, jam, or even chocolate chips. The word likely derives from the German *Mohntaschen,* meaning "poppy seed pastries," though some say the word comes from a combination of *Homen*—the Yiddish name for Haman, and *tash* (pocket or bag), from the Middle High German *tasche.* Although in Israel these pocket pastries are called *oznei Haman* (Haman's ears), elsewhere the cookie's three corners are said to represent Abraham, Isaac, and Jacob—the three patriarchs whose merit saved the Jews. *Hamantashen* have also been said to represent the wicked minister Haman's hat. In any case, eating these cookies has proven a tasty way to commemorate Esther's cunning in saving the Jews.

For the past few years, thanks to magazines like *Joy of Kosher,* I have noticed many creative ways of celebrating Purim. Julia Braun, a chef and educator in Berkeley and a friend of my daughter Merissa, sent me this very modern recipe for a savory *hamantashen.* When I looked at it, I had my doubts, but I made it anyway. To my surprise, everybody loved the savory *hamantashen* and wanted the recipe. I have since tweaked it a bit. I now start *and* close my Purim dinner with *hamantashen*! (See page 311 for sweet *hamantashen.*)

This caramel is a simple yet fancy palate teaser on its own—just sprinkle some Maldon salt on top, put the caramelized olives in a bowl with toothpicks, and serve.

_____

1. **to make the dough** Cream the sugar and butter or coconut oil in a food processor fitted with a steel blade.

2. Add the whole egg and one yolk, the coffee, and the molasses. Then gradually add the cocoa powder, flour, salt, and ground caraway seeds, processing just until the dough forms into a ball. Wrap the dough in plastic wrap and refrigerate for at least a half hour.

yield: about 2 dozen *hamantashen*

CARAMELIZED OLIVE AND DRIED PLUM FILLING

½ cup (100 grams) sugar

½ cup (100 grams) Kalamata olives, drained and pitted, or other good-quality salty olives, plus 2 tablespoons of the olive brine

½ cup (100 grams) dried plums, pitted

DOUGH

1½ tablespoons sugar

2 tablespoons (28 grams) unsalted butter or 2 tablespoons (28 grams) coconut oil

2 large eggs, one left whole and the other separated into white and yolk

1 teaspoon instant coffee

1 tablespoon molasses

1 tablespoon unsweetened cocoa powder

About ¾ cup (100 grams) unbleached all-purpose flour

¼ teaspoon salt

1 tablespoon ground caraway seeds

Maldon salt for dusting

Thyme, fennel, or caraway for seeds for garnish

3. **to make the filling** Stir the sugar and olive brine together in a small saucepan, making a paste. Cook over medium-high heat, stirring frequently to prevent burning, until the sugar darkens and caramelizes, about 5 minutes. Add the olives to the sugar and continue stirring for another 2 minutes. Remove from heat and drain the olives, reserving and setting aside the caramel.

4. Transfer the olives and the dried plums to a food processor and process until chunky—you will want some texture.

5. Remove the dough from the refrigerator, preheat the oven to 350 degrees, and line a baking sheet with parchment paper.

6. Roll out the dough to about ⅛ inch thick. Cut into 1½-inch rounds and fill each with a heaping teaspoon of the olive-plum filling. Rub a little egg white around the rim of each circle. Fold up each round by pinching 3 points of the circle together to make a triangle. After the *hamantashen* are formed, add a dollop of caramel to each cookie.

7. Bake for 20 to 25 minutes or until the filling has set. Sprinkle a pinch of Maldon salt on each *hamantashen* and dust with a little thyme, fennel, or caraway.

Halleq, Persian *Haroset* with Dates, Apples, Pistachios, and Pomegranate Juice

Every Passover, I make about five kinds of *haroset* from different parts of the world. For me, the various blends, representing the mortar used to make bricks in slavery in ancient Egypt, reflect the regional dispersal of the Jews throughout history.

Haroset, a popular dipping sauce for feasts in Babylon, was brought to Jerusalem and later added to the Passover Seder after the destruction of the Second Temple. For centuries, the sauce, originally made of dates, was slowly cooked in copper pots, used to cook down the fruit into a syrupy honey, making the biblical date honey. Then it was topped with ground walnuts (see my *Jewish Cooking in America,* page 387). Later, in Baghdad (about thirty miles from Babylon), it was traditional to buy the dates, press them through a special machine, letting the syrup ooze out, and then heat the dates very slowly in a copper pot until they were the thick consistency of a jam-like syrup. I have heard stories about men and women who would roam the streets of Baghdad hawking this date honey served with clotted cream on bread or matzo for breakfast.

As Jews settled on the Silk Road or throughout the Mediterranean, they either brought with them their recipe for *haroset,* if they could find all the ingredients, or created new ones, based on ingredients where they lived.

Egyptian *haroset* includes raisins, dates, and nuts, and Persian *haroset,* called *halleq,* is filled with nuts and dried fruits, pomegranate juice, bananas, and cardamom as the prominent spice, but uncooked.

———————

yield: 6 cups

1 cup (140 grams) almonds

1 cup (125 grams) roasted, shelled pistachios

1 cup (100 grams) walnuts

1 cup (150 grams) black raisins

1 cup (150 grams) golden raisins

1 cup (175 grams) dates, pitted

2 teaspoons cinnamon

2 teaspoons ground cardamom

1 teaspoon ground ginger

½ teaspoon ground nutmeg

1 large apple, peeled, cored, and quartered

1 large pear, peeled, cored, and quartered

2 bananas, peeled

2 to 3 tablespoons cider vinegar

½ to 1 cup (120 to 240 ml) pomegranate juice

½ to 1 cup (120 to 240 ml) sweet kosher wine

1. In a large food processor, combine the almonds, pistachios, walnuts, black and golden raisins, dates, cinnamon, cardamom, ginger, and nutmeg. Pulse until the nuts are coarsely chopped.

2. Add the apple, pear, and bananas, then pulse until coarsely chopped. Add 2 tablespoons of the vinegar, ½ cup of the pomegranate juice, and ½ cup of the wine. Pulse again, adding more vinegar, juice, or wine to taste or as needed to make a coarse paste. Do not purée; the mixture should retain some crunch.

Ferrara *Haroset* with Chestnuts, Pine Nuts, Pears, and Dried Fruits

It was not a jolly [Passover] supper [in the spring of 1939]. In the center of the table, the basket that, along with the ritual "morsels," contained the bowls of *haroset*, the clumps of bitter herbs, the unleavened bread, and the special hard-boiled egg . . . under the cloth of blue and white silk, embroidered forty years ago by Grandmother Esther . . . I looked at my father and mother, both aged considerably in the last few months; . . . one by one, around me, I looked at uncles and cousins, most of whom, a few years later, would be swallowed up by German crematory ovens: they didn't imagine, no, surely not, that they would end in that way, but all the same, already, that evening, even if they seemed so insignificant to me, their poor faces surmounted by their little bourgeois hats or framed by their bourgeois permanents, even if I knew how dull-witted they were, how incapable of evaluating the real significance of the present or of reading into the future, they seemed to me already surrounded by the same aura of mysterious, statuary fatality that surrounds them now, in my memory. . . . But who could tell? What can we know, of ourselves, and what lies ahead of us?
—Giorgio Bassani, *The Garden of the Finzi-Continis*, 1962

As I sat on the terrace of Residenza Casanuova, a charming bed-and-breakfast in Florence, I watched swallows flying above the red-tiled roofs over the turquoise dome of the great synagogue. With me was Dora Bassani Liscia, the niece of Giorgio Bassani, the novelist cited above. Giorgio was describing his Seder and that of his friends, the Finzi-Contini children dramatized in his book and the subsequent 1970 Academy Award–winning film of the same name.

These families were typical of many Jews in Italy who, when deportations started in the fall of 1943, realized that they had to get out of town and mix with the general population. Giorgio's parents quickly understood that they had to leave Ferrara, because his father was a well-known doctor and could have been easily recognized. They went to Florence, where they were hidden throughout the war.

To my surprise, Dora lived just down the road from my hotel in a tiny garden apartment. Down the road even farther is the building where her mother and her father, as children during the war, were hidden separately in separate apartments. Her parents later met and married.

As I walked down Via della Mattonaia, I wondered about the war in Florence, where 248 of the 2,700 Jewish inhabitants were killed. Most of the survivors, like the Bassanis, were hidden by Italian gentiles.

Before we parted, Dora presented me with a lovely illustrated cookbook by her artist mother, Jenny Bassani Liscia.

The pages are filled with mushroom lasagnas, couscous, and *baccalà,* all crafted in Jenny's kitchen and the kosher restaurant that she ran right next door to the magnificent synagogue. The synagogue, completed not long after the

yield: about 4 cups

1 apple, cored and roughly chopped

2 pears, cored and roughly chopped

1 banana, peeled and roughly chopped

2 tablespoons black or golden raisins

3 dried plums

8 dates, pitted

3 dried figs

¼ cup (35 grams) almonds

¼ cup (30 grams) pine nuts

½ cup (118 ml) kosher for Passover wine or grape juice, or as needed

¼ cup (60 ml) orange juice, preferably fresh

Juice and grated rind of ½ lemon

¼ teaspoon salt

3 tablespoons sugar

1 cup (115 grams) cooked shelled chestnuts

independence of Italy in 1882 (when Jews were recognized as free citizens), represented both Italy's long Jewish past and its future, as no one knew what would happen during the Nazi period.

In the movie *The Garden of the Finzi-Continis,* a scene shows the entire assimilated family seated at their last Passover Seder, probably in April of 1943, before the family was deported and killed in Auschwitz.

In her cookbook, Jenny says that her grandmother would prepare this flavorful *haroset* in the fall when the famous Ferrara pears were at their best, the raisins were at their sweetest, and there were fresh grapes for wine. She would then bottle the rest of the juice and put both away until Passover.

———————

1. Put the apple, pears, banana, raisins, dried plums, dates, figs, almonds, and pine nuts in a large pot. Add the wine or grape juice, orange juice, lemon juice and rind, salt, and sugar. Bring to a boil, stirring occasionally, then simmer, uncovered, until the fruit starts to break down, about 30 minutes. Then stir in the chestnuts and put in a food processor and pulse.

Brazilian *Haroset* with Apples, Dates, and Cashews

On a visit to Recife for the marriage of my nephew, I met with members of the Jewish community, some of whose ancestors came there as Portuguese fleeing the Inquisition. This *haroset* represents the marriage of the apple and nut of the classic eastern European *haroset* and the date and raisin of Middle Eastern versions. You can also mold them into little balls about the size of an olive and serve as our Spanish and Portuguese forebears did until the Inquisition drove them out of their countries to Morocco, Brazil, the Netherlands, and even New York, where their families continue this tradition to this day.

————————

1. Put the apples, cashews, raisins, dates, and cinnamon in a food processor or a large bowl. Pulse or chop until well blended, adding only enough wine to absorb the fruits and nuts. Put the mixture in a large bowl and add sugar to taste.

2. If you want, mold the mixture into balls about the size of a large marble, making sure that each person has one to eat. You can also serve it in a shallow bowl as a spread.

yield: about 4 cups, or about 40 to 50 balls

3 medium tart apples, unpeeled and cut in eighths

1¾ cups (265 grams) chopped cashews

1 cup (150 grams) raisins

1 cup (175 grams) dates, pitted

½ teaspoon cinnamon

About ¾ cup (180 ml) sweet wine for Passover

1 to 2 tablespoons sugar (optional)

Maine *Haroset* with Blueberries, Cranberries, and Ginger

This recipe developed from a conversation years ago as Judy Stein and some friends in Belfast, Maine, tasted *haroset* variations from various places around the world. Together they concocted what has become their traditional Maine *haroset,* with blueberries, cranberries, and, as a nod to eastern European *haroset,* an apple. *Haroset* should resemble the mortar used to build the pyramids, so Judy felt that it should include something long and thin to resemble straw and added ginger (definitely not from Maine). The wine vinegar adds the bitter taste to remind us, as always, of the bitterness of the time in Egypt with the pharaohs.

————————

1. Soak the dried blueberries and cranberries in ¾ cup of the wine for several hours, or overnight, until soft.

2. Put the berry-wine mixture with the apple, ginger, raisins, wine vinegar, and cinnamon in a medium saucepan and cook over medium heat about 10 to 12 minutes, or until the apples are soft. Process in a food processor until combined, but not completely puréed. Add maple syrup or honey to taste and, if needed, ¼ cup more wine.

yield: about 2 cups

¾ cup (125 grams) dried blueberries

¾ cup (105 grams) dried cranberries

¾ to 1 cup (180 ml) sweet kosher wine

1 tart apple, diced and peeled

⅓ cup ginger (30 grams), peeled and sliced into toothpick-size strips

⅓ cup (50 grams) golden raisins

¼ cup (60 ml) wine vinegar

½ teaspoon ground cinnamon

2 tablespoons maple syrup or honey

Nutless *Haroset* with Apples, Dried Fruit, and Wine

One Passover regular at our Seder, Colette Chen, asked if we had any *haroset* without nuts. We did not. She said that her Sunday school teacher had a great version for those who don't like, or can't eat, nuts. Here it is.

———————

1. Put the apples, mixed dried fruit, cinnamon, sugar, and grape juice or sweet wine in a medium bowl. Cover and let sit in the refrigerator overnight.

2. The next day, strain the fruit and discard the juice. To make it "pasty," pulse the fruit in a food processor equipped with a steel blade for a few seconds. Then let it rest again in the refrigerator overnight to make it juicy.

yield: about 2 cups

4 apples (1¾ pounds/ 765 grams), cored and quartered

6 ounces (170 grams) mixed dried fruit, diced

1 tablespoon cinnamon

¼ cup (50 grams) sugar, or to taste

¼ cup (60 ml) grape juice or sweet kosher wine

Salads

Everyday Leafy Green Salad with My Favorite Vinaigrette

Green Salad with Baby Lettuce, Flowers, and an Argan Oil Dressing with Shallots

Homemade Herbed *Labneh* with Beets and Puy Lentil Salad Bowl

Quinoa Salad with Squash, Feta, and Pecans

Carrot Salad Indian-Israeli-Style

Persian Cucumber and Radish Salad with Hungarian Paprika

Matbucha, North African Cooked Tomato Salad

Herbert Samuel's Tomato Salad

Spanakit, Racha's Spinach Salad with Walnuts and Cilantro

Melitzanosalata, Salonikan Eggplant Salad

Rama's Eggplant and Pomegranate Salad with Aioli

Bulgarian Red Pepper and Tomato Salad

Tunisian Carrot Salad with Cumin, Coriander, and Caraway

Moroccan Beet and Orange Salad

Seven Sacred Species Salad with Wheat Berries, Barley, Olives, Figs, Dates, Grapes, and Pomegranate

Tabbouleh with Apples, Walnuts, and Pomegranate

Everyday Leafy Green Salad with My Favorite Vinaigrette

Minutes later Stefania began questioning me about America, particularly about the foods Americans ate. "They eat lettuce, I hear," she said. I confirmed that it was true. Though she grew lettuce on the farm, she was still skeptical. "Let's see if you're a real American," she challenged. She soon brought out a large plate filled with freshly washed lettuce. "Eat," she commanded.
—Lucy S. Dawidowicz, *From That Place and Time: A Memoir, 1938–1947*, 1989

We take lettuce for granted in the United States, but people like Stefania, who lived in Vilnius, Poland (now Lithuania), in 1938, did not. She ate cooked beet salads and potato salads, yes—but not raw lettuce salad. Lettuce salads were, however, common in France and England, and were eaten in ancient Rome.

I first learned to make this dressing, which I have been making for years, from French cousins when I lived in France during my junior year abroad. I have yet to find one that I like better. Just remember to reserve your best-quality extra-virgin olive oil for salads.

---

yield: 4 to 6 servings

2 cloves garlic, pressed

2 tablespoons red wine vinegar

1 teaspoon Dijon mustard

Pinch of salt

Pinch of sugar

2 slices red onion, diced, or 2 shallots, diced

4 tablespoons good-quality extra-virgin olive oil

4 handfuls of greens or 1 intact and cleaned head lettuce

Handful of chopped basil, tarragon, parsley, or cilantro

1. Put the garlic in the bottom of a small bowl. Add the red wine vinegar, Dijon mustard, salt, sugar, and red onion or shallots. Gradually whisk in the olive oil and leave in the bowl.

2. Gently put the lettuce leaves and herbs in a bowl and toss with the vinaigrette. Or, if you prefer, take a beautiful head of lettuce in the summer, cut through the stem so that it will stand upright in a bowl, part the leaves to look like a flower, and, just before serving, pour the vinaigrette over all.

Note I make this dressing once a week so that it is always ready for me in the refrigerator. Once you see how easy it is to make a delicious homemade vinaigrette, you will discard all your prepared ones.

For extra texture, try adding some thinly sliced, raw rainbow beets or matchstick slices of kohlrabi, with edible flowers like nasturtium for color.

Green Salad with Baby Lettuce, Flowers, and an Argan Oil Dressing with Shallots

The first prime minister of Israel, David Ben-Gurion, envisioned the south portion of Israel as a place where the desert would bloom. Although he has been gone for many years, his prophecies are now taking root.

A few miles south is Orly, an argan oil farm, started by Yoni Sharir and his wife, Orly, who make their living training camels. Argan oil, mentioned in the Bible by King Solomon as oil for the furniture of the Temple in Jerusalem, is often used in Morocco but was barely known in Israel until recently. After Yoni read a *National Geographic* article on the oil, he decided that he wanted to grow argan trees on the hills surrounding his camel ring.

So he roamed the Internet and found that a man in Galilee collected species of trees from all over the world, including a few argan samples from Morocco. The man sent him some saplings and Yoni started growing them on his farm. Today, he has hundreds of young trees, some already producing the precious nuts. When they have time, he and his wife crack the shells and extract the oil using a machine.

Today, argan oil is gaining popularity all over the world for its effect on the skin, cuticles, and hair, as well as the nutty flavor it adds to salads.

Moroccan-born Mourad Lahlou, who is the chef-owner of Aziza and Mourad in San Francisco, makes an absolutely delicious salad with argan dressing. The trick is to have a light, fruity vinegar like rice or cider to complement the strong flavor of the argan oil.

yield: 4 to 6 servings

1 shallot

1 clove garlic

2 tablespoons rice or apple cider vinegar

4 tablespoons argan oil

2 tablespoons extra-virgin olive oil

Salt and freshly ground pepper to taste

A pinch or so of sugar

4 cups greens

Tiny edible flowers like nasturtiums, bee balm, baby's breath, or violets

1. Dice the shallot and mince the garlic. Put in a small bowl. Add the vinegar and whisk in the 2 oils. Add salt and pepper to taste and a pinch of sugar and let sit for 30 minutes or so until ready to serve. Then strain the garlic and the shallots and discard.

2. Assemble a mix of salad greens, like arugula and whatever greens you can get. Add a few flowers, dress the salad, and serve.

Making Cheese at the Edge of Israel

I am sending you what has no importance or value, namely white sugar, a bottle, in a tight basket filled with raisins and in a container a pound of Maghrebi kohl, . . . molds of kosher cheese.
—Joseph B. Abraham, in a letter sent to Ben Yiju, found in the Cairo Genizah, twelfth century C.E.

On a trip to Israel, my husband and I drove to what seemed like the end of the world, passing miles and miles of desert and high-tech greenhouses growing cherry tomatoes. Finally we reached Ezuz, a hippie community of about fifty Israelis living in trailers in the farthest western reaches of Israel's Negev Desert, where the Negev meets the Sinai on the Egyptian border. We met Dror and Sarah Friede, who have lived there for thirty years. In this former Nahal outpost, Dror tends to about one hundred goats, while Sarah makes yogurt and cheese in a makeshift kitchen next to their home. They produce yogurts flavored with coffee and mint, semihard and ripened artisanal cheeses, and *labneh*—a strained yogurt with a creamy texture—mixed with *za'atar* (see page 9) and olive oil, and sell their dairy products out of their shop, located in a converted Ottoman-era railroad car.

Sarah, a native of Kenya, told us that their desert farm in Ezuz, with its palm-and-acacia-covered veranda overlooking the Sinai, reminds her of Africa. Just eighty kilometers (or about fifty miles) from their farm lies Mount Sinai, where Moses delivered the Ten Commandments.

Visiting Ezuz is, in many ways, going back in time. "In ancient Israel, they had two ways of preparing cheese," Dror told me. One was using an enzyme (pepsin) that was taken from the stomach of a lamb and added to warm milk, which then separated the curds from the whey. The other was to use sour milk as a starter for yogurt and the strained *labneh*. These are the two ways basically used today. A clay pot strainer for separating the curds and the whey to make cheese is depicted on hieroglyphics, so it has been assumed that cheese making existed at least 6,000 years ago. Recently, archaeologists in Kujawy, Poland, found an intact ceramic bowl with small holes, remarkably similar to a colander, with traces of cheese processing still remaining. This vessel dates back almost 7,500 years. The twelfth-century letter cited above shows that kosher cheese was being shipped throughout the trade routes by ocean vessels.

Bedouins—who live nearby in the Sahara Desert, where people have been making goat and sheep cheese for thousands of years—use salt to draw out the moisture, resulting in a very hard, dry cheese that is preserved throughout the year, without refrigeration. Before being eaten, it is softened and rehydrated with water. And to make butter, they shake the milk in a specially designed goatskin.

"People come down from Jerusalem and Tel Aviv to buy our cheese," Sarah told me, taking a break from making her *labneh*. "The weekend around Shavuot is the busiest of the year for us." Late spring was the time in the ancient world when more animals were born and more greenery appeared, bringing a surplus of milk from cows, goats, and sheep. In many ways, the seasonal cycle of cheese making is the same today.

Homemade Herbed *Labneh* with Beets and Puy Lentil Salad Bowl

Shana Boltin—an occupational therapist from Australia and a pickler and volunteer for Gefiltefest, London's annual Jewish food fair—prepared this salad for MedVeg, the kosher vegetarian pop-up restaurant she runs with an American friend.

You can buy *labneh* from Middle Eastern markets, but it is so easy to make yourself from yogurt, as long as you allow an extra twenty-four hours—the process is described below. Make this salad in steps and make it your own by varying the dish seasonally and to your own taste. Here is my take on Shana's unique and tasty recipe.

———————

1. **to make the *labneh*** Put the yogurt of your choice in a cheesecloth-lined strainer over a medium bowl in the refrigerator overnight. The whey will drip out of the yogurt, leaving a thick, creamy *labneh*. Discard the whey and scrape the *labneh* into a bowl. Then add the salt and garlic and mix well with a spoon.

2. Put the spices or herb combination that you choose in a small bowl. Wet your palms and roll about 2 tablespoons of the *labneh* into a very soft ball. Gently roll the ball in your spice or herb mix.

3. Pour a little olive oil into a pint-size (or so) glass Mason jar. Put each ball in the jar, then pour in oil just to cover. Don't worry about wasting the leftover oil—it makes a great salad dressing.

4. **to make the salad** Preheat the oven to 350 degrees. Rub the beets with the olive oil, sprinkle with salt and pepper, and wrap individually in foil. Bake on a pan about 1 hour, until tender but not completely soft when punctured with a fork. Let the beets cool, then peel. Using a sharp knife, slice the beets very thinly.

5. Spread the oats on the pan and put them in the oven for 10 minutes.

6. Meanwhile, cook the lentils in a medium pot with water to cover and boil for about 30 minutes, until cooked but not mushy. Strain and set aside.

7. Scatter the lentils, oats, peas, walnuts, and arugula in a serving bowl. Sprinkle with salt, pepper, and a drizzle of the oil from the *labneh* balls, then dot some of the *labneh* balls over all, reserving any leftovers for a later use. Arrange the beet slices around the edge of the bowl and serve.

Note Play around with this dish, adapting it to the seasons. In the summer, I like to substitute tomatoes for the beets and use a combination of fresh herbs from my garden with the *labneh*. If you don't want to make your own *labneh*, you can buy it or substitute crumbled feta or any other cheese with this dish.

yield: 4 to 6 servings

HERBED LABNEH

2 cups (500 grams) plain yogurt

½ teaspoon salt

1 clove garlic, grated on a Microplane

1 tablespoon *za'atar* (see page 9), oregano, or other herbs (see note), or crushed chili

1 cup (235 ml) good-quality extra-virgin olive oil

BEET AND PUY LENTIL SALAD BOWL

2 large orange and red beets, trimmed but with a little stem left on

1 tablespoon olive oil

Salt and freshly ground pepper to taste

½ cup (50 grams) rolled oats (not instant)

½ cup (100 grams) dried French lentils, preferably Puy

½ cup green fresh or frozen peas, thawed if frozen

¼ cup (25 grams) chopped walnuts

Handful of arugula

6 to 8 herbed *labneh* balls (recipe above)

Quinoa Salad with Squash, Feta, and Pecans

Quinoa, originally from the Andes in Peru, was barely known until a few years ago. Today, this gluten-free seed is everywhere. For the Jewish community, it is especially popular because it can be served at Passover—it is not related to the forbidden grains, but rather a member of the goosefoot family (which includes spinach, chard, and beets). Chef Meir Adoni of Tel Aviv inspired me with this quinoa dish at his restaurant, Mizlala. I have varied his recipe by substituting red and black quinoa, whose texture and colors I like, replacing the apricots with the less sweet butternut squash, and adding chopped pecans for crunch. The salad is especially perfect in the fall, when butternut squash and pecans are at their best.

———————

1. Preheat the oven to 450 degrees and brush a tablespoon of the olive oil on a baking tray. Arrange the squash on the tray, coat with 1 more tablespoon of olive oil and a little salt and pepper, and cook for 20 to 25 minutes, stirring halfway through, until tender and slightly browned. Be sure not to overcrowd the squash. Use two baking sheets if necessary.

2. Warm a small skillet over medium heat and toast the quinoa, stirring often, for 2 to 3 minutes, just until the quinoa smells nutty. Meanwhile, bring 2 cups (470 ml) of water to a boil in a medium saucepan. When the water is boiling, add the quinoa and a large pinch of salt. Simmer covered for about 15 minutes, or until the quinoa is *al dente* and a light, spiral-like thread appears around each grain. Drain the quinoa and put in a large, attractive bowl, then gently fluff with a fork.

3. Layer the quinoa with the squash. Sprinkle the scallions, pecans, mint, cilantro, and finally feta over the quinoa and squash. Just before serving sprinkle with more salt and black pepper to taste, add the lemon juice, and drizzle the remaining 2 tablespoons of olive oil over all and gently toss the ingredients to combine.

Note This salad is so adaptable to the seasons. You can substitute sliced, dried apricots for the butternut squash and add Swiss chard or spinach cut in *chiffonade* (thin strips). Or, in the spring and early summer, try adding roasted asparagus or sugar snap peas.

yield: 6 to 8 servings

4 tablespoons olive oil, divided

½ butternut squash, peeled and cut into ½-inch cubes (about 5 cups/700 grams)

Sea salt and black pepper to taste

1 cup (190 grams) uncooked red or black quinoa

1 bunch scallions, sliced

½ cup (65 grams) toasted pecans, chopped

1 cup (60 grams) fresh mint, chopped

1 cup (60 grams) fresh cilantro, chopped

1 cup (150 grams) crumbled feta or goat cheese, or to taste

Juice of 1 lemon

Carrot Salad Indian-Israeli-Style

When I was in India, everyone I met in the tiny remaining Jewish community of Kochi, the capital of Kerala, told me that on my next trip to Israel, I must visit Nevatim, a *moshav* (cooperative agricultural settlement) populated since 1954 by Kochi Jews and located about two hours south of Tel Aviv near Beer Sheva. The synagogue has an exquisite duplicate of a gold Torah that came originally from Parur, then Ernakulam. Also at the *moshav* is a museum filled with artifacts gathered from the two-thousand-year history of the South Indian Jews.

When I visited, I met a group of women, guided by Geula Nehemia, who had learned about their past by looking through Indian cookbooks in Hebrew. "When my mother died, I started cooking her food," Geula told me in her kitchen. "For four years, eight of us cooked our heritage. Otherwise, we knew it would go away. We make our food less spicy than our parents did but now our grandchildren like it spicy again."

The women prepared an elaborate vegetarian Indian lunch, including rice, chapati, and *parathas*—from recipes gleaned from the Israeli cookbook of Indian food—followed by lemongrass tea. For weddings and other social and life-cycle events, the women of the *moshav* now cook Indian food—and sometimes, as in this carrot salad, make the recipes half Israeli and half Indian.

————————

1. Cut the carrots into thirds and put into a food processor with a steel blade. Add the garlic, ½ bunch of cilantro, and hot pepper and process until the carrots are finely diced but not puréed. Remove to a medium bowl and stir in the bell pepper, lime juice, and olive oil or mayonnaise. Sprinkle with salt and pepper to taste, top with the pistachios and about 2 tablespoons of chopped cilantro, and serve.

yield: 4 to 6 servings

6 carrots (about 10 ounces/283 grams), peeled

4 cloves garlic

½ bunch cilantro, plus 2 tablespoons chopped cilantro for garnish

¼ teaspoon hot pepper

½ green bell pepper (4 ounces/113 grams), julienned

Juice of 1 lime (about 2 tablespoons)

3 to 4 tablespoons extra-virgin olive oil or mayonnaise

Salt and freshly ground pepper to taste

¼ cup (25 grams) pistachios, coarsely chopped

Persian Cucumber and Radish Salad
with Hungarian Paprika

The court clerk, cantor, and schoolmaster Solomon, son of the judge Elijah, jotted this shopping note on the reverse side of a letter of his, which was returned to him:

Cucumber, *faqqus* (cucumber), parsley
apples, bread, mul[ukhiya?]
a chicken, asparagus.
Pocket money for the wife.
Expended on Friday.

—thirteenth-century shopping list found in the Cairo Genizah,
from S. D. Goitein, *A Mediterranean Society*, 1967

Persian cucumbers, as old as the Bible but relatively new to Western markets, do not need to be peeled, stay crunchily crisp, and taste the way cucumbers should! The seeds for them came from Iran, but like many products affected by politics, they crisscrossed first through Israel and Turkey, then to California and other places around the globe. Try them in this dish.

———————

1. In a small bowl, whisk together the vinegar, sugar, paprika, and salt and pepper to taste. Add the diced shallot or scallions, then set aside until almost ready to serve. Adjust the sugar to your taste.

2. About 15 minutes before serving, put the cucumbers and radishes in a serving bowl, then toss with the vinegar mixture and sprinkle with more paprika.

yield: 6 to 8 servings

⅓ cup (80 ml) flavorful, light vinegar, such as white wine or white balsamic vinegar (or an infused vinegar such as tarragon, lemon, etc.)

1 teaspoon sugar

¼ teaspoon sweet Hungarian paprika

Salt and freshly ground black pepper to taste

1 large shallot or the white part of 2 scallions, peeled and diced

6 tiny Persian cucumbers, thinly sliced (preferably with a mandoline)

4 radishes, thinly sliced (preferably with a mandoline)

Matbucha, North African Cooked Tomato Salad

Also use tomatoes, which are fresh and healthy, and they have seeds that are thick and juicy and make rich sauce and are good to eat. There ought to be pepper of the Indies all around, in the island, in New Spain, in Peru and in all the other discovered places; so that, like corn is the main grain for bread, so garlic is the most common for sauces and stews.

—José de Acosta, *Historia Natural y Moral de las Indias* (Natural and Moral History of the Indies), 1590

Because of priests like José de Acosta, who spent most of his life in Mexico, and merchants who went back and forth from the New World to the Old, little by little tomatoes began to catch on in Europe. Most came to the then-Spanish port of Naples from Mexico and were distributed and grown in the southern climates of Italy, Spain, and North Africa.

Today, these many renditions of summer cooked tomato salads in North African kitchens have spread all over the world through immigration, cookbooks, and the Internet.

Two generations ago, North African women were so proud of their cooking that they would not reveal the recipes even for their salads. I sometimes think that this pride is really a fear that if the cat is let out of the bag, everyone will make the recipes themselves and no one will come to visit.

I love tomatoes in the summer but sometimes, especially in my garden, there is a point when there are just too many ripe ones to deal with. So I do as North African women have done for generations: cook them down with peppers and spices, and serve them as a cooked salad.

Called *matbucha, salade cuite, frita, madurma,* or *salade juive,* this make-ahead salad is so very practical for the Sabbath or any dinner party, as it tastes better made a day or two in advance.

_____

1. Preheat the oven to 450 degrees and roast the peppers on a roasting pan until charred, turning every 10 minutes, about 20 to 30 minutes. Put them in a paper or plastic bag for a half hour (this helps loosen the skin), then peel, remove the seeds and juice, and slice in long slivers.

2. In a large skillet over medium heat, warm the oil with the garlic and add the peppers and the 6 chopped tomatoes, slowly cooking uncovered for about an hour and stirring occasionally, until the liquid evaporates. Add the coriander, cumin, salt and pepper, and a pinch of sugar and adjust the seasonings to taste.

3. To serve, arrange the salad on an attractive flat plate, then thinly slice the last tomato decoratively on top and sprinkle with cilantro.

yield: about 4 cups, or 8 servings

3 red bell peppers

2 tablespoons olive oil

2 to 3 cloves garlic, minced

7 large tomatoes, 6 chopped in chunks (about 5 pounds/2⅓ kilos)

1 teaspoon ground coriander

1 teaspoon ground cumin

Salt and freshly ground pepper to taste

Pinch of sugar

2 tablespoons chopped cilantro

Note You can also sprinkle with fresh basil, parsley, or whatever you have on hand. North African women would first pop the tomatoes into boiling water and skin them. I don't bother.

Herbert Samuel's Tomato Salad

The freshest and most delicious tomato salad I ever ate was served at Herbert Samuel, a restaurant in Tel Aviv. Here it is with my adaptations. The lemon dressing, so simple, is my other go-to dressing (besides the vinaigrette on page 92), and I make it when I want to use lemon rather than red wine vinegar. A good recipe like this should turn you loose, especially in the summer. Have fun with it!

––––––––––

1. Arrange the tomatoes attractively on a platter or plate. Add the olives, radishes, chili pepper, red onion, scallions, basil, oregano, thyme, pea shoots or other greens, and the feta or goat cheese.

2. To make the dressing, squeeze the lemon juice into a bowl. Add the garlic and a little salt, then whisk in the olive oil and toss over the salad.

yield: 6 to 8 servings

6 medium tomatoes, halved or sliced

1 pint (275 grams) mixed red and yellow cherry tomatoes, halved

2 mini Tiger or other heirloom tomatoes, halved or sliced

20 black olives, pitted and halved

6 radishes, thinly sliced

½ green jalapeño or other hot chili pepper, thinly sliced

½ red onion, thinly sliced

2 scallions, diced

10 basil leaves, cut in *chiffonade*

2 teaspoons fresh oregano leaves

3 teaspoons fresh thyme leaves

1 cup (70 grams) pea shoots or other garden greens

4 ounces (113 grams) feta or goat cheese

LEMON DRESSING

Juice of 1 large lemon, or to taste

1 garlic clove, crushed

Sea salt to taste

4 tablespoons extra-virgin olive oil

Spanakit, Racha's Spinach Salad with Walnuts and Cilantro

This is my favorite spinach salad *ever*. It is a very old recipe, with origins in Persia (its name comes from the word *aspanakh,* meaning "spinach"). There is something delectable about the juxtaposition of ground nuts and ground spinach, and the recipe has seemed to follow my travels. I first tasted it many years ago when I went to Georgia (then part of the Soviet Union), in the late 1980s, then again years later in Brighton Beach, Brooklyn, at the restaurants along the boardwalk. Most recently, I tasted it at Racha, a Georgian restaurant in downtown Jerusalem.

Today, most of the Jews from Georgia have immigrated to Israel; others have moved to the United States.

Two of them who came to Israel as children in the 1970s were Lily Ben Shalom, who became a post office employee, and her brother Israel Shahar, an electrical engineer. They had a dream of opening a restaurant, so they saved their money and family mementos of the distant colony of Racha, the western province of Georgia, whose Jewish community dates back 2,600 years.

A few years ago, they opened a charming restaurant in a stone British Mandate–era office building, right across from the office of the original *Jerusalem Post*. They scavenged an aunt's cupboards to fill the restaurant with family pictures on the walls, white lace curtains on the windows, Georgian music, and recipes passed down through generations in the kitchen, ultimately re-creating the ambiance of the country they left behind.

"We cook how they cooked at home," said Israel, the chef. "We don't have any cookbooks. The recipes come from the head and the hand."

yield: 6 to 8 servings

2 pounds (907 grams) spinach or 1 pound (453 grams) kale

2 bunches cilantro, most of the stems included

1½ cups (150 grams) walnuts

3 cloves garlic, peeled

2 to 3 tablespoons red wine vinegar

½ teaspoon hot pepper or pepper flakes, or to taste

Salt and freshly ground black pepper to taste

---

1. If using kale, massage with olive oil. If using spinach, bring a large pot of water to a boil and add the spinach. Blanch for about 30 seconds, just to wilt, then put in a bowl of ice water to retain the bright green color. Remove from the water, squeeze, and dry well.

2. Put the spinach or kale, cilantro, walnuts, and garlic in a food processor with a steel blade and pulse almost to a paste but still leaving some crunch. Remove to a bowl.

3. Stir in the vinegar, hot pepper or pepper flakes, and salt and pepper to taste. Serve at room temperature.

Melitzanosalata, Salonikan Eggplant Salad

When I visited Sandy Amariglio in Athens, we immediately took a walk from her white stucco home to Biologiki Agora Psychikou, the organic market a few blocks away. While there, she picked up several eggplants, handling them as only an expert can, making sure they were firm, black, and smooth. So-called "Jew's apples," there were big ones for salad, thin long ones for stuffing, and tiny ones for pickling or candying.

Sandy's ancestors on both her father's and her mother's side fled Spain during the Inquisition. Her father's forebears went to the island of Rhodes (see page 323), and her mother's went with about twenty thousand others to Salonika, a thriving trading hub where Jews eventually became the major players.

As life was good, most Jews—about seventy-seven thousand—stayed in Salonika until World War II. After the Germans captured the city in 1943, they ghettoized the Jewish population and took most of them by train to Auschwitz, killing the great majority in just a few days.

Sandy's grandmother, however, was one of the lucky ones. Warned about the approaching Germans, she and her husband fled to Athens. Just before the Germans occupied the city, she sewed her Greek sovereigns inside her girdle and hid other money in her husband's shaving cream. Then they fled to Tel Aviv, where they lived off the gold coins throughout the war because Sandy's grandfather couldn't find work. Eventually, after the war, they returned to Greece, where Sandy's parents met and married.

Since the Amariglio family has lived in Greece for so long, their cooking has become Greek, but with many traditional recipes learned in Spain still used, especially for holidays.

"My grandmother would first thing in the morning drink a spoonful of olive oil and a glass of water for her system," Sandy told me.

That day in Sandy's kitchen, we made several dishes, including *melitzanopita,* eggplant pie, a variation of the Bulgarian *pashtida* on page 192; an *almondrote,* basically an eggplant gratin; and this very simple but iconic *melitzanosalata,* Jewish eggplant salad. Often called eggplant caviar, because of the tiny eggplant seeds within, this dish, like the Jews, has wandered all around the world.

Both Sandy and I agree that when an eggplant is cooked over a grill, it has a smokier flavor than when it is just pricked and put in the oven. Sandy suggests eating this simple preparation with a spoon, or even using it as a topping for a carrot or cabbage salad.

---

yield: 4 to 6 servings

1 large eggplant, at least 1 pound (453 grams)

Juice of 1 lemon

¼ red onion, diced

Sea salt and freshly ground pepper to taste

2 tablespoons extra-virgin olive oil, or to taste

½ cup chopped parsley

1. Cover the top of a burner on a gas stove with tin foil. Then place the eggplant on top and cook, moving occasionally with tongs, until soft. It will take from 5 to 10 minutes. (You can also prick the eggplant and cook it in an oven at 450 degrees for about 20 minutes, or until it is soft.) By grilling the outside, you make the inside soft—something you want to do. When the eggplant is soft all around, remove from the heat and let cool in a wooden bowl.

2. Remove the juice and the charred skin. Then either chop in the bowl with a chopper or pulse in the food processor with the lemon juice, diced red onion, salt and pepper, and olive oil. Adjust the seasonings and serve sprinkled with parsley.

Note For an Azerbaijani twist, add a cup of chopped grilled or raw tomatoes and a handful of chopped cilantro.

Rama's Eggplant and Pomegranate Salad with Aioli

Over twenty years ago, Rama's Kitchen was born in the Judean Hills of Jerusalem. Rama Ben Zvi, a dancer, and her husband, Uzi, a gardener, joined forces and moved to the mountaintop village of Nataf, where they started a nursery. With a fabulous biblical garden, Rama was inspired to cook and she did. "Food has to be a part of the experience," she told me at a lunch in her kitchen. The herbs and vegetables are grown at the restaurant, the free-range eggs come from chickens grazing nearby, the cheeses and yogurt come from boutique cheese makers in the surrounding hills, and the flour for the restaurant is grown and ground in a neighboring village.

In the beginning, Rama made quite a splash with her local, organic food, serving it only when the garden was in bloom. I love this dish, which combines grilled eggplant with a Provençal aioli mayonnaise rather than the more traditional tahina. Serve it with crudités or warm pita.

———————

1. If grilling on your gas stovetop, you may want to first line the surface with foil to make cleanup easier. Grill the eggplants on an open flame on a grill or gas stovetop until charred and soft, rotating often with tongs, about 15 to 20 minutes. Remove to cool and drain in a colander set over the sink.

2. While the eggplants are cooling, prepare the aioli. First, in a food processor equipped with a steel blade, pulse the egg yolks, mustard, garlic, and salt and pepper to taste. When they are smooth, very gradually drip the oil into the mixture and continue to run the food processor until the sauce is a mayonnaise-like texture.

3. Peel the cooled eggplants and mash with a fork in a large bowl and stir in half of the pomegranate seeds with half the aioli. Spoon the eggplant on a plate, sprinkling with the lemon juice, remaining olive oil, and salt and pepper to taste. Then scatter the remaining pomegranate seeds on top and serve the remaining aioli in a small bowl on the side with pita bread or cut-up vegetables for scooping.

yield: 6 to 8 servings

3 medium eggplants, preferably *baladi* (about 3 pounds/1⅖ kilos in all)

2 large egg yolks

1 tablespoon grainy Dijon mustard

3 cloves garlic

Fine-grained salt and freshly ground black pepper to taste

½ cup (115 ml) plus 2 tablespoons extra-virgin olive oil

Seeds of 1 large pomegranate, divided

Freshly squeezed lemon juice to taste

Sliced warm pita bread or cut-up vegetables for scooping

Bulgarian Red Pepper and Tomato Salad

After the Italians introduced paprika to their country (from Spain), the Turks, who had many contacts with the Italians, took the seeds from Italy to the Balkans, then part of the vast Ottoman domain. In the sixteenth century the Ottoman Empire included Bulgaria as well as most of Hungary in its realm. The Bulgarians, known as the "gardeners of Europe," have always been famous for being able to make almost anything bloom. Having learned to cultivate paprika from the seeds given them by the Turks, many Bulgarian gardeners emigrated to Hungary during the sixteenth century, partly attracted by the far more favorable soil and climate, and partly fleeing the Turks. Also, some Bulgarians were forced to serve in the Turkish army; others were servants of the Turkish officers. This is the source of most of the mistaken scholarly conclusions about the Turkish role. There is ample evidence that the Bulgarians brought paprika to Hungary and started its cultivation. —George Lang, *The Cuisine of Hungary,* 1971

The late George Lang, whose words on paprika we read above, was one of the most brilliant food personalities and a native of Hungary. Equipped with seeds brought to the fertile Danube valley, Bulgarian farmers grew large green peppers, often called Bulgarian peppers, that turned red when ripe.

I love this quick make-ahead salad; the few simple ingredients combine into something complex and delicious. Note that the first step needs to be done a day in advance of serving.

yield: 6 to 8 servings

10 to 12 red bell peppers
(5 pounds or about 2⅓ kilos)

2 tablespoons olive oil or
vegetable oil

1 pound (450 grams) fresh
tomatoes (4 to 5 medium
tomatoes), roughly chopped

1 teaspoon sugar

Salt and freshly ground black
pepper to taste

2 tablespoons chopped parsley

1. Broil the peppers in the oven for 20 to 30 minutes, turning every 5 minutes with tongs, until they blister and are soft. Put the peppers in a plastic bag to steam. Once they are cool enough to handle, peel the peppers, remove the seeds and stems, and drain any liquid. If necessary, rinse the peppers to remove all the seeds. Cut the flesh into squares about 1 by 1 inch. Let rest overnight in a covered bowl.

2. Warm the oil in a large skillet over medium heat. Add the peppers, tomatoes, sugar, and salt and pepper to taste. Sauté about 30 minutes, until the juices have mostly evaporated and the tomatoes are cooked through. Taste and adjust for seasoning, then sprinkle the chopped parsley over top. Serve at room temperature.

Tunisian Carrot Salad with Cumin, Coriander, and Caraway

yield: 6 to 8 servings

Sitting under an almond tree in Saleilles, a village just outside Perpignan, nestled in the French Pyrenees, my husband and I had lunch with a group of women who were reviving Jewish life in southwest France.

Their ancestors, many of whom were Marranos, or "secret Jews," during the Spanish Inquisition, fled to North Africa. Their descendants lived there for hundreds of years, until the 1950s and '60s, when about 250,000 Jews from North Africa returned to France. Some of them now make up the Jewish community of Perpignan, currently numbering about 450 families. When I asked Corynne Mas, a woman born in France to eastern European parents but married to an Algerian Jew and now an avid Algerian cook, when she cooks for her children, she replied, "We cook every day and our children like to eat our food. Food is a transmission of culture. Living in a small town, we don't lose time in traffic. So we have time to cook."

Guidebooks on the region, for the most part, omit the early history of the Jews. The sole reference I saw to these centuries of history was in the Michelin Blue Guide, which did state quite simply that when the Jews were banished from the ancient port of Narbonne by King Philippe le Bel in the fourteenth century, the city suffered, never again to regain its earlier greatness.

Narbonne, one of the chief centers of Jewish culture during the Middle Ages, has a deep and ancient Jewish past. A letter from a bishop in the twelfth century attested to the fact that there were two thousand Jews in the town. Today there are twenty-three Jewish families living there.

No wonder these women talked about food. It has all gone full circle. Their ancestors probably came from towns like this centuries ago before being expelled, and now they are back again, creating a new and vibrant Jewish life grounded in tradition but with the addition of new foods from the Americas, like hot peppers.

"Jewish cooking is like an umbilical cord; it is never cut from the family," said Carole Chaouat, one of the ladies. "Food is our identity. It is our tradition and our roots," she continued as she dipped two fingers in a jar of hot *harissa* and dabbed the hot sauce on the cooked carrots in this salad. The recipe below calls for adding a sprinkling of *dukkah,* the Egyptian spice combination, for additional texture and taste.

---

2 pounds (907 grams) carrots, peeled

1 teaspoon sea salt or to taste

3 tablespoons olive oil

1 teaspoon ground cumin

1 teaspoon ground caraway

1 teaspoon ground coriander

Freshly ground black pepper to taste

Juice of ½ lemon

1 teaspoon *harissa* or to taste (see page 10)

1 tablespoon *dukkah* (optional)

1. Bring a pot of water to a boil and add the carrots and the teaspoon of salt. Cook for about 15 minutes, until the carrots are easily pierced by a fork but still retain a bit of bite. Remove the carrots from the pot and put immediately into an ice bath.

2. Drain the carrots, cut into rounds and put them in a flat serving dish, then sprinkle with the olive oil, cumin, caraway, coriander, salt, pepper, and lemon juice.

3. Just before serving, dip your index and middle fingers into the *harissa* and dab it over the salad. Then sprinkle on the *dukkah,* if using. Serve at room temperature.

Note You can substitute red new potatoes for the carrots in this salad. Just don't forget to dot with the *harissa* at the end for added color and flavor.

Moroccan Beet and Orange Salad

The Abaye said, "Now that you have said that an omen is significant, at the beginning of each year, each person should accustom himself to eat gourds, fenugreek, leeks, beets and dates."

—Babylonian Talmud, Kerisus 6a

yield: 8 to 10 servings

6 to 8 medium beets

2 tablespoons olive oil

2 to 3 navel oranges

Juice of 1 lemon

2 cloves garlic, minced

1 teaspoon ground cumin, or to taste

Salt and freshly ground black pepper to taste

4 tablespoons extra-virgin olive oil

½ bunch fresh parsley, chopped

2 tablespoons chopped green pistachios

The cultivated beet, known botanically as *Beta vulgaris,* evolved from the wild sea beet, a native of coastlines from India to Britain. The sea beet, in the same family as chard, was first domesticated in the eastern Mediterranean and the Middle East, most specifically Iraq, with only the leaves eaten initially. Although the bulbous beets evolved early on, none of the extant medieval Arab cookbooks mention them. My guess is that with the kind of communal eating they used to have, using fingers to handle food would make eating beets messy, staining both fingers and clothes—beets were also used as a red dye.

But within the Jewish community, especially in Iraq, where I found many recipes for beets, the vegetable has been popular since earliest times. It was used as a way to ward off diseases like leprosy and *ra'anan,* a skin disease causing extreme debility and nervous trembling.

Beets are symbolic at Rosh Hashanah, and before the arrival of potatoes in eastern Europe, they played a greater role in the everyday diets of the Jewish people: as a vegetable, as soup, even as a candy. And of course, much later (see page 302), beets were processed into sugar.

Today, with their health benefits properly understood, beets are finding a new popularity. I even like them raw, grated or sliced thin in salads (see my *American Folklife Cookbook*). You can, of course, find the typical red beets in grocery stores—and sometimes you can even find them peeled, cut, and prepared under *sous vide* as they have been in France for several years. If you go to a farmers' market, you'll likely encounter multicolored beets or, my favorite, the splendid striped watermelon variety, like those that I grow from Renee's Garden seeds. And please do not throw out those greens. Sauté them for breakfast with eggs or at dinner with pasta and as a bed under your meat.

At Rosh Hashanah, I love to serve beets and bright oranges as one of several colorful salads. According to the Gemara, the component of the Talmud comprising rabbinical analysis of and commentary on the Mishnah, written in 200 C.E., you are supposed to serve at least seven vegetables for the new year, including beets.

---

1. Preheat the oven to 350 degrees. Rinse the beets, rub them with the olive oil, and then wrap them in foil and put them on a baking sheet. Roast them for about 1 hour, until tender when poked with a fork. When cool enough to handle, peel the beets and cut into bite-size pieces.

2. With a sharp knife, cut off the tops and bottoms of the oranges. Slice off the peel and the white pith, and cut in between the white membranes to extract individual segments.

3. Mix the lemon juice, garlic, cumin, and salt and pepper to taste in a small bowl. Whisk in the olive oil, then toss with the beets. Let sit for a few hours at room temperature. Just before serving, add the orange segments and sprinkle with the parsley and pistachio nuts for color.

Seven Sacred Species Salad with Wheat Berries, Barley, Olives, Figs, Dates, Grapes, and Pomegranate

For the Lord your God is bringing you into a good land, a land with streams and springs and fountains issuing from plain and hill; a land of wheat and barley, of vines, figs, and pomegranates, a land of olive trees and honey; a land where you may eat food without stint, where you will lack nothing; a land whose rocks are iron and from whose hills you can mine copper. When you have eaten your fill, give thanks to the Lord your God for the good land which He has given you.
—Deuteronomy 8:7–10

Julia Braun grew up in Bandon, Oregon, where hers was the only Jewish family. After college, while teaching in New Orleans, she realized that she wanted to move back to the West Coast, and so she joined Urban Adamah, a Jewish urban farm that offers a three-month food-justice fellowship in Berkeley, California. While there, she recognized that she loved cooking Jewish food and found it a way to connect to her religion. "My mom taught me Judaism through food," she told me. "Often on Fridays she would bake challah and make matzo balls. It is cultural, emotional, and satisfying work to make beautiful food for people that also has spiritual significance for me," she said.

After studying at the Center for Kosher Culinary Arts in Brooklyn, Julia again returned to Berkeley, where she catered a Tu B'Shvat celebration for one hundred people at Urban Adamah. In one dish, she incorporated the seven species (the main produce of the land of ancient Israel) mentioned in Deuteronomy into a salad that can happily be served all year round.

———

1. Stir the balsamic vinegar, garlic, honey, mustard powder, and salt and pepper together in a mixing bowl. Gradually whisk in the olive oil and let sit.

2. Fill a medium saucepan with water and add the wheat berries and ½ teaspoon salt. Bring to a boil and simmer for about 10 minutes. Then add the barley and continue to simmer uncovered for another 20 minutes, until the wheat berries and the barley are almost *al dente*.

3. Drain and rinse under cold water to stop them from cooking and transfer to a bowl and let cool completely. Then stir in the dates, figs, and grapes.

4. Add the red onions, scallions, garlic, parsley, olives, and pomegranates. Put the greens out on a flat plate, cover with the salad, sprinkle on the feta or goat cheese, if using, and drizzle some of the dressing over all. Toss and serve immediately.

yield: 8 to 10 servings

DRESSING

½ cup (115 ml) balsamic vinegar

1 clove garlic, minced

1 tablespoon honey

½ teaspoon mustard powder

Salt and freshly ground pepper to taste

½ cup (128 ml) extra-virgin olive oil

SALAD

¾ cup (170 grams) wheat berries

½ teaspoon salt

¾ cup (170 grams) pearl barley

½ cup (90 grams) dates, chopped

½ cup (75 grams) figs, chopped

1 cup white or red grapes, halved

1 small red onion, chopped fine

5 scallions (green onions), sliced thin

3 garlic cloves, minced fine

1 cup (25 grams) parsley, basil, or cilantro, chopped

1 cup (180 grams) olives, chopped

½ cup (87 grams) pomegranate seeds

2 handfuls of salad greens

1 cup (150 grams) feta or goat cheese, crumbled (optional)

Tabbouleh with Apples, Walnuts, and Pomegranate

I met Mike Solomonov and visited his restaurant Zahav in Philadelphia several years ago. We recently traveled together to Israel to visit the apple orchard on the Lebanese border where his brother David died as a soldier. He had volunteered to cover for a religious friend who wanted to celebrate Yom Kippur with his family, and was killed by sniper fire. As we sat in this beautiful spot, munching on apples that the farmer gave us and looking across at a Lebanese village, I thought of the sadness of this never-ending conflict. Mike must think of it every time he makes his *tabbouleh* with apples.

Tabbouleh, whose name comes from the Arabic word *taabil*, meaning "seasoning," is traditionally made in the mountains of Lebanon, Jordan, Israel, and Syria with wild herbs, bulgur, tomato, lemon juice, and olive oil. In the Middle East, most *tabboulehs*, like this one, are served with lettuce or endives to scoop up the chopped salad.

---

1. Mix the parsley, pomegranate seeds, apples, and red onion in a medium bowl. Stir in the pepper or paprika, honey, lemon juice, and olive oil. Season to taste with salt and mix thoroughly. At this point, you can, if you like, cover the mixture and refrigerate it for up to 2 days.

2. In a dry skillet over medium heat, stir the walnuts until toasted, about 3 minutes. Remove from heat. Sprinkle the walnuts with a pinch of salt and crush them with the side of a knife or in a mortar and pestle until coarsely chopped.

3. Stir in the crushed walnuts. If the *tabbouleh* has been refrigerated, set it out at room temperature for an hour before adding the walnuts.

4. Scoop it up with cabbage, romaine lettuce, endive, or fresh grape leaves.

yield: 6 to 8 servings

1 bunch flat-leaf parsley, finely chopped

½ cup (87 grams) fresh pomegranate seeds

1 cup (120 grams) diced, cored, unpeeled apples (from about 1 apple), preferably Pink Lady

½ medium red onion, diced

1½ to 2 teaspoons ground Urfa pepper, smoked paprika, or chipotle chili pepper

1 to 2 tablespoons honey

¼ cup (60 ml) fresh lemon juice

¼ cup (60 ml) extra-virgin olive oil

Coarse kosher salt to taste

½ cup (50 grams) walnuts

Cabbage leaves, romaine lettuce, endive leaves, or fresh grape leaves for scooping up

Soups and Their Dumplings

Tchav, Chilled Soup with Sorrel, Rhubarb, and Other Greens

Curried Beet Borscht with Apples and Ginger

Minestra di Fagioli, White Bean Soup

Harira, Spiced Moroccan Vegetable Soup with Chickpeas, Cilantro, and Lemon

Jerusalem Sunchoke Soup with Celery Root and Slivered Almonds

Winter Squash Soup with Coconut Milk and Hot Pepper

Lentil Soup with Ginger and Cumin

Hearty Russian Minestrone with Green Peas, Zucchini, and Dill

Yemenite Chicken Soup with Dill, Cilantro, and Parsley

Lagman, Noodle Soup with Meat, Red Peppers, and Green Beans

Abgoosht, Persian Chicken Soup with *Gundi* (Chickpea Dumplings)

Vegetarian Matzo Ball Soup

Butternut Squash and Leek Soup with Kurdish *Kubbeh* (Meat Dumplings)

Tchav, Chilled Soup with Sorrel, Rhubarb, and Other Greens

Sour soup was eaten with bread and potatoes. In the spring, the soup was made of sorrel mixed with some thin sour cream or sour milk. During the height of summer, beet leaves were cooked with sorrel, which gave the soup a naturally sour taste. . . . A really good housekeeper produced a tasty sour soup—"Like wine," women would often brag.

—Hirsz Abramowicz, *Profiles of a Lost World,* translated by Eva Zeitlin Dobkin, 1999

Rhubarb has been around since ancient Persian times. It has mostly masqueraded as a fruit in the United States since a New York court in 1947 deemed it so for the sake of regulations. Coming from Western China, Tibet, Mongolia, and Siberia, these cold-weather vegetable stalks (don't eat the leaves, they are poisonous) migrated to places like Ukraine.

The modern word "rhubarb" derives from the ancient Greek *Rha* (the ancient name for the Volga River) and *barbaron,* meaning "foreign." Rhubarb is found in older dishes, such as the Greek Jewish fish with rhubarb sauce (see my *Jewish Holiday Cookbook*) and the Persian *choresh* with rhubarb and rice.

Icy tart sorrel soup, called *tchav,* has been something that eastern European Jews, especially those from Lithuania, Belarus, and Ukraine, have always loved. Sour-tasting foods were and are known throughout this area once called the Pale of Settlement, established by Russian empress Catherine the Great in 1791.

I was not surprised to see that Ukrainians serve *tchav* for the holiday of Shavuot, a time of the year when milk is more plentiful because cows, goats, and sheep are nourished by abundant springtime grass. Even in the biblical world, milk, turned into butter, yogurt, cream, and cheese, was more important than meat for an everyday diet.

Years ago, I discovered that they also added to their *tchav* rhubarb along with greens like Swiss chard, spinach, or even lettuce. I happen to have a prolific rhubarb patch (you'll see more of the tart vegetable in this book), and so I happily adopted this tradition, adding whatever greens are ready to what has become a delicious tart summer soup.

I like to top the soup with a swirl of Greek yogurt or crème fraîche, fresh radishes, new onions or scallions, and cucumbers from my garden. A garnish of peppery nasturtium leaves with their vibrant edible flowers makes this a simple yet elegant soup, perfect for a warm summer's night, enjoyed with friends. You will see your guests' taste buds awaken with the new, yet very old, tart flavor.

yield: 4 to 6 servings

2 cups diced rhubarb
(about 2 stalks/200 grams)

12 ounces (340 grams)
combined fresh sorrel,
spinach, beet greens, and/or
Swiss chard (preferably the
kind with red stems)

Handful of nasturtiums with
their leaves (optional)

1 tablespoon sea salt

½ teaspoon freshly ground
pepper to taste

1 to 2 tablespoons sugar,
if needed

½ cup (100 grams) sour cream,
yogurt, or crème fraîche

2 sliced scallions

1 small cucumber, peeled and
diced (about 150 grams)

4 radishes, sliced
(about 100 grams)

2 tablespoons fresh chervil
or other herbs

1. Cover the rhubarb with about 3 cups (710 ml) of water and bring to a boil in a large pot. Lower to a simmer and cook for about 10 minutes or until tender.

2. Chop the sorrel, spinach, beet greens, and/or Swiss chard and chard stems. Add the greens, including, if you like, a few nasturtium leaves, to the rhubarb. Continue to simmer for about 5 more minutes or until the greens are wilted and cooked but still green, then scoop out the greens with a strainer, preserving the broth, and put in an ice bath. Cool the greens, then purée in a blender or food processor. Put back with the broth, add salt and pepper to taste, adding some sugar if too tart.

3. Refrigerate for several hours and serve with a dollop of sour cream, yogurt, or crème fraîche, a sprinkle of scallions, cucumber, and radishes, and a yellow or orange nasturtium for color and feathery chervil for an anise kick.

Note When my garden is in full bloom, I often just pick haphazardly, mixing the greens and adding a little cilantro, dill, basil, chervil, or whatever is growing in the garden.

Curried Beet Borscht with Apples and Ginger

Although I have read that in Europe beet soup started to be popular only in the sixteenth century, it was eaten much earlier in Babylonia. Called *tuh'u* (red), a recipe for beet borscht appears in a cuneiform tablet of 1700 B.C.E. and calls for lamb, beer, onion, arugula, coriander, cumin, leeks, and garlic, and, of course, beets. It was garnished with cilantro. The food scholar Nawal Nasrallah prepared it for students at Harvard.

It used to be that American Jews would eat a dairy borscht with no meat in the summer. The marvelous cookbook writer Elizabeth David, in *Mediterranean Food*, tells us of a *zuppa ebrea,* Hebrew soup, that she read about in *Il Gastronomo Educato,* by Alberto Denti di Pirajno (Editions Neri Pozza, Venice, 1950). "The author recalls eating this soup in a Jewish house in Livorno," writes David, "and recommends it to all his friends—'baptized Christians, circumcized Moslems, idolaters or fire-worshipers.'" This cold borscht was thickened with three eggs and served with a hot potato cooked in goose fat or butter at a time well before Mother's Borscht, now owned by Manischewitz, became so popular.

I prefer my cold beet soup less sweet than most bottled borscht and without eggs stirred in. This curried borscht is what I make when beets are growing in my garden. It is slightly sweet, and slightly spicy, more in tune with my tastes today.

——————

1. Heat the oven to 350 degrees. In a bowl, drizzle oil over the beets. Put the beets on a baking sheet lined with aluminum foil and bake for about an hour, or until the beets can be pierced with a fork. When cool, peel the beets and chop into large chunks.

2. In a large, heavy-bottomed pot, melt the butter. Add the onion and sauté until it is almost caramelized, about 30 minutes. Add the chopped apples, beets, ginger, *harissa,* 1 teaspoon of the curry powder, ½ teaspoon of the cumin, salt, pepper, and 4 cups (940 ml) water. Stir to combine and bring to a boil over high heat. Lower the heat to medium-low and simmer, uncovered, about 10 minutes, or until the apples are soft.

3. Pour the mixture into a food processor and purée, in batches if necessary, until smooth. Taste and adjust seasoning, adding more water if you'd like a thinner soup. Stir in the lemon juice and serve warm or cold with a dollop of crème fraîche, sour cream, or yogurt.

Note If I have any dill or cilantro in the refrigerator, I'll garnish the soup with a few sprinkles of it. If I am roasting beets for this soup, I'll always cook a few extra that I can toss into salads that week.

yield: about 6 to 8 servings

2 tablespoons vegetable oil

3 large beets
(2½ pounds/1¹⁄₁₀ kilos)

4 tablespoons (½ stick/
56 grams) unsalted butter

1 medium Vidalia or any
sweet onion (235 grams),
chopped fine

2 to 3 apples (450 grams),
finely chopped (no need
to peel)

1-inch piece fresh ginger,
peeled and grated
(about 1 teaspoon)

2 teaspoons *harissa*
(see page 10)

1 to 2 teaspoons curry powder,
or to taste

½ to 1 teaspoon ground cumin,
or to taste

1 teaspoon salt, or to taste

Freshly ground black pepper
to taste

Juice of 1 lemon, or to taste

½ cup (100 grams) crème
fraîche, sour cream, or yogurt,
to serve

Minestra di Fagioli, White Bean Soup

Laundry day was always a big event. All the work took place in our courtyard with a big fire with fuel to warm up a pot of water for the laundry. . . . At midday our cook Inez would bring *minestra di fagioli* (white bean soup) to the laundry area. . . . And to tell you the truth everybody liked the soup. . . . In fact, the *minestra di fagiole,* which is considered a common food for the poor, if cooked with care becomes incredibly flavorful. And it is not necessary to fry the onions in the manner that you usually do. You can put the raw ingredients in and you get an equal result with less indigestion.

—Jenny Bassani Liscia, *La Storia Passa dalla Cucina* (History Goes Through the Kitchen), 2000

As this lovely passage written by Jenny Bassani Liscia, the sister of the writer Giorgio Bassani, tells us, laundry day in Ferrara, Italy, before World War II, was anticipated each week as much for the simple bean soup cooked that day as for the clean clothes.

The nostalgia from the aroma and flavor of this soup is, of course, not restricted to the Jewish world. It is universal. One of the oldest soups known to mankind is the simple mixture of fava beans and water. Slowly, slowly, onions and carrots entered, and after the Columbian Exchange, the more digestible white beans from the New World replaced the fava beans of the Old (for more on fava beans, see page 52), followed by tomatoes and tomato paste. Spices like cumin or coriander are sometimes added, as are pastas from Emilia-Romagna, where Ferrara is located, like *maltagliati* (hand cut in a random way), *ditalini* (tiny tube-shaped), or *gramigna* (thin, short, and curled), enhanced with butter and Parmesan cheese, from nearby Parma.

Note that the beans require an overnight soak in water.

———

1. Soak the beans overnight in cold water in a soup pot. Drain the beans and replace the water to cover by about 2 inches. Bring to a boil and simmer, covered, for an hour, skimming off any froth that forms. Drain the water, rinse well, and put the beans back in the pot with 1 teaspoon of salt and cover with water by at least 2 inches. Then add the onions, garlic, carrot, and the tomato or tomato paste. Bring to a boil again, lower to a simmer, and continue cooking uncovered over a low heat for another hour or until the beans are soft and the flavors blend.

2. When about ready to serve, reheat the soup and boil the pasta in boiling salted water. Then drain the pasta and add to the soup.

3. Stir in the butter and Parmesan cheese, then season with more salt and pepper to taste. Serve sprinkled with the parsley.

yield: 6 to 8 servings

1 pound (453 grams) *Borlotti* beans (also called cranberry beans) or small white beans

Salt to taste

1 large onion, diced

1 clove garlic, chopped

1 large carrot, peeled and cut into ¾-inch-thick rounds

1 large tomato or 1 heaping tablespoon tomato paste

2 cups (7 ounces/200 grams) uncooked *maltagliati, ditalini,* or *gramigna* pasta

2 tablespoons unsalted butter

2 tablespoons Parmesan cheese

Freshly ground pepper to taste

2 tablespoons chopped parsley

Note You can purée half the beans to make the soup thicker, and can add to the soup other vegetables to make it your own.

Harira, Spiced Moroccan Vegetable Soup with Chickpeas, Cilantro, and Lemon

This is by far my favorite comfort soup. Until I met Meme Suissa, who comes from Casablanca, I had been making a different version. But I swooned after trying her recipe, enhanced with an egg-lemon sauce, that she may have learned from a Turkish forebear. She has been making this for almost eighty years, first watching her mother, then cooking for her five children after she immigrated, like many Moroccan Jews, to French-speaking Montreal.

A Muslim staple to break the daily fast of Ramadan, it has crossed over to the Moroccan Jewish tradition of breaking the fast of Yom Kippur. Although many cooks make this with meat, I have turned it into a vegetarian version and make it whenever I can.

---

1. Heat the oil in a large skillet over medium heat and sauté the onion, celery, and carrots until the onion turns translucent and begin to brown, about 5 to 10 minutes. Add the turmeric, cumin, *harissa* or chili flakes, 1 teaspoon of salt, 1 cup each of the parsley and cilantro, tomatoes, and the stock or water and bring to a boil. If using the soaked chickpeas, drain them and add to the pot. Simmer uncovered for 25 minutes, then add the lentils, another teaspoon of salt and a teaspoon of pepper and continue simmering until the chickpeas and lentils are cooked, about 20 minutes more. If using canned chickpeas omit the first 25 minutes of simmering and add with the lentils.

2. Whisk the flour, egg, and lemon juice into 2 cups (470 ml) of water. Stir into the soup. Simmer the soup about 5 minutes more and serve, sprinkled with the remaining cilantro and parsley. And don't forget to have some extra *harissa* in a plate on the side.

Note This, like most soups, is such a flexible recipe. Whereas Meme adds chicken and noodles to her broth, I prefer to serve it as is. But sometimes I replace all or some of the lentils with whole grains. If using whole farro, barley, freekeh, or wheat berries, put them in with the chickpeas, as they take about 40 minutes to an hour to cook. But do keep in mind that pearled farro and barley as well as cracked freekeh take about 25 minutes to cook.

yield: 8 to 10 servings

4 tablespoons olive oil

1 large onion, diced (about 2 cups)

3 stalks celery, diced (about 1½ cups)

3 large carrots, peeled and cut in rounds

½ teaspoon ground turmeric

1 teaspoon ground cumin

½ to 1 teaspoon *harissa* (see page 10) or dried red chili flakes, plus more for serving

Salt to taste

1 bunch parsley, chopped (about 1½ cups/75 grams), divided

1 bunch cilantro, chopped (about 1½ cups/75 grams), divided

One 15-ounce (425-gram) can tomatoes, crushed, or 2 cups (450 grams) tomato sauce

7 cups (1⅔ liters) chicken or vegetable stock

1 cup (200 grams) dried chickpeas, soaked overnight and cooked (see page 10) or one 15-ounce (425-gram) can chickpeas, drained

1 cup (370 grams) green lentils

1 teaspoon freshly ground black pepper

2 tablespoons all-purpose unbleached flour

1 large egg

Juice of 2 lemons (about ¼ cup)

Jerusalem Sunchoke Soup with Celery Root and Slivered Almonds

The last arrival [from the New World] was the Jerusalem artichoke, and though its value as food both for man and animal in temperate climates is not much less than that of the potato, it has so far failed to win the masses of the people in any country.

—Redcliffe Salaman, *Journal of the Royal Horticultural Society,* 1940

This comment from Redcliffe Salaman, a Jewish British botanist, is not wrong, although the Jerusalem artichoke, perhaps more commonly known as the sunchoke, has gained in popularity today.

It was the French explorer Samuel de Champlain who, while surveying Cape Cod in 1605, wrote, "Saw an abundance of Brazilian beans, many edible squashes of various sizes, tobacco and roots, which they [the native Americans] cultivate, the latter having the taste of artichokes." Two years later in Nova Scotia, he found "certain small roots, the size of a small nut," that tasted like "truffles, which are very good if roasted or boiled."

French and Dutch gardeners sent specimens of this artichoke-like tuber to England, where Dr. Venner of Bath grew them in his garden, Ter Neussen. They quickly became known as "artichokes *ter neussen*." According to Salaman, when hawkers cried out "artichokes *ter neussen*," nobody understood what was being sold. Eventually, as the Holy Land was in vogue in the late seventeenth century, the humble artichoke *ter neussen* was dubbed the "Jerusalem artichoke." In parts of Europe, animals ate them as fodder, but eventually people came around to cooking and eating them as well.

In Lady Judith Montefiore's *Jewish Manual,* the first kosher cookbook written in English, published in London in 1846, a recipe for Palestine Soup is featured with Jerusalem artichokes (plus four other recipes using the tuber!). However, the term "Jerusalem artichoke" was soon under fire. In an 1877 issue of *The American Journal of Science,* American botanist Asa Gray assured us that the Native Americans in Virginia called the knobby, twisted tuber *kaischuc penauk,* meaning "sun roots," and therefore, "sun-root" would have been the most suitable name.

Almost a hundred years later, in 1966, Frieda Caplan, founder of Frieda's Inc., trademarked the name "Sunchoke." Frieda says she preferred that name because "they are not from Jerusalem and not an artichoke, although they are reminiscent of the artichoke heart flavor, and because they are the root of a sunflower-like plant." Later Frieda received a postcard asking how you get rid of flatulence from sunchokes. The postcard was signed, "Julia Child."

yield: 6 to 8 servings

2 tablespoons olive oil

1 large onion, diced

1 celery root (about 1 pound/ 453 grams), peeled and cut into ½-inch cubes

2 pounds (907 grams) sunchokes, peeled and cut into ½-inch cubes

2 large carrots, peeled and left whole

Leaves from 2 sprigs thyme, or ½ teaspoon dried thyme

6 cups (about 1½ liters) vegetable broth, see page 139

Salt and freshly ground pepper to taste

¼ cup sliced or slivered and toasted almonds, to garnish

2 tablespoons chopped parsley, to garnish

I stumbled on this root vegetable soup at lunch one day with Jodi Rudoren, the *New York Times* correspondent in Israel. We were in search of Majda, the tiny outdoor restaurant near Jerusalem mentioned in Anthony Bourdain's *Parts Unknown*. Michal Baranes, a Jewish Israeli, opened this homey eatery with her Arab Israeli husband Yakub Barhum in his village of Ein Rafa, right next door to Abu Ghosh, an Arab town in Israel.

Jodi and I loved this Jerusalem artichoke soup. Now it is my go-to winter soup when I want something warming but simple.

---

1. Warm the oil over medium-high heat in a heavy pot with a tight-fitting lid, then sauté the onion until translucent, about 5 to 10 minutes.

2. Add the celery root, sunchokes, whole carrots, and thyme, and continue to sauté for a few more minutes.

3. Add the vegetable broth, salt, and pepper to taste. Bring to a boil, then simmer uncovered for about 30 minutes, or until the vegetables are completely soft. Pulse most of the vegetables in a food processor, blender, or using an immersion blender, leaving about a fourth of the soup chunky to add a more rustic texture. Taste and adjust seasonings.

4. Serve garnished with a sprinkle of the almonds and parsley.

Winter Squash Soup with Coconut Milk and Hot Pepper

Once, when I visited Cyrel Deitsch, one of the editors of the Lubavitcher cookbook *The Spice and Spirit of Kosher-Jewish Cooking*, in Crown Heights, Brooklyn, we decided to eat at Basil, a new upscale dairy restaurant that I had read about in the *New York Times*. How things have changed! When I used to visit Cyrel, who is an old friend, there was only one kosher restaurant near her house—a terrible pizza place.

To my surprise, Basil is a small attractive restaurant with welcoming wood-framed windows and a marble bar and tabletops, as well as a wood-burning oven for trendy pizzas. When the restaurant first opened—the first of its kind at the crossroads of a very Orthodox community—there was a lot of controversy, but good food, prepared in a traditional Orthodox manner, won out.

I followed Cyrel's lead and ordered several salads, a pizza with kale, hot pepper, and cheese, and a squash soup. When the two Hasidic gentlemen at the next table said the pizza was very spicy, we pooh-poohed them, thinking they didn't know spicy food. We were wrong—the pizza was delicious, and *very* spicy. But the best dish was the squash soup—I had never tasted one so good. It was made with two kinds of squash—a roasted acorn squash sat bathed in a chunky kabocha squash soup made with coconut milk, broth, and hot peppers and sprinkled with fried kabocha skin.

After tasting this squash soup, I asked to meet the chef, José de Soto. No wonder it was so good—José had worked at New York's Savoy and other major restaurants for many years. When he took this new job at Basil, the owner said, "Go with your creativity and culinary background." And he did. Using two kinds of squash, the kabocha of his native Honduras for flavor and the acorn for effect, he created not only a visual knockout, but also a soup delectable in taste. If you can find tiny acorn squash, use them for the visual effect. Otherwise omit the acorn squash and the flavor will be just as delicious.

yield: at least 8 servings

8 small acorn, honeynut (tiny acorn), or delicata squash (optional)

1 kabocha or butternut squash (about 4 pounds), peeled with a paring knife, seeded and cut into chunks, reserving the peels for garnish

6 tablespoons olive oil, divided

Salt and freshly ground pepper to taste

5 small shallots

2 Idaho potatoes, peeled and chunked

1 cup (235 ml) coconut milk

1 chili de árbol or ½ to 1 teaspoon crushed red pepper flakes

¼ to ½ cup (50 to 100 grams) brown sugar

Salt and freshly ground pepper to taste

6 to 8 cups (1⅖ to 1⁹⁄₁₀ liters) vegetable broth (see page 139)

Sour cream or Greek yogurt, for garnish

Chopped parsley, for garnish

---

1. Preheat the oven to 350 degrees. Cut off about 2 inches from the top of the small acorn, honeynut, or delicata squash, if using, then scoop out and discard the seeds. Smear the inside of the squash, and some of the kabocha or butternut peels with about 3 tablespoons of the olive oil and season with salt and pepper. Roast the squash and peels for about 25 minutes or until tender when pressed with a fork. Set aside the cooked acorn squash and their tops, if using.

2. Heat the remaining olive oil in a soup pot and add the kabocha or butternut squash, shallots, and potato chunks, sautéing for about 10 minutes.

3. Add the coconut milk, chilies or red pepper flakes, brown sugar, salt and pepper to taste, and about 6 cups (1⅖ liters) of vegetable stock or enough to cover by about 4 inches. Cook for about 20 minutes, or until all the ingredients are soft, then purée the soup. Taste and adjust seasonings to find a balance of sweet, tart, and spicy.

4. To serve, put a ladle of soup in a wide soup bowl. Then add the acorn, honeynut, or delicata squash and their tops if using, ladle more soup inside and around, add a dollop of sour cream or yogurt, and sprinkle with diced parsley and reserved squash peels, if using.

Lentil Soup with Ginger and Cumin

Once when Jacob was cooking a stew, Esau came in from the open country, famished. And Esau said to Jacob, "Give me some of that red stuff to gulp down, for I am famished"—which is why he was named Edom (red). Jacob said, "First sell me your birthright." And Esau said, "I am at the point of death. So of what use is my birthright to me?" But Jacob said, "Swear to me first." So he swore to him and sold his birthright to Jacob. Jacob then gave Esau bread and lentil stew; and he ate and drank, and he rose and went away. Thus did Esau spurn the birthright.   —Genesis 25:29–34

When I wanted to find a good lentil soup recipe, I went to Saba, a simple Yemenite restaurant in Fairfax, Virginia. The chef told me what spices he was using and I fiddled with them in my own kitchen. I added a dollop of Greek yogurt, the grated zest of a lemon, and a sprinkling of cilantro.

This earth-colored soup—*edom* means "earth," not "red" in Hebrew—is fancier than the one Jacob gave Esau, and I'll bet it looks and tastes better too, with the vast variety of colored lentils and spices we can use today.

Sometimes I use Puy green lentils, which require a longer cooking time. Make as directed below, but cook the lentils for 30 minutes before adding the onion-ginger mixture and tomato paste.

For a fancier two-colored twist, make two half batches of the recipe, with green lentils in one pot and red lentils in another. Then, to serve, first ladle some of the green lentil soup on the bottom of a bowl, top with a little of the red lentil soup, and then swirl with a knife. Add a dollop of Greek yogurt and garnish with cilantro.

------

yield: 10 to 12 servings

3 cups (600 grams) lentils

½ teaspoon ground turmeric

2 tablespoons vegetable or olive oil

1 large onion, chopped

1-inch knob of fresh ginger, peeled and minced

4 cloves garlic, minced

2 tablespoons tomato paste

½ bunch cilantro, chopped, plus 2 tablespoons chopped cilantro for garnish

2 teaspoons ground cumin, or to taste

2 teaspoons sea salt, or to taste

1 teaspoon freshly ground black pepper, or to taste

Greek yogurt for garnish

Grated lemon zest for garnish

1. Put the lentils in a soup pot and cover with 8 cups (about 1¾ liters) of water. Bring to a boil over medium-high heat, then lower the heat and simmer, uncovered, for 15 minutes, skimming any foam off the top and adding more water as necessary. After you've skimmed the foam, stir in the turmeric.

2. Meanwhile, warm the oil in a medium skillet set over medium-high heat, then add the onion and cook until it begins to soften, about 5 minutes. Add the ginger, garlic, and tomato paste and sauté a few minutes more. Add to the lentils and cook uncovered for 10 to 15 minutes more, adding water as necessary if the soup is too thick. Stir in the ½ bunch chopped cilantro during the last few minutes of cooking.

3. Purée the soup to desired consistency in a food processor or using an immersion blender. (I prefer a chunkier soup, but a super-smooth soup is nice as well.) Stir in the cumin, salt, and pepper to taste, then serve dolloped with Greek yogurt and sprinkled with the lemon zest and the remaining cilantro.

Hearty Russian Minestrone with Green Peas, Zucchini, and Dill

All winged swarming things that walk on fours shall be an abomination to you. But these you may eat among all the winged swarming things that walk on fours; all that have above their feet, jointed legs to leap with on the ground—of these you may eat the following: locusts of every variety; and all varieties of grasshopper.

—Leviticus 11:20–22

After I gave a speech at the Orthodox Palm Beach Synagogue, located in a store-front in the downtown shopping area, Nechama Dina Scheiner, the rabbi's wife, asked me if I had eaten. Despite having demoed many dishes from my books, I had not eaten anything myself. I started to invite her to go out but realized that, as a Hasidic Jew, she would not accept. "I'll make you an omelet," she said.

As I walked to her yellow stucco home, past the Everglades Club (where Jack Kennedy and Jacob Javits were both rejected—one because he was Catholic and the other because he was a Jew), I realized how Palm Beach has changed.

Dina's son, Uziel, opened the door for me and told me that his mother was upstairs putting another child to bed.

Two teenage daughters, Malka and Hindy, were in the cluttered but homey kitchen of a busy family.

Moshe Scheiner, the rabbi, came in and heated up some vegetable soup for me while Hindy started to prepare a simple salad. Because observant Jews are very concerned about removing insects from food (see the quote above), she examined each romaine leaf, spraying it with Fit, a fruit and vegetable wash, then carefully washed the leaves in cold water before drying them.

As I dipped my spoon into the soup, thickened with yellow and green split peas and infused with zucchini, sweet potatoes, and carrots, I listened to Uziel tell the story of Dina's father, whose roots go to Lubavitch, the little town in Russia where her grandfather studied as a teenager before World War II. Dina makes her mother's recipe for this hearty soup, so similar to what I have tasted in many Russian Jewish homes. Much like in the old days, Dina regularly changes the soup and uses the vegetables that are in season. With a family of eight and extra pop-in guests like myself, she makes homemade soups about twice a week. Although there were very few prepared foods in the house, Dina occasionally adds the soup sleeves that Manischewitz and others produce for added flavor, ingredients her forefathers never got in Russia.

Most winter soups consist of soup bones, dried beans, barley, chickpeas, and so on—foods that could last throughout the long winter. Since I made this one vegetarian, I don't bother with the soup bones, but I do add a little allspice for extra flavor. This is a very hearty soup that can be played with as you wish.

yield: about 20 cups, or 10 to 12 servings

4 tablespoons vegetable or olive oil

2 large sweet onions, peeled and diced

4 large carrots, peeled and diced

4 stalks celery, diced

1 pound (453 grams) dried green or yellow split peas, or a combination of both

1 large sweet or white potato, peeled and cut into 1-inch cubes

1 celery root (425 grams), peeled and cut into 1-inch cubes

3 zucchini, peeled and cut into 1-inch cubes

6 cloves garlic, peeled and crushed

1 teaspoon ground allspice

2 teaspoons sea salt, or to taste

1 teaspoon freshly ground black pepper, or to taste

½ bunch chopped fresh dill, or to taste

1. Heat the oil in a large, heavy-bottomed pot over medium-high heat. Sauté the onions, carrots, and celery until softened and beginning to brown, about 5 to 10 minutes.

2. Add the peas and 4 cups (1 liter) of water, or enough to cover the vegetables by about an inch. Bring to a boil and simmer, covered, over medium-low heat for about 20 minutes.

3. Add the sweet or white potatoes and celery root and cook another 30 minutes. Then add the zucchini and continue cooking another 10 minutes, or until the peas are well cooked and almost falling apart. Add the garlic, allspice, salt, and pepper and cook for another 10 minutes. If you like, purée all or half the soup in a food processor or with an immersion blender. Remove from heat and stir in the fresh dill.

Yemenite Chicken Soup with Dill, Cilantro, and Parsley

Chicken soup . . . is recommended as an excellent food as well as medication.
—Moses Maimonides, *Medical Aphorisms*, twelfth century c.e.

Moses Maimonides was not the first to recognize the healing properties of chicken soup, but he did understand it as a cure.

One of the first to see the curative potential of chicken soup was Discorides, a Greek army surgeon in the first century who served under the emperor Nero. Discorides discusses the healthy properties of chicken soup in his *Materia Medica*.

A century later, Aretaeus of Cappadocia—a Greek of possibly Jewish origin—described how boiled chicken can treat respiratory tract disorders. Later, Maimonides prescribed chicken soup for many ailments, like leprosy, weight gain (in those days one used an old hen for soup, with the fat left on), and to help those convalescing from illness. Chicken soup also seemed to help people with fevers from white bile, coughs from asthma, and melancholia, what today we call depression. Fenugreek, dill, parsley, and turmeric were all added to the soup for medical reasons at different points in history.

Before the printing press, people did not usually write down recipes (the only recipe books at that time were those in the courts of the Arab potentates in the thirteenth and fourteenth centuries). But artifacts from ancient Jewish communities include documents, scribbled on paper or sheepskin, that refer to chicken soup—shopping lists of foods to be bought or notes from doctors, giving prescriptions for chicken soup with garlic. We see some twelfth-century shopping lists in the Genizah for buying hens for Friday night or holidays, which were then often cooked in a soup or stew.

Perhaps the oldest extant recipe for chicken soup comes from the Yemenite Jews. Separated from the mainstream of Judaism at least two thousand years ago, Yemenite Jews developed their recipe, flavored with turmeric, chili peppers, fenugreek, dill, parsley, and cilantro. As important as the protein of chicken is in the soup, so is the spice. It is carefully infused with three components. *Hawayij* is the Yemenite spice combination for stews and soups. You should also serve it with *zhug* (see page 12). The third component is *hilbe* (see page 134), which means "fenugreek" in Hebrew. Although many people today only add *zhug* to the soup, to be technically correct you add all three, then sip it slowly, as the abstemious Yemenites do.

I first tasted this delicious soup many years ago, sitting cross-legged on the floor on pillows at the home of the late Jerusalem jeweler, rabbi, and patriarch Yosef Zadok. Zadok had come to Israel with his family and thousands of other Jews from Yemen in 1948 on Operation Magic Carpet, when what they thought

yield: 6 to 8 servings

1 whole 3- to 4-pound
(1⅓- to 1¾-kilo) chicken

2 large onions, peeled
and roughly chopped

8 cloves garlic, peeled and
left whole

1 large tomato, almost
quartered but not cut all
the way through

2 stalks celery, left whole

2 tablespoons salt, or to taste

1 to 2 tablespoons *hawayij*
(recipe on facing page)

3 large carrots, peeled and
sliced into ¼-inch thick rounds

3 potatoes
(about 1½ pounds/
680 grams), peeled and cut
into 1-inch cubes

½ bunch parsley, finely
chopped, divided

½ bunch dill, finely chopped,
divided

½ bunch cilantro,
finely chopped, divided

Zhug to taste (see page 12)

Hilbe to taste (recipe on
page 134)

was a big bird landed in a field near Aden, sweeping them up as if by magic to what is now Ben Gurion International Airport.

The only modern additions to this ancient comfort soup are tomato, potatoes, and chili peppers in the *zhug*. Not only does it taste very good, it will help cure anything that might ail you.

---

1. Put the chicken in a large stockpot and cover with cold water by about 3 inches. Bring to a boil, skimming off the foam that forms on the top, and cook for 30 minutes, continuing to skim as necessary.

2. Add the onions, garlic, tomato, celery stalks, salt, and 1 tablespoon of the *hawayij*. Simmer for another 30 to 45 minutes, or until the chicken is almost tender.

3. Then add the carrots, potatoes, and half of the parsley, dill, and cilantro. Simmer until the vegetables are cooked through. Serve as is, sprinkling each bowl of soup with more of the fresh herbs, or remove the skin and bones from the chicken, then put back in the soup, and refrigerate overnight. The next day, skim off the layer of fat from the top of the soup and reheat, garnishing the soup with the remaining herbs. Serve either way over rice with *zhug*, *hawayij*, and *hilbe*.

Hawayij

---

yield: about 5 tablespoons *hawayij*

Filled with warming spices like pepper, cumin, and coriander, this traditional Yemenite spice blend also contains nigella seeds (see page 7), cardamom (see page 5), turmeric, and saffron. I prefer to blend my *hawayij* as needed to ensure a deeply potent flavor that shines through the soup.

2 tablespoons black peppercorns	10 cardamom pods, peeled
1 tablespoon nigella seeds	2 teaspoons ground turmeric
1 teaspoon cumin seeds	1 pinch saffron, optional
1 teaspoon coriander seeds	

1. Either pound all ingredients in a mortar and pestle or use a coffee grinder to grind to a powder. It is okay if you have a few stray bits of whole spices.

Hilbe

It is no wonder Yemenites eat this soup for Friday night, with a big dollop of *hilbe,* made of mostly fenugreek seeds and seasoned with garlicky *zhug*—both fenugreek and garlic are considered aphrodisiacs!

3 tablespoons fenugreek powder	**Juice of ½ lemon**
1 generous teaspoon *zhug* (see page 12)	**1 teaspoon salt, or to taste**

1. Soak the fenugreek powder in ½ cup (120 ml) water for at least 3 hours, until the mixture is gelatinous.

2. Add the *zhug,* lemon juice, and salt. Using an electric hand mixer or a whisk, beat until smooth. Adjust seasonings to taste. The sauce should be very spicy.

Note You can either make *hawayij* and *hilbe* yourself or buy them online through Pereg Gourmet at www.pereg-spices.com.

Lagman, Noodle Soup with Meat, Red Peppers, and Green Beans

At Tandoori Food and Bakery in Rego Park, New York, known for its Uzbek home cooking, I tasted *lagman,* a tasty comfort soup. *Lagman* noodles, thick noodles pulled from one long strand of dough, evolved from the lo mein of nearby China, symbolic of long life. According to the late Gil Marks, the word *lagman,* denoting the quintessential Uzbek noodle, comes from the Chinese *liang mian,* meaning "cold noodle." It is related to *lo mein,* meaning "pulled noodle." *Lokshen,* Yiddish for "noodles," similarly comes from the Khazars, who brought them to Central Asia.

This piquant soup is filled with beef or lamb, yellow and red peppers, string beans, hot pepper, celery, chives, onions, cilantro, and hot oil. It is truly a meal in itself, and is also great served with a colorful salad.

———————

1. Heat the oil in a large heavy pot over medium heat. Add the meat and brown on all sides, stirring occasionally. Cover with about 8 cups (1.88 liters) of water and simmer, uncovered, for about an hour, removing any foam that accumulates on top.

2. While the meat is cooking, put the onions into a medium skillet and sauté until translucent, about 10 minutes. Add the garlic, peppers, green beans, and celery and sauté for another 10 to 15 minutes.

3. Add the carrots, tomatoes, tomato paste, cumin, hot pepper, cayenne pepper, and salt and pepper to taste. Simmer for 20 minutes, uncovered.

4. Put 4 cups (1 liter) of water in a small pot and bring to a boil. Add the noodles and cook about 4 minutes or until *al dente.* Put a heaping portion of the noodles in each of 6 large soup bowls. Ladle the soup on top, and sprinkle with fresh cilantro and dill. Serve with Bukharan flatbread (see page 158) or pita.

yield: 6 to 8 servings

2 tablespoons vegetable oil

1 pound (453 grams) boneless beef or lamb chuck or shoulder, cut into 1-inch cubes

3 medium yellow onions, chopped

3 cloves garlic, peeled and minced

1 red pepper, diced

1 green pepper, diced

8 ounces green beans

4 celery stalks, diced

2 large carrots, peeled and diced

1 cup peeled, seeded, and chopped tomatoes, fresh or canned

1 tablespoon tomato paste

½ teaspoon ground cumin

1 hot pepper, such as jalapeño

½ teaspoon cayenne pepper, or to taste

Salt and ground black pepper to taste

1 sleeve or 8 ounces (226 grams) Oriental-style fresh noodles, about ⅛ inch thick

¼ cup chopped fresh cilantro for garnish

¼ cup chopped fresh dill for garnish

Abgoosht, Persian Chicken Soup with *Gundi* (Chickpea Dumplings)

Although the food of Iranian Muslims and Jews is essentially the same, except that Jews don't use butter with meat, there is at least one specifically Jewish dish in Iran. Served at the start of Sabbath dinners for centuries, *gundi* are plump chicken and chickpea dumplings flavored with cardamom and tinted with turmeric, then cooked in chicken broth. *Gundi* are delicious, evocative, satisfying, and a must on Friday night.

In Iran, men would traditionally come home from synagogue on Friday night and drink a little *arrack,* and sometimes eat the *gundi* alone as an appetizer, without soup. *Gundi* are often served rolled up in a piece of flat *lavash, taftan,* or *sangaak* bread, with scallions and a big plate of *sabzi* (fresh herbs), with the soup eaten on the side. I prefer tiny *gundi* to the typical golf ball size, and I also prefer eating these dumplings in the soup.

For the gluten-free, these are your dumplings!

---

1. **to make the broth** Set aside the breast and put the rest of the chicken in a large soup pot with a lid and cover with water. Bring to a boil and remove any froth that accumulates.

2. Add the onions, garlic, peppers, salt, freshly ground pepper, cardamom, and turmeric. Simmer, covered, for 40 minutes or until the chicken is almost cooked. Add the chickpeas and continue cooking until the chicken is done. Squeeze in the juice of a lemon. Cool and strain the soup, reserving the chicken for a salad or putting chunks into the broth and returning the peppers and chickpeas to the broth. You should have at least 14 cups of broth.

3. **to make the *gundi*** Using a food processor fitted with a steel blade, pulse onions until finely chopped. Transfer to a bowl and set aside. Then pulse the chicken until it has the consistency of ground meat.

4. Mix the onions and chickpea flour in a medium bowl until well combined. Add the ground chicken, oil, salt, pepper, turmeric, cardamom, and cumin. Mix well, adding a bit of water if needed to make dough about the consistency of meatballs. Refrigerate until well chilled, about 3 hours.

yield: 8 servings

BROTH

One 3-pound (1⅓-kilo) chicken, cut in 8 pieces, separating at least ¼ pound (113 grams) of the breast

2 large onions, peeled and diced

1 clove garlic

1 sweet green pepper, thinly sliced

1 sweet red pepper, thinly sliced

1 sweet yellow pepper, thinly sliced

1 tablespoon sea salt, or to taste

½ teaspoon freshly ground black pepper, or to taste

½ teaspoon ground cardamom, or to taste

½ teaspoon ground turmeric, or to taste

1 cup cooked chickpeas (see page 10) from ½ cup dried or from half a 15-ounce (213-gram) can

Juice of 1 lemon

GUNDI (CHICKEN AND CHICKPEA DUMPLINGS)

2 medium onions, peeled and quartered

4 ounces (113 grams) skinless, boneless chicken breast (from chicken above)

(continued)

5. Dip your hands in cold water and make balls about the size of a walnut—you should have about 20 portions. Bring the soup to a boil, then gently add the dumplings one at a time. Simmer, covered, for 15 to 20 minutes, until the dumplings are cooked completely. Meanwhile, in a small bowl, toss together the basil, parsley, mint, and cilantro.

6. Ladle the soup and dumplings into serving bowls, sprinkling with the mixed herbs.

4 ounces/113 grams (about 1 cup plus 2 tablespoons) chickpea flour

1 tablespoon olive oil

1 teaspoon salt

1 teaspoon freshly ground black pepper, or to taste

¼ teaspoon ground turmeric

½ teaspoon ground cardamom, or to taste

½ teaspoon ground cumin

14 cups chicken broth (from above)

Handful each of finely chopped basil, parsley, mint, and cilantro

Vegetarian Matzo Ball Soup

One of the most ardent and energetic cooks that I know is Suellen Lazarus, who prides herself on her vegetarian matzo balls and the broth that goes with them.

Suellen also has a great sense of carrying her family with her. When she slices the carrots for the broth, she thinks of her mother, who thought "it was not matzo ball soup unless the carrots were properly, diagonally sliced."

When creating the matzo ball recipe, Suellen often makes ghee—the clarified butter used in Indian cooking—instead of butter or vegetable oil, and, I must say, it makes a delicious matzo ball. Of course, you can also order ghee online.

***

1. **to make the broth** Put the onions, carrots, celery, leeks, tomatoes, bay leaves, thyme, and parsley in a large stockpot. Season with salt and pepper to taste, then add 15 cups (about 3½ liters) of water, bring to a boil, then simmer over low heat, uncovered, for 45 minutes.

2. Remove from heat and let cool to room temperature, then strain through a sieve, and set the broth aside. You should have about 12 cups of broth.

3. **to make the ghee** Melt the butter in a small saucepan over medium heat. When the butter comes to a boil, reduce the heat to low and simmer, stirring occasionally to prevent scorching, until the butter turns golden brown and dark solids sink to the bottom, about 20 to 30 minutes. Let cool for a few minutes. Strain through a fine-mesh strainer into a glass jar. Store in the refrigerator for up to 2 weeks, or freeze for up to 6 months.

4. **to make the matzo balls** In a medium bowl, whisk together the eggs, ¼ cup (60 ml) of water, ¼ cup of the melted and cooled ghee, ginger, 1 teaspoon of the salt, and the pepper. With a wooden spoon, stir in the matzo meal and mix well. Refrigerate for at least 30 minutes or overnight.

5. Dipping your hands first into cold water, then the matzo mixture, form into balls slightly larger than a walnut.

6. Bring a large pot of water to a boil. Add the remaining ½ teaspoon of salt and carefully drop the matzo balls one at a time into the water. When they have all floated to the top, reduce the heat, cover, and simmer slowly for 20 to 30 minutes. To see if they are done, remove one matzo ball with a slotted spoon and cut in half—it should be the same color and texture throughout. When the matzo balls are cooked, use a slotted spoon to remove them from the boiling water and put them into the vegetable broth. Gently reheat the soup and serve warm, with a sprinkle of fresh dill in each bowl.

yield: about 12 to 14 matzo balls, or about 12 servings

VEGETABLE BROTH

2 large onions, cut in quarters

6 large carrots, peeled and cut in large chunks

3 stalks celery, cut in large chunks

3 leeks, white and light green parts only, cleaned and cut in large chunks

3 canned or fresh plum tomatoes, coarsely chopped

2 bay leaves

3 branches fresh thyme

A few sprigs fresh parsley

Salt and freshly ground pepper to taste

GHEE

1 cup (2 sticks/226 grams) unsalted butter

MATZO BALLS

4 large eggs

¼ cup (60 ml) ghee

1 small chunk ginger, shredded on a Microplane grater (about 1 teaspoon)

1 teaspoon salt or to taste, plus ½ teaspoon for the water

Freshly ground pepper to taste

1 cup (115 grams) matzo meal

½ bunch fresh dill, chopped

Butternut Squash and Leek Soup with Kurdish *Kubbeh* (Meat Dumplings)

Babylonian soups made with dumplings called *kubbeh* came from the Fertile Crescent thousands of years ago. Cooks learned the concept of stuffing one thing with something else, preferably a protein, then floating them in soups as a hearty meal. In the book of Samuel, it says that when Tamar visited her brother Amnon, she prepared dumplings (*lebibot*) for him. Chances are they were like *kubbeh*.

Years ago I became infatuated with *kubbeh* at a tiny hole-in-the-wall restaurant called Morduch in Jerusalem, where every day they served a different variety. I thought they were exotic and complex with unusual flavor combinations—but most importantly, they were amazingly delicious. I couldn't wait to learn how to make them, so I found a woman from Kurdistan who was willing to show me how. When I entered her house, she was sitting on the floor molding *kubbeh* as she did each Friday for sixty members of her family who would come to pick them up and eat them with her or at home.

Then, a few years ago, I was invited to what was called the *Kubbeh* Project in New York City. Before pop-up restaurants were popular, this group transformed tiny Zucker's Bakery on the Lower East Side into a restaurant with one long table each night for about two weeks. Lines of curious customers had a choice of soup with three kinds of *kubbeh* dumplings: an Aramaic one with lemon and celery and traditional *kubbeh,* made of bulgur and stuffed with meat; another with a broth of beets, plums, and celery (see my *Foods of Israel Today* for recipes for both); or the following butternut squash and leek soup. We need more *kubbeh* projects, to ensure that old recipes like this are coming alive again.

———————

1. Preheat the oven to 375 degrees. Cut the top and bottom off the squash, scoop out the seeds, and slice lengthwise into quarters. Brush with some of the oil and roast for 30 to 40 minutes, until mostly cooked but not completely soft. Let cool slightly and scoop out the flesh, cutting into ½-inch chunks.

2. While the squash is roasting, start making the *kubbeh:* Mix the semolina or farina and 1¼ teaspoons of the salt in a bowl. Gradually add about 1 cup (225 ml) hot water, mixing with a fork until the consistency of Play-Doh. If necessary add a bit more water. Cover and refrigerate for at least 20 minutes.

yield: 8 cups soup and 35 dumplings, or 8 to 10 servings

SOUP

1 medium butternut squash (about 2 pounds/907 grams)

2 tablespoons vegetable oil or olive oil

1 small onion, diced

2 leeks, cleaned and diced

5 cloves garlic, minced

¼ cup (30 grams) diced celery root

2 tablespoons fresh lemon juice, or as needed

1 teaspoon sugar, or as needed

1 teaspoon cinnamon

½ teaspoon nutmeg

1 teaspoon paprika

½ teaspoon ginger

¼ teaspoon coriander

¼ teaspoon allspice

2 tablespoons chopped fresh mint leaves

3. Meanwhile, start the soup. In a large pot, warm the oil over medium heat and add the diced onion, leek, and garlic, sautéing until golden. Add the celery root and squash cubes. Cover and cook, stirring occasionally, for about 5 minutes.

4. Add 6 cups (1½ liters) of water, bring to a boil, and reduce the heat to low. Gently simmer until the squash is completely tender, about 10 minutes, then stir in 2 tablespoons of lemon juice, 1 teaspoon sugar, cinnamon, nutmeg, paprika, ginger, coriander, and allspice. Remove the soup from the heat and set aside. As the soup is cooking, you can finish the dumpling mixture.

5. In a food processor, combine the quartered onions, celery leaves, and parsley or cilantro. Pulse until finely chopped but not puréed and transfer to a large bowl. Add the meat, black pepper, and remaining 1 teaspoon salt, mixing well with your hands.

6. Remove the dough from the refrigerator and knead again in the bowl until pliable. Set a small bowl of water near your work surface and line a baking sheet with parchment paper. Dip your hands in the water, then take a walnut-size portion of dough and flatten it as thinly as possible in the palm of your hand. Place 1 heaping teaspoon of the meat mixture in the center, then completely enclose the meat in the dough and roll it into a ball between your hands to seal. Keeping your hands wet, repeat with the remaining dough and filling, setting the prepared dumplings on the tray.

7. Bring the soup to a boil and gently add the dumplings. They will sink. Cover and simmer gently until cooked through, about 30 minutes, adding water if soup becomes too thick. The dumplings will rise back to the top. Add more lemon juice and sugar if needed. Ladle into bowls, garnish with mint, and serve.

Note The soup may be prepared up to one day ahead of time and refrigerated. Dumplings may be frozen on baking sheets, then tossed into plastic bags and put in the freezer. Do not thaw before dropping into the simmering soup.

KUBBEH

2 cups (325 grams) semolina or farina

2¼ teaspoons salt, divided

3 small onions, quartered

2 tablespoons chopped celery leaves

1 packed cup chopped parsley or cilantro (about 30 grams)

8 ounces (226 grams) lean ground beef or lamb

1 teaspoon freshly ground black pepper

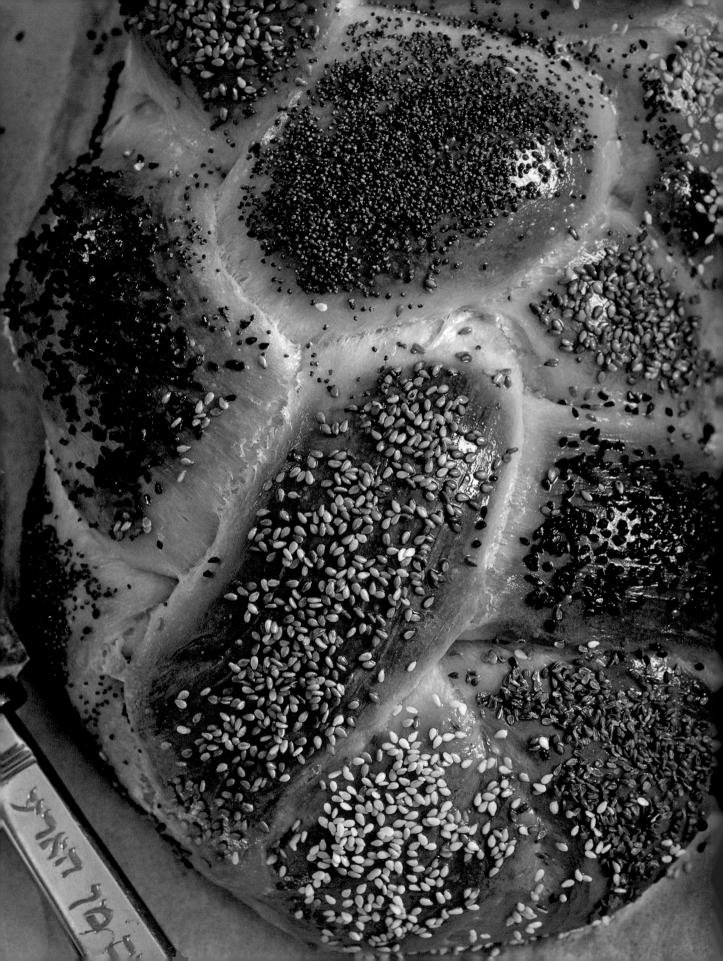

Breads

SABBATH BREADS

Pita Bread

Multi-Seeded Fennel-Flavored Challah

Vegan Challah

***Defo Dabo,* Ethiopian Sabbath Bread**

Spiced and Fried Matzo

***Kubbanah,* Yemenite Overnight Breakfast Bread**

***Noni Toki,* Bukharan Dome-Shaped Crisp Flatbread**

WEEKDAY BREADS

***Ka'ak,* Middle Eastern "Pretzels"**

***Pletzel,* Onion and Poppy Seed Flatbread**

Pumpernickel Rye Bread

Potato Rolls

Pita Bread

You shall take choice flour and bake of it twelve loaves, two-tenths of a measure for each loaf. Place them on the pure table before the Lord in two rows, six to a row. With each row you shall place pure frankincense, which is to be a token offering for the bread, as an offering by fire to the Lord. He shall arrange them before the Lord regularly every Sabbath day—it is a commitment for all time on the part of the Israelites.
                                                                        —Leviticus 24:5–8

Most likely, the twelve loaves made for Solomon's Temple resembled the flat pita breads made in a *tabun* oven that we find occasionally today in the Old City of Jerusalem on the outskirts of Mea Shearim and, I am told, in countries throughout the Middle East, including Iran and Iraq. Since ancient times, people in arid climates have made thin flatbreads that cook quickly over a short-lived hot fire fueled not only by whatever timber happens to be within reach, but also by olive pits and even animal dung.

Some of these flatbreads, made without yeast, are what matzo originally was like. Flatbreads have always been easy to cook, either over an open fire as the Bedouins do—mostly without yeast, as it "corrupts" their bread—on an iron wok-shaped griddle. The breads can also be slapped on the walls of a *tabun* oven and cooked at a high temperature, where they crisp up and cook quickly. Or, if they are fried on a griddle, as in Yemen, they are thicker, floppier, and more flavorful in a different way.

Whatever their preparation, none of these flatbreads looked much like the mechanized pita bread of today.

The word "pita" comes from *pitter*, an ancient word that means "split," referring to the pocket created in pita as steam splits the dough. One trick to making good pita bread is to roll it out, let it rest a few minutes, and then, just before you put it in a hot oven, roll it out again.

---

yield: 8 pita breads

1 tablespoon active dry yeast

1½ cups (200 grams) whole-wheat flour

1½ cups (200 grams) unbleached all-purpose flour, plus extra for work surface

1 teaspoon salt

1. Stir the yeast into 1½ cups (355 ml) lukewarm water, then add the flour and salt and mix in a standing mixer equipped with a dough hook for about 5 to 10 minutes, until a smooth, wet dough forms. Cover the bowl with a damp cloth and let stand for 1 hour, or until almost doubled.

2. Punch down the dough and knead again for a few minutes, adding flour if the dough is too sticky. Cover with a damp cloth and let stand another hour, or until doubled.

3. Preheat the oven to 500 degrees and set two baking sheets in the oven to heat up. Lightly flour your work surface and tear off a few sheets of parchment paper.

4. Divide the dough into 8 small balls, then flatten the balls with a rolling pin until they are as flat and round as a tortilla. (If you have one, a tortilla press would work well for this.) Put the discs of dough on the pieces of parchment. Then, just before positioning on the hot baking sheets, roll out again quickly. Bake for 10 to 15 minutes, or until the breads are lightly golden. Cool on a wire rack.

Ergotism, Holy Fire

Throughout history, since the first likely outbreak in 944 C.E. in the southwest area of France, Jews and others who ate rye bread often came down with a mysterious set of ailments, including distended stomachs, feeling coldness or numbness in their extremities, and symptoms similar to being on an LSD trip. Caused by ergot, a fungus that grows predominantly on rye, ergotism was thought to be the cause of both death and mystical, even witchlike behavior. Some say that ergotism coincided with the rise of Jewish mystic movements such as the Jewish pietist movement in Germany in the twelfth and thirteenth centuries.

Multi-Seeded Fennel-Flavored Challah

yield: 2 challahs

I learned to make challah years ago from an elderly woman in Brookline, Massachusetts. Her hands were racked with arthritis, but no matter how terrible the pain, every week she made the bread. I have never forgotten the verve for life this woman received through the act of dipping her hands in the dough and baking a simple loaf.

Since then, I have picked up tips from challah bakers the world over. I've learned that several risings make a better loaf, and if you want an especially brioche-like texture, let the dough rise slowly in the refrigerator for one of the three risings. The secret to a glossy loaf is to brush with an egg wash twice, once just after braiding and then again just before baking. My new favorite challah adds fennel seeds to the dough with a variety of more seeds—nigella, fennel, poppy, and sesame—sprinkled on top.

The eastern European concept of a sweetened bread probably began in the Mediterranean, but it was not just a Jewish phenomenon. The Greeks serve a rich, braided egg bread called *tsoureki* at Easter; the Portuguese also make a sweet bread, infused with many spices not typically found in challah; the Russian nobility ate a rich egg bread called *kulich*; and the Czechs ate a bread exactly like challah, called *vanocka,* or "Christmas bread." Eastern European Jews adapted these traditions for an enriched egg bread to usher in their Sabbath.

Thus, by the late Middle Ages, when twisted breads were popular in central and eastern Europe, the twelve circular loaves described in Leviticus (see page 144) as offerings in the Temple became two braided loaves with six strands each, representing the two portions of manna given to the Jews for the Sabbath, as well as the two rounds of bread in the Temple.

From about the fifteenth century in eastern Europe, according to Rabbi Avi Keller of the Lubavitcher community in Brooklyn, the word "challah" came to mean a twisted, sweet, almost brioche-like bread, instead of the portion of dough tossed into the oven.

I usually make the dough a day ahead and put it in the refrigerator to rise slowly so that I can maintain control and adjust the baking to my schedule. When my children were young, I made the dough before they came home from school, then asked them to punch it down and braid it. Shaping dough was the perfect task for young cooks, especially as a distraction if they had been bickering.

Although I am partial to a six-braided challah, when I am in a hurry, I make a long cylinder, fold it over, and then twist three times to form a spiral sort of braid. Then I squish the braid together so it will be squatter and fatter, or I stretch it longer and swirl it into a circle. Hot from the oven, my challah begins every Sabbath or holiday meal.

The recitation of the blessing over the challah, thanking God for the gift of food from the earth, is followed by one or two very important customs, telling you about your background or maybe even your personality. The head of the house-hold either tears pieces of the bread and tosses them to the family and guests, or slices the challah with a knife and passes the pieces around the table. My family is full of tearers and tossers.

———————

1. In the bowl of a standing mixer, dissolve the yeast and 1 tablespoon sugar in 1½ cups (360 ml) of lukewarm water.

2. Using the paddle attachment, stir the oil into the yeast mixture, then add 2 eggs, one at a time, the remaining sugar, the salt, and 2 teaspoons of the fennel. Switch to the dough hook and gradually add 6 cups (810 grams) of flour, kneading for about 5 minutes and adding more flour as needed to make a slightly sticky, smooth and elastic dough.

3. Grease a large bowl, turn the dough into it, and put the greased side up. Cover with plastic wrap and let rise in a warm place for 1 hour, or refrigerate for a few hours or overnight.

4. When the dough has almost doubled, punch it down, remove it to a lightly floured counter, knead it briefly until smooth, and divide it in half. Roll each piece into a cylinder about 27 inches long, making sure there are no seams in the dough, and cut each in 3 pieces. Braid each loaf, and put on a parchment-lined baking sheet at least 4 inches apart. You can also twist the loaves into a circle if you like; the dough is very malleable.

5. Beat the remaining egg and egg yolk and brush about half the mixture on the loaves, reserving the rest. Let the dough rise uncovered another half hour or overnight in refrigerator.

6. If dough has been refrigerated, bring to room temperature. Heat oven to 350 degrees and either combine in a small bowl or keep separate the remaining fennel seeds and the poppy and sesame seeds. Brush the loaves with egg again and sprinkle with seeds, making your own design.

7. Bake for 35 to 40 minutes or until golden and firm when tapped with a spatula. Cool on a rack.

1½ tablespoons (2 packages) active dry yeast

1 tablespoon plus ⅓ cup (70 grams) sugar

⅓ cup (80 ml) vegetable or canola oil

3 large eggs, plus 1 egg yolk

1 tablespoon salt

1 tablespoon fennel seeds, divided

6 to 7½ cups (810 to 1012 grams) unbleached all-purpose flour, plus more as needed

2 teaspoons poppy seeds

2 teaspoons roasted sesame seeds

Vegan Challah

Late one recent summer, I visited Ramah in the Rockies, a Habonim camp about two hours southwest of Denver, and was bowled over the Jewish precepts being taught, the sheer beauty of the place, and the efforts to serve sustainable kosher food that, whenever possible, was also organic and local.

What they do with the soil, the environment, and the food captivated me, all done in the spirit of Rabbi Eliav Bock, formerly a Wall Street trader, who quit that profession for camping, something that he always loved as a child.

The rabbi thought hard about the kind of camp—mostly vegetarian with a bit of kosher meat occasionally served—he wanted to run. "I want the food to be local," he said.

The camping program experiments with dehydrating thinly sliced fruits and vegetables like zucchini, watermelon, peaches, etc., that they will turn into food on camping trips. (No store-bought beef jerky for Ramah in the Rockies!) The children make their own tomato paste, which sometimes becomes fruit leathers, which are much lighter to carry than sauce, as well as dried-out hummus that comes out like little pellets.

When I biked with Rabbi Bock to the vegetable garden, passing through fields of pine trees colored with lupine, lavender, and black-eyed Susans, I couldn't help but think of the short growing season in the Rockies. At the garden, which is tended by the campers, we saw carrots, turnips, radishes, and other vegetables that sustained many of these children's eastern European forebears. As they work the garden, the children learn about the life cycle of the Jewish year, and they learn how to care for animals along with tending to themselves.

I left feeling hopeful for a new generation of young people who will put into practice Rabbi Bock's thoughtful Jewish thinking about food, the cycle of the year, and the tenets of Jewish law.

Each Friday, Robyn Goldstein, a vegan counselor and now the head of their farm program, makes this four-braided vegan challah that the children braid themselves and, of course, love to eat.

---

yield: 2 challahs

2½ to 3 cups (338 to 465 grams) whole-wheat flour

2½ cups (338 grams) unbleached all-purpose flour, plus more as needed

1 tablespoon active dry yeast

1 tablespoon salt

⅓ cup (75 grams) sugar

¼ cup (60 ml) plus 3 tablespoons olive oil

3 tablespoons maple sugar

Sesame seeds

1. In the bowl of a standing mixer, mix the flour, yeast, salt, and sugar with a whisk. Attach the dough hook, then add 2 cups (470 ml) of warm water and mix on low until the consistency is tacky and fairly sticky.

2. With the motor running, add the ¼ cup oil and mix for a few minutes to incorporate, pausing to scrape down the sides if necessary. Then turn the dough onto a lightly floured surface and knead with your hands, adding small amounts of flour until the dough does not stick to your fingers.

3. Put the dough into a greased bowl, cover with a damp towel, and let rest for at least 2 hours, or until it is about doubled in volume.

4. Punch the dough down, then turn onto a lightly floured surface. Divide the dough in half, then cut each half into 4 pieces. Roll each strand into strands about 18 inches long. Put the strands next to each other and pinch together gently at the top. Starting from the left side, take the outside strand and weave it over the next strand, under the third and over the fourth. Always continuing from the left, keep weaving the strands as long as you have strands. Tuck the ends under and mold with your hands. Continue with the second dough, making two challahs.

5. Arrange the braided breads on a parchment-lined baking sheet and let rest for about 30 minutes. Preheat the oven to 350 degrees.

6. Dissolve the maple sugar in the remaining 3 tablespoons of olive oil and mix, then brush over the loaves and sprinkle the sesame seeds on top.

7. Bake the challahs for about 30 minutes, or until they are golden brown and sound hollow when tapped.

Defo Dabo, Ethiopian Sabbath Bread

yield: 1 large *dabo*

One Friday night, a group of twenty-somethings met at a shared house on the Leichtag Foundation's sixty-seven-acre agricultural ranch in coastal Encinitas, California. The foundation is using this space to develop a Jewish community farm where members till the land and work at food security organizations in the nearby San Diego area. As more and more young people seem to do, they were celebrating Shabbat together, saying prayers and singing songs.

That week, Ethiopian-born Avi Asnkow volunteered to have his friends cook an Ethiopian Shabbat dinner for me. Using cookbooks and the Internet, each person found an Ethiopian Jewish recipe for a different vegetarian *wat* (stew)—spinach, wild mushroom, *aleecha* (vegetable), red lentil, and yellow pea—served with a chopped salad and all seasoned with *chow,* an Ethiopian spice paste of garlic, ginger, mustard seeds, turmeric, and dry red chilies.

Then, visibly touched by the efforts his friends had made, Avi, who moved to Israel when he was five from Gunder, a village in the mountains of northern Ethiopia, talked about the food and life of the Ethiopian Jews. "In our village, we all ate together," he said. "What was special about Shabbat," he continued, "was the food was cold." This custom was started by the Karaites, an ancient sect of Judaism who believed that lighting a fire on the Sabbath was work and therefore was forbidden. Today, this sect of Judaism of about forty-four thousand people still lives by the word of the Torah, not the meanings interpreted by the Talmud.

"At Shabbat," he said, "parents ate first, before the children. We usually ate vegetable stews except for weddings, or at feasts when we moved to a new house. Meat was scarce. But when we ate it, it was cow, goat, lamb, or chicken." Each year just before Passover, Ethiopian Jews broke the clay dishes they use for eating and started anew with new clay dishes that they would use until the next Passover.

Avi's girlfriend, Tzvia Adler, who grew up on a kibbutz near Jerusalem, made *dabo,* the Ethiopian challah, a round loaf flavored with nigella seeds and sometimes turmeric. Using Avi's memory of what the bread tasted like, Tzvia combed through recipes on the Internet until she found a few that sounded just right, piecing together the perfect loaf. Beneath the *dabo* on the table was a typical Ashkenazic challah, and next to the breads was a platter of *injera,* the large Ethiopian flatbread made from fermented teff, a grass that grows in Ethiopia.

Defo dabo, meaning "homemade large bread" in Amharic and often called simply *dabo,* is a special bread for holidays for all Ethiopians. During the week, teff is the primary ingredient used to make *injera,* which is used to scoop up all the spicy stews served in Ethiopian cooking. Because the Bible mandates serving bread made out of different kinds of wheat for the Sabbath, Jews have tried to find the precious but often rare types of wheat for the special day.

Dabo dough is traditionally formed into a ball and enveloped in banana leaves, which you can find in sheets in the frozen section of Latin supermarkets. Parchment paper is an acceptable, though not as romantic, substitute in our standard ovens.

Spices in the dough can also differ as they do in Ethiopia, depending on where you live, what your tastes are, and what is available. This recipe includes coriander, the ground seeds of the cilantro plant that some people believe is the manna sent by God to the children of Israel. In fact, the two *challot* symbolize the double portion of manna, as cited above, sent on the sixth day so the Israelites would not have to gather it on the Sabbath.

After we said the blessings over the food and sang Sabbath songs, Avi showed us how to scoop up each stew with either the *dabo* or *injera*. Sitting on the floor, we all ate, using only our right hand as everyone used to do in the Middle East.

———————

1 tablespoon yeast

3 tablespoons sugar

3 tablespoons honey

2 teaspoons sea salt

1½ teaspoons nigella seeds (see page 7)

¼ teaspoon turmeric

¼ teaspoon ground coriander

Scant ½ cup (120 ml) vegetable oil

6½ cups (875 grams) unbleached all-purpose flour, divided, plus more as needed

1 large egg (optional)

1. In the bowl of a standing mixer fitted with the dough hook, stir together the yeast, sugar, honey, salt, nigella seeds, turmeric, ground coriander, and 2½ cups (590 ml) of warm water. Add the oil and mix well.

2. Add 6 cups (810 grams) of the flour and mix until a very wet, sticky dough forms. Cover with plastic wrap and let the dough rest for 40 minutes.

3. Uncover the dough, let it breathe, and stir in ½ cup (65 grams) more flour with a wooden spoon. Cover the dough again with plastic wrap and let it rest for another 40 minutes.

4. Cover a baking sheet with parchment paper and preheat the oven to 375 degrees.

5. Punch down the dough with the spoon, and then, using the spoon or a spatula, add enough flour to the dough so that it can be handled easily. Put it on the parchment-lined baking sheet. If you want, beat the egg and brush the top of the bread.

6. Bake for about 1 hour and 15 minutes, or until the top is golden brown and the bottom sounds hollow when tapped.

Note If you prefer to make two smaller *dabos*, line two 8-inch round baking pans with parchment paper, then pour half the dough into each. The baking time will be reduced to about 30 to 40 minutes.

Spiced and Fried Matzo

[Karaites] make their Passover matzoh of barley flour rather than wheat, as a reminder of the "bread of affliction" mentioned in the Torah.
—Benjamin of Tudela's twelfth-century writings, in Sandra Benjamin,
The World of Benjamin of Tudela: A Medieval Mediterranean Travelogue, 1995

The Karaites, a sect of Judaism with about forty-four thousand members who endeavor to live by the word of the Torah, not the meanings interpreted by the Talmud, can now make their matzo easily with barley flour available to us today. Remember, though, according to the laws, that as soon as the water touches the barley, or any other flour, it has to be kneaded and baked within eighteen minutes or it will have risen and therefore not be considered kosher for Passover. And, if you are strictly kosher, the barley flour has to be kosher for Passover, and that will be impossible to find. However, there are so many different kinds of kosher-for-Passover matzo available today that there will surely be a widely available barley matzo soon.

Matzo, the central element of the Passover Seder, is similar to the very flat bread that we get today at Middle Eastern stores—but without the yeast. It was quickly fried in a *tabun* oven or a rounded griddle on an open fireplace. The word "matzo" comes from the Old Babylonian *maassaartum,* which means "barley." It was the first grain harvested in the Middle East and was used for centuries before wheat appeared, about 4000 B.C.E.

Until 1838, when an Alsatian Jew named Alex Singer invented the first mechanized matzo-dough-rolling machine, people bought their matzo round from the local kosher bakery, ordering, say, one pound of matzo per person during Passover. By the end of the century, the Manischewitz Company of Cincinnati had covered the globe with machine-made square matzo.

Today, we may not eat a pound of matzo per person at Passover, but we still want variety in our matzo preparations during the eight-day holiday.

I tasted this spiced and fried matzo from JoeDoe restaurant on the Lower East Side of Manhattan. Use this mix of spices or make your own. Serve them anytime or at Passover dipped into one of the *harosets* (see pages 85 to 90).

---

yield: 10 to 15 whole fried matzos

1 tablespoon plus 1 teaspoon salt

2 tablespoons plus 2 teaspoons sugar

1 teaspoon celery seed

2 teaspoons minced garlic

¼ teaspoon turmeric

¼ teaspoon cayenne

¼ teaspoon black pepper

4 cups (945 ml) canola oil, for frying

10 to 15 whole matzos

1. In a small bowl, mix the salt, sugar, celery seed, garlic, turmeric, cayenne, and black pepper. Mix well.

2. Heat a 14-inch or larger skillet to medium, and pour in the oil. Heat the oil to 350 degrees. Set aside a baking sheet or plate lined with paper towels.

3. Lower a whole matzo into the oil using tongs, pressing down gently until well submerged. Fry for 20 to 30 seconds, then transfer the matzo from the oil to paper towels to drain. The matzo will crisp and change to light golden brown after it is removed from the oil.

4. Sprinkle the top of each warm matzo with about a teaspoon of the spice mix. Serve immediately, or cover with a kitchen towel and set aside in a warm place for up to several hours.

Kubbanah, Yemenite Overnight Breakfast Bread

The Yemenite Jews eat just like non-Jews except for their Sabbath inventions—and there are lots of them. *Jahnoun,* from the city of Aden, as well as its equally buttery, deeply flavored leavened cousin called *kubbanah,* from the north of Yemen, are both breads, baked overnight with hard-boiled eggs. My guess is that Yemenite Jews, who had frequent commerce with Indian traders, learned the technique of making these laminated doughs smeared in butter or ghee from the Indian *paratha.* The technique spread to Iraq and eventually to Spain and from there everywhere. Also, when Yemen became part of the Ottoman Empire, the technique became absorbed into the *borek,* where it was introduced to Hungary and Vienna. There, it became puff pastry, and eventually the croissant.

When I lived in Israel in the 1970s, these breads were typically only eaten at home, not yet found in mainstream restaurants or frozen-food sections of Israeli and kosher supermarkets around the world as they are today.

Kubbanah is like a miracle. The bread, slathered with butter, ghee (called *samneh* in Yemen), or oil, is tucked into an 8-inch classic aluminum *kubbanah* pot and steamed overnight in a very low oven before the Sabbath starts, emerging the next day as a buttery, deeply flavored, highly risen bread. I first tasted *kubbanah* years ago at the home of a Yemenite family in Jerusalem, who were keeping the prohibition against cooking on the Sabbath. It is served for breakfast Saturday morning with grated tomatoes, *zhug* (see page 12), and a hard-boiled egg.

As cultures have exchanged ideas about food, *kubbanah* baking has changed dramatically, with Israeli chefs trying their hands at it, embellishing the dough with more sweetness and sometimes using all-white flour, resulting in an almost brioche-like bread.

Adeena Sussman, a prolific writer and great cook, is also an excellent *kubbanah* baker. She taught me her recipe, learned many years ago when she was doing an article for *Gourmet* magazine on Yemenite cooking. Unfortunately, the *Gourmet* test kitchen was concerned that home cooks wouldn't want to keep their ovens on overnight. (Not to mention topping it with nigella seeds [see page 7], which no one would have heard of then!) So the article was published without the recipe.

There is a saying that whenever a *kubbanah* is in the room, all breads should bow to it.

I totally agree.

---

yield: 8 servings

1 tablespoon active dry yeast

1 teaspoon plus ⅓ cup (70 grams) sugar

½ tablespoon salt

5 tablespoons (70 grams) unsalted butter, melted and cooled slightly, plus about 1 cup (2 sticks/226 grams) butter, at room temperature

3 to 3½ cups (360 to 420 grams) unbleached all-purpose flour

4 to 8 large eggs in the shell, rinsed

1 teaspoon nigella or black sesame seeds (optional)

1. In the bowl of a standing mixer with the paddle attachment, dissolve the yeast and 1 teaspoon of sugar in ⅓ cup (80 ml) warm water. (The water should be only slightly warmer than room temperature, not boiling.) Let the mixture sit for 5 to 10 minutes, or until the yeast activates and bubbles.

2. Add the remaining ⅓ cup sugar, the salt, 5 tablespoons melted butter, and ¾ cup (180 ml) more warm water, stirring well. Switch to the dough hook and knead in 3 cups (390 grams) of the flour, kneading until a smooth, glossy, and only slightly sticky dough forms. Add more flour if necessary.

3. Remove the dough and grease the bowl with some of the remaining butter, then add the dough, turn to coat, and cover the bowl with a towel. Let the dough rise for at least 30 minutes, then punch the dough down and let rise another hour. You can also let the dough rise for 8 hours or overnight in the refrigerator, then bring to room temperature and let rise another hour before proceeding.

4. Divide the dough into eight equal pieces and set the room-temperature butter next to your work surface. Butter an aluminum *kubbanah* pan or 8- to 9-inch oven-safe pot with a tight-fitting lid and set aside. Preheat the oven to 225 degrees.

5. Liberally butter your work surface, using about 2 tablespoons of the butter. Then, using your fingers, spread a piece of the dough out into a rectangle about 11 by 13 inches. The dough will be quite thin; don't worry if some parts rip or tear. Again using your fingers, spread 1½ tablespoons of the butter over the dough. With your fingers, roll the dough lengthwise like a jelly roll, then flatten the dough into a 2-inch-wide rectangle. Next, fold the dough over onto itself in threes or fours, making a spiral. Put the spiral, open side up, into the prepared pan, then repeat with the remaining spirals of dough, arranging in one even layer.

6. Nestle the eggs between the pieces of dough, then sprinkle the nigella or sesame seeds over the top, if using. Cover the pan and bake for 12 hours.

Note The 8½-inch round aluminum *kubbanah* pans with a tight-fitting cover are next to impossible to find in the United States, but you can use an oven-safe pot with equally delicious results.

Noni Toki, Bukharan Dome-Shaped Crisp Flatbread

When I grew up in Providence, we would go to an Armenian store and get mounds of crisp flatbread that seemed to last forever. On a recent visit to Rokhat Kosher, an Uzbek bakery in Queens, I was happy to discover *noni toki*, a similar dome-shaped bread, fresh from the oven.

Although I did not achieve the perfect crispy result that I found in the bakery when I attempted to make the bread, I made these so-called hubcap matzos myself at home—with the help of a trick I learned in the late Copeland Marks's *Sephardic Cooking*—and the result is a great substitute. I should have known that Marks, whom I so admired as a cookbook author, would find a way to make the bread in his home kitchen after traveling all the way to Uzbekistan to get the recipe. For brunch, I like to serve individual breads (that I make the day before) with an Azerbaijani omelet (see page 15) and fruit salad.

———

1. In a standing mixer equipped with a dough hook, mix the flour, baking powder, cumin seeds (if you like), salt, sugar, and oil with 1 cup (240 ml) water for about 2 minutes, until the dough comes together and is stiff. Cover and let the dough rest for about 30 minutes.

2. Preheat the oven to 450 degrees and search your kitchen for two heavy (ovenproof) aluminum medium-size mixing bowls.

3. Divide the dough into four pieces and knead each piece for a minute or so, by hand. Then roll out, as thin as possible, on a marble slab or between two pieces of parchment paper until the dough is at least 12 inches in diameter. Put the mixing bowls upside down so the dome shape is on top and spray with vegetable spray. Roll out the dough again and carefully pick it up with your hands and swing it over the dome. Repeat with the remaining pieces.

4. Move the oven rack to the middle (if using mixing bowls). Bake in the oven for about 8 to 10 minutes or until it starts to brown a bit. Remove from the oven. Wait a minute or two, then gently insert a spatula beneath the *toki* to release it and flip it over onto a serving plate. Continue baking until you have used up all the dough.

yield: 8 servings

4 cups (540 grams) unbleached all-purpose flour

3 teaspoons baking powder

1 tablespoon cumin seeds (optional)

2 teaspoons sea salt

1 teaspoon sugar

¾ cup (175 ml) soybean or vegetable oil

Note Although it's not very Uzbek to do so, during the summer I add rosemary, thyme, fennel, and fennel fronds or whatever fresh herb I am growing. Sometimes I also make this bread *au naturel* so that it doesn't conflict with whatever else I am serving.

If you prefer, you can omit the dome shape, divide the dough into four pieces, roll them out paper-thin between two pieces of parchment paper to about 14 by 9 inches, let sit for 30 minutes, then gently cut almost through the dough to make long strips about 2 inches wide, before baking as above. Bake and break up the perforated strips. I serve these with dips or with cheese.

Ka'ak, Middle Eastern "Pretzels"

I have been eating and loving *ka'ak* (the word means "cake" in Arabic) for years. After I first tasted one of these crackers in Jerusalem, they found me again in Syrian and Lebanese markets and then all the way in Puglia, Italy, where they are known as *taralli*. This trail started in ancient Egypt, where the Egyptians made circular rolls with a hole in the center, which are depicted in the hieroglyphics on the pyramids. Through the centuries, these rolls journeyed to Syria, Lebanon, Turkey, and to Puglia, where, like so many dishes, the same technique is used, but the spices are different. Depending on where they lived along spice routes, cooks flavored the *ka'ak* with cumin, anise, coriander, *za'atar,* or *mahlep,* the inside of cherry pits.

Travelers eventually brought *ka'ak* to Poland, where along the way they became everyone's favorite roll with a hole, the bagel. But that is quite another story! (See page 29.)

---

1. Dissolve the yeast and sugar in 1 cup (235 ml) of warm water in the bowl of a standing mixer. Add the butter or oil, salt, anise, coriander seeds, and flour and mix with a dough hook until the dough comes together, adding more flour if necessary. Put the dough in a greased bowl and let rise for 1 hour.

2. Preheat the oven to 375 degrees and line two baking sheets with parchment paper. Put the sesame seeds in a small, shallow bowl.

3. Divide the dough into 4 pieces, then divide each piece into 8 (achieving 32 pieces). Roll one piece into a rope about ¼ inch in diameter, then cut the rope in half. Twist each half around two or three fingers, pinching to seal the circle closed. (You may make the *ka'ak* larger or smaller if you wish, but the thinner you roll them, the crisper they will be.)

4. Brush each *ka'ak* with a little olive oil, dip the tops in the sesame seeds, and put on prepared baking sheets. Repeat with the remaining pieces of dough.

5. Bake for 25 to 30 minutes, rotating sheets halfway through, until the *ka'ak* are golden brown and crisp.

yield: about 5 dozen *ka'ak*

2 teaspoons active dry yeast

½ teaspoon sugar

8 tablespoons (1 stick/ 113 grams) butter, at room temperature, or ½ cup (120 ml) extra-virgin olive oil

2 teaspoons salt

2 teaspoons anise seeds

1 teaspoon coriander seeds, lightly crushed in a mortar and pestle

3½ cups (465 grams) flour, plus more for dusting

4 to 5 tablespoons sesame seeds

3 tablespoons olive oil (about), for brushing

Pletzel, Onion and Poppy Seed Flatbread

Before there was pizza, there were *pletzel:* flatbreads topped with onions and baked in the oven.

In Bialystok these were called *Bialystoken Tzibele Pletzel Kuchen,* or "Bialystok Onion Pletzel Cakes." Also called "onion boards" when large, these *pletzel* became bialys on the Lower East Side of New York. As far as I am concerned, nothing can beat the flavor of the sweetness of the dough with the caramelized onions, topped with poppy seeds and a little coarse salt.

My favorite place to buy them fresh from the oven is at Florence Kahn Bakery and Delicatessen in Paris's Marais.

Because *pletzel* are not exactly mainstream American, I was surprised to see them on the website of Cold Moon Farms, a bed-and-breakfast in Jamaica, Vermont. My niece and nephew went there with their young son Charlie, who enjoyed gathering eggs and milking the goats. The owners of the farm, remarkable transplanted New Yorkers from Brooklyn who run a school for children with special needs, serve *pletzel* for their guests the way other innkeepers serve blueberry muffins at breakfast or scones for tea. (Their *pletzel* are also a hit with chili for Super Bowl parties.) Of course, these breads are not just for special occasions.

———————

1. Stir together the eggs, yeast, salt, and 1¾ cups (415 ml) warm water in the bowl of a standing mixer with the paddle attachment. Add the ½ cup oil and honey and mix well.

2. Switch to the dough hook and gradually add the flour. Knead in the mixer until you have a soft dough, adding more flour if necessary so the dough is not too sticky.

3. Grease a large bowl with extra oil or nonstick spray, put the dough in the bowl, turn to coat, and cover the dough with a towel. Let the dough rise for 2 hours.

4. While the dough is rising, caramelize the onions. Heat 4 tablespoons of the olive oil in a large, heavy-bottomed skillet over medium heat. Add the onions and cook, stirring occasionally, until the onions start to sizzle, about 3 minutes. Continue to cook the onions over low heat, stirring every 10 minutes and more frequently at the end, until the onions caramelize and turn deeply golden, about 20 to 30 minutes. Add more olive oil if the onions begin to stick. This can be done a few days in advance.

5. Thirty minutes before you are ready to begin baking, preheat the oven to 375 degrees and line three baking sheets with parchment paper.

yield: 6 large *pletzel*

DOUGH

4 large eggs

1½ tablespoons active dry yeast

1 tablespoon kosher salt

½ cup (120 ml) olive oil

¼ cup (60 ml) honey

7 to 8 cups (945 to 1080 grams) unbleached all-purpose flour, plus more for rolling

TOPPING

4 to 6 tablespoons olive oil

4 large yellow onions, thinly sliced into half rounds

2 tablespoons poppy seeds

2 teaspoons kosher salt

6. When ready to bake, divide the dough into six pieces. Lightly flour your work surface and roll each ball into large rectangles about 7 by 10 inches. Put two pieces of dough on each baking sheet.

7. Top the dough with the caramelized onions, poppy seeds, and kosher salt. Bake for 20 to 25 minutes, or until golden brown.

The Sacredness of Bread

And Solomon made all the furnishings that were in the House of the Lord; the altar of gold; the table for the bread of display of gold.

—1 Kings 7:48

Nothing is more basic than a loaf of bread. The cookbook author Paula Wolfert once told me that when she lived in Morocco, her housekeeper did not sleep well unless there was a sack of wheat in the house to make bread.

Bread is always sacred and therefore so are the grains used to make it. But for Jews, there are Sabbath and everyday breads. In many lands where wheat was scarce, the Sabbath was the only day you could have wheat bread. On the others you would eat bread made from barley, oat, spelt, teff, or rye.

It made sense, then, for Jewish merchants to go into the grain business, which they have done for centuries all over the world. Like the concept of the futures market, merchants would buy the wheat at harvest, then store it until needed, when, ground into flour, it would fetch a higher price. Take the classic example of Joseph, who, in the book of Genesis, cleverly stored the pharaoh's grains in times of plenty to later sell during famines.

To me, though, the most beautiful thing about bread is that one of the Hebrew words for bread, *lechem,* is close to the word for life, *l'chaim,* and in Arabic *aish* means both life and bread.

On Pumpernickel and Rye

The day Mrs. London's Bakery opened in 1977, we were sold out of everything except for one loaf of pumpernickel rye bread. Two women were holding on to the last loaf of pumpernickel. "Ladies, let's be civil about this. I'll be Solomon and we'll split the loaf." Instead, one of the women yanked the bread out of the other's hand, put down her money, and ran.

—Michael London, Mrs. London's Bakery, Saratoga Springs, New York

Pumpernickel and other rye hearth breads are most often found in cold climates where there is an abundance of water and timber. Enclosed ovens can hold the heat for long periods, being fed by wood, coal, and now gas. (It is interesting to compare this long, slow, and low-heat baking technique to that for flatbreads, which require a quick, high heat.)

Years ago I learned to make a sour, also called "cement," from Michael London, cited above. This fermentation of flour and water caused by wild yeasts in the air, helped along with a little active dry yeast, does the trick to start the bread.

In the last few years, there has been a renaissance in traditional bread making in the United States and around the world. In Tel Aviv, San Francisco, Ann Arbor, Washington, D.C., and, of course, New York, to name some places, bakers are experimenting with old-fashioned grains like rye in all kinds of artisan breads, including those needing a sour starter, a defining element of pumpernickel rye.

SOUR STARTER

2 medium onions, coarsely chopped

1 tablespoon caraway seeds

1 tablespoon active dry yeast

5 cups (675 grams) rye flour,
plus 1 tablespoon for sprinkling

1. Put the onions and the caraway seeds in a cheesecloth bag and tie shut.

2. Dissolve the yeast in 3½ cups of water in a large bowl and sprinkle with 4 cups of the flour. Stir to mix until it attains the consistency of cement. Submerge the cheesecloth bag of chopped onions and caraway seeds in the center. Sprinkle the tablespoon of rye flour over the surface. Loosely cover with plastic wrap and set aside overnight on the counter. The sour needs air to breathe, but not too much or it will dry out.

3. The next day, remove the onion-caraway bag and discard it. After about 15 hours, the sour should smell somewhat acidic. "Feed" it with the remaining cup of flour and ½ cup (120 ml) of water, or enough to maintain the thick consistency. Mix and cover again and let the sour sit until the area between the "cracks" in the dough spreads, about 4 hours. You want to capture as much of its strength as possible.

4. After it rises again, in about 4 hours, you will have about 6 cups of sour starter and you can begin to use it. If keeping the starter on a countertop, "feed" it once every 24 hours with 1 cup (130 grams) flour and ½ cup (120 ml) water. The sour can stay several days in the refrigerator without being fed, but as Michael London says, never take a sour for granted. It needs to be nourished. You can also freeze it and, when you want to use it, bring it to room temperature and "feed" it as above.

Pumpernickel Rye Bread

This rye bread was inspired by a batch of freshly harvested and ground rye flour sent to me from farmers on Martha's Vineyard. Pumpernickel and whole rye flour are the same, but coarsely ground pumpernickel tends to yield a more strongly flavored and dense bread.

yield: 2 loaves

2 cups (about 460 grams) sour starter (see page 163)

1½ tablespoons molasses

1 tablespoon yeast

1½ tablespoons sea salt

2 tablespoons coarsely ground caraway seeds (optional)

7 cups (700 grams) rye or pumpernickel flour, plus additional for sprinkling

———————

1. In the bowl of a standing mixer fitted with the dough hook, stir together the sour starter, 2 cups (480 ml) of water, the molasses, and the yeast.

2. Add the sea salt and caraway seeds, if using. With the motor running, gradually add the flour. Using the dough hook, mix for about 5 minutes, until well incorporated, scraping down the sides of the bowl, adding more flour if the dough is really sticky. Remove the dough to a lightly floured surface and knead by hand for a few minutes, until a smooth, slightly tacky dough forms.

3. Form the dough into a ball and put it in a greased bowl, turning to coat the dough, then cover with a towel and let the dough rise for 1 to 1½ hours, until doubled in size.

4. Punch the dough down, and if it is still sticky, knead in more flour. Divide the dough in half, gently form two round or oblong loaves, and let them rest 10 to 15 minutes on a floured work surface. Remove the loaves to a floured cookie sheet, cover very loosely with plastic wrap, and let them rise for another 1½ hours, or until almost doubled in size.

5. Preheat the oven to 400 degrees, set a rack in the middle, and set a brick or pizza stone on the lower rack.

6. Brush or spray the loaves with water, then sprinkle some of the rye flour on top. With a single-edge razor or very sharp knife, make 5 cuts across each loaf, shorter ones on the end, longer in the center. Slide the loaves into the oven, then throw a few ice cubes onto the oven floor to generate steam. Bake the loaves for 35 to 45 minutes, or until they sound hollow when tapped with a spatula.

Note You can omit the caraway seeds and throw in whole almonds, pecans, apricots, or dried plums instead.

Potato Rolls

yield: 20 rolls

As I thumbed through the many potato recipes in a family cookbook written in the early twentieth century, I recalled my father telling me stories he had learned in school about the American-born Sir Benjamin Thompson, also called Count Rumford. A British loyalist who fled to England after the American Revolution, Count Rumford became head of the Bavarian army and reorganized it, encouraging the chefs to cook potatoes for human consumption, rather than tossing them to animals.

Although the Spanish conquistador Gonzalo Jiménez de Quesada brought potatoes from Peru to Spain in the mid-1500s, a hundred years later the potato was still—like corn and Jerusalem artichokes—regarded as better suited for livestock than humans. The Russian Orthodox Church even looked down on the humble spud, noting that there is no mention of potatoes in the Bible.

Prussian king Frederick II—more fondly known as Frederick the Great or "Old Fritz"—saw the budding potential of using potatoes to feed the masses, and provided cuttings for the peasants to grow. During the Seven Years' War (1756–63), Antoine-Augustin Parmentier, a pharmacist from Paris, was captured by the Prussians and forced to eat only potatoes to survive. Although the experience was less than pleasant, his time in prison and the role the potato had certainly played in his sustenance led him, in 1772, to propose the potato as a nourishing food for those suffering from dysentery. Shortly after, Paris's Faculty of Medicine declared potatoes edible, and, at an auspicious moment no less, potatoes started to be planted in France.

As famine led to the French Revolution and subsequent Reign of Terror, potatoes, planted in the Tuileries Gardens and other places in Paris, saved the day (or at least the stomachs). By the beginning of the nineteenth century, potatoes were being added to recipes all around Europe, but still were a harder sell than tomatoes and peppers. Parmentier encouraged people to eat potatoes by serving them at fancy dinners for the Parisian elite and visiting foreigners such as Benjamin Franklin. Eventually the French got used to and even enjoyed eating potatoes, especially when they learned that they were cheaper than flour. And, for many of the best French chefs today, potatoes are the favorite vegetable.

At about the same time, the Jewish communities of southern Galicia, a former kingdom in between Poland and Ukraine, caught on to potatoes, which soon worked their way into *cholent* and kugels. *Berches,* the challah of German Jews (see *Joan Nathan's Jewish Holiday Cookbook* for a recipe), began containing potatoes, as did dinner and breakfast rolls. And, of course, Ukrainian potato pancakes, called latkes by Jewish immigrants, became beloved all over Europe.

According to Shmil Holland's fascinating cookbook, *Schmaltz,* northern Europeans baked or boiled potatoes and mixed them with rye flour to make bread in the nineteenth century. The late Hirsz Abramowicz, in his *Profiles of a Lost World*

(1999), said that before World War II in Lithuania, the following potato rolls, baked in a very hot oven while set on top of green cabbage or oak leaves—there was no parchment paper in those days—were a meal with a side of hot milk or pickles. Wealthy people ate them as a side with butter and sour cream. I remember them fondly from the bread basket at Hammer's Dairy Restaurant on the Lower East Side.

2 medium russet potatoes (426 grams)

¼ cup (60 ml) warm milk

3 teaspoons (15 grams) active dry yeast

¼ cup (50 grams) sugar

4 tablespoons (56 grams) unsalted butter, melted and cooled slightly, or vegetable oil

1 large egg plus 1 egg yolk

1 teaspoon sea salt

3 cups (405 grams) unbleached all-purpose flour, plus more for kneading

2 medium onions (28 grams), thinly sliced

1 tablespoon vegetable oil

3 tablespoons (8 grams) poppy seeds

1 teaspoon coarse sea salt

1. Scrub the potatoes, then boil in water to cover for 15 to 20 minutes, or until cooked through. Remove from the water to cool and reserve the cooking liquid.

2. While the potatoes are cooking, mix the milk, yeast, and sugar in the bowl of a standing mixer and let it sit.

3. Peel the potatoes, then purée with ¼ cup (60 ml) of the cooking liquid. Add 1 cup (240 ml) of the purée (saving the rest for another use) to the standing mixer with an additional ¼ cup (60 ml) cooking liquid, the butter or oil, the whole egg, and the salt. Whisk to combine, then, with the dough hook attached, gradually add the flour. Knead for 5 to 10 minutes, until a smooth, slightly sticky dough forms. Remove to a large greased bowl, cover with a towel, and let rise for 1 hour.

4. Gently punch the dough down and knead a few minutes on a lightly floured surface, then put the dough back in the bowl, cover, and let rise for another hour.

5. Meanwhile, cook the onions over low heat in a large nonstick sauté pan with 1 tablespoon of vegetable oil until lightly caramelized, about 20 to 30 minutes. Remove from the heat and set aside.

6. Divide the dough into 20 portions, then, with floured hands, shape into balls and put 2 inches apart on the parchment-lined baking sheets. Brush with the egg yolk and sprinkle with poppy seeds, coarse salt, and the caramelized onions, then let rise uncovered for another 30 minutes. Preheat the oven to 375 degrees.

7. Bake the rolls until golden, about 30 minutes, rotating the baking sheets halfway through cooking.

Note After you've let the dough rise twice, but before shaping into rolls, you can refrigerate the dough overnight and finish shaping them the next day—just bring the dough to room temperature before baking.

Grains and Such

Crunchy Saffron Rice

Hand-Rolled Couscous

Fideos Tostados, Toasted Pasta in a Cinnamon-Spiked Tomato Sauce

Kishke, Stuffed Derma with Matzo Meal, Spices, and Onions

Orecchiette with Rosemary Oil, Chickpeas, and Broccolini

Kasha Lasagne with Mushrooms and a Confit of Onions

Jerusalem Kugel

Sweet and Crunchy Kugel

Matzo Muffins

Farfl, Egg Barley Noodles with Fresh Thyme and Onions

Crunchy Saffron Rice

When I visited Sandra Di Capua, one of my former assistants, and her family in North Miami Beach, I tasted dishes and listened to stories from Colombia, Panama, Italy, and Lebanon. In the early 1920s, when the United States often refused Jewish refugees from pre–World War II Europe, Colombia welcomed them. Sandra's mother's Polish family found refuge in Barranquilla, a city near Cartagena and once the most important port in Colombia. Her father's parents had come there from Italy and Lebanon, where they joined a relative who had founded a textile factory, subsequently bringing other refugees from Europe and the Middle East.

Eventually, Barranquilla's Jewish community grew to about two hundred families and Bogotá's to about one thousand families. Both cities had a Sephardic and an Ashkenazic synagogue, offered ample work opportunities, boasted beautiful country clubs, maintained Jewish schools, and provided a good life. When Sandra's father, Riccardo, married her mother, Raquel, they lived in Bogotá until fighting between local drug lords ushered in a period of violence and instability in the 1980s. Many families, like the Di Capuas, left Colombia for Miami.

Like Jews from Tunisia, Morocco, Cuba, and so many other places where there were at one time mostly merchant Jewish enclaves, many Colombian Jews have regrouped in Florida. The foods at a dinner with all these friends and family at the Di Capuas' modern apartment included, among other dishes, Syrian *laham b'ajeen*, Italian artichokes, chicken with eggplant, and for dessert, guava *kamishbroit* (see page 317). Added to the hodgepodge were fried plantains and Sandra's stunning butterflied and boned snapper (see page 239) served with preserved lemon, sautéed onions and capers, and the following crunchy saffron rice.

Rice has been a staple in the Middle East ever since it came from China through Persia thousands of years ago. This recipe uses the Latin American technique of browning the rice first. The crunchy, nutty bottom, called *a'hata*, is similar to the crispy Iranian rice, and is always fought over in Lebanese and Iranian homes. I have added saffron to make this like the Jewish *pilav* that traveled from medieval Persia to southern France, where today it is considered a traditional French dish.

yield: 6 to 8 servings

4 tablespoons olive oil

3 cups (600 grams) basmati or Carolina Gold rice

1 tablespoon sea salt, or to taste

A few pinches of saffron or ¼ teaspoon turmeric

---

1. Heat the olive oil in a nonstick frying pan that is at least 3 inches deep and 12 inches in diameter. Add the rice and sauté for about 5 minutes, stirring, just to toast. Then add the salt, saffron or tumeric, and 5½ cups of water. Bring to a boil, then cover. Reduce the heat to the lowest setting and simmer very, very slowly for an hour. Raise the heat to medium and continue cooking for another 5 to 10 minutes, just to toast the bottom. Remove the cover, put a knife around the bottom, then place a serving platter on top. Carefully flip the rice onto the platter and serve. The golden crust will be on top.

Hand-Rolled Couscous

While visiting Mejlaw, a tiny village in northwest Morocco, I was enchanted by the sight of a group of women at a food cooperative, sitting on the floor with their legs outstretched, expertly mixing water with semolina, then raking the grain with their fingers in sweeping circular motions as they prepared couscous from scratch.

I returned home longing for the fresh, wheaty flavor and light, steamed texture of homemade couscous, which is far superior to what you get from a box.

By coincidence, a few weeks later, I found myself in Brooklyn, at the Smorgasburg food market in Williamsburg, where I encountered a booth emitting the fragrance of fresh couscous and stew. The booth, New York Shuk, was operated by Ron Arazi and his wife, Leetal, young chefs from Israel who run an artisanal food company in Brooklyn showcasing handcrafted Middle Eastern pantry staples, specializing in harissa, spice blends, and hand-rolled couscous. From them I learned how simple and satisfying it is to make your own couscous.

All you need is some semolina, water, a little oil, a strainer, and a steamer. Once you have practiced the technique a few times, it is easy—even magical.

Ron learned to make couscous from his mother, who was born in Mogador, now Essaouira, a town in Morocco once known for its expert Jewish couscous makers. "I, the only son in my family, love to preach about it," he said, "and even taught my sisters how to make it."

Ron taught me how to make couscous in the tiny kitchen of his Crown Heights apartment. Watching him work with his hands was mesmerizing. He poured about four cups of semolina in a large mixing bowl, dampening it by spraying it with water. Holding the bowl in his left hand, he patted and circled his fingers gently over the semolina until the grain started to clump into tiny balls. Then he steamed it over water.

"Moroccan Jewish cooks always steam couscous over a stew or a soup," he said, but "then you can't taste the natural wheat flavor of the semolina." Transferring the couscous to a mesh sieve, he gently shook the grains through. Soon it was ready for a little more water, before going back into the steamer. He repeated that step once again and then the fourth and final steaming came when he served it with braised lamb with a plum and apricot sauce (see page 292).

---

yield: about 6 servings

2¾ cups (500 grams) coarse semolina

1½ teaspoons salt, or to taste

⅓ cup (80 ml) canola, soybean, or vegetable oil

1. Put the semolina in a large mixing bowl. Fill a spray bottle with ½ cup (120 ml) water and salt and shake well to dissolve the salt in the water. Spray the semolina, stirring the mixture with your hand and gently pressing down while moving your palm in a circular motion. Be careful: It is better to have too little moisture than too much or you'll create a dough. Continue to spray and mix until the water is evenly incorporated into the semolina; it should form tiny granules without clumping. You may not need all of the water.

2. Press the moistened semolina through a strainer or colander with holes about ⅛ inch in diameter (better slightly larger than smaller) and into another large bowl. Add the oil to the sieved semolina and mix well. There may be a small amount of doughy mixture that won't go through the strainer—as much as ⅓ cup—and this may be discarded.

3. Pour 4 to 5 inches of water into the bottom of a *couscoussiere* or vegetable steamer, then bring it to a boil. Add the rolled semolina to the top part of the steamer and steam uncovered for 10 to 15 minutes, or until you see that the steam goes through the couscous easily and the mixture is completely clumped. Put it into a large bowl and, using a fork, break up the clumps. Add about ½ cup (120 ml) of water and mix well. Put the couscous back in the steamer for another 15 minutes.

4. Transfer the couscous to a bowl, and add about ⅓ (80 ml) to ½ (120 ml) cup more water. Stir gently with a fork. Then put the couscous back in the steamer for the third steam. After about 10 to 15 more minutes, take the couscous out of the steamer again. Stir it with a fork and add another ⅓ cup (80 ml) of water, then return the couscous back to the steamer for one last steam.

5. After 10 to 15 minutes of steaming, when the couscous is perfectly cooked to a light airy texture, remove the couscous to a bowl, then pass the couscous through the sieve into another bowl. This important stage will help rid the couscous of all the hard bits that are not light and airy. Let cool to room temperature. When ready to eat, steam briefly until it is hot again. Fresh couscous will keep well for up to 7 days, so you can always make it a few days beforehand. Just splash a little water on top before reheating in the microwave or steaming again.

Fideos Tostados, Toasted Pasta in a Cinnamon-Spiked Tomato Sauce

For years I have been making *fideos,* a dish I learned from women from the island of Rhodes. The thin vermicelli coils made out of durum wheat, first browned for flavor and to better separate the strands in cooking, then simmered in broth, were originally made by hand in Sicily as early as the tenth century.

Rabbi Binyamin Mussafia, in his concordance to the 1140 c.e. *HeAruch* (a glossary of terms in the Talmud), interprets noodles as *itrin,* an Aramaic word for long, thin dried or fresh strands of dough that are boiled in water or fried in oil. But the word had already appeared in the fifth-century Jerusalem Talmud, six centuries before Marco Polo supposedly brought pasta from China. Later Rashi called these vermicelli noodles *vremselles.* I assume that these earliest of noodles became known as *fidellos tostados*—also called simply *fideos*—in Spain and were brought by Muslims and Sephardim after the Inquisition to other parts of the Mediterranean, and in turn by the Spanish explorers to the Americas, where they are served today in Mexican homes and restaurants as *sopa seca.* In the last few centuries, with tomatoes added, *fideos* plays the roll of a savory kugel-like dish or *pashtida* for the Jews of Spain and their Diaspora.

I like to make this dish with the flavorful tomato sauce I tasted on the Greek island of Kea, when I was visiting Aglaia Kremezi's cooking school. Her sauce is infused with orange and cinnamon, a wonderful complement to any pasta, but especially this dish from the island of Rhodes.

———

1. **to make the sauce** Warm the oil in a medium heavy-bottomed saucepan set over medium-high heat, then sauté the onion until it begins to soften, about 5 minutes. Add the tomato paste and cook, stirring, for 1 minute, then add the wine, Aleppo pepper or crushed red pepper flakes, and currants. Simmer for 2 minutes, then add the tomatoes, cinnamon stick or ground cinnamon, orange peel, and 2 teaspoons of salt. Bring to a boil, then reduce the heat to low, cover, and simmer for 15 to 20 minutes, or until the sauce thickens.

2. Remove the cinnamon stick, if using, and the orange peels, then purée the sauce with an immersion blender or in a food processor fitted with a steel blade.

3. Adjust seasonings to taste. The sauce can be made 5 days ahead of time and kept stored in an airtight container in the refrigerator.

yield: at least 8 servings

SAUCE

2 tablespoons olive oil

½ large red onion, chopped (about 1 cup or 135 grams)

1 tablespoon tomato paste

1 cup sweet wine, such as Manischewitz or Marsala

1 teaspoon Aleppo pepper, or ¼ to ½ teaspoon crushed red pepper flakes

½ cup (50 grams) dried currants

One 28-ounce (794-gram) can whole plum tomatoes or 3 pounds (1⅖ kilos) whole fresh tomatoes

1 cinnamon stick, or 1 to 2 teaspoons ground cinnamon

Two 4-inch pieces fresh orange peel

2 teaspoons sea salt, or to taste

FIDEOS

1 pound (453 grams) very thin angel hair pasta

1 cup (235 ml) olive oil

4 cups (945 ml) vegetable stock or water

4 cups (945 ml) tomato sauce

1 tablespoon salt, or to taste

4. **to make the *fideos*** If you are not using *fideos* noodles, which come in round clumps, then break the dry pasta into thirds. This allows the pasta to become more manageable in the skillet. Line a baking sheet with paper towels.

5. Warm the olive oil in a large sauté pan over medium heat. Add the pasta, in batches if necessary, making sure the oil is completely covering the pasta. Use tongs to stir the pasta, cooking until golden brown. Remove the pasta to drain on the baking sheet, then repeat with any remaining batches of pasta. Drain all but 3 tablespoons of oil from the pan, saving the oil for another use if you'd like.

6. In a large saucepan, stir together the stock or water, sauce, and 1 tablespoon of the reserved oil and bring to a boil over medium-high heat.

7. Add the salt and the browned pasta, cover, and cook over medium-high heat for about 10 to 15 minutes, or until the *fideos* are tender and the liquid is absorbed, depending on the type of pasta.

8. Before serving, preheat the oven to 350 degrees, grease a 10- or 11-inch pan, and spoon the *fideos* into the pan. Brush the remaining 2 tablespoons of oil over the coils of pasta and bake for a half hour or until the top is crunchy. Serve warm as an accompaniment to fish or chicken or as the main course of a vegetarian meal.

Kishke, Stuffed Derma with Matzo Meal, Spices, and Onions

Kishke, an ancient delicacy, consists of the intestines of an animal stuffed with meat or a grain and a fat, and then cooked in a stew. Today *kishke* is usually either packaged and made with a vegetable casing or made as below in parchment paper. The word *kishke* comes from Yiddish but is akin to the ancient Arabic word *kishk,* also meaning "to enrich stews." *Kishk* was probably the first instant dried food.

I saw *kishk* being made in an Arab village in the north of Israel. This version was made from drained yogurt, salt, and freshly harvested bulgur, kneaded, shaped into loaves, and then dried in the sun for nine days on rooftops. This sun-dried food is kept for the winter to enrich soups and stews.

The Jewish equivalent of the dish does not contain yogurt and is used to enrich stews like *cholent* (see page 277). It is served as a side dish and is really tasty!

———————

yield: about 8 servings

6 tablespoons vegetable oil or chicken fat, divided

1 medium to large onion, cut into 1-inch pieces

1 clove garlic, chopped

1 stalk celery, cut into chunks

1 large carrot, peeled and cut into chunks

1 cup (115 grams) matzo meal

1 teaspoon salt, or to taste

⅛ teaspoon freshly ground black pepper, or to taste

⅛ teaspoon hot paprika

1. Preheat the oven to 425 degrees. Line a baking sheet with a double layer of foil 12 inches long, topped with a sheet of parchment paper the same size.

2. In a skillet over medium-low heat, heat 4 tablespoons of the fat or vegetable oil, and sauté the onion and garlic until soft and golden, about 5 to 10 minutes. Cool slightly and pour everything, including fat, into a food processor equipped with a steel blade.

3. Add the remaining 2 tablespoons fat or oil, celery, carrot, matzo meal, salt, pepper, and paprika to the food processor. Pulse until the vegetables and fat are incorporated into a paste. Transfer mixture to parchment paper, and shape into a knockwurst-like cylinder about 9 inches long and 1¾ inches in diameter. Enclose the parchment and foil firmly around the cylinder, folding the ends under.

4. Either bake for 30 minutes and then add it to a *cholent* (see page 277), or bake for 30 minutes, then reduce the heat to 350 degrees and cook until the *kishke* is solid, about 45 to 60 minutes more.

5. Unroll the *kishke* to expose the surface and return to the oven just until the top is lightly browned and slightly crisped, 10 to 15 minutes. Cool slightly and cut into rounds. If desired, serve as a side dish with pot roast or roast chicken (see page 266).

Orecchiette with Rosemary Oil, Chickpeas, and Broccolini

Luscious-looking roasted carrots in varying colors and eggplants topped with pomegranates in large white bowls greeted me as I walked into NOPI, Yotam Ottolenghi's showcase restaurant in London's Soho district.

During lunch, I tasted new dishes for the menu. As we ate, Yotam and his business partner Sami Tamimi, with whom he coauthored *Jerusalem* and *Ottolenghi,* came by to taste and talk. While they critiqued the dishes, I could see their high standards, flowing from two sons of Jerusalem to our global world of food. Fortunately for the British, they landed in London.

Born in Jerusalem of an Italian Jewish father from an old Italian family and a mother whose parents came there from Germany, Yotam now takes inspiration for his cooking from his roots and the whole world.

Earlier that week, I was invited for dinner at Yotam's home, where I met his partner Karl and young son Max. As we played with this very active and fun-loving baby on the patio, Sami walked in. Sipping wine as we got acquainted, we all sat down to a casual family dinner in the kitchen at a long table hewn from one huge piece of wood so long that half the table was outside and half inside the house. Eventually, when Max went to bed, Yotam put the finishing touches on our dinner that he had started before I arrived: chickpeas and broccolini over *orecchiette* for starters, then zucchini, roasted garlic, and mint, an Italian *braciole*—a *rollade* of beef with fresh tomatoes—and for dessert, simple strawberries with ice cream. The meal was delicious, with Yotam and Sami suggesting, as all cookbook writers and chefs do, how each recipe could be better.

The dish I liked best that night was this *orecchiette* with chickpeas and broccolini, a recipe with ancient roots being made new again today with anchovy, cumin, a dash of hot pepper, and broccolini—a modern, unfussy spin to unite two dishes that go back almost two thousand years.

---

1. Warm ¼ cup (60 ml) of the olive oil in a large sauté pan set over medium heat. Add the rosemary and fry gently for 5 minutes, turning once or twice, until the leaves are crisp. Use tongs to remove the rosemary and set aside to drain on paper towels.

2. Add the garlic to the pan and cook for 1 minute, then add the chickpeas, anchovies, cumin, ¼ teaspoon of salt, and a few grinds of black pepper. Cook for 6 to 8 minutes, stirring occasionally, until the chickpeas start to crisp and there is plenty of oil still left in the pan. Remove from heat and set aside.

yield: serves 2 as a meatless main course or 4 as a starter

Up to ½ cup (120 ml) olive oil

8 sprigs rosemary

2 cloves garlic, crushed

2 cups (950 grams) cooked chickpeas (from 1 cup/190 grams of dried chickpeas, see page 10, or from one 15-ounce can)

3 anchovies, finely chopped

1 teaspoon ground cumin

¼ teaspoon salt or to taste

A few grinds of pepper

1 bunch broccolini (about 8 ounces/226 grams), quartered lengthwise

8 ounces (226 grams) *orecchiette*

⅓ cup finely grated Parmesan cheese

3. Bring a medium pot of salted water to a boil over high heat. Add the broccolini and blanch for 2 minutes, until crisp-tender. Drain and put in a large bowl of ice water for 1 minute, then drain again and add to the chickpeas.

4. Refill the pot with salted water and bring to a boil over high heat. Add the pasta and cook for 12 minutes (or according to the package instructions). Drain, reserving ½ cup (120 ml) of the cooking liquid. Pour the pasta into the pan with the chickpeas, stirring in the Parmesan and enough pasta water to create a sauce. Add more oil if you like as well. Warm over low heat, then sprinkle with the crispy rosemary leaves and serve.

Note Back in D.C., I tasted a similar dish using house-made *cavatelli* at the Red Hen, a restaurant in the small but vibrant Bloomingdale neighborhood. There, chef Mike Friedman used his Jewish roots and love of Italian food to make *cavatelli* with spinach and chickpeas, topped with a black pepper mascarpone—a blend of 1 pound mascarpone (450 grams), 2 tablespoons freshly cracked black pepper, and 1 tablespoon of salt. When I'm feeling extra indulgent, I'll whip up this savory cheese and add a dollop onto Yotam's *orecchiette*.

Kasha Lasagne with Mushrooms
and a Confit of Onions

When I visited Zamosc, Poland, the Italian Renaissance town near Lublin where my in-laws' families lived for generations, there was not one restaurant in sight. A few years after my visit, my son David ate at Muzelane Ormianski Piwnice, a restaurant across the street from the building in a square patterned after Siena where my mother-in-law, Peshka, lived before she left hurriedly at the start of World War II. The restaurant was filled with dishes for buckwheat groats: cabbage stuffed with buckwheat and bacon, and dumplings stuffed with buckwheat and cottage cheese, but not that beloved dish that we call *kasha varnishkes,* a comfort food favorite in our family, made with homemade noodles cut with a knife into sizes about two inches by four inches and then pinched together like a bow tie.

Recently, I tasted a version that is much more authentic and more delicious than the one we all eat today. Like a lush lasagne with kasha (buckwheat groats), a confit of onions, and wild mushrooms, it comes from a Polish Israeli cook who served it to a friend who left Poland during the war and was nostalgic for this Friday night dish of her past.

It is a true *kasha varnishkes.*

Varnishkes, a Yiddish form of the Russian *varnashekis,* actually means a stuffed dumpling. Isn't lasagne, one of the oldest pastas known to man, similar to that? The dough is first boiled as dumplings are, then filled with buckwheat groats, caramelized onions, and loads of mushrooms and baked.

You can use boxed lasagne noodles instead if you wish, but it will not be nearly as fun to prepare. If you want, make the noodles and filling a day ahead of serving, then just assemble and bake for your guests. It is great as a vegan or vegetarian main dish or a side dish anytime.

yield: at least 8 servings

3 cups (360 grams) all-purpose flour or 1½ cups (202 grams) all-purpose flour and 1½ cups (202 grams) durum flour, plus more for dusting

½ teaspoon kosher salt, plus salt to taste

4 large eggs, plus 3 large egg yolks

3 to 4 cups (710 to 940 ml) vegetable or chicken broth

2 cups (190 grams) buckwheat groats

4 to 6 tablespoons olive oil or rendered chicken, duck, or goose fat, or as needed

6 large onions, sliced in half circles (about 8 cups)

8 cups shitake or other sliced mushrooms

Freshly ground black pepper to taste

---

1. Put the flour and the salt into a food processor fitted with a steel blade and add 3 of the whole eggs and all the yolks. Pulse until mixed, then slowly add 2 to 3 tablespoons of iced water until the dough comes together in a ball. Remove, wrap in plastic, and let rest at room temperature or the fridge for 1 hour.

2. Cut 4 pieces of parchment paper bigger than a 13-by-9-inch pan or about the size of the pan you will be using and have them ready. Using a dough cutter, divide the dough into 4 pieces and roll out one piece on a floured surface into a rough 9-by-13-inch rectangle, making it as thin as possible. I sometimes stop for a moment when I think the dough is as thin as possible, let it

rest, then roll it some more. Transfer to the parchment paper. Repeat with the other pieces and let the lasagne noodles dry for at least an hour. Then, if you want, you can keep them in the refrigerator, between layers of waxed paper in sealable plastic bags, until ready to use, up to 3 days. (Or store in the freezer for up to 3 months.)

3. Bring a pot of salted water to a boil and prepare an ice bath. Cook each lasagne leaf separately for about 20 seconds. Then carefully, using tongs, move to the ice bath for about 5 minutes. Then move back to the parchment paper. Repeat with the rest.

4. Bring the chicken or vegetable broth to a boil in a small pan.

5. Meanwhile, warm a skillet with a lid over medium heat and add the groats, stirring them for a few minutes until they smell like toasted nuts. Pour 3 cups of the hot broth into the skillet. Simmer, covered and stirring occasionally, for about 20 minutes, or until cooked, adding more broth if needed.

6. In a large skillet, warm the olive oil or schmaltz over medium heat. Cook the onions until they are lightly browned and caramelized to a "confit," golden brown, almost black, and sweet smelling. Then add the mushrooms except about 6 slices for garnish and just cook through. Season with salt and pepper. Mix with the buckwheat groats.

7. To assemble the lasagne, preheat the oven to 375 degrees and rub a little olive oil or schmaltz on the bottom of a 9-by-13-inch Pyrex or other baking pan.

8. Carefully lay one of the lasagne leaves in the pan. Spoon on one-third of the groats-onion-mushroom mixture, then lay the second leaf on top, ending up with a lasagne layer. Mix the remaining egg with a little water and brush the top. Arrange a few of the remaining cut raw mushrooms on top.

9. Bake for 40 minutes or until golden on top. Let cool for a few minutes, then with a very sharp knife, cut into squares.

Note Try to use Bob's Red Mill Buckwheat; it is made of white groats which are raw, so you can smoke them yourself.

Jerusalem Kugel

For many Jews, kugel is the taste of childhood. They want exactly the kind of kugel their mother made, whether as a weekly Sabbath treat or served only on holidays. In fact, Allan Nadler, a professor of religious studies at Drew University, told me that the homey casserole of noodles or potatoes has been credited with mystical powers.

"Clearly the spiritual high point of the meal is the offering of the kugel," he told me. "At that moment the rabbi has the power to bestow health and food, and even to help couples conceive."

But despite kugel's deep tradition, the dish is changing, especially in Brooklyn, a current center of kugel cooking. One afternoon at Hungarian Kosher Catering in Borough Park, I saw at least eighteen kinds of kugel for sale, as customers discussed them in Yiddish, English, and Hungarian. Most Jews know about noodle (*lokshen*) and potato kugel. But salt and pepper kugel? Blueberry and rhubarb kugel? Or three-layer kugel with sweet potato, broccoli, and cauliflower?

The word *kugel* comes from the German word for "ball." It is traditionally a round, baked sweet or savory pudding or casserole made of noodles or potatoes. Originally kugel was the second dish for the Sabbath, made of leftover bread, fruits, and eggs. It was baked in an upside-down, flower pot–shaped dish alongside the main Sabbath dish in Ashkenaz (modern-day Alsace-Lorraine) in the eleventh and twelfth centuries. Today, in Alsace it has morphed into a delicious bread pudding of pears and dried plums (see my *Quiches, Kugels, and Couscous* for the recipe) and in America and elsewhere has evolved into elaborate noodle puddings.

Allan, who grew up Orthodox in Montreal, is adamant about his kugel. "Everything is a kugel these days. I grew up in a home where my grandparents were from Russia. We ate salt and pepper kugel, and cut it up in soup. Now, *that's* kugel."

One really delicious kugel I almost always see in religious communities, especially in Jerusalem, is a sweet and peppery version called *Yerushalmi*, or Jerusalem kugel. Supposedly it originated in Jerusalem with followers of the Gaon of Vilna, a Jewish scholar, in the late eighteenth century. Made with thin noodles, pepper, salt, and sugar, it is tricky because it has a caramel base that can stick or burn. My guess is that this was a sweet take on the salt and pepper kugel that people like Allan Nadler grew up with. When well made, it is a favorite kugel.

---

yield: 12 servings

1 cup (200 grams) sugar, divided

½ cup (120 ml) vegetable oil, plus more for greasing the pan

1 tablespoon sea salt, or to taste

1 teaspoon black pepper

½ teaspoon cinnamon

1 pound (453 grams) fine noodles, like vermicelli or angel hair

4 large eggs, well beaten

1. Put ½ cup (100 grams) of the sugar and the ½ cup oil in a heavy 3-quart saucepan. Stir constantly over medium-high heat until caramelized, about 5 to 10 minutes. The sugar might seize up a little, but with constant stirring it will eventually smooth out and become golden brown. Remove from the heat. Let harden and cool for 15 minutes.

2. Pour 5½ cups (about 1⅓ liters) water into the saucepan with the sugar mixture and bring to a boil. Preheat the oven to 350 degrees and grease a 10-inch round baking pan.

3. Add the salt, pepper, cinnamon, and the remaining ½ cup of sugar with the noodles to the boiling water. Cook, stirring occasionally, until the water is almost evaporated, about 15 to 20 minutes.

4. Remove from the heat and cool for 10 minutes, then stir in the eggs. Mix well and pour into the greased baking pan.

5. Bake the kugel for 1 hour, or until golden brown and crusty on top. The longer you cook it, the better people like it. Run a knife around the edges of the kugel, turn out onto a plate, and serve.

Sweet and Crunchy Kugel

Through the years, Madison Avenue has had its way with kugel. Boxed noodles replaced homemade noodles, canned pineapple and cranberries replaced raisins, and processed cream cheese, sour cream, and cottage cheese were swapped for farmer cheese and other European dairy products. And, as if all this weren't enough, crunchy plain and frosted cornflakes became preferred American toppings for kugel.

The Kellogg Company introduced Frosted Flakes in 1951. By 1963, the *New York Times*'s Craig Claiborne wrote a Rosh Hashanah article about his friend Martha Hadassah Nadich, the wife of Judah Nadich, the rabbi of the Park Avenue Synagogue in New York City. The article included recipes for challah, gefilte fish, strudel, and a noodle pudding topped with cornflakes. The postwar synagogue cookbooks in the 1950s and '60s are full of such recipes.

This kugel, my daughter Merissa's favorite, is adapted from a friend's aunt Lorraine, who lived in Brooklyn. It is one that my children grew up eating for years at potluck Shabbat dinners. Covered with frosted flakes, it is sweet and very American. The unbaked kugel needs to sit overnight (or a day and a half) in the refrigerator. The secret to the frosted flakes is not using any at the bottom of the box, as they will be way too sweet.

You can, if you prefer, use plain cornflakes instead of frosted flakes. But then you will be tampering with Aunt Lorraine's tradition. And speaking of tampering with tradition, I don't bother boiling the noodles in advance.

---

yield: 12 to 16 servings

Two 8-ounce (226-gram) packages low-fat cream cheese or Neufchâtel cheese, softened

8 tablespoons (1 stick/113 grams) lightly salted butter, at room temperature

¾ to 1 cup (150 to 200 grams) sugar

8 large eggs

4 cups (945 ml) nonfat milk

⅓ cup (83 grams) low-fat sour cream plus sour cream for serving

⅓ cup (80 grams) cottage cheese

2 teaspoons ground cinnamon

2 teaspoons vanilla extract

14 ounces medium or wide (dried) egg noodles

About 2 cups frosted flakes cereal, such as Kellogg's

1. Lightly grease an 11-by-16-inch baking dish with nonstick cooking spray. Mix the cream cheese or Neufchâtel cheese, butter, and sugar in the bowl of a standing mixer, blending on medium speed for a few minutes, then add the eggs one at time, incorporating after each addition. Reduce the speed to low and add the milk, sour cream, cottage cheese, cinnamon, and vanilla extract; the mixture will be very wet. Add the uncooked noodles to the baking dish and pour the cream cheese mixture on top; use a slotted spoon to lift some of the noodles so that the liquid is well distributed. The noodles should be just about covered with the mixture; cover and refrigerate overnight.

2. When ready to bake, preheat the oven to 350 degrees and uncover the kugel. Bake for 40 minutes, then pull the kugel out of the oven and lightly crush handfuls of cereal over the top, spreading the cereal evenly. Return to the oven and bake for 20 minutes more, or until light to medium brown around the edges and no longer liquidy inside. Shake the pan to see if the kugel seems solid. Cut into squares and serve warm.

Matzo Muffins

Chef Adam Sobel of RN74, a Michael Mina restaurant in San Francisco, remembers fondly these matzo "cupcakes" (I call them muffins) that his great-grandmother brought with her from Russia. "When my mother makes the matzo cupcakes," Sobel told me, "they are awesome. Our family are dunkers, and they are great for soaking up the juices from the brisket." Try them alone or with my take on Sobel's brisket (page 294).

---

1. Preheat the oven to 375 degrees and grease 12 muffin tins.

2. Break up the pieces of the matzo farfel or the matzo in a bowl. Add warm water to cover and soak for 3 minutes. Then carefully squeeze out the excess water, passing the wet matzo through a fine-meshed sieve.

3. Wipe the bowl and whisk the eggs in it, then stir in the matzo.

4. In a large skillet set over medium heat, warm the chicken fat or vegetable oil and sauté the sliced onions until soft, tender, and beginning to brown, about 10 to 15 minutes. Then stir the onions, olive oil, and parsley into the matzo-egg mixture. Season with salt and pepper to taste, then spoon into the muffin cups, dividing evenly.

5. Bake for about 25 minutes, rotating the pan every 8 minutes during baking. Remove when golden brown and let rest for 15 minutes before serving.

6. The muffins can be frozen and reheated in a 350-degree oven before being served.

yield: 12 muffins

3 cups (396 grams) matzo farfel or 6 whole matzos, processed in a food processor

4 large eggs

¼ cup (55 grams) chicken fat or vegetable oil

2 large yellow onions, sliced (about 3 cups)

1 cup (235 ml) extra-virgin olive oil

¼ cup diced fresh parsley

1½ teaspoons salt, or to taste

Freshly ground black pepper, to taste

Farfl, Egg Barley Noodles with Fresh Thyme and Onions

Supper consisted of a dairy soup made with milk, especially a soup made with *farfl.* Flour would be combined with water (and, if they were lucky, egg), then the mixture was kneaded well. The dough would be cut into thick slices which were then reduced to bits with a chopping knife. This *farfl* was made of a dark meal that was a ground mixture of peas, barley, rye, and buckwheat. It had a distinctive flavor and was used mainly in summer, when there was a good supply of sweet milk. When new potatoes appeared, they were scraped and added to the *farfl.* In wealthier homes, *farfl* were made of wheat flour.

—Hirsz Abramowicz, *Profiles of a Lost World,* translated by Eva Zeitlin Dobkin, 1999

yield: 6 to 8 servings

Every cuisine has little tiny bits made of flour, egg, oil, and salt. The Italians call them pasta *grattata,* the Tunisians call them *nikitouche* (see my *Quiches, Kugels, and Couscous*), and Jews from Eastern Europe call them *farfl,* or egg barley, because they are formed in the shape of barley.

Hirsz Abramowicz, in his marvelous *Profiles of a Lost World,* describes *farfl* for Lithuanian country Jews (see quote above). Later on in the passage, he says that they ate *farfl* with lentils—and, I imagine, also with onions—as a dish during the week, much as the Lebanese eat the delicious dish *mujeddra,* with lentils, rice, and topped with lots of fried onions.

Farfl is something Chef Ian Boden also makes in his tiny restaurant called the Shack, in Staunton, Virginia. "My grandmother Pauline used to buy boxed egg barley made by Manischewitz, and it was always the highlight of Thanksgiving, served with brisket, for us growing up," said Ian at his humble restaurant, literally a shack. "When I was a cook in New York working at Judson Grill, she sent me a care package full of her stuffing—the best!—and her egg barley," he told me as he prepared dinner for the twenty-six diners who would sit at the seven mis-matched tables with chairs to match the yellow walls.

Whatever Ian serves in Staunton (which boasts a long-standing Jewish com-munity and historic synagogue), his grandmother's egg barley, always drying in the kitchen, will be grated, then browned in the oven, and boiled and cooked into one of his dishes. Make your own egg barley or use tiny bits of prepared pasta.

"I really like it as a stand-alone dish," he told me. "Whenever we make it at the Shack, I have to do a large batch because my cooks and I will eat a good bit of it."

Note that after making the dough, you need to let it rest for 24 hours.

1. Put the flour into the bowl of a standing mixer fitted with the dough hook. In a small bowl, stir together the eggs, the vegetable oil, and 1 teaspoon of the salt. Then, with the mixer running on low, gradually add the egg mixture to the flour, kneading until the dough forms into a ball, about 3 minutes. You may have to add a tablespoon or so of water.

2. Remove the dough from the mixer and put on a lightly floured surface. Knead by hand, folding the dough over itself and pressing with the heels of your hands. Continue folding and pressing, turning the dough after each press, until the dough is smooth and elastic, about 3 to 5 minutes.

3. Divide the dough into two and flatten into discs about 2 inches thick and let stand, uncovered, for 24 hours, to let it dry.

4. The next day, preheat the oven to 300 degrees and line 2 baking sheets with parchment paper.

5. Grate the dough on the coarse side of a box grater, letting the gratings fall onto the baking sheets. Continue to move the grater so that the dough spreads to one thin layer over the entire sheet. Bake for between 30 and 40 minutes, stirring the egg barley every 10 minutes and rotating the sheets top to bottom, until evenly browned. Remove from the oven and cool completely. Once cool, the egg barley can be stored in an airtight container at room temperature for up to a week.

6. When ready to cook the egg barley, warm 3 tablespoons of schmaltz or vegetable oil in a large, heavy-bottomed pot set over medium-low heat. Add the onion, garlic, the other teaspoon of salt, the bay leaf, and thyme sprigs. Cook, stirring occasionally, until the onions are translucent, about 10 minutes.

7. Add the egg barley, stir to coat, then pour in the broth or water. Bring to a low simmer and cook uncovered for about 15 minutes, or until the barley has soaked up most of the sauce but still has some chew, similar to cooked barley. Season to taste with salt and especially black pepper. Serve as a side with brisket or a main course with vegetables or lentils with fried onions.

Note To serve the egg barley with lentils, as Lithuanians did, cook about 1 cup of green or brown lentils, then mix them with 1 cup of the cooked *farfl*. Top with 2 slowly cooked crisp onions for a vegetarian main course or accompaniment to meat or fish.

2⅓ cups (315 grams) unbleached all-purpose flour

3 or 4 large eggs

1 tablespoon vegetable oil

2 teaspoons kosher salt, plus more to taste

3 tablespoons schmaltz or vegetable oil

1 large Spanish onion, diced

3 cloves garlic, minced

1 fresh or 2 dried bay leaves

2 sprigs fresh thyme

3 cups (710 ml) chicken or vegetable broth or water

Freshly ground black pepper to taste

Vegetables

Slow-Cooked Silky Spinach and Chickpeas

Spinach with Pine Nuts and Currants

Concia, Crispy Fried Zucchini with Garlic, Basil, and Balsamic Vinegar

Bulgarian Eggplant and Cheese *Pashtida*

Grilled Eggplant with Tahina, Feta, and Pomegranate

Vegetarian Tagine of Peppers, Onions, Zucchini, Eggplant, and More

Slightly Sweet and Sour Cabbage

Whole Roasted Head of Cauliflower with Whipped Feta and Goat Cheese

Green *Chile Relleno* Latkes

Pomodori a Mezzo, Baked Tomato Halves

Kolokuthokeftedes, Zucchini Fritters

Yuca Latkes with Cilantro Cream

Mashed Sweet Potato Latkes with *Zhug*

Paprikás Krumpli, Hungarian Roasted Potatoes with Onions

Sweet Plantain Guava Kugel

Slow-Cooked Silky Spinach and Chickpeas

When Rachel Sasson learned that she'd won first prize in a cooking competition in Athens, she immediately brought a bouquet of flowers to her Romaniote grandmother's grave. Rachel, the main kosher caterer in Athens, thought her grandmother would have been proud that she won with the simple hand-me-down family recipe for chickpeas with spinach.

Romaniotes have ancestors who settled in Greece during the Hellenistic period, beginning in the third century B.C.E. The Greek influence on this group is so great that they have a distinct and separate way of worshipping, surviving to this day in only a few synagogues, including Kehila Kedosha Janina, a tiny congregation on New York's Lower East Side. Now listed with the National Register of Historic Places, the slightly disheveled town house where it is housed shows the daily life of this community that uses a Graeco-Hebrew form of vernacular Greek in its services and follows the Roman rites, also dating back two thousand years. This group of Jews once inhabited towns like Salonika, the island of Rhodes, and about thirty other distinct places throughout Greece, joined by Jews fleeing there from Spain during the Inquisition. During the last century, the Nazis destroyed 80 percent of the Jewish population of Salonika in just a few days. Now Rachel and the lucky few whose families returned to Athens after the war are doing their best to revive Judaism. For posterity, Rachel has written a cooking pamphlet of her recipes in Greek, including many like this one that have been around for two thousand years.

When I first saw this recipe, one of those dishes that was once cooked in a communal oven overnight, I thought the cooking time must be way too long. But as I do often when trying new dishes, I tested it just as the recipe had been written. To my surprise, the chickpeas held up beautifully and became toasty, almost like roasted chestnuts; the spinach, dill, and parsley achieved a smooth, silky texture. When I suggested retesting to shorten the cooking time, friends and family said, "No!"

---

yield: serves 4 to 6

1 cup (200 grams) dry chickpeas, soaked overnight (see page 10) or one 15-ounce (425-gram) can chickpeas

4 scallions, cut in slivers, or ½ medium onion, chopped (about ½ cup chopped/100 grams)

¼ cup (60 ml) olive oil

1 cup (235 ml) vegetable broth (see page 139)

1 teaspoon salt

½ teaspoon freshly ground pepper

2 pounds (907 grams) fresh spinach or three 10-ounce (283½-gram) packages of frozen chopped spinach, thawed and drained

1 bunch fresh dill, chopped, with 4 tablespoons reserved

½ bunch parsley, chopped, with 2 tablespoons reserved

Juice of ½ lemon, or to taste

---

1. Preheat the oven to 350 degrees. Drain the chickpeas and put them with 2 cups (470 ml) of fresh water in a 3½-quart Dutch oven or other oven-safe pot and bring to a simmer over medium-low heat.

2. Once simmering, add the scallions or onion, oil, vegetable broth, salt, and pepper. Then, using two wooden spoons, gently fold in the fresh spinach a handful at a time, adding more as it wilts. (Or, if using frozen spinach, simply stir it in.) Cover the pot, transfer to the oven, and bake for 1 hour.

3. Remove from the oven and stir in all but 4 tablespoons of the dill and all but 2 tablespoons of the parsley. Cover the pot and bake for 30 minutes. Remove the cover, stir, and bake for another 30 minutes, checking occasionally to make sure the mixture isn't too dry, adding a little water if necessary.

4. Remove from the oven and adjust the seasonings to taste, stirring in the lemon juice. Garnish with the reserved dill and parsley and serve accompanied with rice, wheat berries, or couscous.

Note This is one of those recipes I love because it is so adaptable. You can use spinach, kale, arugula, lettuce, Swiss chard, or whatever greens you have available. Just chop them up and add your favorite herbs.

You can also prepare the dish hours in advance and reheat it gently on the stove before serving, but don't add the reserved fresh herbs until you are ready to serve, as they wilt quickly.

Spinach with Pine Nuts and Currants

I have been making this recipe for years. Onions, pine nuts, and raisins are a sure sign of an early Jewish Italian recipe, possibly prior to the first century, when the first Jews moved to the island of Sicily. There, they must have learned about the superior flavor of nuts from the Italian stone pines that grow near Mount Etna. And who knows? Perhaps this dish was served to the great Rabbi Akiva during his visit to Syracuse in the first century. If so, I am sure that he liked it.

---

1. Cover the currants with hot water to plump them up.

2. Rinse the spinach well and remove the stems. Drain slightly but do not dry the spinach. Put in a large sauté pan and cook over medium heat, stirring until wilted, just a few minutes. Strain well, and set aside.

3. Add the olive oil to the now empty pan, heat, then sauté the onion until tender, about 8 minutes. Add the pine nuts and brown them, then drain the currants and add with the spinach, sautéing briefly to warm the spinach. Season with salt and pepper to taste and serve warm or at room temperature.

yield: 4 to 6 servings

2 tablespoons currants

1 pound (453 grams) fresh spinach

1 to 2 tablespoons olive oil

1 small yellow onion, minced

2 tablespoons pine nuts, toasted

Salt and freshly ground pepper to taste

Concia, Crispy Fried Zucchini with Garlic, Basil, and Balsamic Vinegar

On a trip to Rome, I tasted freshly made *concia,* the Italian Jewish preserve made from thinly sliced and fried Costata Romanesco—an Italian heirloom zucchini—flavored with garlic and herbs, then cured with vinegar and oil. With the interplay of the fried slices of zucchini and the vinegar, which adds a real tang, it was so delicious that it has become a mainstay of my kitchen.

At the end of the nineteenth century, Italians began breeding zucchini, based on a New World squash, to grow just the size of a cucumber, rather than the large squash that they were used to eating. Now we are happily seeing Costata Romanesco in our markets and seed catalogues. But if you can't find it, any medium-size zucchini will do.

In the summer, you can season this dish with fresh basil, mint, or oregano; in the cooler months, fresh rosemary, sage, or thyme. I love deep-frying the zucchini slices to quickly crisp them, but you could sauté the slices if you wish to use less oil. Once you are done frying, you can strain and refrigerate the oil for future use.

---

1. Trim the ends off the zucchini and cut in very thin rounds. A mandoline is great for this but a sharp knife will do. Arrange the zucchini in a single layer on paper towel–lined baking sheets and sprinkle liberally with salt. Let sit for at least 2 hours to draw out the water.

2. Heat about 4 inches of the oil in a large pot or electric wok to 375 degrees. While the oil is heating, rinse and completely dry the zucchini slices.

3. Fry the zucchini for 3 to 5 minutes, until deep gold brown but not black, using tongs or a large slotted spoon to turn the slices after 2 to 3 minutes. Drain the fried zucchini on paper towels.

4. Taste a zucchini slice to determine if it needs more salt. To assemble, put a single layer of the fried zucchini in a flat glass serving dish. Next add a bit of the garlic, a light sprinkle of vinegar, salt and pepper to taste, and a scattering of the basil. Repeat with another zucchini layer and the garlic, vinegar, and basil, until you have used all the zucchini, ending with the garlic, vinegar, and basil on top.

5. Either serve immediately or cover and refrigerate at least 2 hours and up to a day before serving. This is delicious as part of an antipasto or as a side dish.

yield: 6 to 8 servings

3 pounds (about 1⅓ kilos) medium-size zucchini

4 to 5 tablespoons coarse sea salt, or to taste

Olive oil for frying

2 cloves garlic, peeled and diced or pressed through a garlic press

A few tablespoons of good-quality balsamic vinegar or white wine vinegar, to sprinkle on zucchini

Freshly ground pepper to taste

Small bunch of basil, thinly sliced

Note You can also use thin Japanese eggplant or a yellow summer squash for this dish. Another, more traditional way to draw out the water is to thinly slice the vegetables and let them sit in the hot sun all day, or dry them in a 210-degree oven for a few hours before frying.

Bulgarian Eggplant and Cheese *Pashtida*

I am always amazed how I fall into recipes. On a visit to Israel, I found myself at a party in an Ottoman building in Jaffa chatting with a dapper gray-haired gentleman. When he learned that I wrote about food, he asked what I was going to make later that week for Shavuot. I hadn't really thought about it, but I knew that I didn't want to make a cheesecake. He said that he was going to make a Bulgarian eggplant *pashtida* (Hebrew for "savory pie") that he had learned from a friend's cleaning woman. Afterward we emailed back and forth so that I could get the correct recipe. (Somehow you know when someone is a good hobbyist cook.) He kept insisting that I grill the eggplants over an open fire—all ten of them—until they were really black, then drain them in a plastic strainer overnight before mixing them with the various goat cheeses and baking in the oven.

This dish, which originated in Spain, is basically the same throughout Greece and all over the Balkans, with the short crust often made with vegetable oil instead of butter. The eggplant is sometimes mixed with *brinza,* a salty sheep's milk cheese found in Romania, Slovakia, and Bulgaria. It is similar in creaminess to Brie and Camembert and similar in flavor to feta, so I try to use a creamy Bulgarian feta. *Kashkaval* is a harder, mild sheep's milk cheese, similar in texture to Emmental or cheddar. Luckily, today in major cities around the world, cheese choices are many, so you do not have to substitute as you had to in the past.

When I returned to my own kitchen, I decided to try the dish as is but to cook it in a Bundt pan. It is beautiful served with roasted peppers in the center, and is absolutely delicious as a first course or as a side course with fish.

---

1. **to make the filling** Cook the eggplants over a grill or gas stove, turning occasionally with tongs, until charred and soft, about 15 to 20 minutes, or prick the skin and put in a 450-degree oven for 20 to 25 minutes. Leave in a plastic strainer to drain on the counter for a few hours or overnight.

2. Peel and roughly chop the eggplant, then mix with the cheeses, the whole egg, a little salt, and lots of black pepper and set aside. Taste and adjust seasonings.

3. **to make the dough** Using a standing mixer with a paddle, mix the sour cream or yogurt with the butter or the oil. Gradually stir in the flour, baking powder, and salt, then slowly, if needed, add a tablespoon of cold water, using just enough water to form a dough. Let the dough rest for 30 minutes.

4. Preheat the oven to 350 degrees and grease a 9-inch pie or baking pan with butter. On a lightly floured work surface, roll out two-thirds of the dough

yield: about 8 servings

FILLING

4 eggplants
(about 1 pound/453 grams each)

½ to ¾ cup (75 to 113 grams) *brinza* or Bulgarian feta cheese

½ cup (50 grams) grated *kashkaval* cheese or Emmental

1 large egg

Salt and freshly ground black pepper, to taste

DOUGH

½ cup (125 grams) sour cream or yogurt

8 tablespoons (1 stick/ 113 grams) unsalted butter, softened, or ½ cup (110 ml) vegetable oil

1½ cups (200 grams) all-purpose unbleached flour

1 teaspoon baking powder

½ teaspoon salt

1 egg yolk

into a round or square as thinly as you can and line the bottom and sides of your pan with the dough.

5. Add the eggplant mixture, smoothing the surface with a knife. Trim the dough so that about ½ inch hangs over the edges. Roll out the remaining dough to a rough round that will fit on top of the dish. Lay it on top and crimp the edges together, cutting slits to allow steam to escape.

6. Put the egg yolk in a little bowl and, with your fingers or a pastry brush, paint the top of the dough. Bake the *pashtida* for 45 minutes, or until the top of the dough is golden brown.

7. Either serve in the baking pan or put a plate on top, flip, then flip again onto a serving plate.

Note You can add a little fresh basil or chopped chives to the eggplant.

Grilled Eggplant with Tahina, Feta, and Pomegranate

When I lived in Israel in the 1970s, everyone ate eggplant dips that were swirled with mayonnaise, soy sauce, pickles—you name it. Not anymore. Today, Israeli eggplant dishes are simpler and at the same time more sophisticated.

This grilled eggplant, a recipe I adapted from chef and cookbook author Erez Komarovsky and Toto restaurant in Tel Aviv, looks beautiful on the plate and has a lovely, smoky flavor obtained by cooking over an open flame. Like the eggplant itself, the toppings can easily be adapted to suit your own tastes.

Cooking over an open fire, grill, or gas stove imparts a delicious flavor to the eggplant. You can, of course, bake it in the oven, but you will not get the same flavor as you do from the direct heat. And don't forget that garnishes are only the accent to the smoky flavor of the eggplant.

———————

1. Grill the whole eggplant over a charcoal grill, turning carefully with tongs for several minutes as the eggplant softens. You can also use the flame from a stovetop gas burner, but first line the stovetop grate with aluminum foil to make cleanup easier.

2. Continue grilling until soft, about 15 to 20 minutes. If you want to skip the grilling (which can get messy), you can instead prick the eggplant skin with a fork and bake in a 450-degree oven for about 30 minutes, or until soft.

3. Working gently to keep the eggplant intact, use tongs to remove the eggplant to a strainer. Allow to drain and cool, then carefully transfer the eggplant to a serving plate, split open slightly, sprinkle with salt and freshly ground pepper to taste, and drizzle with lemon juice, olive oil, pomegranate molasses or date jam, and tahina or tahina sauce. Sprinkle with cilantro, parsley, or mint to taste. Garnish with the pomegranate seeds, Greek yogurt, or feta, and serve.

Note My preferred eggplant for this dish is the bulbous *baladi* (the word means "municipality"), found in the Middle East and occasionally at farmers' markets around the world. But a pear-shaped eggplant will do, as long as it is very dark and fresh. Also, I prefer a pure pomegranate molasses, not one that contains rose water.

yield: 4 servings

1 large eggplant
(about 1 pound/453 grams)

Sea salt and freshly ground pepper to taste

Juice of 1 lemon

1 to 2 tablespoons extra-virgin olive oil

Pomegranate molasses or date jam, to taste

¼ to ½ cup tahina or tahina sauce (see page 67), or to taste

Cilantro, parsley, or mint, to taste

Pomegranate seeds, to garnish

Greek yogurt or feta, to garnish

Vegetarian Tagine of Peppers, Onions, Zucchini, Eggplant, and More

yield: 6 to 8 servings

The best way to understand Asilah, a fortress town on Morocco's Atlantic coast about eighteen miles south of Tangier, is to let your eyes and your nose lead you through the narrow streets where only foot traffic is allowed.

In Asilah, like everywhere else in Morocco, the home cooks make the most flavorful food. But not all of their cooking is done at home.

One morning, I happened upon a crowd of women, along with a few men and small boys, all balancing boards on their heads piled with rounds of dough. I followed them into a small stucco building where smoke poured out from the chimney. Inside, a baker stood calmly underneath a portrait of King Mohammed VI. He carefully placed the mounds of shaped dough on long wooden paddles and slid them into a *ferrane*, a brick public oven fueled with eucalyptus branches.

From 8 a.m. to 8 p.m. each day, customers arrived in a steady stream, paid a few dirhams—about 25 cents—and then left. About twenty minutes later, they returned to pick up their golden rounds of bread, and later in the day, when the ovens were cooler, people brought tagines and other dishes to be cooked at a lower temperature.

For hundreds of years, until the late 1950s, the Jewish kosher public oven, now boarded up, was just meters away. These communal ovens were a major part of life, not just in Morocco, but all over the world.

In my own travels, I have encountered public ovens only rarely: in Jerusalem's Old City; in Arab villages in Israel and the West Bank; on the Caribbean island of Montserrat; and in Moroccan towns.

Today, as many people in Morocco have stoves or propane cooktops at home, the communal ovens are disappearing. Traditional cooks in Asilah wake around dawn each morning to knead and shape their bread dough. They let it rise for a few hours before carrying it to the public oven.

In Asilah, Jews and Arabs lived next to each other and very often ate the same foods until the 1950s, when the Jews left. Sometimes Jews learned recipes from the Arabs and vice versa. How could they not? One whiff of the famous *dafina* or *s'keena*, the overnight Sabbath dish made here with chickpeas and cow's feet, would tempt anyone. Many of the Moroccans I spoke with have a collective memory of the *dafina*, most likely from their parents.

As I wandered around the town, peeking into public ovens, I could see how the Jews picked up ideas from their neighbors and vice versa.

When, later that day, I tasted this vegetable tagine at our friend's home, I reflected on the different varieties of tagine in Morocco. It occurred to me that Moroccan recipes are proud secrets embedded in families, transferred by word of mouth from generation to generation. A little more cumin, a little less cinnamon? Should the vegetables be diced in rounds or squares?

This dish would make a perfect Shabbat meal, slowly cooked in a Dutch oven or tagine until the vegetables have soaked up the seasonings, the cilantro, and the onions—a beautiful and delicious alternative to roasted vegetables for a party or dinner or a main course for a vegetarian meal. It is best served with cous-cous (see page 170) or saffron rice (see page 169).

———————

4 tablespoons olive oil, divided

2 garlic cloves, minced

½ bunch cilantro, chopped, divided

½ bunch parsley, chopped, divided

½ teaspoon ginger

½ teaspoon turmeric

½ teaspoon cumin

½ teaspoon cinnamon

½ teaspoon hot paprika

Salt and freshly ground pepper to taste

2 small sweet potatoes (about ⅔ pound/300 grams), peeled and quartered lengthwise

2 small white potatoes (about ⅔ pound/300 grams), peeled and quartered lengthwise

4 medium carrots (about ⅔ pound/300 grams), peeled

1½ large onions, peeled and cut in thirds

4 long, tapered, mild peppers like Italian sweet peppers, cubanelle, Anaheim, or banana peppers, washed but left whole

4 small zucchini (about ⅔ pound/300 grams)

4 medium ripe tomatoes, cut in quarters (about 1 pound/450 grams)

1. Smear about 1 tablespoon of the olive oil over the bottom of about a 12-inch tagine or Dutch oven.

2. Stir together the garlic with the remaining olive oil and all but 2 tablespoons each of the cilantro and parsley, then smear the mixture over the vegetables. Mix the ginger, turmeric, cumin, cinnamon, paprika, and salt and pepper to taste and sprinkle the spices over all.

3. Mound some vegetables in the center, cutting up to fit. Then arrange the rest in a circle in the pan, piling them up and alternating the type of vegetable and the color. Make at least 2 layers. They should look like the spokes of a wheel.

4. Simmer the vegetables over a low heat, covered, until they are soft but still hold together, about 45 minutes to an hour. Serve immediately in the tagine, sprinkled with the remaining parsley and cilantro, and drizzled with some of the sauce from the vegetables.

Slightly Sweet and Sour Cabbage

yield: 4 to 6 servings

This recipe comes from Sara Yaech, a woman whom I met on a trip to Havana the week before Barack Obama visited Cuba. Descended on her father's side from Turkish Jews who came from Istanbul to this Spanish-speaking country in the 1920s, Sara grew up with Turkish and Ladino food. An amazingly alive woman in her early seventies, Sara has always been the one to teach many of the now six hundred or so Jewish women in Havana about their culinary past in the Sephardic synagogue (one of three in Havana today). Like many of the Cuban Jews descended from Bessarabia and Poland, she learned cooking from her grandmother and from her mother, who was descended from Jews who came to Cuba in the far past, perhaps those who came from Spain with Christopher Columbus after 1492, when Jews were often stowaways on the ships.

At a lunch in her simple house surrounded by fledgling pomegranate bushes grown from seeds she brought from Israel and banana, orange, and many other trees, she made food with some of the simple subsidies she gets each month from the Cuban government—three pounds of rice, red and black beans, sugar, brown sugar, and eggs. The chicken and beef allowed to her and her husband now that her two children are grown and live in Mexico and Israel are brought live to the local *shochet* of the Jewish community and slaughtered in the kosher butcher shop near the Orthodox synagogue in Old Havana, and she picks them up once a month. Anything more she must buy.

A few years ago, during a difficult period in Cuba, Sara's joints started puffing up and she felt stiff and uncomfortable. Her doctor told her to change her diet from beans and rice, which she did, going directly back to the unprocessed Sephardic food of her ancestors. At a lunch in her garden, she served her own challah and a variety of eggplant dishes from a new book she wrote entitled *Veinte Recetas de Berenjena*—"hummus" from eggplant, thin strips of eggplant with meat inside, a sweet eggplant purée with toasted coconut on the side—as well as a cabbage dish and wine made from the fruit growing in her garden. The food was delicious but the salad made from cabbage, a universal ingredient that I saw everywhere in the Cuban kiosks that act as supermarkets, intrigued me as a symbolic Jewish food that really went around the world. In fact, Sara told me that once she made this dish for a Jewish woman from Russia who was delighted because her mother in Moscow made the very same sweet and sour dish. To show how very old this dish is, it swaps tamarind, the acid used by Sara's ancestors until the advent of the tomato, for the tomato sauce.

---

1. Heat a sauté pan with the oil. Add the onion, pepper, and garlic and sauté until the onion is golden. Then stir in the cabbage, brown sugar, salt, wine vinegar, and tomato sauce. Cover and simmer for about 15 minutes, or until most of the liquid has disappeared and the cabbage is soft. Adjust the seasonings and serve, sprinkled with the parsley.

Note For a beautiful visual effect, make this recipe twice—once with a purple cabbage and once with a white one. Then, just before serving, mix the two.

2 tablespoons vegetable oil

1 small onion, thinly sliced

½ sweet red pepper
(175 grams), sliced thin

2 teaspoons finely chopped
garlic

4 cups (400 grams) finely
chopped cabbage, purple
and/or white, thinly shredded

2 tablespoons brown sugar

1 teaspoon salt

4 tablespoons wine vinegar

4 tablespoons tomato sauce

2 tablespoons parsley

Whole Roasted Head of Cauliflower with Whipped Feta and Goat Cheese

Once a year, I host a brunch for chefs visiting Washington for Sips and Suppers, a charity event I chair with chefs Alice Waters and José Andrés. And once a year, Alon Shaya, chef of Shaya's in New Orleans, brings cooked cauliflowers in his suitcase to serve the invited chefs. The whole, slightly browned cauliflowers look stunning, and, as Alon, one of the nicest human beings around, says, "The beauty that God has gifted this vegetable with does not change from earth to plate. That is what I love most about whole vegetable cooking. I enjoy preserving an ingredient's natural look as well as its natural flavor." Alon serves the cauliflowers with local whipped goat cheese from a farmer in nearby Mississippi. You can serve it as you wish but just remember, the whole cauliflower is an eye-catcher!

———————

1. Trim the green leaves off the bottom of the cauliflower, leaving the thick stem intact.

2. Fill a 4-quart saucepan or one large enough to hold the cauliflower easily with 6½ cups (1.56 liters) cold water and set over a medium heat. Add the wine, kosher salt, bay leaf, lemon juice, chili flakes, sugar, butter, and 5 table-spoons of the olive oil, mix, and then add the cauliflower, top side up.

3. Bring to a simmer, then with two slotted spoons or prongs, flip the cauli-flower over so it cooks bottom side up. Simmer for about 15 minutes, or until you can easily insert a knife through the center. Be careful not to overcook the cauliflower, or it will fall apart when you remove it from the pan. Using two slotted spoons, carefully remove the cauliflower from the poaching liq-uid and put it bottom side down onto a rimmed baking sheet. You can do this several hours ahead of serving if you like.

4. Just before serving, preheat the oven to 500 degrees or to its highest setting, then bake until the cauliflower is golden all over the top, about 10 minutes. Turn it on its sides to brown all over, taking care not to burn it.

5. Remove from the oven and sprinkle with the remaining tablespoon of oil and a little coarse sea salt. Serve immediately with the whipped cheese.

6. **to make the whipped feta and goat cheese** Put all the ingredients together in a blender or food processor fitted with a steel blade and blend until smooth. Remove to a bowl and chill well before serving.

yield: 4 to 6 servings; 1½ cups whipped cheese

1 whole large head cauliflower

2⅓ cups (550 ml) dry white wine

4 tablespoons kosher salt, plus salt to taste

1 bay leaf

Juice of 1 lemon

4 teaspoons crushed Aleppo pepper or red chili flakes

2½ teaspoons sugar

2 tablespoons (28 grams) unsalted butter

5 tablespoons plus 1 tablespoon extra-virgin olive oil

Coarse sea salt

Whipped feta and goat cheese (see below), for serving

WHIPPED FETA AND GOAT CHEESE

½ cup (120 ml) heavy cream

½ cup (75 grams) good Bulgarian feta cheese

¼ cup (72 grams) goat cheese

5 tablespoons (120 grams) mascarpone, cream cheese, or crème fraîche

1 tablespoon extra-virgin olive oil

Note This makes a delicious dip with raw vegetables as well.

Green *Chile Relleno* Latkes

Through the years, I have received recipes for so many variations of latkes from friends and readers around the globe. These Green *Chile Relleno* Latkes were created on a Hanukkah night in the hills of Placitas in northern New Mexico at the home of Tom and Joanne Ashe, avid cooks who are always having family gatherings.

"We were under way cooking potato latkes as we do every year, but that night my niece, Marisa Johnson, and her nephew Ethan came up with a new twist. Ethan was also cooking something for his New Mexico history class," wrote Joanne in an email. "He had to choose a dish that reflected New Mexican culture and tradition, photograph his cooking adventure, and then write about it. He chose the beloved green *chile relleno*. He was prepping alongside Tom, waiting for some stovetop space to fry his *rellenos,* when he had the brilliant idea to top each latke with an un-battered *relleno*. The Green *Chile Relleno* Latke was born! The cheese inside the roasted chili melts and sticks the chili to the latke, creating total latke '*relleno*' perfection." Indeed it does.

———————

yield: 12 latkes

12 whole green chilies,
such as Anaheim, Poblano,
or Hatch

12 ounces (340 grams) white
cheddar or Jack cheese, sliced
widthwise into 12 short pieces

2 pounds (1.11 kilos) russet
or baking potatoes
(about 3 large), peeled

1 medium onion, peeled

2 large eggs

⅓ to ½ cup (30 to 55 grams)
panko or regular breadcrumbs
or matzo meal

Salt and freshly ground pepper
to taste

Vegetable or grape-seed oil
for frying

1. Preheat the oven to 375 degrees and line a baking sheet with foil. Put the whole chilies on the baking sheet and roast for 40 minutes to an hour, flipping every 20 minutes, until the chilies are blackened all over. Let cool and then remove the stems and skin from each chili, leaving them as intact as possible. Then cut a slit almost the full length of each chili and carefully pull out the seeds. Put a piece of cheese inside each chili.

2. While the chilies are roasting, make the latkes, keeping the potatoes in cold water until ready to grate them.

3. Starting with the onion, alternately grate some of the onion in a food processor fitted with a steel blade or on the large holes of a large box grater and some of the potatoes on the smallest. (Doing it in this order will keep the potato mixture from blackening.) When you have finished, put the potato and onion mixture into a clean dish towel and squeeze out the water into a medium bowl, allowing the potato starch to settle at the bottom. Carefully pour off the water, but leave the potato starch at the bottom of the bowl.

4. Once the liquid has been drained, put the potato mixture back in the bowl with the potato starch that has accumulated in the bottom. Add the eggs, the breadcrumbs or matzo meal, and salt and pepper to taste and mix well.

5. Heat an inch of oil in a frying pan. Drop about 2 heaping tablespoons of mixture for each latke into the skillet and fry for a few minutes, turning

once. You should have 12 latkes. When golden and crisp on one side, drain on paper towels.

6. After all are browned on one side, gently lay a stuffed chili on the top of each latke and carefully flip the latke over so that the chili is face down.

7. Fry for a few minutes more until the cheese is melted and slightly crisped in spots and the latke is golden brown. Drain, latke side down, on paper towel–lined baking sheets and then serve immediately.

8. Top with a dollop of sour cream or serve it on the side, and drizzle with a New Mexico red chili sauce or Yemenite *zhug* (see page 12).

Pomodori a Mezzo, Baked Tomato Halves

When I go to Rome, the Eternal City, and am invited to a home for a cooking session or for dinner, the hosts serve me *pomodori a mezzo*—no matter the season! These tiny, candy-like, oven-browned cherry and grape tomato halves are always gobbled up immediately.

I couldn't find *pomodori a mezzo* in any of my Italian cookbooks—until I checked Donatella Limantani Pavoncello's *La Cucina Ebraica della Mia Famiglia* (Jewish Cooking from My Family), published in 1880.

Although the Columbian Exchange brought tomatoes to Europe via the port of Naples in the sixteenth century, they were used vary rarely by the general population other than as an ornamental plant until the late eighteenth century. People were reluctant to eat tomatoes because they are, like eggplants, members of the nightshade family and were thought to be poisonous (see page 16). However, Roman Jews knew better. Many Jewish physicians knew of tomatoes' and eggplants' healthy properties and spread the word within the community about them. And Jews, too, were often the merchants selling this new produce around the ports of Europe.

---

yield: 4 to 6 servings

2 pounds (907 grams) tomatoes, such as grape, Campari, or large cherry tomatoes

4 tablespoons olive oil, divided

1 clove garlic, minced

1 teaspoon sea salt, or to taste

½ teaspoon freshly ground pepper, or to taste

1 teaspoon sugar

½ teaspoon dried or 1 tablespoon fresh basil

½ teaspoon dried or 1 tablespoon fresh oregano

---

1. Cut the tomatoes in half lengthwise. Remove the seeds by squeezing the tomato half with one hand and scraping out the seeds with a paring knife in your other hand.

2. Preheat the oven to 450 degrees. Rub a 15-by-10-inch glass or ceramic baking dish with 2 tablespoons of the olive oil and fill with the tomato halves, skin side down. Sprinkle the garlic, salt, pepper, and sugar over the tomatoes. If using dried herbs, sprinkle them on now. Drizzle the remaining 2 tablespoons of olive oil over the tomatoes.

3. Put the tomatoes in the oven and lower the heat to 350 degrees. Bake for about an hour, or until the tomatoes are extremely soft and a little black. The cooking time will depend on the size of the tomatoes. If using fresh herbs, sprinkle them over the tomatoes as soon as they come out of the oven. Cool to room temperature and serve as an antipasto or a side dish.

Note This is perfect in the summer, when tomatoes are at their best, but you can make it in the winter with large grape or Campari tomatoes found in the grocery store.

Kolokuthokeftedes, Zucchini Fritters

Across from the ancient Agora in Athens is a line of outdoor restaurants with stunning views of the Parthenon. At one, called *To Kouti*, meaning "The Box," are served the best zucchini fritters in Athens, even better than those I used to eat in Jerusalem, many years ago.

———————

1. Cut the zucchini on the grating blade of a food processor or a box grater. Toss with the sea salt and the lemon juice. Let sit for about 15 minutes. Then squeeze the zucchini very hard in a strainer to remove the excess juices and put in a large mixing bowl.

2. Add the mint, fennel, dill, thyme leaves, and the spring onion or scallions to the drained zucchini. Stir in the feta cheese, egg yolks, and wine vinegar, then gently fold in the flour.

3. Create small patties about the size of a golf ball and dust lightly with flour, using a small strainer. Arrange on a tray covered with parchment paper. Freeze them for at least 20 minutes. This will make them hold together better when frying.

4. When you are ready to serve them, fill a wok or deep fryer with about 3 inches of oil and heat until it is 375 degrees. When ready, fry about 5 at a time for a few minutes on each side. Drain on paper towels and serve immediately.

Note I make all kinds of these vegetable fritters, serving them as a side or an appetizer, sometimes substituting eggplant pulp, carrots, a mixture of vegetables, and of course potatoes, calling them latkes in the winter.

yield: about 36 fritters

6 small zucchini, about 3 pounds (1⅓ kilos)

1 teaspoon sea salt, or to taste

Juice of 1 lemon

¼ bunch fresh mint, chopped

1 tablespoon fennel fronds, chopped

2½ teaspoons fresh dill, chopped

1 tablespoon fresh thyme leaves (lemon thyme is fantastic here)

1 spring onion or 4 scallions, diced

8 ounces (226 grams) feta cheese, crumbled

2 large egg yolks

1½ tablespoons white wine vinegar

1 cup (135 grams) unbleached all-purpose flour, plus more for dusting

Canola or vegetable oil for frying

Yuca Latkes with Cilantro Cream

El Salvador, a country with about six million people, has a minuscule Jewish population of about a hundred. Most of their families came in 1920 to the capital city, San Salvador, from Alsace-Lorraine and Germany after the First World War. A few had already settled there in the 1870s, opening Paris Volcán, a department store with French perfumes, and Goldtree Liebes, a hardware store. Many of the adults there today can tell stories of their grandfathers going by donkey into the countryside and peddling wares for these stores. These families, who have prospered through the years, often bought land in the country and cultivated coffee, more as a hobby than a vocation.

"It was a great way to grow up," said Jean Geismar, in his sixties, whose parents came from Alsace to work at Paris Volcán. "We were like one big family. We did everything together."

Jewish Salvadorans have to think way ahead for holidays. As a community, they order matzo, matzo meal, kosher meat, and kosher bouillon cubes in October to get them by April. "When the order comes in from Israel, someone drives to Guatemala and picks them up," said Delia R. Cukier, the president of the sisterhood of the country's one synagogue, Cumunidad Israelita de El Salvador. For Passover each family celebrates the first night with their family or extended family and the second night as a community, this year in the synagogue.

When Mrs. Cukier, who was born in Cuba, was asked to bring a dish to a potluck Shabbat dinner that I attended, she brought her yuca latkes, which she prefers to potato. They are similar in taste to *nuegado de yuca,* a Salvadoran doughnut that is served as a dessert in a syrup made from dark brown sugar. Do not skip the step of soaking the shredded yuca—the soak reduces any bitterness and produces a crisper, less dense, gluten-free latke.

yield: about 10 to 12 latkes

1¾ pounds yuca

2 teaspoons sea salt, divided

½ cup Salvadoran crema, Greek yogurt, or sour cream

2 tablespoons chopped cilantro, divided

3 large eggs

½ cup grated onion (from about 1 small onion)

4 tablespoons cornmeal (or masa harina)

½ teaspoon freshly ground pepper

Vegetable oil, for frying

Guacamole, for serving (optional)

---

1. Peel the yuca and cut it in large chunks. Shred, using a food processor with the shredding attachment. (Or peel and keep the yuca whole, then shred on a box grater.) Rinse the shredded yuca in a mesh strainer until the water runs clear, then put in a bowl with cold water to cover. Sprinkle in 1 teaspoon of salt, stirring briefly to mix. Let soak at room temperature for 1 hour.

2. Meanwhile, in a small bowl, mix the Salvadoran crema, Greek yogurt, or sour cream with half the chopped cilantro. Sprinkle the remaining cilantro on top. Chill, covered, until ready to serve the latkes.

3. Drain the yuca in the mesh strainer, pressing against the strainer to squeeze it as dry as possible. Put the yuca in a large bowl, then add the eggs, grated onion, cornmeal or masa harina, remaining 1 teaspoon salt, and the pepper. Mix well and form into patties the size of an egg, then flatten between your palms and put on a plate.

4. Heat a thin film of oil in a large nonstick pan and fry the yuca patties in batches for about 3 minutes on each side, or until golden and cooked through. Drain on paper towel–lined plates. Serve warm with the cilantro crema or, as I often do, with guacamole.

Note Jews from Costa Rica make these out of green plantains, which are starchier than ripe ones. They are made the same as above, but you won't need eggs, making them especially nice for vegans. To these latkes, I add a touch of vinegar for balance.

Mashed Sweet Potato Latkes with *Zhug*

The sweet potato originated in either Central or South America, with the oldest known remains being dried roots from the caves of the Chilca Canyon of Peru, dated at eight thousand to ten thousand years old (but it's not known if these remains are wild or domesticated sweet potatoes). The oldest remains of sweet potatoes that we know were definitely cultivated come from the Casma valley of Peru, dated around 2,000 B.C.E. The sweet potato traveled to Europe with Columbus, who discovered the tuber in Hispaniola and Cuba during his first voyage and brought a few samples back to Europe. Once grown in Europe, the sweet potato spread to Africa (where it joined the yam, and from there it probably came to India), then went back to the Americas in slave ships, was brought to the East Indies by Portuguese explorers, and to the Philippines by Spanish traders.

There are many theories, however, that the sweet potato somehow (samples floating on logs, seeds traveling in birds' stomachs, etc.) made its way westward, from its homeland of Central or South America, to Polynesia long before the Columbian Exchange. It seemed that this tuber was already well established in Polynesia by 1521, when Ferdinand Magellan traveled around the world carrying specimens of, among other things, sweet potatoes. The tuber is even thought to have reached Polynesia sometime during the first century C.E. Unfortunately, although the pre-Columbian existence of sweet potatoes is a strong theory, it remains just a theory without definitive archaeological evidence. In any case, today the sweet potato is adored the world over.

---

yield: about 10 to 15 latkes

½ cup (55 grams) panko breadcrumbs, plus more as needed

3 large sweet potatoes (2 to 2½ pounds/907 grams 1⁷⁄₁₀ kilos)

2 teaspoons coconut oil, melted

1 large egg

1 teaspoon salt, or to taste

Freshly ground black pepper, to taste

Vegetable oil, for frying

Zhug, for serving (see page 12)

---

1. Preheat the oven to 350 degrees and line a baking sheet with foil. Pour the panko in a shallow bowl or baking dish and set aside.

2. Scrub the potatoes clean, then pierce with a knife and rub with the coconut oil. Bake for 30 minutes, or until a knife is easily pierced through the potatoes. Let cool and then peel (you can peel the skin off easily with your fingers).

3. In a medium bowl, mash the potatoes with a potato masher or the back of a fork. Mix in the egg and then season with salt and pepper to taste. Form into patties about ¼ inch thick and 3 or 4 inches in diameter, then coat with the panko.

4. Warm a ⅛-inch-thick sheen of vegetable oil in a large frying pan and fry the latkes until golden on each side, about 3 to 4 minutes per side. Drain on paper towel–lined baking sheets.

5. Serve with *zhug* or any hot sauce you like, or omit the sauce if you like less spice.

Paprikás Krumpli, Hungarian Roasted Potatoes with Onions

In Hungary, *paprikás krumpli* originated with two ingredients from the Americas—potatoes and chilies. Frying these potatoes in lard or bacon made this an entire meal for poorer families. Of course, Jews used chicken fat instead for frying.

When Eva Weiss Cooperman, whose parents survived Auschwitz, was growing up in the Bronx, *paprikás krumpli* was sometimes the sole entrée on Sunday evenings. Later, when her own children were growing up in Greenwich, Connecticut, she served it with roast chicken or fried cutlets. As it did for Eva, the dish became comfort food for her children.

In my version of this recipe, I roast rather than steam the potatoes and add a bit of cayenne to the sweet paprika for the kick we all love today. This is a wonderfully addictive way to roast potatoes. Serve them with lemon chicken (page 266) and spinach with pine nuts and currants (page 190).

---

yield: 4 to 6 servings

2 to 3 tablespoons of vegetable oil or schmaltz, divided

1 large onion, roughly chopped

1½ tablespoons sweet Hungarian paprika (about)

¼ to ½ teaspoon hot or smoked paprika, or cayenne pepper

1 teaspoon salt or to taste

2 pounds (907 grams) red bliss or Yukon gold potatoes, peeled, and cut into bite-size quarters, or eighths if the potatoes are large

---

1. Preheat the oven to 375 degrees and lightly grease a 9-by-13-inch baking dish with a tablespoon of the oil or schmaltz.

2. Heat the remaining oil or schmaltz in a frying pan over medium heat. Add the onion and cook until translucent, about 10 minutes. Stir in the sweet paprika, hot or smoked paprika or cayenne pepper, and salt, and cook, stirring frequently, for about 3 minutes. Take care to not let the paprika burn. Add the potatoes, stirring to coat with the onion-paprika mixture, then put everything into the prepared baking dish.

3. Roast for about 30 to 40 minutes, stirring halfway through, or until the potatoes are cooked through and beginning to crisp on the edges.

Note It is important to use a high-quality sweet paprika from Szeged, or from Turkey or Israel. The quality of the paprika is very important for this dish.

Hot Paprika

When searching for hot paprika in grocery stores, and even my local spice shop, I noticed that the spice is not always available. If you can't find it, worry not—you can mix together sweet Hungarian paprika with spicy cayenne pepper, in a ratio of one part sweet to one-quarter part spicy, to make your own. Of course, if you prefer less spice, then reduce the amount of cayenne.

Sweet Plantain Guava Kugel

When Susie Lustgarten of So Heavenly Catering in Miami makes this very popular kugel, she buys boxes of ripe plantains and has them sit for a week to ripen them even more. "For those who like something sweet with a savory brisket [see page 294] this plantain kugel with guava is a great alternative to a super-sweet noodle kugel," Susie told me as she made it in her kitchen. "It is really not a kugel, but my customers like to call it a kugel."

yield: 8 to 10 servings

6 very ripe and soft plantains (about 4 pounds/2 kilos)

Vegetable oil for frying

8 ounces (226 grams) guava paste

½ cup (116 ml) orange juice, divided

---

1. Peel and slice the plantains in thirds lengthwise. Heat a half inch of oil in a large nonstick pan over medium-high heat and line a baking sheet with paper towels. Fry the plantains in batches until lightly browned on each side, about 2 to 3 minutes per side. Drain on the prepared baking sheet.

2. Preheat the oven to 350 degrees. Melt the guava paste with ¼ cup (55 ml) of the orange juice in a small saucepan. Grease a 9-by-13-inch baking dish with nonstick spray.

3. To assemble the kugel, arrange a layer of plantains in the prepared baking dish, then spread a thin layer of the melted guava paste mixture. Keep layering for up to three layers of plantains, ending with the guava paste mixture. Drizzle the remaining orange juice over the top.

4. Bake for 20 to 30 minutes, until the plantains are very soft. Serve warm as a sweet side dish.

Fish

Sarde in Saor, Sweet and Sour Sardines with Pine Nuts and Raisins

Escoveitch with Salmon and Scotch Bonnet Peppers

Aharaimi, Arctic Char in a Spicy Tomato Sauce

Salmon Gefilte Fish Mold with Horseradish and Beet Sauce

Gravlaks with Mustard Sauce

Pickled Herring Spread

Herring and Apple Bites with a Dill and Caper Dipping Sauce

Bene Israel Fish Curry with Fresh Ginger, Tamarind, and Cilantro

Haddie Paddies, Nova Scotian Fried Haddock Cakes

Couscous con le Sarde, Sardines with Fennel, Onions, Currants, and Pine Nuts over Couscous

Cod with Tomatoes, Dried Plums, Onions, and Pine Nuts

Snapper with Preserved Lemon and Capers

Brazilian-Belarusian Grouper with Wine, Cilantro, and Oregano

Fish *B'stilla* with Rice Noodles and Vegetables

Poached Salmon with Ginger-Cilantro Butter and Spinach

In the center of Sidon [biblical name for Saida, the third-largest city in Lebanon] is a certain spring of water famed for its fish. The fish are small, about the length of a finger but fatter; they have tiny fore and hind legs, which are partly hidden; their male and female organs are evident. In the spring months men catch these fish and dry them. When a man feels inclined toward more sexual activity than that for which he has the force, he scrapes one of these dried fish and eats it: it is an aphrodisiac.

—Benjamin of Tudela's twelfth-century writings in Sandra Benjamin,
    The World of Benjamin of Tudela: A Medieval Mediterranean Travelogue, 1995

Water is 70 percent of the world. We all came from fish, so it is right that they are the first things we eat for the Sabbath.

—a Sabbath saying

Sarde in Saor, Sweet and Sour Sardines with Pine Nuts and Raisins

On a visit to Venice, my husband, Allan, and I bumped into Anna Campos Calimani, a librarian who has a food blog and is considered one of the best cooks in Venice's small, 450-member Jewish community. After chatting with us during the intermission at the opera, Anna and her husband, Dario, invited us over for a simple Friday night dinner before they took off for their weekend home in the nearby countryside. A table for two was set in their kitchen with two tiny challahs, covered with a napkin. I loved the fact that even with their children gone, and after a night out at the opera, they still made the effort to mark the specialness of Friday night.

Anna brought out jars of *concia,* preserved zucchini (see page 191), then from the freezer goose sausage that she had made from a recipe from her grandmother, who came from the Gentili family. They lived in a big house with geese running free outside in San Daniele del Friuli, a sausage- and prosciutto-making center in northeastern Italy, where a Jewish community settled after the Inquisition in Spain. But the most tempting thing that she told me about was her *sarde in saor,* which she didn't have time to make but that I found a recipe for on her blog.

Almost every good restaurant in Venice has this Jewish specialty on its menu. I love the briny flavor of the sardines with the sweetness of the raisins and caramelized onions, mixed with the tartness from the red wine vinegar and the crunchiness of the toasted pine nuts. My guess is that this dish traveled up from Sicily to Spain and Venice through the centuries and has stayed there ever since.

---

yield: 4 to 6 servings

Flour for dredging

2 pounds (907 grams) fresh sardines, cleaned and dried

Olive oil for frying

4 medium onions, about 2 pounds (907 grams), chopped

½ cup (120 ml) red wine vinegar, or to taste

Salt to taste

½ cup (75 grams) raisins

½ cup (50 grams) pine nuts, toasted

---

1. Put the flour in a wide bowl. Then dip the sardines into the flour, and shake off any excess flour. Heat a skillet with a thin film of oil and brown for a minute or two on each side, then drain on paper towels.

2. Wipe out the skillet, heat, and add a little more oil. Fry the onions until golden. Add ½ cup (120 ml) water, cover the skillet, and continue to cook slowly until the onions begin to brown. Pour a few tablespoons of vinegar over them and season with a little salt. Add more vinegar and the raisins until the onions are completely covered. Bring to a boil, cook for a minute, then remove from heat. Allow the onion mixture and fish to cool.

3. In a flat pan, sprinkle 1 to 2 tablespoons of the onion mixture and cover with a layer of sardines. Scatter another 1 to 2 tablespoons of the onion mixture and then some pine nuts over the sardines, and continue—onions, sardines, and pine nuts—until all the ingredients are used up. Pour the remaining onion and vinegar mixture over everything. Stir, then cover, and refrigerate for 24 hours, stirring occasionally. Serve cold or at room temperature.

Escoveitch with Salmon and Scotch Bonnet Peppers

In the waiting room of New York's Penn Station, I met Anna Ruth Henriques of Jamaica, who is quarter Chinese, quarter black, and half Jewish. Anna Ruth, whose Jewish family tree goes back to thirteenth-century Spain and Portugal, conducts tours of the twenty-one Jewish cemeteries in Jamaica. Her father, Ainsley Henriques, is one of the few remaining keepers of the traditions of the Jews of Jamaica. During the Inquisition, the Henriques family scattered far and wide: to Holland, Brazil, Denmark, Curaçao, and Jamaica. Travelers and traders, they were constantly on the move. Some were stowaways on Christopher Columbus's ships. Moses Cohen Henriques, the famous pirate of the Caribbean, was an ancestor, as was Beatrice Enríquez de Arara, Columbus's mistress and the mother of his son Fernández. And, of course, many were in the sugar trade, bringing sugar processing to the island and founding the first sugar mill there in the early 1500s.

Although most of the three thousand or so Jews Anna Ruth grew up with as a child have either left Jamaica or intermarried, the old recipes have remained. Like other immigrants to the island, they adopted jerk chicken and rice and beans, but they also adapted recipes, adding Scotch bonnets, one of the hottest peppers in the world and indigenous to Jamaica, to their *escabeche,* a fried and pickled fish dish for the Sabbath, that is often served in hot climates.

According to Dan Jurafsky's book *The Language of Food,* the word *escoveitch* comes from *sikbāj,* the name of an ancient Persian sweet and sour sauce served over meat and beloved by Khosrow I, who ruled the Sassanid Persian empire in the late sixth century C.E. Although the dish was originally made with meat, sailors and no doubt merchant Jews (like the Radhanites), traveling the oceans and trading in the Abbasid Muslim empire, fried the fish, then steeped it in an acidic sweet and sour sauce to preserve it for the Sabbath, when they could not cook. Eventually *escabeche* reached Spain, principally Catalonia, and then moved on with other sailors—who perhaps had lemons, limes, and oranges in the holds of their ships—to the New World. The dish became *escoveitch* in Jamaica, with the local allspice and Scotch bonnet peppers adding extra kick. If you don't like that much heat, use a milder red or green pepper.

---

yield: 6 to 8 servings

2 pounds (907 grams) salmon, tuna, halibut, or kingfish fillets

Juice of 1 lime (about 2 tablespoons)

1 teaspoon salt, or to taste

½ cup (120 ml) white vinegar

1 small red onion, sliced in rounds and cut in quarters

1 Scotch bonnet pepper or other hot pepper, seeded, deveined, and diced

10 to 12 allspice berries (also called *pimentón*) or 2 tablespoons ground allspice

6 whole black peppercorns

1 small carrot, peeled and sliced in rounds

1 red pepper, seeded and sliced into thin strips

1 garlic clove, finely diced

Freshly ground pepper to taste

2 tablespoons vegetable oil

2 tablespoons chopped chives

1. Cut the fish in 6 to 8 equal-sized pieces and put in a glass bowl. Squeeze the lime juice over all and sprinkle with the teaspoon salt. Let sit for an hour or two.

2. While the fish is marinating, combine ¼ cup (60 ml) water and the white vinegar in a small saucepan and bring to a boil. Add the onion, Scotch bonnet pepper, allspice, black peppercorns, carrot, red pepper, and garlic and bring to a boil, just to meld the flavors. Then turn it off.

3. Remove the fish from the lime juice, pat dry, and season with black pepper.

4. Heat a frying pan with a thin film of oil and fry the fish for a few minutes on each side, just to brown but not to cook all the way through. Then pour the liquid with all the vegetables and spices over the fish. Let cool to room temperature and cut the fish into bite-size pieces. Before serving, drain off some of the liquid, then sprinkle with chives and serve as an appetizer or first course with crackers or bread.

5. The *escoveitch* will last for several days in the refrigerator. It develops more flavor as it marinates.

Aharaimi, Arctic Char in a Spicy Tomato Sauce

There were wild fruits of various kinds, some of which our men, not very prudently, tasted; and upon only touching them with their tongues, their mouths and cheeks became swollen, and they suffered such a great heat and pain that they seemed by their actions as if they were crazy and felt obliged to resort to cooling applications to ease the pain and the discomfort.

—letter from Dr. Diego Álvarez Chanca, 1494, describing the Scotch bonnet chili peppers of Jamaica on the second voyage of Christopher Columbus to America

Aharaimi is a traditional post–Columbian Exchange Libyan dish popular among the Mediterranean seafood restaurants, especially in Tripoli but also throughout the Maghreb. It is a kind of fish tagine or casserole (the sauce is always thick), fragrant, hot, and spicy.

yield: 8 servings as a first or 4 as a main course

For the Jews of Libya, who are now mostly in Israel and Italy, *aharaimi* begins the Sabbath meal. The secret is the spice kick, called in Israel *pilpel tsuma,* a mixture of garlic and red pepper once ground by every Libyan home cook and today available from the Israeli-Libyan spice company called Pereg Gourmet.

Abraham Pereg started the company in a small stall with no electricity in the marketplace of Tripoli, where he sold hot peppers, cumin, ginger, and cloves. When the family immigrated to Israel after 1948, his son Victor soon opened a spice market in Lod, about twenty-five minutes from Tel Aviv.

"Immigrants came from all over the world asking for spice combinations," said Chaim Pereg, Victor's son and the owner of the certified kosher company. "The Moroccans asked for sweet paprika with oil, so we started growing peppers here. Yemenites wanted *zhug,* and showed us how many grams of cumin, cardamom, caraway, cilantro, pepper, and coriander went into this hot sauce. That is the way we learned how to make everything." The Peregs added *pilpel tsuma,* a blend of pepper and garlic that they used in Tripoli. As Israeli appetites for peppers and other spices grew, so did Pereg Gourmet, which now has boutiques all over Israel and even ships abroad to the United States and other countries.

According to Nawal Nasrallah, a specialist in Arabic cooking and the author of *Delights from the Garden of Eden,* some say that the dish was originally called *harr ya'mmi* ("Mom, it's hot!"). Others say that when the delicious aroma of this dish spread throughout the neighborhood, Muslim Libyans would visit their Jewish neighbors in hopes that it would be shared. To discourage them, the Jews would say it was *haraimi* (from *haram*), i.e., that Muslims were forbidden from eating it.

Until the twentieth century, chili peppers, like the hot Scotch bonnets from Jamaica first described by Christopher Columbus's doctor above, were dried on a cloth outside in the sun, often laid on flat roofs. Then they were ground with garlic and mixed with salt, caraway, and sometimes cumin. Serve this spicy fish as a first or main course, with saffron rice (see page 169) or a colorful salad, like *matbucha* (page 101), carrot (page 99), and beet (page 112).

---

1. Heat the olive oil in a heavy frying pan with a cover. Sauté the onion until golden, then add the garlic, tomato paste, and hot pepper and stir, sautéing for about a minute.

2. Add 1½ cups (355 ml) of water, stirring until the paste is dissolved. Then add the cumin, caraway, and salt. Simmer for several minutes, until the sauce is very thick. Taste and add a little *pilpel tsuma* or harissa if not hot enough.

3. The traditional way to prepare this is to slip the fish pieces into the sauce and spoon the liquid over them, adding a little water if necessary to create more sauce. Simmer slowly, covered, until the fish is just cooked through, or for no more than 12 minutes. You can also transfer the sauce to a baking dish and put the fish on top of the sauce, skin side up, and bake in a 450-degree oven for 10 minutes and switch to a broiler for an additional 2 minutes.

4. Using two spatulas, gently transfer each piece of fish with the sauce to a serving platter. Adjust the seasonings to taste, lay the red pepper slices over the fish, sprinkle with cilantro or parsley, and sprinkle the lemon juice over all. Serve either hot or at room temperature.

⅓ cup (80 ml) extra-virgin olive oil

1 small onion, diced

7 to 8 cloves garlic, diced

3 heaping tablespoons tomato paste

1 tablespoon diced small hot red pepper like habanero, Scotch bonnet, or cayenne

1 teaspoon ground cumin

1 teaspoon ground caraway

1 teaspoon sea salt

2 pounds (907 grams) arctic char, grouper, tuna, whiting, yellowtail, or bonito, cut into 8 pieces

1 roasted red pepper, sliced into lengths

2 tablespoons diced cilantro or parsley

Juice of 1 lemon

Salmon Gefilte Fish Mold with Horseradish and Beet Sauce

yield: 15 to 20 slices

For centuries, Jewish women schlepped to the fish market, choosing the best fish "by the look in its eyes" before transforming it into the quintessential Sabbath gefilte fish. Using a wooden bowl and a half-moon-shaped chopper, they cut up the fish with onions, crying a little, chopping a little, until the mix was just the right consistency, later to be shaped into ovals or balls and poached in fish broth.

Today, cooks often turn to commercially prepared frozen loaves of ground fish, sometimes even spiked with jalapeños or almonds and raisins. These new, more American flavors are rapidly replacing the more distinctively fishy blends made from carp, whitefish, and pike, and have a smooth texture that indicates they have never felt the blade of a hand chopper.

Fish has always been a mainstay of the Jewish diet, and fish balls, a precursor to gefilte fish, can be traced backed to Spain in the Middle Ages, and possibly even earlier to the Middle East.

Traditionally, the fish mixture was stuffed back into the skin (thus *gefilte,* meaning "stuffed") and baked in a crust or poached, with leftover filling formed into patties, covered with fish skin, and simmered in the same pot. When Jews migrated to eastern Europe after their expulsion from Spain and France, they continued the tradition. Using the flesh of large, freshwater kosher fish, cooks added onions, garlic, a little egg, and matzo meal and stuffed the filling into the skin of the fish, poaching and sometimes baking it. On the Sabbath, it was, of course, served cold.

As the fish crossed the ocean to America with the large-scale eastern European immigration, the artful but laborious stuffing step was discarded and the patties became the gefilte fish eaten today.

Although gefilte innovation like the first jarred fish and the frozen loaves are taking over now, I still, as with many things, prefer the taste of homemade that I make twice a year for Passover and Rosh Hashanah. Before Passover, at what we call a "gefilte-in," friends assemble in my kitchen with their own pots, fish, carrots, eggs, and matzo meal to make these old-fashioned fish patties. (See *Jewish Cooking in America* for my homemade classic gefilte fish recipe.) For Rosh Hashanah, I make a light, circular fish terrine that looks beautiful and has the components of gefilte fish, but is much easier to make, baked in a Bundt or tube pan in a bain-marie. This is also a great make-ahead recipe, as it requires several hours of refrigeration before serving.

Turned out onto a platter and featured as one of many foods at a buffet, it is always a big success. Even those who swear they would never eat gefilte fish come back for seconds, provided you serve horseradish sauce with it.

1. Have your fish store grind the fillets or pulse them yourself, one at a time, in a food processor or meat grinder. If using a food processor, pulse the fish in short bursts, being careful not to purée the fish—you want some texture. Preheat the oven to 325 degrees. Grease a 12-cup Bundt pan and fill a larger pan (such as a large Pyrex dish) with 2 inches of hot water.

2. In a large pan over medium-high heat, sauté the diced onions in the oil for about 5 minutes, until soft and transparent but not brown. Set aside to cool.

3. Put the fish, onions, eggs, 2 cups (470 ml) water, matzo meal, carrots, 4 tablespoons dill, salt, pepper, mustard, and sugar in the bowl of a standing mixer equipped with a flat beater. Beat at medium speed for 10 minutes.

4. Pour the mixture into the Bundt or tube pan, then put the pan inside the larger water-filled dish (called a bain-marie). Smooth the top with a spatula. Cover with aluminum foil and bake for 1 hour, or until the center is solid. Remove the Bundt or tube pan from the water dish, then allow the terrine to cool slightly for at least 20 minutes. Slide a long knife around the outer and inner edges of the Bundt or tube pan, then carefully invert the terrine onto a flat serving plate.

5. Refrigerate for several hours or overnight. If any water accumulates on the serving dish, carefully drain it away before serving. Slice the terrine as you would a torte and serve as an appetizer, garnished with parsley and dill and served with Horseradish and Beet Sauce. Leftovers keep for up to 5 days.

2 pounds (907 grams) salmon fillets

1 pound (453 grams) cod, flounder, rockfish, or whitefish

3 medium red onions, peeled and diced (about 2 pounds/907 grams)

3 tablespoons vegetable or canola oil

4 large eggs

4 tablespoons matzo meal

2 large carrots, peeled and grated

4 tablespoons snipped fresh dill, plus more for garnish

1 tablespoon salt, or to taste

2 teaspoons freshly ground pepper

1 teaspoon Dijon mustard

2 tablespoons sugar

Parsley, for garnish

Horseradish and Beet Sauce (see below)

Horseradish and Beet Sauce

yield: about 4 cups

Wherewith does one show his delight therein? . . . With a dish of beets, a large fish, and cloves of garlic.
—Babylonian Talmud: Tractate Shabbath, Folio 118a

Jews serve horseradish, sliced as a root or ground into a sauce, at Passover to symbolize the bitterness of slavery. It was in Ashkenaz, what is now Alsace-Lorraine and southern Germany, that the horseradish root replaced the romaine and arugula of more southerly climates as the bitter herbs at the Passover dinner.

Today, farmers in France dig up horseradish roots and peel and grate them outdoors, making sure to protect their eyes from the sting. Then they mix the root with a little sugar and vinegar and sometimes grated beets, keeping it for their own personal use or selling it at local farmers' markets.

Horseradish with beets originally came from farther east in Poland, to which Jews immigrated from the west in the fourteenth century, and from the east probably earlier. It was a condiment served at Easter and represented the blood of Jesus Christ, something that I will bet most Jews did not know when they bought it from farmers at outside markets in Poland.

A few years ago, I ate an adaptation of this tasty sauce at the short-lived Kutsher's Restaurant in New York. I have played with it and now it is a keeper at our Passover Seder.

3 large beets (about 2 pounds/ 907 grams), trimmed but not peeled

3 tablespoons extra-virgin olive oil

4 ounces/113 grams (about 1 cup) peeled and roughly chopped fresh horseradish root

2 tablespoons white vinegar

1 teaspoon kosher salt

1 teaspoon black pepper

1 to 2 tablespoons fresh lemon juice

1. Heat the oven to 350 degrees. Rub the whole beets with 1 tablespoon of olive oil and wrap in foil. Bake the beets for about an hour or until tender in the center when pierced with a knife. Remove from the oven, allow to cool, then peel and cut into large chunks.

2. In the bowl of a food processor, mix the horseradish and the vinegar. Process with the steel blade until finely chopped; do not purée. Add the beets and remaining olive oil. Pulse until the beets are coarsely chopped, but not puréed. Transfer to a bowl and add the salt, pepper, and lemon juice to taste.

3. Adjust the seasonings as needed. Cover and refrigerate for at least a day. Serve as an accompaniment to the gefilte fish mold (see page 223).

Gravlaks with Mustard Sauce

I rarely host a cocktail party without making *gravlaks,* which means "buried salmon" in Scandinavian languages. The practice comes from Scandinavian fishermen who, after catching and curing salmon, once buried it in the ground to keep it cool. Today, we do not have to go to all this trouble. Homemade gravlaks, so easy to prepare by curing salmon in salt and sugar, is much less expensive than buying it already made. People love it, especially when it is served with a homemade mustard sauce on pumpernickel bread (see page 164 for a good one).

Although I have been making gravlaks for years, it was not until I met Runa Ross, who hails from Denmark, that I learned how to make a truly authentic version. Runa is the granddaughter of Jewish immigrants from Russia who came to Copenhagen in 1904.

Growing up in Copenhagen, Runa learned from her father, who was in the restaurant business, how to pick out the fattest and freshest salmon possible. Now, living in Palm Beach, she loves to use wild salmon for her gravlaks, even though the result is less consistent due to more variables, because it tastes better than farmed salmon. She also does not weigh the salmon down and adds splashes of aquavit to her recipe. What could be better!

———————

1. Roughly chop three-fourths of the dill (stems and all), saving a little for the garnish. Mix the chopped dill with the pepper, salt, and sugar in a bowl and set aside.

2. Cut the salmon in half widthwise and put one half skin side down on a cutting board. Sprinkle the dill mixture on top, splash with aquavit, gin, or brandy, and sandwich it with the other half of the salmon, skin side up. Slide the salmon into a large zip-top plastic bag and set in a large, rimmed dish (such as a Pyrex) to prevent leaking. Allow the salmon to cure in the refrigerator for 2 to 3 days, flipping it every day. The longer cure will result in a firmer and saltier gravlaks.

3. After 2 to 3 days, remove from the refrigerator, scrape off the dill mixture, and pat the fish with paper towels. Transfer the fish to a cutting board and, with a very sharp knife, slice thinly at an angle almost parallel to the board. Discard the outer skin.

4. There are many ways to present the gravlaks. To serve at a cocktail party, diagonally cut each slice of bread, creating two small triangles, then butter the slices and top with a few slices of gravlaks, a dollop of mustard sauce, and a sprig of the remaining dill. You can also, as a first course, serve it on a plate with dill, cucumber slices, and a dollop of mustard sauce. Or slice all

---

yield: about 30 appetizer servings and about ½ cup mustard sauce

1 large bunch of dill, divided

2 tablespoons coarsely ground pepper

½ cup (220 grams) coarse kosher salt

½ cup plus 2 tablespoons (225 grams) sugar

1 whole fillet of salmon, the fattiest you can find, about 3 pounds (1⅓ kilos), preferably with the skin on

¼ cup (60 ml) aquavit, gin, or brandy

Mustard sauce (see below)

1 sleeve of Mestemacher or other sliced pumpernickel bread, for serving

Unsalted butter, for serving

MUSTARD SAUCE

2 tablespoons Dijon mustard

2 tablespoons white vinegar

½ teaspoon sea salt, or to taste

2 to 2½ tablespoons sugar, or to taste

⅓ cup (80 ml) vegetable oil

¼ cup chopped dill

the gravlaks, arrange them on a beautiful platter, along with little bowls of fresh dill and mustard sauce and slices of bread, cucumber, or endive, and let your guests serve themselves.

5. **to make the mustard sauce** Stir together the mustard, vinegar, salt, and sugar. Then slowly whisk in the oil until the sauce is emulsified. Add the dill and set aside until ready to use.

Note When I buy a whole fillet of salmon, I cut off about 3 inches from the lean end and serve it for dinner that night. Or, do as Runa does during the holidays and grind it with your gefilte fish. If there is any leftover mustard sauce, don't throw it out. Just add it to a salad dressing.

Pickled Herring Spread

Gehackte herring (chopped herring), which is usually served as the first dish at the Sabbath dinner, is made by skinning a few herrings and chopping them together with hard-boiled eggs, onions, apples, sugar, pepper, and a little vinegar.   —Jewish Encyclopedia, 1906

Sometimes you just need tradition.

Visiting London is a pleasure for me. I like to stay with my friends Geoffrey and Rachel Paul, whom I knew in Jerusalem many years ago. At the time, Rachel was foreign press attaché to the Government Press Office, and Geoffrey was a correspondent for the *Jewish Chronicle* of London.

Today, the two live a traditional Jewish life in northwest London, where I celebrated Shabbat with them, going to the Golders Green synagogue. Once, their rabbi, Dr. Harvey Belovski, gave a talk, "Getting It in the Neck: Are Giraffes Kosher?" at Gefiltefest, an annual Jewish food festival celebrated across Golders Hill Park. Another year, he discussed and cooked locusts, which are (usually) kosher. He did not cook a giraffe, although it is technically kosher.

What surprised me at this synagogue was the long praise for the health of the queen and the royal family. But then, this is Great Britain.

Services ended at about noon, and then we had a sumptuous lunch with the Pauls' friends, starting with single-malt whiskies and a delicious herring spread, asparagus soup, several fresh pasta salads, slices of corned beef, and fresh fruit and apricot pie for dessert.

The herring, something that Rachel makes all the time, was a particular winner.

———————

1. In the bowl of a food processor fitted with a steel blade, pulse the onion and the almonds, then add the apple and the egg, pulsing just to combine.

2. Pour off the sauce and onions from the jar of marinated herring, then add the herring to the food processor and pulse just to chop. Place the mixture in a serving dish and serve as is or sprinkled with dill to garnish.

yield: about 6 to 8 servings

2 tablespoons chopped red onion

2 tablespoons almonds

½ Granny Smith or other tart apple, peeled and cored

1 large egg, hard-boiled and peeled

One 12-ounce (340-gram) jar marinated herring tidbits

1 tablespoon fresh chopped dill

Herring and Apple Bites with a Dill and Caper Dipping Sauce

I reduced all the beauty in the world to a small pickled fish.
—Leon Voskovec, the herring merchant, in Woody Allen's *Love and Death*

Once thought of as poor shtetl food, herring, heavily salted in wooden barrels, has been popular with northern European Jews for centuries. Tales of herring slingers were the stuff of Jewish folkways, as was a weekly diet of the salted fish, a cousin of the shad, anchovy, and sardine. Since Jews could not eat pork, herring was their chief source of protein, battered in egg and flour, then fried or pickled with cream sauce, always accompanied by potatoes and fresh onions.

Herring's resurgence comes as the sources and quality of much of the world's seafood have come under suspicion. Once one of the most abundant fish in the world, herring is still caught from sustainable wild stocks. Inexpensive and high in omega-3 fatty acids, it is approved for low-fat, high-protein diets. Herring used to be pickled in only wine sauce or cream sauce for Jewish holidays. No more. Now it can be found in dill sauce, in curry sauce, with pickles, with mustard sauce, and at most chain grocery stores.

"It is true that in Minnesota and Florida, when every old Jew or Scandinavian dies, we lose a case of herring," added Lorne Krongold, the owner of Feature Foods in Toronto, Ontario. "Luckily, in the eighties and nineties, the new immigration from the former Soviet Union replaced the aging generation of herring lovers."

Traveling in huge shoals of millions of tiny fish and caught with enormous nets, herring is left to dry, cured with the salt left from the sea, and sprinkled with extra salt. Herring slingers like Lorne's grandfather—who followed herring from Poland to Canada, where most of the herring we Americans eat is caught—would buy barrels of the fish from the fishermen and sell them to processors.

Known as the "herring czar" of Canada, Lorne makes these simple bites from bottled herring in wine sauce.

yield: about 20 bites

One 12-ounce (340-gram) jar herring tidbits in wine sauce

1 bunch scallions or 1 red onion

1 small Granny Smith or other tart apple

4 tablespoons mixed sour cream, mayonnaise, and/or yogurt

1 tablespoon chopped dill, divided

1 tablespoon capers, divided

---

1. Remove and discard the jarred onions from the herring fillets. Arrange the herring pieces on a flat dish.

2. Slice the scallions or onion and the apple into bite-size pieces and put on top of each piece of herring and secure with a toothpick to hold the garnish in place.

3. In a small bowl, stir together the sour cream, mayonnaise, or yogurt and half the dill and capers. Sprinkle the remaining dill and capers on top.

4. Put the herring on a serving plate with the dip in the center.

Couscous con le Sarde, Sardines with Fennel, Onions, Currants, and Pine Nuts over Couscous

I fell in love with this dish years ago in Washington when I took a cooking lesson with a charming woman named Mimmetta Lo Monte. I still remember the surprise when Mimmetta, knowing my interest in the food of the Jews, said that this was a Jewish Sicilian dish. But of course! The recipe includes sardines and no shellfish and uses pine nuts, fennel, and currants, all telltale signs of Jewish dishes in Italy.

After I tasted the dish, I never forgot the lovely combination. Recently, I stumbled on a recipe for the dish when I couldn't find fresh sardines in the market and didn't want to substitute canned, so I made it with a fillet of arctic char. You can also make it without fish as a vegetarian main course.

————————

1. Prepare the couscous. If using precooked couscous, then follow the instructions on the box. (Or you can make your own, following the recipe on page 170.) After adding the boiling water and covering for 5 minutes, put the couscous in a strainer over boiling water and steam while preparing the fish.

2. Heat a tablespoon of the oil in a small skillet, add the almonds, stirring constantly until they make a crackling sound. Drain and let them cool. Cut by hand or pulse in a small food processor to a medium chop and set aside. Then add a bit more oil to the skillet and add the pine nuts. Stir-fry them for a few minutes until they are golden and set aside.

3. In a larger pot with a cover, like a Dutch oven, add 2 more tablespoons of oil and add the onion, fennel, and fennel seeds, sautéing until the onion is golden.

4. Lay the fish on top of the vegetables and sprinkle some salt, pepper, and lemon juice over them. Add the currants, cover, and simmer over low heat for about 6 minutes for sardines and 10 minutes for other fish, or until it is soft. Then cut the fish, if using instead of the sardines, into 6 servings.

5. Put the couscous on a platter, then, using a spatula, place the fish on top of the couscous and surround it with all the vegetables. Sprinkle with the pine nuts, almonds, and fennel fronds and serve immediately.

Note If using fresh sardines, cut off the head and tail with a sharp knife. Then extend a sharp knife down the back to the tail of the fish. Then, using your index finger and thumb or a butter knife, carefully lift out the bone, starting at the tail end. The sardine should remain intact and open up like a butterfly; close it to cook.

yield: 4 to 6 main servings, or 8 as an appetizer

8 ounces (226 grams) boxed couscous or from scratch (see page 170)

4 to 6 tablespoons olive oil, divided

⅓ cup (47 grams) almonds

¼ cup (34 grams) pine nuts

1 large onion, diced

1 fennel bulb, diced, fronds reserved

½ teaspoon fennel seeds

1½ pounds (680 grams) fresh sardines (see note below) or 3 pounds (about 1⅓ kilos) arctic char, salmon, grouper, tuna, whiting, bass, or bluefish fillets

Salt and freshly ground pepper to taste

Juice of 1 lemon

3 to 4 tablespoons currants

Cod with Tomatoes, Dried Plums, Onions, and Pine Nuts

yield: 4 to 6 servings

Some friends and I drove up the winding roads bordered by olive trees and grapevines to Perugia, the university town, capital and mercantile center of Umbria, Italy. After parking our car, we walked toward Piazza 4 Novembre, passing the cathedral and Sandri, the luscious chocolate store in the square, tempting us inside. I thought back to the Middle Ages, before there were chocolate stores, before anyone in Europe knew about chocolate! The tiny Jewish population here, most of whom were small merchants, physicians, and moneylenders, worked on these same streets.

Little trace remains of the group of about one hundred Jewish families who lived in Perugia for three hundred years. In the latter part of the thirteenth century, the local authorities invited some five hundred Jews to move there from Rome and Sicily, where they were joined at the end of the fifteenth century by Sephardic Jews fleeing Spain and Portugal.

With difficulty we found Via Vecchia, where the Jews once lived and prayed in two synagogues on a narrow street behind the *duomo*. The few who did not convert were a distinct minority, the "other" in this city of Catholics. As these stubborn Jews would not eat pork in a country where wild boar and pork were local specialties, and because they needed special wine prepared by Sabbath-observant Jews, they were never treated like other Perugians, and the city taxed them heavily and had many laws defining what they could and could not do regarding kosher meat, dating, marriage, and even burial.

But despite all these burdens, the Jews of Umbria survived and thrived during this period, until they were all exiled in 1569 by papal decree and went to other parts of Italy or headed eastward through Germany and then Poland.

Today, it is hard for us to understand the need to keep such a low profile. As I mused about this, a parade of white-masked gay and lesbian activists passed me by on the piazza in front of the *duomo* near the Fontana Maggiore with piped-in music from Carl Orff's *Carmina Burana*. Jews of Perugia during the Middle Ages could never have marched so publicly.

The following flavorful and festive ancient baccalà, a salted cod dish known to have originated with the Jews, is still served at Christmas by many in Perugia. The cod, heavily preserved in salt when caught, is refreshed by soaking in cold water. The method of preserving the fish in salt is thousands of years old and is credited to the Basque fishermen, who used the same method of salting and drying to preserve whale meat. Salting and drying the cod not only enhanced the taste, but also preserved it for several years, making it less expensive than fresh fish.

This recipe can be made with baccalà (see note below) or, as I have done, with fresh cod. Either way, it is a delicious, old Italian dish highlighted by the distinctly Jewish tradition of combining sweet and sour flavors from raisins, pine nuts, onions, and dried plums. The inclusion of tomatoes is relatively recent and a welcome addition, after the fruit came to the kingdom of Naples from the New World in the sixteenth century.

_____

1. Warm 1 or 2 tablespoons of oil over medium heat and sauté the onion, garlic, and a pinch of salt and pepper until the onion is soft and translucent, about 5 to 10 minutes.

2. Increase the heat to medium-high and add the brown sugar, wine, and 2 tablespoons vinegar. Stir to mix, and cook until the liquid is almost completely evaporated, adding more vinegar if you'd like a more tart sauce.

3. Add the tomato, dried plums, raisins, pine nuts, apple, and lemon zest. Season with a bit more pepper and mix well to let the flavors mingle, adding a few tablespoons of water to create a sauce. Cook gently for about 15 minutes, covered. You can do this up until a day ahead.

4. Meanwhile, remove the skin and bones from the prepared baccalà or fresh cod, cut it into 2-inch pieces, pat dry, and dust lightly with flour. Warm 2 to 3 of the remaining tablespoons of oil in a large nonstick sauté pan set over medium-high heat and fry the fish until golden, a few minutes per side, adding more oil as needed.

5. Remove to a large platter and spoon the sauce over and sprinkle with the chopped mint and chives.

Note Baccalà can most often be found in Hispanic markets, where it will be called bacalao. If using baccalà, rinse and then soak the fish in water for at least 12 hours and up to 36, changing the water at least twice.

4 to 5 tablespoons olive oil, divided

1 large red or sweet yellow onion, thinly sliced

1 clove garlic, chopped

Salt and freshly ground black pepper to taste

1 tablespoon dark brown sugar

½ cup (120 ml) white wine

2 to 4 tablespoons red wine vinegar

1 pound (453 grams) tomato pulp or chopped canned peeled tomatoes

10 pitted dried plums

2 tablespoons black or golden raisins

2 tablespoons lightly toasted pine nuts

1 apple, peeled and chopped in chunks

Zest of ½ lemon

About 2 pounds (907 grams) salted cod (baccalà) or fresh cod (see note)

About 4 tablespoons flour for dusting the fish

Handful of chopped mint and chives for garnish

Snapper with Preserved Lemon and Capers

Also when they shall be afraid of that which is high,
And terrors shall be in the way;
And the almond-tree shall blossom,
And the grasshopper shall drag itself along,
And the caper berry shall fail;
Because man goeth to his long home,
And the mourners go about the streets.

—Ecclesiastes 12:5

The Talmud says that the caper berry is a fruit that arouses sexual passion as well as the appetite. But this speech by Koheleth, a son of David, shows that everything, even the caper berry with all its provocative properties, can fail.

Whether or not capers, one of the oldest flavor enhancers, really excite an amorous appetite, they clearly enhance the flavor of any meal. This simple fish dish, which I first tasted in Florida (see page 169), is delicious. You can use snapper, flounder, fillet of sole, or any delicate fish.

———————

1. Preheat the oven to 425 degrees and brush a 9-by-13-inch baking pan with 1 tablespoon of the olive oil, then gently put the fillet in the prepared dish.

2. Sprinkle the fish with pepper. Then scatter the preserved lemon, the spring onions, and the capers on top. Dust with the sumac and squeeze the lemon all around.

3. Bake for about 10 to 15 minutes, or until done. Serve with saffron rice (see page 169).

Note If using a thicker fillet like salmon, cook it for about 20 minutes. You can also cook the fish with a sprinkle of *za'atar* on top with the preserved lemon instead of the capers.

yield: 6 servings

2 tablespoons olive oil, divided

1 filleted snapper, flounder, striped bass, or other similar fish, about 3 pounds (1⅓ kilos)

Freshly ground pepper to taste

1 preserved lemon, diced (see page 11)

2 spring onions, diced

2 tablespoons capers

½ teaspoon sumac

Juice of 1 lemon

Brazilian-Belarusian Grouper with Wine, Cilantro, and Oregano

On a trip to the Brazilian city of Recife for a family wedding, I visited the Centro Israelita de Pernambuco, a community center that houses a synagogue and a school. Outside, three children were playing hide-and-seek beneath the mango trees. Awaiting them inside were coconut-filled sweets, potato pies, and other Brazilian goodies, some made by their grandmother Mathilda Steinberg.

Later that week, the children would sit down to a Passover Seder with food prepared by Mathilda, reflecting both their family history and local culture.

It is believed that the first Jews in Brazil, some three hundred families from Spain and Portugal, arrived in the northeastern port of Recife in 1631, seeking safe haven from the Spanish Inquisition. Hundreds of years later, in the 1920s, another wave of Jews arrived from what is now Belarus, fleeing persecution, pogroms, and forced conscription in the Bolshevik army. The twelve hundred or so Jews who live here now are more Russian in heritage than Mediterranean, and so is their cuisine.

In close-knit communities like this one, classic Jewish recipes, long forgotten elsewhere, can still be found, though altered somewhat by the use of local ingredients. Most of Recife's Jews speak Portuguese and a little Hebrew (with the older ones speaking some Yiddish). They hold on to the recipes of their past, much as the Jews of Montreal, originally from Romania, Ukraine, and Poland, hold on to their pierogi and smoked beef, and the Jews of South Africa, originally from Lithuania, hold on to their stuffed matzo balls.

At Mathilda's Seder, traditional eastern European gefilte fish, chicken soup, and pot roast tell this family's history. But the gefilte fish is made with snapper, hake, grouper, or whiting, all local fish, instead of the traditional mix of carp, whitefish, and pike.

The Jewish community in Recife is too small for stores to carry many Passover supplies, so ingredients come from São Paulo or Israel. The people who pay dues to the Centro Israelita receive a free box of matzos, but they must order wine and matzo meal specially.

Since horseradish root is not found in Brazil, Mathilda uses wasabi powder mixed with beets, sugar, salt, and vinegar for the bitter herb at the Passover Seder. Her grandmother used mustard greens.

"By making these dishes, at least the kids will have a taste of things Jewish," Mathilda told me. "The Jewish people have been through so many changes. My grandparents thought they would not make it out of Belarus. I hope that the next generation will feel the desire to pass on these foods. That's the way the Jewish people have always continued."

yield: 6 to 8 servings

3 pounds (about 1⅓ kilos) grouper, striped bass, red snapper, pollock, whiting, or sea bream fillets

5 cloves garlic, peeled

1 teaspoon salt, or to taste

Freshly ground pepper to taste

2 bay leaves

2 cups (470 ml) dry white wine

¼ cup (60 ml) olive oil

1 cup chopped cilantro (from about 1 bunch), divided

¼ cup fresh chopped or 1 tablespoon dried crumbled Mexican oregano

½ green bell pepper, diced

1 large tomato, diced

¼ cup snipped chives

As a main course for holidays, Mathilda serves what she calls "holiday fish," poached with wine, cilantro, and oregano, typical flavors of this coastal province. As she tells me, "I have integrated the herbs and spices that are here into what my grandmother used to cook in Europe."

---

1. Heat the oven to 375 degrees. Put the fillets in a large Pyrex dish or other baking pan. With a mortar and pestle or a small food processor fitted with a steel blade, blend together the garlic, salt, and pepper, and spread on fish.

2. Place the bay leaves over the fish. Pour enough wine and olive oil over the fish to almost cover it, then sprinkle ½ cup of the cilantro and the oregano on top. Cover the pan tightly with foil and bake for about 30 minutes, spooning pan juices over the fish two or three times. Cool to lukewarm.

3. Remove the bay leaves and mix the remaining cilantro with the green pepper, tomato, and chives. Sprinkle over the fish and serve.

Fish *B'stilla* with Rice Noodles and Vegetables

The public oven in Moroccan towns is where families announce weddings, anniversaries, and other special occasions, whether they want to or not. When someone brings a *b'stilla*—a chicken or pigeon pie made with nuts, sugar, cinnamon, and orange blossom water that is one of the jewels of Moroccan cooking—everybody knows that a big celebration is on the way. After all, no one would take the trouble to make *b'stilla* on just any old day. This delicious pie is topped with *warqa* leaf, a thin dough that is made by bouncing fistfuls of wet batter on a hot grill until it miraculously comes together. Filo can easily be substituted in this recipe.

This celebratory pie, sometimes also spelled *pastilla,* is usually made with chicken, nuts, an egg custard, and cinnamon sugar. But this fish version, which I tasted as the first course at a fancy dinner given for my husband's birthday in Morocco, is equally delicious and more modern.

According to cookbook author and Moroccan cuisine expert Paula Wolfert, Mohammed Boussaoud, the executive chef at the Mamounia Hotel in Marrakech, created the *b'stilla* with whiting (a cousin of cod), squid, and shrimp. When he became the chef at Darna, a glatt kosher restaurant in Jerusalem, he switched the fish to just whiting.

Fish *b'stilla* has spread throughout Morocco and often has an Asian flavor, with soy sauce added to the rice noodles. The version I tasted had only whiting, nori (seaweed flakes), preserved lemon, and *harissa.* I have added more vegetables, like carrots, celery, and Swiss chard or spinach, into the mix and often double the recipe as a stunning main course for a buffet surrounded by North African cooked vegetable salads (see pages 101, 110, and 112).

———————

1. Preheat the oven to 400 degrees and grease a 9-inch round baking or paella pan.

2. Cut the fish into roughly 2-inch pieces and season with salt and pepper. In a large nonstick skillet, melt the butter and sauté the fish for a few minutes on each side to take on some color. When browned but not cooked through entirely, set aside on a plate.

3. Add the onions, carrots, and celery to the pan and sauté until the onions are golden and the carrots are slightly tender.

4. Add the spinach or Swiss chard, parsley, garlic, and pinch of saffron and sauté for a few minutes. Remove from heat and set aside.

yield: 6 to 8 servings

1½ pounds (680 grams) whiting, cod, or tilapia

Freshly ground salt and pepper to taste

4 tablespoons (½ stick/ 56 grams) unsalted butter, plus 5 tablespoons (70 grams), melted

2 medium-large onions, diced

2 large carrots, diced

2 celery stalks, diced

10 ounces (283 grams) chopped spinach, Swiss chard, or other greens

½ bunch parsley, chopped (about 1 cup loosely packed)

4 cloves garlic, chopped

1 pinch saffron threads

6 ounces (170 grams) Chinese rice vermicelli

1 teaspoon each cinnamon, ginger, or cumin or, if you have it, 1 tablespoon *Ras el Hanout*

1 teaspoon *harissa* (see page 10)

1 preserved lemon, diced, with 1 teaspoon of its juice (see page 11)

1 large egg

One 1-pound (55-gram) package filo dough (about 8 sheets)

5. Submerge the rice vermicelli in a bowl of hot water for 5 minutes. Drain and cool, then cut into 1-inch pieces and set aside.

6. Mix the vegetables, cinnamon, ginger, cumin, or *Ras el Hanout, harissa*, preserved lemon, and lemon juice. Then add the rice vermicelli and lastly the fish.

7. In a small bowl, whisk the egg with 1 teaspoon of water, creating an egg wash.

8. Arrange 4 filo sheets over the prepared pan, letting ⅓ of each piece of dough hang outside the pan, so that there are 4 "flaps" outside the pan—one at the 12 o'clock position, one at 3 o'clock, one at 6 o'clock, and one at 9 o'clock. Brush each sheet with melted butter, then put a fourth sheet in the center. Brush the dough again with the butter, then with the egg wash. Fill the center with the filling and enclose with the overhanging filo sheets, brushing each sheet with butter after you fold it over the filling. Once all sheets are folded over, brush the whole thing with the egg wash. Finally, layer more sheets of filo on top, brushing each with butter, then brush the top layer with the egg wash.

9. Bake for 20 to 30 minutes or until golden.

The *Warqa* and Filo Question

Since filo dough is often substituted for *warqa,* it is important to note that although the ingredients might be the same, the process of making filo is totally different, as it is rolled, then stacked.

Strudel, on the other hand, is a stretched, high-gluten dough, requiring two people working together to stretch it.

Poached Salmon with Ginger-Cilantro Butter and Spinach

David Tanis is known for being many things: a longtime chef at Chez Panisse, an acclaimed cookbook author, and the City Kitchen columnist for the *New York Times.* Being Jewish isn't one of them.

Born in Dayton, Ohio, David calls Jewish food his "culinary roots." "Our family was kind of a funny family," he said. "We always did Friday night, but it usually wasn't at our house but at Aunt Edith and Uncle Marvin's, who were good family friends. We didn't do the whole nine yards, but we did do matzo balls or *chremsel.* I was totally into it, I was bar mitzvahed, Hebrew school. But then I ran away into the large wide world."

A few years ago when I visited Berkeley to moderate a Deli Summit, I met David for the first time and, lucky for me, he was behind the stove at Chez Panisse. The first course, a salmon *à la nage,* consisted of a three-inch square of sweet wild Pacific salmon, the kind that is available for only a few weeks a year. David made a court bouillon, a light vegetable broth with white wine, and added Asian ingredients like star anise and lemongrass. Then he poached the fish in the broth and served it with a cilantro-ginger butter that melted on top. The result was refreshingly delicious. I serve and savor it as a main course, with a salad, for a summer dinner.

———————

1. **prepare the court bouillon** Put the carrots, celery, onion, lemon, thyme, lemongrass, and parsley in a noncorrosive pot large enough to later hold the salmon pieces side by side with room to spare. Add 3 cups (705 ml) of water, the Sauvignon Blanc, and salt. Bring to a simmer, cover, and cook very slowly for 20 minutes.

2. **in the meantime, prepare the herb butter** Mix the butter together with the shallot, ginger, lemon zest, cilantro, salt, and pepper. Set aside in a small bowl and keep it at room temperature.

3. Taste the court bouillon and correct it to your taste for salt. Bring the court bouillon to a bare simmer and add the salmon. Gently poach the salmon slices in the hot liquid for about 2½ minutes. Do not raise the heat during this time. Transfer the salmon to warm soup bowls and put a dollop of herb butter on each slice. Add the spinach to the hot court bouillon, cooking until it just wilts, remove the lemon thyme, and ladle the liquid with the spinach over the butter and salmon, adding some of the vegetables from the pot to each bowl, and serve, sprinkled with the chives.

yield: 4 servings

1 small carrot, peeled and very thinly sliced in rounds

½ celery stalk, very thinly sliced

½ medium yellow onion (about ½ cup/55 grams), sliced in rounds

3 sprigs fresh lemon thyme

2 stems lemongrass, pounded

1 large sprig Italian parsley

½ cup (120 ml) Sauvignon Blanc

1½ teaspoons salt

Four 4-ounce (113-gram) pieces of salmon, cut 1 inch thick and skin removed

2 handfuls of spinach

½ tablespoon thinly sliced chives

HERB BUTTER

4 tablespoons (½ stick/ 56 grams) unsalted butter at room temperature

1 small shallot, finely diced

1 inch of fresh ginger, peeled and grated

Zest of ½ small lemon

Handful of cilantro, chopped

Pinch of salt and pepper

Poultry

T'Beet, Baghdadi Sabbath Overnight Spiced Chicken with Rice
and Coconut Chutney

Chicken with Eggplant and Swiss Chard

Chicken *Paprikash* with Dumplings

Fessenjan, Persian Walnut and Pomegranate Chicken Stew

Indian Chicken with Cardamom, Cumin, and Cilantro

Syrian-Mexican Chicken with Apricot, Tamarind, and Chipotle Sauce

Gondi Kashi, Rice with Turkey, Beets, Fava Beans, and Herbs

Hungarian Stuffed Chicken

Double-Lemon Roast Chicken

Roast Turkey with Challah-Chestnut-Cranberry Stuffing

How an Exotic Bird from India Became the Standard White Meat: Chicken

The first [dish] is hens or roosters, boiled or broiled in a pit, or steamed, or cooked with chervil, or cooked in water into which green fennel is cast; these dishes are suitable in the wintertime. Those cooked in water to which lemon juice, cedrat pulp or mixed lemons are added, are suitable in the summer time. Those prepared with almonds, sugar, lemon juice and wine are suitable in every season. Those prepared with currants, almonds and a little vinegar are excellent at any time. Those prepared in Isfidbaj with beets or lettuce in the summertime and those prepared with round pumpkins, or spinach, or blite, or with dried plums which the people of Syria call Khawkh (Land of Israel) are all good in the summer.

—Moses Maimonides, *Regimen of Health,* twelfth century

It is hard to imagine a time when chicken was a rarity on the dinner table.

Although domesticated chickens, descended from the Southeast Asian red jungle fowl, came to the Middle East from India about 4,500 years ago, it took a long time for our feathered friends to become the popular protein they are today.

Even as early as 1775 B.C.E., we find quasi-recipes, written on cuneiform tablets from Mesopotamia, for broths and stews with pigeons, turtledoves, ducks, geese, and old chickens.

Neither the Canaanites nor the Egyptians knew of chicken—they had ducks and geese—until the rise of the Persian Empire, when the Persians introduced the breeding of chickens as they advanced toward the west. According to the late and dearly lamented Gil Marks, in his magisterial *Encyclopedia of Jewish Food,* the earliest representation of a chicken is an onyx seal decorated with a rooster, from the sixth century B.C.E.

Although chickens were widespread by the first century C.E., rabbis ruled that the priests (Cohanim) in the Temple couldn't use them because, according to Marks, "they were quite messy and wandered in places they weren't wanted."

During this period and throughout history, roosters were used for cockfighting, something that Jewish law prohibited. Only old roosters and hens that had finished laying their eggs were eaten, mostly in chicken stews.

One of the earliest Jewish recipes that is still in existence is *t'beet,* the Sabbath chicken overnight baked dish of the Babylonian Jews (see page 249).

By the twelfth century, during the time of Moses Maimonides and the Cairo Genizah, hens and cocks were often used in soups and stews as a curative and as a holiday and Friday night dish. Maimonides, in his *Medical Aphorisms,* suggested that the consumption of fowl helps asthmatics and increases sexual potential, all the more reason to serve it on Friday night, when men are supposed to perform their marital duties. Maimonides also prescribed a soup or stew with an old hen or cock as a curative for leprosy and other ailments like asthma or the common cold. From other Genizah documents, we learn that live chickens and quails were sent back and forth in cages as gifts.

In the thirteenth century, from the Andalusian cookbook *Anwa' al-Saydala fi Alwan al-At'ima* (A Compendium of Dishes and Their Healing Benefits, writer anonymous), we find fowl prepared in an elaborate way, such as the "Jewish Dish of Chicken" with a stuffing of hard-boiled eggs, pine nuts, cinnamon, and other spices.

By the nineteenth century, German and Jewish cookbooks show more of a variety of birds used in cooking. But until the strides of industrialization, most recipes were still for a stewed and occasionally roasted chicken.

Throughout history, the by-products of fowl were almost as important as the meat. Until the late nineteenth century, for example, chicken plucking was a time-consuming communal event in the homes of Jews in many lands. "While engaged in plucking feathers, people would tell wondrous tales, which either had come down through tradition, or were new ones that someone had heard somewhere or had read in a storybook," wrote Hirsz Abramowicz in his *Profiles of a Lost World* about life for Lithuania's country Jews. "The guests might include Christian women and girls from the neighborhood. They would sing songs in Yiddish, Lithuanian, Polish, Belorussian and Russian. . . . At the time, feather plucking was an established tradition in every Jewish family. The feathers, which came from geese and ducks, were collected in sacks or pillow cases. In poorer homes, the feathers of chickens and roosters were also collected. Every daughter (and in those days it was rare for a Jewish family to have only one daughter) had to be provided with pillows and feather beds. The girl closest to marriageable age made a special effort to acquire as many feathers as possible, so that she might be in a position to be proud of her bedding."

Another communal custom performed in many Jewish communities before Yom Kippur, the Day of Atonement, was *Kapparot,* where an animal was used as a substitute offering. A man held a cock and a woman a hen and swung it around the head three times while the right hand was put upon the animal's head. Three times in Hebrew they said, "This be my substitute, my vicarious offering, my atonement. This cock [or hen] shall meet death, but I shall find a long and pleasant life of peace!" After this the animal was slaughtered and given to the poor. Today Jews who want to practice this custom instead give money to the poor.

Believe it or not, until very recently chicken was one of the most expensive types of meat. That is why *coq au vin*, made from an old rooster, and Jewish chicken soup with root vegetables, made with a hen, became perennial favorites.

In the twentieth century, with mechanization, inoculation, and the breeding of broilers beginning in the 1930s, chicken has become an inexpensive and very popular protein, albeit with some pitfalls. The good news is that with increased concerns about health, chickens raised humanely and with minimal antibiotics as well as organic free-range chickens—so much tastier than the tired, wan-looking birds often found in supermarkets, and well worth the higher cost—are widely available.

As soon as the freezer came into being, it became profitable for Joseph Katz, an immigrant from Austria, to mass-produce kosher chickens in Liberty, New York. With refrigerated trains and trucks, he could ship them throughout the country. Katz's company, founded in 1938, eventually became Empire Kosher, today the largest kosher producer in the world, now located in Mifflintown, Pennsylvania.

Today, more and more people are going local in their reaction to frozen kosher chickens and industrial slaughter. Small kosher meat growers and slaughterers, who use only animals raised humanely, with minimal antibiotics, are springing up all over the world wherever there are sizable Jewish populations.

When I lived in Jerusalem in the 1970s, boiled chicken was a norm on hotel menus. No more. Today, in Israel and elsewhere, we are using exciting—and ancient—spices like cardamom and cumin, chili peppers, and fruits like dates, tamarinds, and pomegranates to liven up our chicken dishes.

T'beet, Baghdadi Sabbath Overnight Spiced Chicken with Rice and Coconut Chutney

yield: at least 8 servings

One of my favorite ways to prepare a chicken comes from medieval Iraq. Called *t'beet*, which is derived from the Arabic *tabayit*, meaning "to be cooked overnight," this Sabbath chicken dish is stuffed with rice, meat, and spices, then buried in more rice and cooked all night over charcoal embers before being served warm for lunch.

T'beet, in some form, may date back to the destruction of the First Temple, when Nebuchadnezzar II welcomed the Jews to Babylon starting around 597 B.C.E., thus beginning a centuries-long Jewish presence in what later became Iraq. By 1940 there were 180,000 Jews living in Baghdad alone. (Today there are practically none.)

On a recent trip to London, I visited Eileen Dangoor Khalastchy, one of those naturally great cooks, who lives in an apartment overlooking Baker Street.

Eileen, now in her late eighties, may have left Baghdad in 1975, but the family dishes, decorated with rosebuds and fragrant with cinnamon, cloves, nutmeg, cardamom, and turmeric, remain in her thoughts and perfume her kitchen.

During a delightful day, I learned recipes and listened to stories about Eileen's early life, when some twenty people, mostly family—when family meant everything—lived in a big house overlooking the Tigris River.

"At home we used the rice my husband's family grew," Eileen told me in her kitchen. "The rice often had small stones in it, so we had to clean it before we washed it, then we washed it again. And again. The rice we get today is clean, but we Iraqis still wash it three times and soak it for a few hours. In Baghdad we only ate fruits and vegetables in season. So we had to make and store what we needed for the whole year.

"We even made tomato purée for our cooking," she added. "In the summer, everybody bought a lot of tomatoes, squeezed the juice out, sieved them to remove the seeds and the outer skin, and put the juice in a big container on the roof of the house and kept it there for a few days in the sun until it became thick."

Friday was the day to start *t'beet*. There were no home ovens at that time in Baghdad, so the *t'beet* was cooked on charcoal overnight for Sabbath lunch.

"On top of the cover, we put eggs in their shells, then covered it again," she said. "On top of everything was a folded blanket to keep the heat. We ate the eggs Saturday morning with tomatoes, onions, and lemon salad, with pickles or with spring onions and parsley."

Today, most cooks have learned speedier ways to make *t'beet* than the one I described above. When I make *t'beet*, I follow some traditional customs like using fresh spices I grind, and cleaning the chicken with a lemon. Also, I make sure to produce enough *h'kaka,* known in Iran as *tadig,* the prized crust of rice that forms on the bottom of the casserole.

——————

1. Rinse the rice in water until the water runs clear, then soak in lukewarm water for a half hour.

2. While the rice is soaking, heat 4 tablespoons of the oil in a 7-quart wide, oven-safe, heavy-bottomed pot and sauté the onions until golden. Add the tomatoes, stir and cook for a few minutes, then remove and put the mixture into a small bowl.

3. Rub the chicken with lemon, then mix the salt, ground cardamom, cinnamon, allspice, nutmeg, cloves, ginger, paprika, and pepper in a bowl and rub over the chicken. Add another tablespoon of oil to the pot if needed, brown the chicken on all sides, and remove from the pot to a large bowl with the onions. You can do these two steps a day ahead, then refrigerate until ready to finish cooking.

4. Drain the rice, drizzle 2 more tablespoons of oil into the pot, and spoon half the rice into the pot. Add the onions and tomatoes, then press the chicken pieces into the rice mixture and cover with the remaining rice. Stir the tomato paste and the parsley into the 5 cups of broth or water and add to the chicken. Top with the eggs, if using, and bring to a boil.

5. If cooking overnight, preheat the oven to 150 degrees and cover the pot and transfer to the oven until ready to serve the next day or, cook the dish in a 275-degree oven, covered, for about 4 hours. When done, the chicken will be very tender, the water absorbed, and the bottom rice crunchy.

6. Before serving, set the bottom of the pan in cold water. This will make it easier to detach the *tadig* or *h'kaka* (the delicious bottom crust of the rice). Spoon the *t'beet* onto a large serving dish, with the chicken skin side up in the middle and the crust on top. Sprinkle with the rose petals, if using, and parsley and serve, with chutney (at right) or *amba* (see page 68). Serve the egg for breakfast or with the chicken for lunch or dinner.

3 cups (600 grams) basmati rice

7 tablespoons olive oil, divided

2 large onions, diced

2 whole large tomatoes, cut up

Two 3-pound (1⅓-kilo) chickens, each cut into 8 pieces

1 lemon, cut in half

1 tablespoon salt or to taste

2 tablespoons ground cardamom

1½ tablespoons ground cinnamon

1 teaspoon ground allspice

1 teaspoon ground nutmeg

1 teaspoon ground cloves

1 teaspoon ground ginger

1 teaspoon paprika

1 teaspoon freshly ground black pepper

2 heaping tablespoons tomato paste

Handful parsley plus a little for garnish, chopped

5 cups (1.175 liters) chicken stock or water

6 to 8 large eggs, with the shell (optional)

8 dried rose petals or about 2 teaspoons (optional)

Amba (see page 68)

Coconut Chutney with Cilantro and Green Pepper

yield: about 2 cups

I love this refreshing and flavorful accompaniment to *t'beet*. It is also good served with Indian Chicken with Cardamom, Cumin, and Cilantro (page 259) or Bene Israel Fish Curry with Fresh Ginger, Tamarind, and Cilantro (page 231).

Juice of 2 limes
(about ¼ cup or 60 ml),
or more to taste

2 small green peppers,
cored and roughly chopped

1 jalapeño, cored and roughly
chopped

1 bunch fresh cilantro,
cleaned and stemmed
(about 2 cups/120 grams)

¼ teaspoon salt

½ inch fresh ginger, peeled
and roughly chopped

1 cup (100 grams) finely shredded
sweetened or unsweetened
coconut

1 to 2 tablespoons sugar
(optional)

1. Put the lime juice, green peppers, jalapeño, cilantro, salt, and ginger in a food processor with a steel blade, adding more lime juice if desired.

2. With the machine running, add in the coconut gradually until the mixture is pulsed but still somewhat rough, sprinkling on a few tablespoons of sugar if using unsweetened coconut. Store in an airtight container in the refrigerator for up to a week.

Chicken with Eggplant and Swiss Chard

Expenditure for Shavuoth—if I live so long with the help of the Almighty. Little chickens—1 dirhem; meat—1½ dirhems; a pound of fat tail (of sheep)—½ and ⅙ dirhem; a hen—1½ dirhems; garden mallow—½ dirhem; cubeb and garlic—⅛ dirhem; sesame oil—¼ dirhem; eggplants—½ dirhem; this is for the first day, which is a Friday.

For the Sabbath: a lemon hen—2 dirhems; chard (leaf beets)—⅜ dirhem; onions—¼ dirhem; safflower—¼ dirhem; green lemons—½ dirhem.

—thirteenth-century shopping list of Solomon ben Elijah ben Zechariah

Solomon ben Elijah ben Zechariah wrote the above shopping list in the city of Fustat (now part of modern-day Cairo), the center of Jewish life in old Egypt in the first half of the thirteenth century. According to the documents found in the Genizah, men shopped and lived a public life, while women were confined to the house. (There were even prenuptial contracts specifying this in the Cairo Genizah.)

A major figure of the period, given his various communal responsibilities as cantor and rabbi, Solomon was a childhood friend of Abraham Maimonides, the son of Moses Maimonides, and worked in Abraham's office later in his life. Solomon had a variety of professions: teacher, bookseller, cantor (which he did not like very much), notary, vintner (in partnership with his brother), and cheese merchant.

In the Middle East, during medieval times and even today, it was often the husband who purchased food in the open marketplace for the family. Using Solomon ben Elijah's thirteenth-century shopping list as a guide, I pored through my library of Jewish cookbooks and put together a recipe similar to what this special eggplant chicken dish might have been. According to one of Solomon's letters, his wife, Sitt Ghazal, made the dish in the early summer on the first night of Shavuot, the ancient festival celebrating the giving of the Law on Mount Sinai. A few centuries later, as the recipe went through Spain and eventually to northern Morocco, it became a chicken and eggplant or red pepper dish (see my *Jewish Cooking in America*), served before the fast of Yom Kippur.

The recipe has continued to evolve through the centuries. Following the Columbian Exchange, string beans, tomatoes, and eventually tomato paste were all added.

Although mallow is considered a weed, I sometimes pick the lobed leaves that grow in my backyard for salad or, as Sitt Ghazal did, to serve as a green cooked with chicken. Mallow is becoming more popular in the Middle East, for stuffing vegetables and for use in stews in place of spinach. Who knows—perhaps it will be the next kale?

yield: 6 to 8 servings

6 to 8 tablespoons sesame or olive oil, divided

2 medium eggplants (about 2 pounds/907 grams)

Sea salt, to taste

1 large onion, chopped

2 cloves garlic, diced

One 4- to 5-pound (about 2-kilo) chicken, cut into 8 pieces

1 teaspoon ground cubeb (from about 20 cubeb berries) or allspice

¼ teaspoon ground turmeric, divided

2 cups chicken stock or water

1 dried lime (optional)

1 bunch Swiss chard or spinach (about 1 pound/450 grams), cleaned, trimmed, and roughly chopped

Juice of 1 lemon

1. Preheat the oven to 375 degrees and brush two baking sheets liberally with 3 tablespoons of the oil. Slice the tops and bottoms off the eggplants, then slice into ½-inch-thick rounds and arrange on a single layer on the baking sheets. Brush the rounds generously with some of the oil, sprinkle with a little salt, then bake for 20 minutes, rotating the sheets halfway through. Let cool and then set aside.

2. Meanwhile, in a large, heavy-bottomed pot with a tight-fitting lid, warm the remaining oil over medium-high heat and sauté the onion and garlic until the onion is soft and beginning to brown, about 15 minutes. Remove to a plate and set aside.

3. Sprinkle the chicken pieces with some of the salt, cubeb or allspice, and turmeric. Then add to the pot, in batches if necessary, and brown on all sides, removing when finished browning.

4. Arrange the eggplant slices on the bottom of the pot, cover with the onions and garlic, add more salt, cubeb or allspice, and turmeric, then top with the chicken mixture and about a cup of chicken stock or water and the dried lime, if using. (You may want to add a little more liquid.) Bring to a simmer, then lower the heat to medium-low and cover the pot. Cook for about 30 minutes, then remove from the heat and allow everything to cool before refrigerating overnight.

5. The next day, skim off and discard the layer of fat from the top of the stew. Then add the Swiss chard or spinach to the pot, bring to a boil, cover tightly, and simmer slowly for about 30 minutes, or until the chicken is cooked through.

6. Fish out the lime if used and discard, and arrange the chicken pieces on a platter surrounded by the vegetables. Squeeze the lemon juice over all and serve.

Note You can make the dish in one day but I prefer to make the chicken a day ahead, then refrigerate overnight and remove the layer of fat that rises to the top and reheat with the vegetables to serve.

If you want more heat in this dish, add a little hot paprika or cayenne.

Paprika

The spice of their food is some sort of red beast called paprika—it certainly bites like the devil.
—nineteenth-century Hungarian priest

Among the trendy ingredients chefs are adding to their repertoires to enliven their menus, paprika—the spice made of dried and ground red chili peppers—is the latest darling.

My quest to learn more about this sudden spice starlet, found in cultures the world over, started at an Israeli *moshav* (a type of agricultural settlement), in a poppy-red field flush with chili peppers—a rich contrast to the tall drab tower blocks of Ashdod in the background.

My first impression while standing in this sea of paprika was of color, not aroma. Nearby, an American-made John Deere combine plucked the fruit from the plants, which resemble Anaheim chilies from California in size and shape.

Capsicum is the Latin name for the genus of chili peppers—of which there are five taxonomic varieties: *annuum, baccatum, chinense, pubescens,* and *frutescens*. Originating in Latin America, they were brought back to Spain by Christopher Columbus and Hernán Cortés. The species produces fruits that vary in size, shape, appearance, and pungency, but they all grow on plants that are about three feet tall. Chilies range in length from one-half to eleven inches and

can be long or round, thick- or thin-fleshed. In general, tiny ones have more heat and larger ones more color, although farmers and gardeners are breeding new varieties that break these rules.

After a short drive from the fields to the Negev Spices factory, I watched the industrial production of sweet paprika. To my surprise, the entire process—from picking, to bringing the picked peppers to the nearby factory, to mechanically stemming, washing and drying, milling, and placing in barrels in cold storage—takes only five hours, which, assisted by the hot desert climate of the Negev, thus minimizes mold. If I couldn't smell the peppers in the field, their fruity, vegetal smell permeated the factory as they were processed into the spice.

Thousands of years ago, not far from the Negev Spices factory, King Solomon built his Temple in Jerusalem and sent scouts to search the then-known world by ship and by camel caravan for spices like cinnamon, cardamom, cassia, and black pepper from the East Indies. These were used for their smell, taste, and health benefits, such as helping male potency.

But as soon as explorers made it to the New World, a search was on, one for heat and bright red color from these new "Indian" peppers, as Diego Álvarez Chanca—Christopher Columbus's ship physician—called them in a letter to a friend in 1484.

By 1650 this "Indian" pepper had journeyed with the Columbian Exchange to Spain, then Turkey and Hungary. Traders, many of them Jews, who moved to Ottoman Turkey because of the Inquisition, started introducing merchants and farmers to peppers, tomatoes, and potatoes. Eventually the peppers reached Central Europe via the Balkans, which were under Ottoman rule. Soon they were being harvested in places like the Danube valley of Bulgaria and Hungary as well as Spain and Turkey.

By the nineteenth century, New World peppers were fully integrated into the cooking of the Old World: *pimentón* in Spain, paprika in Hungary, and red pepper in Turkey and North Africa. (Kalocsa, which had a Jewish population who traded in spices until World War II, is famous for its paprika festival in September.) After the Industrial Revolution, the long process of turning pepper to paprika became mechanized, and Szeged became the capital of Hungarian paprika production. The taste for paprika spread like wildfire across Central Europe. When the Jews of Central Europe, of which there were a total of about one million then, came to New York from the Austro-Hungarian Empire during this period, they brought with them, along with their brass candlesticks and mortars and pestles, sacks of red tins of Paprikas Weiss or Szeged Paprika to flavor and color their goulashes, chicken, and salads.

Many Hungarians and Hungarian Jews settled in the Yorkville section of New York City, introducing Americans to the delights of chicken *paprikash*, goulash, and cucumber salads sprinkled with paprika.

Hungarian immigrants also went to Israel when the state was founded, bringing with them paprika seeds so they could still taste the foods of their childhood, such as *leczo*, the Hungarian equivalent of *shakshuka*.

Today paprika is a big crop in Israel, the first country to use a mechanical harvest and one of the first to prohibit the growing of Monsanto seeds; most of Israel's production goes to Europe, where choosy consumers disdain genetically modified crops. Because of the dry, hot climate, good soil, and Israeli drip technology, Israel is particularly productive at growing peppers.

When I left Israel, I carried a big bag of paprika back to Washington, where at my first opportunity I made, what else, chicken *paprikash*.

Chicken *Paprikash* with Dumplings

I found this particular recipe for chicken *paprikash* in a 1960 *New York Times* article about Isadore Weiss, the founder of Paprikas Weiss, a Hungarian store in Manhattan and brand of paprika that both ceased to exist in the 1990s. Homey and delicious, the dish is best served with dumplings.

---

1. Pat dry the chicken pieces with paper towels.

2. Heat the oil or chicken fat in a Dutch oven or a heavy frying pan and sauté the onions for a few minutes until soft. Add the chicken pieces, then raise the heat to medium-high and cook until they are golden brown on all sides, about 10 minutes. Sprinkle with the salt and stir in the sweet and hot paprikas as well as the green pepper.

3. In a small saucepan, heat 1 cup of the chicken broth or water and stir in the tomato paste. Bring to a boil, stirring until the tomato paste dissolves. Then pour over the chicken. Simmer covered over medium-low heat for about 40 minutes, stirring occasionally.

4. **to make the dumplings** Mix the flour with eggs and salt in a medium bowl until a thick dough forms. In a saucepan, bring 4 cups (1 liter) broth or water to a boil. Drop the dumpling dough into the liquid by half teaspoons, simmering for about 4 minutes. The dumplings are done when they plump up and become firm, about 3 to 5 minutes.

5. Drain the dumplings and stir them into the chicken mixture during the last 5 minutes of cooking. Sprinkle with parsley, and serve.

yield: 4 to 6 servings

One 4-pound (1⅘-kilo) chicken, cut into 8 pieces

¼ cup (60 ml) olive oil or chicken fat

2 large onions, chopped fine

1 teaspoon salt or to taste

1 tablespoon sweet paprika

¼ teaspoon hot paprika or to taste

1 green bell pepper, cut in large dice

1 cup (235 ml) chicken broth or water

1 tablespoon tomato paste

DUMPLINGS

6 to 8 tablespoons (42 to 72 grams) flour

2 large eggs

¼ teaspoon salt

4 cups (1 liter) chicken broth or water

2 tablespoons parsley, chopped

Fessenjan, Persian Walnut and Pomegranate Chicken Stew

In Los Angeles's vast Persian community, Farrokh Maddahi is known as the "champion" of *fessenjan,* a traditional chicken-and-walnut stew considered the crown jewel of Persian cooking. Likely named for an old Persian town called Fisinjan, the dish—a delightful combination of sweet, savory, and tart that blends pomegranates, onions, and turmeric—is one of the glories of the old Silk Road.

Farrokh comes from Tehran and traces her roots to the Jews who were exiled to Babylon with the destruction of the First Temple. After settling in Babylon, many of these Jews set off for the Persian Empire, following the trade roads, where they encountered the key ingredients of *fessenjan.* Walnuts are the basis for the sauce, adding a little crunch; the Jewish version adds apricots and dates to sweeten it up and balance the tartness of the pomegranate molasses.

Persians don't care that *fessenjan* often looks "muddy," but I like to add a bit of color and serve the stew over rice, sprinkled with bright red pomegranate seeds and fresh green herbs. Traditionally, a platter of assorted herbs, called *sabzi khordan,* is served with Persian meals such as this; instead, I incorporate the herbs into my favorite everyday salad (see page 92). As the Iranians say when making this dish, *nosh-e jan*—enjoy!

---

yield: 6 to 8 servings

One 3- or 4-pound (1⅓ or 1⅘-kilo) chicken

1 medium onion, peeled and quartered

1 teaspoon sea salt, plus more to taste

½ teaspoon freshly ground black pepper, plus more to taste

1 teaspoon ground turmeric

4 cups (385 grams or ⅘ pound) walnuts, coarsely ground in a food processor

3 cups (¾ liter) pomegranate juice

3 tablespoons (45 ml) pomegranate molasses, or to taste

1 cup (190 grams) plus 2 tablespoons dates, pitted and roughly chopped

½ cup (83 grams) dried apricots, roughly chopped

1 to 2 tablespoons date jam or sugar, or to taste (optional)

Chopped cilantro, to garnish

Pomegranate seeds, to garnish

1. Put the chicken in a large pot and pour water over until almost covered, about 8 to 9 cups (about 2 liters). Add the quartered onion, 1 teaspoon of the salt, the black pepper, and the turmeric, then bring to a boil over medium-high heat. Cover the pot and reduce the heat to a simmer, then cook the chicken until done, about 40 minutes.

2. Use tongs to remove the chicken from the pot and let it cool on a plate. Strain the broth into a large bowl and discard the onion pieces. You should have about 8 cups of broth. Once the chicken is cool enough to handle, use a fork and knife or your clean fingers to remove and discard the skin, then tear off bite-size pieces of chicken, putting the chicken pieces back into the empty pot. Discard the bones.

3. Add the ground walnuts, pomegranate juice, pomegranate molasses, dates, apricots, and more salt and pepper to taste to the chicken, then stir in 2 cups of the reserved chicken broth. Bring to a simmer over medium-high heat, then lower the heat and cook, covered, for 1 hour, stirring occasionally and adding more broth as necessary to prevent sticking. Taste and add more pomegranate molasses and/or the date jam or sugar to reach the desired balance of sweet and tart. (Refrigerate or freeze any remaining broth for another use.)

4. Serve over rice, sprinkled with cilantro and pomegranate seeds, if you like.

Indian Chicken with Cardamom, Cumin, and Cilantro

yield: 4 to 6 servings

I visited Queenie Hallegua, the doyenne of the now tiny Jewish community of about eight people in Kochi's Jew Town. A port city, Kochi was built in 1341 c.e. and many of the Jewish spice merchants migrated there from Iraq and then Spain after the Inquisition.

As I sipped Queenie's pungent Passover wine, which she makes from boiled raisins blended with water, she told me how much fun it was being Jewish growing up in a country that loves all kinds of religious ceremonies. When Queenie was a child, there were several thousand Jews in the area.

"Pesach work began in January when we bought rice, cleaned and washed it, pounding some into rice flour," Queenie told me in her clipped Indian British accent. "We also cleaned chilies, coriander, cinnamon, pepper, ginger, and cardamom and set some aside for Passover." Later, the spices, which had been harvested in December and January, were dried in the sun for two or three days, before being roasted and ground for use.

"In the olden days, we made our own matzo," she said. "We pounded the wheat collected in fields and people gathered to cook it on a grill over a wood fire in our courtyard—sometimes in one-hundred-degree heat." For *haroset,* she still boils down dates to the texture of honey in a copper cauldron. This date jam, called *duvo* here or *halak* by Iraqi Jews, eaten topped with chopped cashews, walnuts, or almonds, was used as honey in biblical times.

"Today Passover comes and goes without much fuss," Queenie told me. Now she can find prepared date jam and machine-made matzos that come from Israel through the consulate in Mumbai.

A day later, I visited Queenie's synagogue, where she once had the fortune to meet Queen Elizabeth. Taking my shoes off, I walked on the blue tiles and enjoyed the beauty of the Paradesi ("foreigner") Synagogue of the Sephardic Jews, built in 1568. Queenie told me that the original synagogue was built in the fourth century in Kodungallur (Cranganore) when the Jews had a mercantile role in the South Indian region (now called Kerala) along the Malabar coast. When the community moved to Kochi in the fourteenth century, it built a new synagogue.

Usually, Queenie buys kosher chicken from Bangalore. Otherwise, she uses one of the two local *shochets* still operating in Kochi. She seasons her chicken with cardamom, cumin, and cilantro; I have added a fresh masala to her dry one, to liven up and add some color to this already delicious recipe that now tastes more Indian than Iraqi.

1. Heat a frying pan over medium heat. Toast the cardamom seeds, cloves, peppercorns or pepper, coriander seeds, cinnamon stick, anise seeds, and cumin seeds for about 5 or 6 minutes, stirring often, until they start to pop. Immediately remove them from the pan and grind them in a small blender or mortar and pestle with the nutmeg, turmeric, and salt. Rub into the chicken and let rest in the refrigerator for a few hours or overnight.

2. In a Dutch oven, sauté the onions for a few minutes in about 2 tablespoons of oil over medium heat until golden. Add the chicken, tomatoes, curry leaves, if using, ½ cup (120 ml) water, and the white vinegar. Bring to a boil, reduce to a simmer, and cook, covered, for about 20 minutes, or until the chicken is soft and cooked through.

3. In a food processor, blend the ginger, garlic, cilantro, mint leaves, and 2 of the chilies. Taste and add more chilies to taste. Add to the chicken and simmer for another 5 minutes. Serve over rice.

Seeds from 4 cardamom pods

6 cloves

6 black peppercorns or 1 teaspoon ground black pepper

3 heaping tablespoons coriander seeds

One 2-inch Ceylon cinnamon stick (see page 5)

½ teaspoon anise seeds

1 teaspoon cumin seeds

½ teaspoon ground nutmeg

½ teaspoon ground turmeric

½ teaspoon salt

3 large onions, diced in large chunks

2 to 3 tablespoons vegetable oil

3 pounds (1⅓ kilos) (about 6 to 8) boneless skinless chicken thighs

3 tomatoes, roughly chopped

4 to 5 curry leaves (optional)

2 tablespoons white vinegar

2-inch piece of fresh ginger

4 to 5 cloves garlic

½ bunch (about 1 cup) cilantro leaves, chopped

¼ bunch mint leaves (about ½ cup), chopped

2 to 3 fresh green chilies, minced

Syrian-Mexican Chicken with Apricot, Tamarind, and Chipotle Sauce

One should not neglect spicing [chickens] with cinnamon bark, mastic, and nard to prevent any harm to the stomach. Those prepared with tamarind and sugar, and those prepared with purslane seeds and sugar, should not be used except in the summer, while those prepared with rose preserves are better in the winter. The one prepared with pistachio and sugar ought to have a little lemon juice added to it.
—Moses Maimonides, *Regimen of Health*, twelfth century

Flora Cohen's family of so-called "Arabian" Jews moved to Mexico from Guatemala and before that Syria, founding the first synagogue in Mexico City at the turn of the last century. In Mexico, she gave cooking classes to young brides.

Flora used ingredients like tamarind, already rooted and used in Mexico, and apricots, which were new and exciting for these women. One of her students, TV personality and cookbook author Pati Jinich, eventually added the chipotle pepper that she found in Mexico to this recipe.

———————————

1. Season the chicken pieces well with salt and pepper. Put a large, heavy skillet over high heat and add the oil. Add the chicken pieces skin side down in a single layer, then reduce the heat to medium and slowly brown, turning occasionally, until browned evenly on all sides.

2. Pour 4 cups (940 ml) of water over the chicken, raise the heat to medium-high, and bring to a simmer. Stir in the dried apricots, apricot preserves, tamarind, sugar, and chipotle sauce, including 1 or more chipotle peppers for more heat, if desired.

3. Simmer uncovered, adjusting heat as necessary, until the sauce has thickened and the chicken is cooked through, about 30 minutes. Adjust salt and pepper to taste, and serve.

yield: 6 to 8 servings

One 4- to 5-pound (1⅘- to 2⅓-kilo) chicken, cut into 8 pieces

1 teaspoon kosher or sea salt, or to taste

½ teaspoon freshly ground black pepper, or to taste

½ cup (120 ml) vegetable oil

¾ cup (142.5 grams) dried apricots, roughly chopped

3 tablespoons apricot preserves

3 tablespoons tamarind concentrate

¼ cup (50 grams) sugar

2 tablespoons sauce from canned chipotles in adobo sauce

1 or more chipotle peppers from a can of chipotles in adobo sauce (optional)

Gondi Kashi, Rice with Turkey, Beets, Fava Beans, and Herbs

yield: at least 8 servings

I met Tannaz Sassooni, an animation software engineer and food blogger whose family hails from Iran, at a dinner at my daughter Daniela's home in Los Angeles.

When I was next in L.A., Tannaz invited me to visit her parents' home in Encino to taste *gondi kashi,* a rice dish her mother makes that, Tannaz claims, is unlike any other.

When I arrived at the house, a plate of walnuts—soaked in water and kept cold with ice—welcomed me, as did chunks of pumpkin preserves spiked with cardamom and perfumed with rose water, and carrot and orange peel candy, similar to the eastern European *eingemachts*. These were served with tea made from carrots, all of which had to be tasted before we started our cooking lesson.

Like so many Iranian Jews in L.A. (by some estimates, there are about forty thousand), Violet Sassooni and her children came in 1979 after the fall of the shah, with Tannaz's father, Saeed, a chemical engineer in Tehran, following later. All Tannaz's grandparents came from Kashan, a city in the province of Isfahan known for its velvet and carpets. Violet, nicknamed Dokhi, which means "little girl," so called as she was the youngest of six, showed me a piece of carpet that her mother had made, with a design woven on both sides. The family traces their links to Persia to at least the fifteenth century, when many Jews came there from Spain.

It used to be that relatives visiting from Tehran would fill their suitcases with spices and dried vegetables. These days, no one has to do that. Most Persian herbs and vegetables have been smuggled through Turkey to the United States and Israel, where they are grown today.

Filled with spices, herbs, meat, beets, and fava beans, *gondi kashi* must have originally been an early spring dish, perhaps for Passover, when fava beans are in season and greens like radishes, spring onions, mint, and tarragon are available.

Gondi kashi is best eaten with *sabzi khordan,* sprigs of fresh herbs. This marvelous Iranian accompaniment can be anything from basil, tarragon, and mint, to parsley, cilantro, chives, and tarragon, along with radishes and spring onions. It reminds me of the Vietnamese equivalent of fresh basil, cilantro, mint, bean sprouts, and lime wedges. Dokhi always has these fresh herbs on hand, but she sometimes uses fresh frozen herbs, purchased at Iranian grocery stores, in the cooked dish.

As we dipped our forks into the perfectly cooked rice, each grain separate and capturing the flavor of all the herbs and meat, Dokhi said, "*Nooshe jan*" ("May your soul enjoy it").

A few days after trying *gondi kashi,* I went to Sqirl, a popular restaurant in L.A.'s Silver Lake neighborhood, with Jonathan Gold, the *Los Angeles Times* restaurant critic. He insisted that I taste a bowl of short-grained rice with herbs and served with a little preserved lemon and a poached egg. The taste reminded me of *gondi kashi,* so I told Jessica Koslow, the owner and chef, about the dish. She wanted to try it immediately. "Those are all my favorite flavors," she said. Inspired by Sqirl, now I too add a little preserved lemon to give my *gondi kashi* a kick.

———

1. Cover the rice in water and soak for a minute, then drain. Repeat the process two times more and set aside.

2. Bring 5½ cups (1⅓ liters) water and the sliced beets to a boil in a heavy large pot.

3. Using your hands, mix the turkey, rice, salt, grated onion, dill, fenugreek, chives, tarragon, basil, and savory very well, breaking up the lumps. Then put them in the pot with the favas, turmeric, pepper, and grapeseed oil and return to a boil.

4. Cover the pot, then lower the heat, and simmer for about 45 minutes, or until the rice is tender and fluffy. Serve accompanied by *sabzi khordan,* an assortment of fresh herbs.

Note You can find fresh fenugreek at Persian, Indian, or sometimes Korean stores. And, if you cannot find one ingredient, don't worry—the dish will still be loaded with flavor.

Vegetarians can substitute the meat with a poached egg on top for protein, but please keep those marvelous fresh vegetables intact.

3 cups (600 grams) basmati rice

3 to 4 small beets (about 12 ounces/350 grams), peeled and sliced thin

1 pound (453 grams) ground turkey, preferably dark meat

1 tablespoon kosher salt, or to taste

1 small onion, grated

1 bunch fresh dill, coarsely chopped

1 bunch fresh fenugreek, coarsely chopped, or ¼ cup dried

1 bunch Persian or regular chives, coarsely chopped

1 bunch fresh tarragon, coarsely chopped

1 bunch fresh basil, coarsely chopped

1 bunch fresh savory, coarsely chopped

2 cups (252 grams) fresh or frozen fava beans, peeled

1 teaspoon turmeric

1½ teaspoons black pepper

1 cup (235 ml) grape-seed oil

½ preserved lemon for garnish (optional) (see page 11)

Hungarian Stuffed Chicken

In the early 1970s, when I lived in Jerusalem, I frequented Leah Brumer's Hungarian restaurant, one of the few at the time that served homey Hungarian cuisine, something I really relished. I have never forgotten Leah nor her stuffed chicken, a crispy, flavorful dish.

On their arms, Leah and her employees bore numbers from the Nazi concentration camps. In the restaurant, they spoke Hungarian and served a very limited but delicious menu of the few dishes of their past that, like this chicken, were traditionally eaten all year long, and especially at Passover, stuffed with matzo.

———————

1. Sauté the finely chopped onion in about 2 tablespoons of the chicken fat or olive oil for a few minutes, until the onions are golden brown. Then add the chicken livers, if using, and the mushrooms, and sauté for a few minutes.

2. Mix the bread or matzo, egg, and parsley with the onions and mushrooms in a bowl. Add salt and pepper to taste, as well as 1 teaspoon of each paprika. Let the stuffing set for a few hours in the refrigerator.

3. Preheat the oven to 375 degrees and rub a little schmaltz or oil into a 9-by-13-inch baking pan.

4. With your fingers, carefully push the stuffing mixture underneath the chicken skin. Brush the skin with schmaltz or oil, sprinkle the top with salt and the remaining hot and sweet paprika, and put the chicken into the prepared pan. Scatter the tomato pieces, coarsely chopped onion, green pepper, celery, and garlic around the chicken. Then pour the wine over all. Roast, uncovered, in the oven for about an hour and a half, covering the chicken with foil if the skin browns too quickly.

Note If you prefer using a cut-up chicken, then stuff the breast, the leg, and the thigh and bake stuffed side up.

yield: 6 to 8 servings

2 medium onions, 1 finely chopped and the other coarsely chopped

⅓ cup (79 ml) schmaltz (rendered chicken fat) or olive oil, divided

2 chicken livers (3 ounces/84 grams), finely chopped (optional)

8 ounces (226 grams) mushrooms, stems removed and chopped

3 slices white bread or 3 matzos, dampened slightly in water and squeezed dry

1 large egg, slightly beaten

4 tablespoons chopped fresh parsley

Salt and freshly ground black pepper to taste

1½ teaspoons hot paprika, divided

1½ teaspoons sweet paprika, divided

1 large 7- to 8-pound (3⅕- to 3⅗-kilo) roasting chicken

1 tomato, coarsely chopped

1 green pepper, coarsely chopped

1 celery stalk, roughly chopped

2 cloves garlic, minced

1 cup (240 ml) white wine

Double-Lemon Roast Chicken

Wherever I am, comfort food is roast chicken. Like many people, I learned from Julia Child. As I travel the world I have added to and subtracted from the dish. Now I pop one of my preserved lemons (see page 11) into the belly of the chicken, season it with fresh herbs, *za'atar,* and sumac, and scatter carrots, celery, zucchini, black olives, and sun-dried or fresh tomatoes around for an easy, beautiful, and—most important—delicious and colorful one-pot meal. I used to serve the chicken whole, but now I cut it up and surround it with the vegetables and sprinkle everything with the preserved lemon from the cavity. For Passover, I use artichokes with the chicken as one of my main courses at the Seder.

———————

1. Season the chicken with salt and pepper, *za'atar* if you like, and sumac. Then rub the outside with the olive oil.

2. Put the chicken in a 9-by-13-inch baking pan. Fill the cavity with half the preserved lemon, 2 garlic cloves, and a sprig each of the thyme, rosemary, and sage. Cut up the remaining preserved lemon and scatter it with the remaining cloves of garlic, the onion, and the rest of the thyme, rosemary, and sage, as well as the regular lemon slices, around the chicken. Add enough wine just to let the chicken sit in the liquid. You can do this the night before and cover with tin foil in your refrigerator.

3. When ready to cook, remove the chicken from the refrigerator for about a half hour to return to room temperature. Here is where you can be creative. Add cut-up celery, carrots, zucchini, and/or fennel, Brussels sprouts, black olives, and sun-dried or fresh tomatoes, or leave as is.

4. Preheat the oven to 375 degrees, then roast the chicken until it is golden brown and crispy, about an hour and 15 minutes, or until the internal temperature says 160.

5. Cut the chicken into roughly 8 pieces, place them on a platter, spoon the vegetables and juices with the preserved lemon and lemon slices over and around the chicken, and serve.

yield: 6 to 8 servings

1 whole 4-pound (1⅘-kilo) chicken

Salt and freshly ground pepper to taste

1 to 2 tablespoons *za'atar* (optional)

1 teaspoon sumac

2 tablespoons olive oil

1 preserved lemon, divided

5 cloves garlic, peeled

Handful of fresh thyme sprigs, divided

Handful of rosemary sprigs, divided

Handful of sage leaves, divided

1 onion, cut into roughly 8 pieces

2 lemons, cut widthwise in thin circles

¾ cup (175 ml) white wine

1 celery stalk, 1 carrot, peeled, 1 fennel bulb, and/or 1 zucchini, all chopped into 2-inch pieces, or a handful of Brussels sprouts, black olives, and sun-dried tomatoes or a fresh tomato, cut up

Roast Turkey with Challah-Chestnut-Cranberry Stuffing

Thanksgiving's festive meal, to me, is a symbol of how Americans can celebrate our unity while still honoring our amazing diversity. Most everyone makes turkey, the North American bird, but the way you make it, what kind of stuffing you use, and which side dishes go with it say who you are. We all celebrate as Americans, but we can put our own ethnic, religious, and regional touches on the meal, whether we serve our turkey with Vietnamese spring rolls or Armenian stuffed grape leaves, tortillas or chopped liver.

Though the turkey is the holiday's commonality, its provenance tells us different stories. Turkeys today can be heritage breed, kosher, organic, fresh, pasture raised, wild, or frozen Butterballs, the favorite of the late Julia Child. That range of choices is a relatively recent development; until the early 1990s almost everybody bought a frozen factory-processed turkey.

A while ago, I spent a day on the tractor with Joel Salatin, immortalized by Michael Pollan in *The Omnivore's Dilemma,* at his family's Polyface farm, in Virginia's Shenandoah Valley. Salatin, a fundamentalist Christian, raises two kinds of free-range turkeys in his pasture and slaughters them humanely with a quick cut across the neck, "in the biblical way," he explains—that is, according to Jewish dietary laws.

Across the country, more and more people are turning to farmers like Salatin, who thinks hard about the life and the death of his animals. Kosher producers like the relatively new (opened in 2010) Grow and Behold Foods are following Salatin's lead. "I feel like a turkey hunter before Thanksgiving," Naftali Hanau, Grow and Behold's CEO and founder, told me. "Thanksgiving is a time when many people who don't generally eat meat indulge," Hanau says, "and when they do, they want birds that are sustainably produced and slaughtered humanely."

Over the years, by trial and error, I've learned a few things about turkey and roasting them: A quick brine is as good as a long one. Kosher turkey is already brined with salt in the koshering process, so it's easy to prepare once you pluck off any lingering feathers; I brine kosher birds too, but use less salt. If you don't use kosher turkey, you can just rub a teaspoon of salt per pound of turkey into the skin, then leave it loosely covered in the refrigerator for about two hours. The brine will quickly permeate the skin. And finally, as long as you put the turkey on a turkey rack and add lots of herbs, onions, and wine on the bottom, the turkey will be aromatic and delicious. Just make sure the skin is crisp and golden, since, as everyone in my family knows, this is the best part of the bird.

———————

yield: 10 to 12 servings with lots of leftovers. After all, what would Thanksgiving be without the leftovers!

Challah-Chestnut-Cranberry Stuffing (see page 270)

One 20- to 22-pound (9- to 10-kilo) turkey

¾ to 1 cup (135 to 180 grams) kosher salt, depending on the size of the turkey

5 cloves garlic, mashed

3 sprigs of thyme, divided

2 tablespoons extra-virgin olive oil, plus extra to grease the pan

½ teaspoon freshly ground black pepper

½ teaspoon paprika

2 large onions

2 celery stalks with leaves, roughly chopped

A few sprigs of rosemary

A few sprigs of sage

1 cup (235 ml) white wine or apple cider

1. Clean the turkey, remove the gizzards, and set them aside.

2. Rub the salt and garlic into the turkey, reducing to ¼ cup (60 ml) if using a kosher turkey, and allow the bird to air-dry in the roasting pan in the refrigerator for an hour or so before preparing for cooking. Put half of the thyme and any remaining garlic around the turkey.

3. Preheat the oven to 450 degrees and grease a roasting pan.

4 Spoon the stuffing in the front and back cavities of the turkey and tie its legs together. Place the turkey, breast side up, on a rack in the roasting pan. Brush 2 tablespoons of oil over the turkey and sprinkle the black pepper and paprika on the bird for color.

5. Cut the onions into eighths and scatter them with the celery, the saved giblets, rosemary, sage, and remaining thyme around the turkey. Pour the wine or cider over the vegetables.

6. Bake in the oven for 15 minutes. Then drop the temperature to 350 degrees, basting with the juices from the bird and vegetables about every hour, adding water if necessary. Make sure the turkey isn't browning too quickly. If it is, tent the turkey loosely with aluminum foil. You should figure 15 minutes of cooking time per pound of turkey.

7. Remove the tent for the last half hour of cooking. Approximately 30 minutes before the turkey is done, baste it every 10 minutes with the wine, or cider, adding more liquid if needed. You will know the turkey is done when a thermometer inserted into the thigh reads 160 degrees.

8. Remove the turkey from the oven and put on a serving platter. Baste again with the juices. Rest for at least 20 minutes and up to an hour.

9. Meanwhile, put the vegetables in a serving dish and put the pan on top of the stove and heat, stirring up the browned bits at the bottom, adding wine or water to deglaze as necessary. Stir until the mixture thickens. Pour gravy into a tall vessel that allows the fat to rise to the top and remove as much of the fat as you deem necessary.

Challah-Chestnut-Cranberry Stuffing

I don't care what the present thinking is, I love my stuffing cooked in the turkey. It is more moist and just more delicious. I take leftover bread, preferably challah, stored in the freezer, cube it and toast it; I have even been known to use commercial stuffing. Then I add chestnuts, dried cranberries soaked in rum, a few vegetables, and chicken or vegetable stock (depending on how many vegetarians we have at our Thanksgiving dinner). After the bird is stuffed, with leftover stuffing in a bowl to bake later, I can breathe a sigh of relief.

2 tablespoons olive oil

2 medium onions, roughly chopped

4 stalks celery, with leaves, chopped

Leaves from 1 sprig thyme

Leaves from 1 sprig rosemary

2 cups chestnuts, cooked, peeled, and cut in half, or jarred

1 cup dried cranberries, soaked in rum to cover for 30 minutes

Salt and freshly ground black pepper to taste

½ loaf challah or other brioche-like bread, cubed and toasted (about 4 cups/960 grams)

1 cup (235 ml) chicken or vegetable broth

1. Warm the oil in a large sauté pan over medium-high heat. Add the onions, celery, thyme, and rosemary and sauté until the onions are golden, begin to soften, and are translucent, about 5 to 10 minutes.

2. Add the chestnuts, dried cranberries and their liquid, and salt and pepper to taste. Remove to a bowl and stir in the challah.

3. Stir the broth into the mixture and set aside while you prepare the turkey.

Meat

Lubia bel-Saeilk, Libyan Lamb or Beef Stew with White Beans and Spinach

Salyanka, Georgian Beef Stew with Red Peppers

Roman *Stracotto,* Beef Stew with Tomatoes, Wine, and Vegetables

Hamim-Cholent Hybrid, Wandering Sabbath Stew

Iraqi False *Mahshi:* Layered Swiss Chard, Beets, and Meat

Bukharan *Plov* with Beef, Carrots, and Cumin Seeds

Kiftes de Prasa, Macedonian Leek and Meat Patties

Keftes Garaz, Syrian Meatballs with Cherries and Tamarind

Pastel di Carne con Massa Fina, Bulgarian Eggplant and Meat Pie

Tagliolini colla Crosta, Crusty Pasta with a Bolognese Sauce

Moroccan Lamb Shanks with Caramelized Onions and *Tanzeya*
(Dried Fruit Sauce)

Slow-Cooked Brisket with Red Wine, Vinegar, and Mustard

Braised Short Ribs with Almonds, Dried Plums, and Star Anise

Home-Cured Corned Beef

Lubia bel-Saeilk, Libyan Lamb or Beef Stew with White Beans and Spinach

When you ask Hamos Guetta how to spell his first name, he will tell you a story about life in his native Tripoli. Shortly after he was born, his mother told an old woman that he was the third son in a row, and the woman made a funny sign. Thinking the old woman was casting a curse on the baby, his mother called him Hamos, instead of Amos (which means "strong" in Hebrew), adding an "h" (the Hebrew letter *het*), the sign for life, to protect him from evil spirits.

After that, he will tell you that one of his earliest memories is of his mother standing him on a chair. She was showing him how to roll meatballs to tuck into potatoes for a dish called *mafroom,* a Friday must for Libyan Jews. (See my *Foods of Israel Today.*)

Hamos, a charming man in his early fifties, moved to Rome after the 1967 Arab-Israeli war, as did 2,500 other Jews fleeing Libya. The remaining Jewish population went to Israel. Thus ended the two-thousand-year history of the Jews in Libya, where at one time there were about 45,000 Jews and forty-four synagogues throughout the country. Today there are none. The main synagogue in Tripoli has been turned into a mosque.

On a recent trip to Rome, Hamos invited me to his apartment for Shabbat dinner. Three of his four daughters were there as well as Smadar, his wife, who comes from the north of Israel. Because Smadar does not know how to cook Libyan food, Hamos, a fashion designer by day, has been videotaping and recording Libyan and Roman Jewish cooks in his spare time. (You can find his videos on YouTube or through his site, www.italiaebraica.it.)

As soon as we sat down, Hamos brought out nibbles for us—chopped fennel, apple, carrots, and cucumber—all dressed with salt and lemon, *bottarga,* the Mediterranean caviar made out of dried mullet roe, *ka'ak,* savory crackers like a tiny bagel (see page 159), and home-cured olives from trees he brought back from Puglia and planted near his clothing factory outside Rome.

When we moved to the table, the candles were already lit for the Sabbath, as the sun had set before we arrived for dinner at 8:30 p.m. Hamos held up a kiddush cup and chanted the prayers, pouring a little wine into our empty cups, then giving his own cup to his daughters to have a sip.

Before saying the blessing over the challah, he lifted two loaves, held bottom to bottom, and blessed them. Then he tore morsels off one of the breads and tossed the pieces to all the guests, a tradition that originated in Baghdad.

Delighted, we all sat down and sampled the delicacies of the Libyan Jews. The first dish was *aharaimi* (see page 221), a piece of grouper bathed in a hot sauce, a dish so good that it has become part of the lexicon of Israeli cooking. Hamos also

yield: 8 to 10 servings

1 pound (453 grams) dry cannellini beans

2 pounds (907 grams) spinach, beet greens, Swiss chard, or a mixture, divided

½ to ¾ cup (110 to 175 ml) olive oil

8 cloves garlic, finely chopped

2 medium onions, chopped

2 pounds (907 grams) lamb shoulder or beef round, cut into 2-inch pieces

½ bunch cilantro, chopped, divided

½ teaspoon ground turmeric

1 teaspoon salt, or to taste

½ teaspoon freshly ground pepper, or to taste

shared another, less spicy dish of chicken livers and a slightly pungent sauce. The main course was couscous with *mafroom*. Accompanying it was a cooked squash and *matbucha,* a pepper and tomato salad, and *lubia bel-saeilk,* the stunning stew of white beans, spinach, and meat, similar to the Tunisian *p'kila,* made with burnt chard or spinach and cooked for hours with dried beans, hard-boiled eggs, potatoes, and meat.

For this Libyan Jewish dish, the greens are first steamed, then sautéed in olive oil with onions and garlic until they turn almost black and even burn a little. They are used as a flavor base to stew the beans and meat.

When making this dish, many Libyans and Tunisians use white beans brought from the New World, rather than the more traditional fava beans or chickpeas that have been in the area for much longer.

Note that you need to soak the beans overnight before making the recipe.

———————

1. Rinse the beans and remove any stones. Put the beans in a large bowl and cover with water by 2 inches. Soak overnight.

2. Wash the spinach, Swiss chard, or beet greens, and pat with a towel to absorb excess water, but do not dry completely. Chop the spinach coarsely, put half in a large nonstick pan, and cook over medium-high heat, stirring occasionally, until it wilts and reduces, about 5 minutes. Add the rest of the greens and continue cooking until all the spinach wilts and the water is mostly evaporated, about another 20 minutes.

3. Add ½ cup (100 ml) olive oil and continue cooking over medium-high heat, stirring occasionally, until the spinach is blackened and beginning to smell burnt, about 15 to 20 minutes. You want the flavor of the burnt spinach for the sauce.

4. Remove the pan from the heat and pulse the spinach in a food processor, adding a little oil if necessary to form a smooth paste.

5. Pour the green purée into a heavy-bottomed pot. Add the garlic and onions and sauté until the onions begin to soften, about 5 minutes.

6. Drain the beans, then add them to the pot along with the meat, all but 2 tablespoons of the cilantro, the turmeric, 1 teaspoon of salt, and ½ teaspoon freshly ground pepper. Add water to cover by a few inches (about 5 cups/1.175 liters) and bring to a boil. Lower to a simmer, cover, and cook for about 2½ hours or until the meat is tender. Season with more salt and pepper to taste. Sprinkle with the reserved cilantro and serve over rice or couscous.

Salyanka, Georgian Beef Stew with Red Peppers

As I first bit into this delicious Georgian beef stew, I was intrigued by the fact that, as with many early Jewish recipes I have found around the world, the beef, often a tough inexpensive cut, is first boiled in water until it is almost tender and then layered with flavor from onions, spices, and bright red bell peppers. No browning the meat first for this recipe! After slowly simmering the beef for a few hours, you are rewarded with a melt-in-your-mouth, silky stew—a perfect main dish for Passover or any special occasion throughout the year. And, as they say in Georgia, დმერთმა შეგარგოთ!—*ghmert`ma shegargos,* or *bon appétit!*

———————

1. Put the meat in a Dutch oven or similar heavy pot and cover with about 3 cups (705 ml) water. Bring to a boil, then lower the heat and simmer, uncovered, for 1 hour and 15 minutes or until almost tender, adding more water if necessary. You might have to periodically skim foam that accumulates on the top.

2. Add the red peppers and the tomatoes, stir, and cook uncovered for another 20 minutes.

3. Stir in the tomato paste, onions, and garlic, reduce the heat to low, cover, and cook for another 40 minutes to 1 hour, or until the beef is very tender and almost falling apart.

4. Season with salt, pepper, and hot and sweet paprika to taste and stir in half the parsley. Serve over rice or potatoes, sprinkled with the remaining parsley.

yield: 6 to 8 servings

2 pounds (907 grams) stewing beef, cut into 1½-inch chunks

2 large red bell peppers (about 1 pound/453 grams), cut into 1-inch squares

10 ounces (280 grams) high-quality canned plum tomatoes (or about 4 fresh plum tomatoes, peeled, crushed with your hands)

2 heaping tablespoons tomato paste

2 large onions, diced (2 cups/200 grams)

5 cloves garlic, minced (2 tablespoons)

Salt and freshly ground pepper to taste

½ teaspoon hot paprika, or to taste

½ teaspoon sweet paprika, or to taste

½ bunch parsley, chopped and divided

Roman *Stracotto,* Beef Stew with Tomatoes, Wine, and Vegetables

"We can't imagine the Italian kitchen without tomatoes," Paola Fano told me in her kitchen in Rome, where she was preparing *stracotto,* a very slowly cooked beef stew with tomatoes, wine, and vegetables, often served at lunch after synagogue by Italian Jews. Paola, who used beef muscle in her stew, set the timer for six hours. "This is one of those recipes," she told me, "that you do when you are home in your house all day." I've changed the recipe only a little, using a slightly more tender cut of meat that lets me reduce the cooking time to about two hours.

---

1. Warm the oil over medium-high heat in a heavy sauté pan. Add the onion and sauté for 3 to 4 minutes, until beginning to soften. Then add the garlic, carrot, and celery, lower the heat, and sauté for a few minutes more. Add the meat and a teaspoon of salt, or to taste, stirring occasionally to brown evenly, and cook for about 20 minutes, or until the water is released.

2. Add the red wine and simmer for 2 to 3 minutes, or until the wine evaporates. Add the tomato purée and cinnamon stick, then season to taste with the hot pepper.

3. Bring to a boil, then cover and simmer very, very slowly over low heat or in a 350-degree oven for about 2 hours. The sauce will turn brown and the meat should be completely tender, falling apart easily when pierced with a fork. Serve it over fettuccine.

yield: about 6 to 8 servings

3 tablespoons olive oil

1 cup diced onion
(from about 1 medium onion)

2 cloves garlic, diced

1 carrot, diced

1 stalk celery, diced

2 pounds (907 grams) chuck
or round roast, cut into
2-by-1-inch cubes

Salt to taste

1 cup (235 ml) dry red wine

4 cups tomato purée,
or one 28-ounce can tomatoes,
puréed

1 cinnamon stick

½ teaspoon ground hot red
pepper or cayenne pepper,
or to taste

Hamim-Cholent Hybrid, Wandering Sabbath Stew

Ani, Anida, or Adafina: Among Sephardic Jews, a dish composed of beans, peas, fat meat, and eggs, placed in an oven over Friday night, and eaten at the Sabbath meal. The Ani, called by the German Jews Schalet, was regarded by the Inquisition as conclusive evidence of Jewish practises against Marranos.

—*The Jewish Encyclopedia,* 1906

This aromatic recipe for overnight Sabbath stew has traveled through the twists and turns of history and geography, just like Eda Eskin's Shaltiel forebears. According to family legend, her father's mother, Tamara, was a member of the Shaltiel family, supposedly descended from one of King David's sons. Zerubbabel Shaltiel was chosen as the leader of the Jewish community in Babylonia at the time of the destruction of the First Temple. The family continued in positions of power until the eleventh century, when Eda's ancestors went to southern Spain.

yield: 12 to 18 servings

Some Shaltiels also left for Narbonne, a scholarly city and trading center, where they became the *parnasim,* or leaders of the Jewish community. Others went to Granada, a vibrant center of Judaic life until it became dangerous for Jews to live in Andalusia. They then went north to live in Barcelona until 1492, when, at the start of the Inquisition, they fled to Salonika, then an independent state. Eventually, Eda's Shaltiel ancestors worked their way to Trieste, then to Yugoslavia, finally finding a safe haven in Sofia, Bulgaria, where her grandparents lived through World War II. After the war, Eda's father, David, moved to New York, where he married Rajna Grubman, who escaped the Holocaust in Poland and, it just so happens, is my husband Allan's cousin.

Recipes like *hamim* (the word comes from *cham,* Hebrew for "hot") or *adafina* (from *dafīnah,* Arabic for "covered" or "hidden"), the Moroccan stew suspiciously similar to *cassoulet,* which eventually became known as *cholent*—the typical Sabbath overnight stew—surface in every land where Jews have lived. These stews can include chickpeas, dried peas, kidney beans, a bit of meat, and some barley, rice, or other grains, as noted above in the 1906 *Jewish Encyclopedia.* They were originally prepared in clay pots and buried in sand surrounded by charcoals. Later they were cooked in public ovens. The hot dish, which had been slowly cooking all night, was served for lunch on Sabbath after services, in accordance with the written laws of the late second-century Mishnah, or teachings of the rabbis.

Today, on Fridays, on almost every street corner in places like Williamsburg, Brooklyn, Ramat Gan, Israel, the twentieth arrondissement in Paris, or other religious Jewish quarters around the world, you see *cholents* and *hamims* from every conceivable background—Hungarian, German, Polish, Argentinian, Moroccan, and Salonikan, to name a few. And of course, these traditions sometimes blend together, creating something entirely new.

As a young girl, Eda often had Shabbat lunch in Tel Aviv with her father. "Once when we were eating the Sabbath stew, my father said that his mother used to make it even more interesting by adding chopped roasted eggplants, as the Bulgarians have a special feeling for eggplant dishes," she told me.

When Eda met an Iranian Jew born in Milan, they married and moved to Italy without a recipe for this favorite dish. She got the basics from a cookbook (not mine, unfortunately). "Not only did I cook it very well, but I actually became well known in Milan for my *cholent*," she told me. Eda made it her own by adding cardamom and turmeric, spices typical of the Middle East, while scattering sautéed onions, garlic, a little paprika, and crushed red pepper between the layers of meat, sweet potatoes, chickpeas, and dried plums. When she introduced her children to this *hamim-cholent* hybrid, she also added hot dogs, which turned out to be a big hit. "Most of all, as a tribute to my father, my grandmother, and our Shaltiel bloodline, I added the delicious eggplants. When I taste it, I remember the beautiful Ashkenazic-Sephardic mix of my past."

Don't let this recipe scare you. It is foolproof and a winter crowd pleaser. (It would be great for a Super Bowl party.) You start two days in advance, but the dish almost cooks itself. You can make it in a slow cooker, something most religious cooks do, or in the oven. The recipe is very flexible; use your imagination and take inspiration from the time of year, what is available in your local farmers' market, and your own dietary restrictions, and you will make it your own.

———————

1 pound (453 grams) dried or canned chickpeas or kidney beans

3 medium eggplants (about 3 pounds/1⅓ kilos total)

1 tablespoon salt, or to taste, divided

2 teaspoons Hungarian sweet paprika, or to taste, divided

1 teaspoon freshly ground black pepper

1 teaspoon cayenne or hot paprika, or to taste

1 teaspoon ground cumin

1 teaspoon ground turmeric

½ teaspoon ground nutmeg

¼ teaspoon ground allspice

¼ teaspoon ground coriander

3 tablespoons olive oil

2 large onions, chopped

3 cloves garlic, minced

2 sprigs rosemary, leaves chopped

½ cup (115 grams) pearled or hulled barley, rinsed and drained

2 pounds (907 grams) stewing beef, cut into 1½-inch chunks

4 to 5 beef bones with marrow (optional)

1 cup (225 grams) dried plums

2 cups (440 grams) roasted chestnuts

5 medium potatoes (about 2 pounds/907 grams total), peeled and cut into 4 pieces

4 medium sweet potatoes (about 2 pounds/907 grams total), peeled and cut into 4 pieces

4 to 6 large eggs in their shells (optional)

1. One day before cooking the *cholent*, cover the dried chickpeas or beans in cold water and soak overnight.

2. Next, cook the eggplants. You can use a charcoal or gas grill or a stovetop gas burner, but first line the stovetop with aluminum foil to make cleanup easier. Grill the eggplants whole, turning carefully with tongs every few minutes. Continue grilling until soft, about 15 to 20 minutes. If you want to skip the grilling process, which can get messy, you can also prick the skin with a fork and bake the eggplants in a 450-degree oven for about 30 minutes, or until they are soft. Whichever way you choose, after you've cooked the eggplants, put them in a colander set over the sink to drain and cool, then peel and mash with a potato masher or the back of a fork in a bowl. Cover and refrigerate until the next day.

3. In the morning, drain the beans and put in a large pot of water to cover. Bring to a boil, then lower the heat and cook, uncovered, for about 20 minutes, until the beans are starting to soften but are not cooked all the way through. (Remember, they'll be cooking for 12 hours in the *cholent*!) Drain the beans and set aside. Skip this step if using canned beans.

4. In a small bowl, stir together 1 teaspoon each of the salt and sweet paprika, as well as the pepper, cayenne or paprika, cumin, turmeric, nutmeg, allspice, and coriander and set aside. (This is a spice blend known as *baharat*—see page 4).

5. Warm the olive oil over medium-high heat in a large (at least 7-quart capacity), oven-safe pot with a tight-fitting lid, then sauté the onions until beginning to soften, about 5 minutes. Stir in the spice blend and cook for 10 minutes longer. Add the garlic and rosemary leaves and cook over medium heat for 5 minutes, then remove from the heat.

6. Now for the fun part—layering! Just remember to *not* stir after adding each ingredient. Scatter the beans in an even layer in the pot, then sprinkle some of the remaining salt and paprika on top. Next add the barley, a little more salt and paprika, then the meat and bones, if using, followed by more salt and cayenne. Add the dried plums, chestnuts, and more salt and paprika. Then arrange the potatoes and sweet potatoes in an even layer and sprinkle with any remaining salt and paprika. Wedge the eggs in their shells between the potatoes, then, if using, layer the hot dogs on the very top.

7. Add water to just cover, then drizzle the honey all over and sprinkle with the crushed red pepper. Bring the mixture to a boil over medium-high heat, skimming off any foam that accumulates. Cover the pot tightly with foil, secure with the lid, and either reduce the heat to the very lowest setting on the cooktop or let it cook for 12 hours in a 250-degree oven or on a *blech* (a metal pad used by observant Jews on the stove), or in a slow cooker (see below). Let cool for about a half hour before serving.

4 to 6 beef hot dogs
(optional, but delicious)
1 tablespoon honey
1 teaspoon crushed red pepper

Modern *Cholent* in a Slow Cooker

The slow cooker began life as the Naxon Beanery All-Purpose Cooker, the brainchild of an inventor living in Chicago. In 1936, Irving Naxon remembered the tales of his grandmother, an immigrant from Lithuania, who talked about bringing *cholent* to the public oven in the old country. While he was wondering how he could make her life easier, a lightbulb went off in his head, and voilà, the bean cooker was born, eventually morphing into the slow cooker. Whenever I visit a modern Orthodox woman on Friday morning, she has turned on her slow cooker, not for baked beans, but for, of course, *cholent*.

Iraqi False *Mahshi:* Layered Swiss Chard, Beets, and Meat

At the Rosh Hashanah Seder, a series of blessings are said over squash, leeks, dates, pomegranates, black-eyed peas, apples, the head of a fish or a lamb, and Swiss chard or beet greens.

The Hebrew word for "beet greens" and "chard" sounds very much like the word for "remove." No wonder, then, that the blessing Jews from Iraq and others recite at their Rosh Hashanah meal before eating beet greens or chard leaves translates roughly to "May it be your will, O God and the God of our forefathers, that our adversaries be removed."

When people ask me about my most memorable meal, I always come back to my first taste of an Iraqi dish with bitter Swiss chard, sweet beets, and beef in a sweet and sour sauce, eaten at a simple picnic in a pine forest near Jerusalem.

I learned it from Esperanza Basson, the mother of Moshe Basson, an Israeli chef. I have followed Moshe's career since he began running a very simple restaurant called Eucalyptus, named for the eucalyptus tree growing right in the center of the tiny dining room, on the outskirts of Jerusalem.

One day when I was visiting Israel, Moshe, who came to the country from Iraq in 1951, invited me to go foraging in the Judean Hills for herbs found in the Bible and the Talmud. As he, his mother, and I scrambled around the forest, he pointed out Jerusalem sage leaves that he stuffs in winter and the sour grapes that were pickled in antiquity and used as lemons.

Then Moshe's mother set out a tablecloth, plates, and cutlery on a wooden picnic table in the forest and pulled a casserole wrapped in a small blanket out of a picnic basket.

When she opened the lid, I was struck by an aroma reminiscent of my mother's sweet and sour stuffed cabbage, but I saw instead bright red beets mixed with Swiss chard and rice.

The traditional dish, one her family had eaten at Rosh Hashanah for generations in Amarah, a city near Basra in southern Iraq, is made by stuffing Swiss chard leaves with beets, onions, rice, and sometimes meat, and then simmering them in a lemon sauce with sugar to mitigate the bitterness of the leaves.

Other cooks, she explained, prepare a sweet and sour sauce that combines tart tamarind with brown sugar or a syrup made by slowly cooking dates, a technique that stretches back to the biblical period.

Esperanza's family has always called the chard dish *mahshi.* (*Mahshi* means "stuffed" in Arabic.) Because she once couldn't find undamaged chard leaves to make the traditional version, she decided to make the dish in layers, calling it "fake *mahshi.*" To her surprise, the dish tasted just as good.

yield: 6 to 8 servings

1½ cups (375 grams) long-grain jasmine rice

2 pounds (907 grams) rib-eye steak, cut into 1-inch cubes

Salt and coarsely ground black pepper

6 tablespoons (89 ml) vegetable oil, divided

2 large onions (200 grams), peeled and diced

2 large beets (about 1 pound/453 grams), peeled, 1 cut into ½-inch dice and 1 grated

1 pound (453 grams) Swiss chard, leaves left whole and stems cut into 2-inch pieces

8 teaspoons sugar, or as needed

4 tablespoons fresh mint or spearmint leaves

1 teaspoon dried mint

4 cloves garlic, peeled and finely diced

Juice of 3 to 4 lemons (about ½ cup/110 ml), or as needed, divided

As I dipped my fork into the vegetables and the meat, I felt as though I were taking a journey into the past. Jewish cooks have always varied dishes depending on where they lived and what was available.

---

1. Put the rice in a mixing bowl and cover with water. Stir, drain off the cloudy water, and repeat until the water runs clear. Pour fresh water over the rice and let soak for about 1 hour.

2. Season the beef with salt and pepper to taste. Heat a Dutch oven over medium heat and add 1 tablespoon of the oil. When the oil is shimmering, add the beef and sauté until well browned on all sides, about 5 minutes. Remove the beef and set aside.

3. Return the pan to low heat and add 2 more tablespoons of oil. Add the onions and sauté until transparent, stirring occasionally, about 5 minutes. Add the diced beets and sauté for another 5 minutes. Then add two-thirds of the Swiss chard stems and continue cooking until the onions are golden, about 5 more minutes.

4. Stir in the beef, cover, and remove from the heat. Spread one-third of the Swiss chard leaves on top of the beef mixture.

5. Drain the rice and return to a bowl. Sprinkle with salt to taste, then add 5 teaspoons of sugar, ½ teaspoon black pepper, 1 tablespoon fresh and the dried mint, garlic, the grated beet, the remaining oil, and the juice of 2 lemons. Stir and spoon half of the rice mixture on top of the meat and chard mixture, and cover with another third of the chard leaves. Spread with the remaining rice, and top with the remaining Swiss chard leaves and stems. You can do this a day ahead and leave in the refrigerator, covered, overnight.

6. Just before serving, mix 1½ cups (355 ml) water with the remaining 3 teaspoons sugar and the juice of another lemon in a small bowl. Taste, adding more sugar or lemon juice so the mixture is both sweet and sour. Pour over the Swiss chard and bring to a boil.

7. Cook partially covered until the chard begins to wilt, 3 to 5 minutes, adding a little water if needed. Poke the handle of a wooden spoon into the mixture in three places, making holes to let the steam rise through the chard. Cover, reduce the heat to very low, and cook until the rice is tender, about 30 minutes. Remove from the heat and let rest for 15 minutes. Just before serving, sprinkle with the remaining lemon juice and fresh mint. Serve, if you like, with fresh cucumbers, mint, dill, and other herbs.

Bukharan *Plov* with Beef, Carrots, and Cumin Seeds

Jews first arrived in Uzbekistan back in the sixth century B.C.E., traveling along the Silk Road from Babylon to the province of Bukhara. In the early 1990s, after the fall of the Soviet Union, 95 percent of Uzbekistan's 200,000 Jews emigrated, with about 60,000 settling near 108th Street in Queens, now dubbed Bukharan Broadway.

On a quiet street of small clapboard houses in Rego Park, Queens, live Aron and Ella Aronov, who were born in Uzbekistan. Their door was open when I arrived, and I peeked into a room filled with Bukharan newspapers, photos, and other ephemera of the life they left behind.

"Would you like to come to a dinner after *schloshim,* the thirty days of mourning for a leader of our community?" he asked. We drove to King David Kosher Restaurant on Queens Boulevard, where about 350 people, all in black, sat at tables—men and women separately. At a center table, the rabbi and the honored of the community, including Aron, sat with pictures nearby of the eighty-six-year-old respected elder who had died a month before. I sat with a table of women. On top of the table, two large dome-shaped cracker breads (see page 158) acted as the centerpiece with a loaf of flat Uzbek bread (see my *Jewish Cooking in America*) nestled inside, topped with *fijuelas* (see my *Jewish Holiday Cookbook*), a circular fried sweet pastry from Spain, which I have seen in Jewish Moroccan homes, dipped in honey, but this time it was covered with confectioners' sugar. The sweet was the first thing eaten after the long service, to break the mourning period, a symbol of the bittersweetness of life.

The meal progressed, interspersed with prayers, the soulful music of the Bukharan Jews, and long reminiscences on the deceased. Huge platters of sour cucumber pickles and cabbage, carrot, eggplant, and beet salads were served, followed by fried tilapia with garlic sauce, meat with cabbage and tomatoes, and, finally, the much-anticipated *plov.*

Arthur Shakarov, the chef and owner of the restaurant, told me that *plov* is served for all special occasions. He makes it outside in huge iron pots for twenty to three hundred people.

As we left, Aron said wistfully, "I left Bukhara because the Soviet Communist system was incompatible with the Jewish way of life. They wanted us to forget about our Jewish identity." Clearly, the food and culture make Bukhara impossible to forget.

This Central Asian recipe uses medium-grain rice like Kokuho Rose Extra Fancy sushi rice and pure sesame oil rather than vegetable oil. I recommend finding the wild Uzbek cumin seed if you can (they *do* exist!) and the tart barberries in your

yield: about 8 servings

¼ cup (60 ml) vegetable oil

2 tablespoons pure sesame seed oil

2 large Spanish onions, diced

2 cloves garlic, minced

3 pounds (1⅓ kilos) beef round or chuck, cut into 1½-inch squares

1 tablespoon cumin seeds, or to taste, divided

1 tablespoon sea salt, or to taste, divided

½ teaspoon freshly ground black pepper

¼ cup (25 grams) barberries, divided

10 large carrots, peeled and cut lengthwise into 2-by-¼-inch slivers, divided

1½ pounds (680 grams) medium-grain rice, preferably Kokuho Rose Extra Fancy

¼ teaspoon cayenne, or to taste

2 scallions, finely chopped, for garnish

Handful of pomegranate seeds, for garnish

local spice market or Persian or Russian store (or even online). Usually prepared with mutton or lamb in Bukhara, it is generally made in this country, as it was when I tasted it, with beef. This dish is definitely a crowd pleaser.

---

1. Heat the oils in a 5-quart pot. Add the onions and garlic and cook for about 10 to 15 minutes, until the onions "taste of the oil" and are golden.

2. Add the beef and cook for about 15 to 20 minutes, until it is browned on all sides. Then add 1½ teaspoons of the cumin seeds, 1½ teaspoons of salt, ½ teaspoon of pepper, half the barberries, and a handful of the carrots. Add enough water to cover, about 10 cups (2⅓ liters). Bring to a boil, then cover the pot, simmering over medium heat for 35 to 40 more minutes.

3. While the meat is cooking, wash the rice in a large sieve with cold water until the water runs clear. Rinse two more times (just to be sure!), then put the rice in warm water for 15 minutes to "open it up." Drain and set aside.

4. When the meat has cooked for 35 minutes, add the remaining carrots with the remaining 1½ teaspoons of salt and the cayenne, adding more water if needed. Cover and cook for a few minutes.

5. Spoon the rice gently on top of the carrots, stirring the rice every 10 minutes while taking care not to disturb the carrots, until the water is evaporated and the rice cooked, about 30 minutes in all. Then cover and cook slowly for 10 to 15 more minutes.

6. To serve, spoon the rice onto a large platter. Top with the carrots and the meat, then sprinkle a few scallions on top along with the remaining cumin, remaining barberries, and the pomegranate seeds.

Kiftes de Prasa, Macedonian Leek and Meat Patties

This is a dish about which Jews from the Balkans wax nostalgic. But the one-hundred-plus-year-old recipe turns out patties that are a bit tired compared to what we eat today. So, when Alana Newhouse, the editor of *Tablet* magazine, told me about the *kiftes* or *kiftes de prasa* made by her maternal grandmother from Monastir (now Bitola), Macedonia, she asked me to tamper with tradition. I roasted the leeks at a high heat instead of boiling them as Alana's grandmother did. Bringing out the flavor made all the difference. This dish, a staple at most holidays for Jews from this part of the former Ottoman Empire, can be made with either meat or potatoes. Alana's grandmother made the *kiftes* with lamb, and served them accompanied by salad, as an appetizer. I like them served the same way, but as a main course.

----

1. Preheat the oven to 425 degrees and rub a large rimmed baking sheet with a little of the oil. Toss the leeks with more oil, 1 teaspoon of the salt, and the pepper. Spread the leeks out in a single layer (use a second baking sheet if necessary) and roast, tossing frequently, until golden brown and crisp at the edges, about 20 minutes. Cool to room temperature.

2. Chop the leeks and mix with the meat or potatoes, eggs, cinnamon, allspice, cayenne, parsley, matzo meal, and salt. Form into 12 patties. Heat a frying pan with a thin film of oil. Brown the patties until golden on each side, making sure they cook through.

Note If substituting potatoes for the meat, add a little Parmesan to the potatoes for some extra flavor.

yield: 12 patties

¼ cup (60 ml) olive oil plus oil for frying, divided

6 cups (about 1 kilo), chopped leeks (from 6 to 8 leeks)

2¼ teaspoons coarse kosher salt, plus more to taste, divided

½ teaspoon black pepper

2 pounds (907 grams) chopped lamb, beef, or boiled potatoes (see note)

3 large eggs

1 teaspoon cinnamon

½ teaspoon allspice

¼ teaspoon cayenne pepper (optional)

½ cup chopped parsley, or to taste

½ cup (55 grams) matzo meal

Keftes Garaz, Syrian Meatballs with Cherries and Tamarind

Ostian meat balls—*Offellæ ostienses*: Prepare the meat in this manner: clean the meat [of bones, sinews, etc.]. Scrape it as thin as a skin [and shape it]. Crush pepper, lovage, cumin, caraway, silphium, one laurel berry, moistened with broth; in a square dish place the meat balls and the spices where they remain in pickling for two or three days, covered crosswise with twigs. Then place them in the oven [to be roasted], when done take the finished meat balls out. Crush pepper, lovage, with the broth, add a little raisin wine to sweeten. Cook it, thicken with roux, immerse the balls in the sauce and serve.

—Apicius, *De re Coquinaria* (Cookery and Dining in Imperial Rome), first century c.e.

One of the great gifts of the Syrian Jews to gastronomy is this meatball dish. Flavored with tamarind sauce and dried and frozen sour cherries, this sweet and sour *keftes* meatball recipe has been handed down for five generations in the family of Melanie Franco Nussdorf, a Washington lawyer who loves to cook the dishes of her ancestors, from Aleppo. We can tell that Melanie's family recipe has been updated over the years, as it contains tomato paste, a relatively recent addition to Old World cooking. If you cannot find sour cherries, frozen Bing or dark sweet cherries will work just fine.

---

1. Preheat the oven to 350 degrees and toast the pine nuts by stirring often, in a small dry skillet over medium heat, until lightly brown, about 5 to 10 minutes. Remove to a medium bowl.

2. **to make the meatballs** Sauté the onions in the oil in a nonstick frying pan until lightly caramelized, about 20 to 30 minutes.

3. Add the onions to the pine nuts, then add the ground beef, garlic, Aleppo or Marash pepper, cumin, allspice, cinnamon, salt, and pepper. Break the eggs into the bowl and stir in the tamarind and tomato paste or ketchup, mixing gently with your hands until just combined, then add just enough breadcrumbs for the meat to become clammy.

4. Take about 1½ tablespoons of meat and slap the beef several times into the center of the palm of your hand to emulsify. Shape into small meatballs, about 1¼ inches in diameter. Put on two rimmed baking sheets and bake for about 20 minutes, or until done but still juicy. You should get about 36 meatballs.

5. **while the meatballs are baking, make the sauce** Heat the oil in a medium saucepan set over medium-high heat. Add the onions and sauté until trans-

yield: 6 to 8 servings

MEATBALLS

½ cup (50 grams) pine nuts

1 large sweet onion, diced (about 1½ cups/350 grams)

2 tablespoons olive oil

2 pounds (907 grams) ground beef

2 cloves garlic, minced

¼ teaspoon ground Aleppo or Marash pepper

½ teaspoon ground cumin

1 teaspoon ground allspice

¼ teaspoon cinnamon

Salt and freshly ground pepper to taste

2 large eggs

1 teaspoon tamarind concentrate

2 teaspoons tomato paste or ketchup

½ cup breadcrumbs, fresh

SAUCE

¼ cup (59 ml) olive oil

1½ onions, diced (1⅓ cups/165 grams)

(continued)

parent, then add the tamarind, pitted sour or frozen cherries, dried cherries, lemon juice, allspice, salt, pepper, beef stock, and wine. Simmer together for about 20 to 25 minutes, until the sauce is slightly thickened.

6. Mix the meatballs with the sauce and serve, sprinkled with chopped parsley or cilantro, over rice.

Note You can make this dish ahead and freeze if you like. Defrost in the refrigerator overnight, then reheat in a pan, covered, over medium heat until warm.

1½ tablespoons tamarind concentrate

2 cups (440 grams) pitted sour cherries or frozen dark red cherries

2 cups (440 grams) dried cherries

Juice of 2 lemons

1½ teaspoons ground allspice

Salt and pepper

1½ cups (355 ml) beef stock

1½ cups (355 ml) red wine

2 tablespoons chopped parsley or cilantro

Tamarind

Tamarind, whose name comes from the Arabic word meaning "date from India," is an ancient sweet and sour fruit that actually originated in Africa but traveled very early to India and throughout the Middle East, then was brought by the Arabs and Jews to Spain and by the Spanish to Latin America. Within Jewish communities, you know a dish has Syrian roots if you find tamarind listed in the ingredients.

Often used the way we use tomatoes today, to add acidity, depth, and sweetness to a sauce, tamarind has been a lovely flavor addition for centuries in Syrian, Persian, Iraqi, Georgian, and Indian Jewish dishes, as well as Sephardic dishes that eventually, in the 1500s, traveled with the Spanish and Portuguese to Mexico, the Caribbean, and other parts of Latin America, where it remains very popular today.

The only catch is that tamarind is somewhat difficult to use—it has to be peeled, soaked, seeded, and then squeezed through cheesecloth and mixed with sour salt, lemon juice, and/or sugar before being cooked down to a concentrate or paste. (Poopa Dweck's beautiful book *The Aromas of Aleppo* describes the process.) As soon as tomatoes came from the New World to the Old, the more easily used red tomatoes replaced tamarind in many dishes. The unique flavor and tartness of tamarind, however, is becoming popular again, with easily dissolvable tamarind paste concentrates and bulk tamarind dissolved in a little water now available from India, other parts of Asia, Latin America, and even Texas.

Pastel di Carne con Massa Fina, Bulgarian Eggplant and Meat Pie

Talk about wandering dishes! Pastels in one form or another have been around forever, but they attained greatness when the Jews went to Spain and were then disseminated with them to Latin America, the Ottoman Empire, and the Balkans. In Kochi, India (see page 231), I tasted a chicken and potato handheld pastel that the Jews called pastel and the Indians *sambousak,* while in Tel Aviv, I sampled a large *pashtida* with eggplants (see page 192), also a large pastel.

_____

1. Preheat the oven to 450 degrees, prick the eggplants with a fork, put them on a foil-lined baking sheet, and bake for about 20 to 30 minutes, until burnt on the outside and soft on the inside. Leave for a while to cool, then peel off the burnt skin and strain in a colander set over the sink or a bowl, squeezing out the excess liquid. Coarsely chop the eggplant, then mix in a large bowl with the lemon juice and half the chopped garlic.

2. In a large sauté pan, warm the oil over medium high heat, then add the onion and the rest of the garlic, cooking for a few minutes. Add the ground beef or lamb, 1 teaspoon salt, pepper to taste, parsley, crushed red pepper flakes, Vegeta or other soup mix if using, wine, and the tomato paste. Cook until the meat is just browned, then set aside to cool slightly.

3. Stir the meat mixture into the eggplant, mixing well and adjusting seasonings to taste. Drain off any fat. (I like to cook the meat a day ahead and leave in the refrigerator overnight, so that I can easily remove the fat.)

4. Preheat the oven to 375 degrees and grease the bottom of a 9- or 10-inch pie plate and scatter the breadcrumbs on top. Roll out one pastry sheet on a board larger than the pie plate and lay it on the breadcrumbs, then spoon the eggplant and meat mixture over it. Roll out the second sheet and lay it on top, trim off the excess puff pastry, and crimp the sides by pinching and turning the edges of the crust. Pierce the top with the tines of a fork to allow steam to escape. Beat the egg in a small bowl, then paint the egg on the crust with a pastry brush. Sprinkle Maldon or other flaky salt over the top.

5. Bake for 25 to 30 minutes, or until golden on top.

Note I sometimes add ½ cup of currants soaked in rum or brandy and warm water.

yield: 6 to 8 servings

2 to 3 eggplants
(about 3 pounds/1⅓ kilos total)

Juice of ½ lemon

3 to 4 cloves garlic, chopped, divided

2 tablespoons olive oil

1 large onion, chopped

1 pound (453 grams) ground beef or lamb

1 teaspoon sea salt, or to taste

½ teaspoon freshly ground black pepper, or to taste

4 tablespoons fresh parsley

¼ teaspoon crushed red pepper flakes, or to taste

½ teaspoon Vegeta (a Balkan spice blend with vegetables) or any vegetable soup mix (optional)

½ cup (120 ml) red wine

2 tablespoons tomato paste

¼ cup (25 grams) breadcrumbs

2 ready-made puff pastry sheets

1 large egg

½ teaspoon Maldon or other flaky sea salt

Tagliolini colla Crosta, Crusty Pasta
with a Bolognese Sauce

Edda Servi Machlin's jewel of a cookbook *The Classic Cuisine of the Italian Jews* includes a favorite recipe of mine, a wonderful pasta with two names: *tagliolini colla crosta* and *ruota di faraone.* The first means "crusty pasta," while the latter means "pharaoh's wheel." This traditional Purim Sabbath dish, which Edda ate as a child in Pitigliano, a mostly Jewish hilltop town in southern Tuscany, is also served throughout the year for the Sabbath. Italian Jews associate the dish with the Israelites' passage through the Red Sea and deliverance from the Egyptians.

It is a typical Italian Jewish dish, and you can find different variations in different towns throughout Italy. The Jews of Venice have a similar dish called *frisensal,* using *luganega,* a sort of sausage, plus oil, raisins, and pine nuts instead of Bolognese sauce. In Edda's version, the pasta is first boiled briefly, then mixed with a rich Bolognese sauce, dotted with pickled tongue, pine nuts, and raisins: an unusual but delicious combination of salty and sweet. Because it can be made ahead of time, it is therefore suitable for the Sabbath.

Years ago I was lucky enough to have Edda prepare the dish for me at her home in Mount Kisco, New York. She baked it in a ceramic mixing bowl, then theatrically turned it out onto a plate.

---

1. Heat a large saucepan and add the oil. Toss in the onions, carrots, celery, and parsley and lightly brown for 2 to 3 minutes, stirring occasionally.

2. Add the meat and brown thoroughly, stirring occasionally. Pour in the wine and raise the heat, allowing the wine to evaporate completely. Then add the tomatoes and tomato paste, cooking over high heat for 1 to 2 minutes, stirring frequently and breaking apart the tomatoes with a wooden spoon. Next pour in the beef broth or water and cook, covered, over very low heat for 45 minutes, stirring occasionally. The sauce should be nice and thick. If it is too thin, cook a few minutes longer until it loses its excess liquid and add salt to taste and the hot pepper.

3. Preheat the oven to 350 degrees and grease a round, 12- to 16-cup-capacity oven-proof baking dish.

4. Fill a large pot with water, add a pinch of salt, and bring to a boil. Add the *tagliolini,* bring back to a boil, and cook for 7 minutes. Drain and put in a large bowl with the meat sauce, raisins, almonds, and pine nuts, tossing quickly and thoroughly to distribute. Put in the baking dish and bake for 1 to 1½ hours, or until a nice crust has formed. Invert onto a platter and serve warm with a leafy green salad (page 92).

yield: 6 to 8 servings

¼ cup (60 ml) olive oil

2 medium onions, peeled and diced (about 2 cups/440 grams)

2 medium carrots, peeled and diced

2 stalks celery, diced

½ cup (12.5 grams) chopped Italian parsley

2 pounds (907 grams) lean ground beef

1 cup (235 ml) dry white wine

One 14.5-ounce (415-gram) can peeled canned tomatoes

One 3-ounce (85-gram) can tomato paste

3 cups (710 ml) beef broth or water

Salt to taste

½ teaspoon dried hot red pepper like cayenne

1 pound (453 grams) *tagliolini* pasta

½ cup (75 grams) dark seedless raisins

½ cup (59 grams) very coarsely ground whole almonds

½ cup (68 grams) pine nuts

Moroccan Lamb Shanks with Caramelized Onions and *Tanzeya* (Dried Fruit Sauce)

They shall eat the flesh that same night; they shall eat it roasted over the fire. . . . Do not eat any of it raw, or cooked in any way with water, but roasted—head, legs, and entrails—over the fire. You shall not leave any of it over until morning; if any of it is left until morning, you shall burn it. —Exodus 12:8–10

In Josephus we read about how hundreds of thousands of Israelites gathered on the hilltops around Jerusalem and roasted a one-year-old lamb as a sacrifice to be eaten with bitter herbs and unleavened bread before dawn that same night. To this day, Samaritans roast lambs outside on Passover, following this age-old tradition.

Until the destruction of the Second Temple, Jews roasted lamb or goat at Passover in a spring festival as the book of Exodus describes above. They slaughtered the animal and daubed the tent posts or doors of their home with blood to ward off evil spirits. After the Temple's destruction, when the Seder became a service to be performed at home, around the dining room table, the rabbis prohibited eating roast lamb at Passover, because the meat became a symbol of the destruction. The only exception was the Jewish community of Rome, who predated the Temple's destruction and therefore didn't place that significance on the roast lamb.

To this day, observant Jews around the world will not eat roast lamb or other roasted meat at Passover out of deference to the ancient Temple. Middle Eastern Jews will eat lamb at Passover, but not roasted. For many Reform Jews, however, exactly the reverse is true: Roast lamb or other roasted food is served to commemorate the ancient sacrifices.

I tasted this heavenly, long-cooked lamb shank with *tanzeya*, a Moroccan sauce. The recipe comes from Ron Arazi, a chef from Israel, who was born in Mogador, Morocco.

------

1. Sprinkle the lamb shanks with salt to taste; if using kosher lamb, less salt will be needed. In a large, wide casserole with a lid, heat the oil over medium-high heat. Working in batches, brown the lamb shanks on all sides. Transfer the lamb to a plate and set aside.

2. Add the onions to the pan and sauté until they begin to brown, about 3 to 5 minutes. Add ½ cup (120 ml) of water and 1 teaspoon salt. Cover, reduce the heat to low, and simmer until the onions are very soft, about 30 minutes. Meanwhile, preheat the oven to 275 degrees.

yield: 6 servings

6 lamb shanks, about 1 pound (453 grams) each

Coarse kosher or sea salt

2 tablespoons vegetable oil

4 large onions, halved root to stem and thinly sliced

Pinch of saffron threads

1 cup (225 grams) Moroccan Jewish *tanzeya* (see opposite)

1 cup (120 grams) blanched whole almonds, toasted

3. Mix the saffron with ¼ cup (60 ml) of warm water and let it stand for about 5 minutes to give time for the water to become yellow, then add to the pan. Stir to mix well for 2 to 3 minutes. Add the lamb shanks to the onions and mix well. Cover and transfer to the oven. Bake until the lamb is very tender, about 2 hours.

4. Stir 1 cup of the *tanzeya* into the onions. Return the pan to the oven and bake, covered, about 15 minutes. Garnish with toasted almonds and serve by itself or over couscous.

Tanzeya, a Moroccan Sauce of Dried Plums, Apricots, Figs, and Raisins

about 3 cups

This scrumptious condiment can now be bought online from Ron and Leetal Arazi at nyshuk.com, or you can make it yourself. I use it on lamb but you could also serve it over chicken, on brisket, or just spoon it on good bread with butter.

1 cup (174 grams) dried plums

1 cup (190 grams) dried apricots

1 cup (149 grams) quartered dried figs

1 cup (150 grams) raisins

1 cup (200 grams) sugar

1 stick cinnamon

1 whole cardamom pod

1 whole allspice berry

Pinch of dried chili flakes

Pinch of salt

1. In a wide, shallow saucepan, mix the dried plums, apricots, figs, and raisins. Add 2 cups (470 ml) hot water, and allow to rest for 15 minutes.

2. Add the sugar, cinnamon stick, cardamom, allspice berry, chili flakes, and salt. Bring to a boil over high heat, then cook, stirring often, for 5 minutes. Reduce the heat to low and simmer, uncovered, until the water has almost completely evaporated, about 45 minutes to 1 hour, stirring occasionally to make sure it does not stick to the bottom of the pan.

3. Discard the cinnamon stick, cardamom pod, and allspice berry. Allow the mixture to cool; if desired, it may be covered and refrigerated for up to 2 weeks.

Slow-Cooked Brisket with Red Wine, Vinegar, and Mustard

My mother made great brisket when I was growing up: slow-cooked, tender, more sour than sweet. We ate it every year for Erev Rosh Hashanah, with *farfl*, Goodman's tiny egg-noodle barley (see page 185). I loved it.

So as a child, I never understood why people joked about dry, overcooked brisket. Now I know: Many people weren't as lucky as I was.

Take Adam Sobel, for example. His Roman Catholic mother had learned to make some Jewish dishes, like sweet and sour meatballs and matzo balls, from Adam's Jewish paternal grandmother, but somehow she never got the knack of brisket. Today, Adam—a chef at San Francisco's RN74—has learned how to do brisket right, slow-cooked and braised in a slightly acidic sauce. Recently, his father, with desperation in his voice, called him before Rosh Hashanah. "Can't you help Ma?" he asked. "Talk to her about her brisket, she needs help."

"I wasn't insulted at all," said Diane, Adam's mom. So, phone in hand, Adam walked his mother through the steps of a good brisket. His tips are simple but useful for anyone who's ever struggled with this Jewish staple.

Brisket is an American invention. Here it has become the Jewish holiday cut of meat par excellence, but it wasn't always so. In some countries, like France, butchers don't even sell this cut of beef.

Before the Civil War, Jews in America would eat dishes like chicken fricassee and meatballs, stuffed veal, or flanken (short ribs) for Rosh Hashanah. Then came refrigerated trains that were able to transport large cuts of meat throughout the country. Jews became enamored with the grainy American cut and cooked it long and braised, or *gedempte fleisch*.

Eventually, brisket became traditional for holidays, like Rosh Hashanah, Hanukkah, and, for many people, Passover. My late mother-in-law told me that years ago in Poland, whole briskets of beef (probably not our cuts, exactly) were reserved mostly for special occasions like weddings. One thing hasn't changed: Brisket is what Jews cook for festive meals when large groups are gathered around the table.

The first important point when preparing a brisket is to buy the right meat and put it in the pan properly. Each brisket has a fattier side, called the point, which should be up when cooking, and a leaner side, called the flat, with more flavor. I often buy a whole choice brisket, at least eight to ten pounds including all the fat, rather than a "first cut," because it's more flavorful, and it saves money. Adam starts his brisket by searing the outside to develop more flavor. Pay attention to how you place the meat in your roasting pan. Cook it with the point side up.

yield: 12 servings

1 high-quality brisket (about 6 pounds/2¾ kilos)

Coarse kosher salt and freshly ground pepper to taste

¼ cup olive oil

6 carrots, peeled and sliced into 3 chunks each, cut on the diagonal

4 large onions, quartered

6 ribs celery, with the greens, cut into 2-inch chunks

5 cloves garlic, smashed and peeled

½ cup (120 ml) red wine vinegar

2 cups (470 ml) red wine

2 tablespoons honey or maple syrup

4 tablespoons fresh grated horseradish

2 tablespoons brown Dijon mustard

4 cups (945 ml) beef broth

2 bay leaves

6 sprigs fresh thyme

½ bunch parsley

Adam's mother was very happy with the results. "He told me exactly what to do," she said. "I don't like to cook. Adam's talent for cooking skipped me and came from my mom and Neal's mom for the Jewish holidays."

If there is one thing I have learned through the years, it's that when cooking tough meat, there has to be something acidic in the mix to help break down the proteins. Adam uses red wine vinegar but suggests that you could add instead tomatoes or tomato sauce. To make a deeper sauce, he suggests using beef broth or red wine.

Like many young chefs of his generation, Adam tries to go back to his family's gastronomical roots at holidays. "I add grated horseradish and all the ingredients that are indigenous to Russia and used in the fall," he said. "The *mirepoix,* diced vegetables that are cooked with the brisket to bring out the flavor, are not finely diced as they are in French dishes. For brisket they should be chunky." I agree.

"My approach to cooking brisket is the same as for corned beef: slower and lower," Adam added. "The muscles get tougher at a higher temperature. I add enough liquid to barely cover, cover it, and let it go."

We may use more spices today in our briskets because we have access to them, but the techniques for flavoring have really not changed much in the past two thousand years.

---

1. Preheat the oven to 250 degrees.

2. Season the brisket liberally with salt and pepper. Then add a few tablespoons of the olive oil to a braising pan or a pot large enough to hold the brisket. Warm the pan over medium heat, then sear the brisket on all sides (this may take as long as 10 minutes per side, and you might have to maneuver the brisket a bit to make it sear evenly). When the brisket is mostly browned on all sides, remove it from the pan and set aside for a few minutes. I have to admit that these days I rarely sear the brisket.

3. If there is not enough fat rendered in the pan, then add a few more tablespoons of oil. Add 3 of the carrots, the onions, celery, and garlic and sauté for a few minutes, stirring occasionally, and sprinkling with more salt and pepper as needed.

4. Stir together the wine vinegar, wine, honey, grated horseradish, and mustard in a small bowl, then pour the liquid into the pan and deglaze, gently scraping up any stuck bits with a wooden spoon. Simmer for 3 minutes, until the sauce is slightly reduced.

5. Return the brisket to the pot and then add enough beef broth to just cover the brisket. Add the bay leaves, thyme, and parsley and bring to a simmer. Cover the pot and put in the oven for 4 hours, checking occasionally. At the end of the fourth hour, add the remaining 3 carrots, and return to the oven for one more hour.

6. Remove from the oven and let sit until the brisket reaches room temperature, then cut the brisket against the grain into slices about an eighth to a quarter of an inch thick, or refrigerate overnight in the cooking pan. When ready to serve, remove the fat that has accumulated on top of the brisket. Heat the liquid in the pan and reduce by half, then strain out the vegetables if you want. I like to keep them. Return the cut brisket to the pan, heat, ladle the carrots on top, pour the sauce over, and serve.

Note I often make a brisket in advance, refrigerate it, then get rid of the fat, slice it against the grain, return it to a baking pan, cover with the sauce, and freeze. Then, when I need it, I just pop it into the oven to reheat before serving.

Braised Short Ribs with Almonds, Dried Plums, and Star Anise

It used to be that kashrut-observant Jews ate short ribs or flanken for Friday night dinner. As soon as the American practice of sawing through the bone instead of carefully cutting around it became popular, butchers started to prefer the large cuts of what they called briskets, which give diners more of the forequarters in one big slab. Today, creative Jewish chefs are once again doing wonders with short ribs. I have riffed on this recipe from Tony Maws, chef at Craigie on Main in Cambridge, Massachusetts, who makes this take on his grandmother's short ribs. The meat is embellished and enriched with dried plums, almonds, and spices like star anise. It is a great recipe to cook one day ahead and just reheat before your guests arrive.

You'll need a piece of cheesecloth and kitchen string or an herb infuser, such as the Pulke herb infuser from Ototo Design.

———————

1. Season the short ribs or flanken with salt and pepper. Set a heavy wide pan over medium-high heat and add the fat or oil, heating until the oil shimmers. Add the beef and sear well on all sides. Transfer to a plate.

2. Add the onion, carrots, celery, garlic, and ginger to the pan, and stir until the onions begin to brown, about 5 minutes. Add the tomato paste, port, and wine, scraping the bottom of the pan with a wooden spoon. Simmer until reduced by half, about 10 minutes.

3. In a large Dutch oven or heavy braising pan, put 1 cup (174 grams) of the dried plums and 1 cup (70 grams) of the almonds. Tie up half of the parsley with the thyme, cilantro, and bay leaf into an herb bouquet and put the cinnamon, clove, star anise, cardamom, coriander, and orange zest in a piece of cheesecloth or herb infuser. Add the herbs and spices to the pot.

4. Add the meat, the vegetable mixture, and enough stock to cover.

5. Preheat the oven to 325 degrees. Then increase the heat under the meat and vegetables to bring to a boil, cover, and transfer to the oven. Cook about 2½ hours, or until the meat is falling off the bones. Cool completely in the pan, then refrigerate overnight or until well chilled.

6. Skim off the fat, then transfer the beef to a large bowl, discarding any loose bones, the herb bouquet, and the cheesecloth packet. Transfer the remaining broth and vegetables to a food processor. Purée, then put in a clean pan. Add the meat and remaining cup of whole dried plums. Heat, stirring occasionally, until gently reheated. Garnish with the remaining parsley and almonds.

yield: 6 to 8 servings

7 pounds (about 3 kilos) beef short ribs or flanken, cut in 4-inch portions

Salt and freshly ground black pepper to taste

¼ cup (60 ml) rendered duck fat, chicken fat, or canola oil

3 large Spanish onions, diced

3 large carrots, peeled and diced

2 stalks celery, diced

3 cloves garlic, peeled and smashed

1-inch piece ginger, peeled and smashed

¼ cup (75 grams) tomato paste

2 cups (470 ml) ruby port

2 cups (470 ml) red wine

2 cups (348 grams) pitted dried plums, divided

2 cups (140 grams) slivered almonds, lightly toasted, divided

½ bunch parsley, chopped and divided

4 sprigs fresh thyme

½ bunch cilantro, chopped

1 bay leaf

1 stick cinnamon

1 clove

3 whole star anise

2 whole cardamom pods

1 teaspoon coriander seeds

Zest of 1 orange, cut in strips

4 cups (1 liter) veal, beef, or chicken broth or stock

Home-Cured Corned Beef

To keep cooked sides of pork or beef or tenderloins: Place them in a pickle of mustard, vinegar, salt and honey, covering meat entirely, and when ready to use you'll be surprised.
—Apicius, *De re Coquinaria* (Cookery and Dining in Imperial Rome), first century C.E.

yield: 8 to 10 servings

One 3-pound (1⅓-kilo) brisket, preferably with fat attached

1 cup (9 ounces/255 grams) coarse kosher salt

Scant ¾ cup sugar (5 ounces/140 grams)

4½ tablespoons (2 ounces/56 grams) brown sugar

1 tablespoon honey

1 scant tablespoon coarsely ground black pepper

2 teaspoons coarsely ground yellow mustard seed

2 tablespoons coriander seed

1 tablespoon crushed red chili peppers

½ teaspoon ground allspice

1½ teaspoons nutmeg

1 cinnamon stick, crushed

6 bay leaves, crushed

1 pinch ground cloves

1 tablespoon ground ginger

1 tablespoon celery juice powder (can substitute ⅖ ounce pink curing salt)

Doug Singer makes great corned beef and everybody knows it. Like many people today, he transitioned from working in a more traditional office setting, in his case the family's ready-made clothing business, to the food world, where he has found his niche pickling corned beef. Now his corned beef dumplings are sold in delis around the Washington area, including the one he has started in Georgetown.

Before Doug moved to D.C., he asked his sister, who was living there, where he should live and where he could get a good corned beef sandwich. He found out where to live, but the corned beef proved to be a problem—so he started making his own for his friends and family, going through about three hundred pounds of brisket while recipe testing. "Every time I made it, I thought it was really good but felt it always could be better," he said. "I kept lowering the salt content because I didn't want the corned beef to be a salt lick." Wanting to make an all-natural product, he uses celery juice powder, which contains naturally occurring nitrites (as opposed to other curing salts that contain added nitrites).

"The love for corned beef was from my grandparents who lived in Detroit and visited us in Cleveland," he told me one day while showing me how to pickle the beef. "The reward for being a good grandson was to go to the Stage Deli in Detroit and Corky and Lenny's in Cleveland for a corned beef sandwich."

The concept of preserving beef in salt is ancient, and that medium morphed into a wet brine—basically a water, salt, sugar, and spice solution similar to what we use today—which morphed again with the arrival of refrigerators in the mid-1800s. With them the curing solution could contain less salt and sugar, resulting in a milder and more tender corned beef.

The basis of the brine is salt, sugar, and celery juice powder (available in 1¼-ounce packages from online suppliers such as waltonsinc.com or sausage maker.com). You can also use pink curing salt, found at well-stocked grocery stores or specialty shops, although Doug prefers the celery juice powder. The rest is just seasoning that, preferably, should be freshly ground as you prepare it, especially the allspice. Corned beef preservers used to rinse off the meat after brining it to get rid of the surface salt, something you don't have to do with this recipe.

"Corning" is preserving ("corn" refers to "corns" of salt, not maize), so corned beef is beef that has been preserved. Although corning goes way back, it hit its peak in Alsace-Lorraine during the early Middle Ages, when many Jews lived there and many were either butchers or cattle sellers, acting as the middlemen between farmers and butchers. My late Polish mother-in-law used to tell me that corned beef was only used for special occasions like weddings or bat mitzvahs. My favorite way to prepare it is with sauerkraut and lots of different kinds of French mustards and gherkins on the side. It's also great, of course, in sandwiches, as part of a classic boiled beef dinner, in *choucroute alsacienne* (see my *Quiches, Kugels, and Couscous*), or made into glazed corned beef (see *Jewish Cooking in America*), once the "ham" of American Jews. The curing is Doug's and the cooking is my way of doing it.

———

1. Fill a non-aluminum container with about a gallon (3.8 liters) of water. Add the brisket to make sure the water covers the meat by about by 2 inches. Remove the brisket and set aside. Then energetically whisk the salt, sugar, brown sugar, honey, black pepper, yellow mustard seed, coriander seed, crushed red chili pepper, allspice, nutmeg, cinnamon stick, bay leaves, cloves, and ginger until everything is dissolved.

2. Add the celery juice powder and whisk to dissolve fully. Put your hand in the brine to feel the bottom to make sure that everything has dissolved.

3. Alternatively you can put 1 quart (944 ml) of water, the spices, and the celery juice powder into a blender (in batches if necessary) and blend until smooth.

4. Put the brisket back in the water, fatty side up, and top with two saucers to submerge the beef. It is important that it is all submerged. Cover with a tight-fitting lid and let it sit in the refrigerator for 8 days.

5. Remove the beef from the container and discard the brine. At this point the outside of the meat will be gray and the "pickled" inside will be bright cherry red.

6. If you want to cook the corned beef traditionally, put it in a suitably sized pot, cover with water, bring to a simmer, and cook for 2½ to 3 hours, partially covered. You can also steam the meat on a rack (like a fish poacher) for 3½ to 4 hours, or until fork tender.

7. Once the beef is cooked, let it rest for 10 to 15 minutes, then slice against the grain and serve.

Sweets

Tahina Cookies

Rugelach with Spicy Chocolate-Nut Filling

Walnut-Almond Macaroons with Raspberry Jam Thumbprint

Schokoladenwurst, Chocolate Sausage

Hamantashen with Poppy Seed, Chocolate, or Apricot Filling

Kamishbroit with Guava

Orange-Almond *Mandelbrot*

Pizza Ebraica, Biscotti-Like Cookies with Dried Fruit and Wine

Salty Anise Butter Cookies

Soufganiyot, Israeli Jelly Doughnuts

Croquante, Almond Brittle

Natillas, Spanish Custard

Dates in Brown Butter with Vanilla Ice Cream, Date Syrup,
and Halvah Crumble

Apple Kuchen

Upside-Down Fruit Cobbler

Free-Form Quince Babka

Roman Ricotta Cheese *Crostata* with Cherries or Chocolate

Fluden de Pasach, Cashew Nut Strudel with Guava and Lime

Classic American Cheesecake with a European Twist

Aranygaluska, Hungarian Golden Pull-Apart Cake with
Walnuts and Apricot Jam

Ginger Almond Sponge Cake with Cardamom and Pistachios

Flourless Chocolate Cake

Libyan *Saefra,* King Solomon's Cake

What Would Sweets Be without Sugar?

Take five Egyptian pounds of sugar, cook it as syrups are cooked, removing its foam, until it acquires a good consistency. Then cast into it one Egyptian pound of good wine, and thicken it into a syrup of the consistency of syrup of roses. This Servant has mentioned this syrup along with the foods only because it resembles them. It should always be taken daily at the beginning of the day, in the wintertime in hot water and in the summertime in cold water.

—Moses Maimonides, *On the Causes of Symptoms,* twelfth century

For thousands of years, human beings in the Fertile Crescent used honey as both a sweetener and a medicine. They ate honey extracted from honeycombs as well as sweet liquids processed from dates, pomegranates, and the white, sweet morning dew called manna that settles on tamarisk trees, often called manna trees.

Halvah, made from date or bee honey and pressed sesame seeds, came to southern India and the Arabian Peninsula from China, and from about the fourth century B.C.E., sugarcane was also an important agricultural crop there. In those days, a type of granulated sugar was made by squeezing the juice out of the cane, evaporating the water, and then separating the molasses and impurities to extract the sucrose. This sugar was used for medicinal reasons in India, and eventually this practice spread to other parts of the Arabian Peninsula, like Persia and Babylonia. Early visitors to India, such as the philosopher Strabo at the beginning of the first century C.E., described sugar as the "reeds that make honey without the agency of bees."

With the Arab conquests starting in the seventh century, the crop spread to other parts of the Near East and to Spain in Europe. During this period, documents found in the Cairo Genizah mention sugar, including recipes for preparing lozenges and for promoting weight gain. In a letter written in Jerusalem in 1196, Abu Zikri, the physician for several Ayyubid rulers, mentions sugar with almonds as a medication. (Today, of course, that sounds like a delicious dessert!)

The great Maimonides, cited above, even discussed sugar's medicinal effects and sang the praises of the taste of roasted sugar. He too recommended sugar with almonds and raisins, drinking sugar and water to strengthen the lungs, and just plain eating food "spiced" with sugar, as was the custom during the Middle Ages. Through the Genizah documents, we also know that Jews played a role in the extraction of sugar from the cane as well as in its production during the time of Maimonides.

Later, with the Columbian Exchange, sugarcane was brought to the Americas from the sixteenth century onward, to Brazil and the West Indian islands—most notably Barbados and Jamaica, owned by the British. Jews and others took part in its production and dissemination, although the vast majority of the work was performed by slaves brought from Africa.

Through the next two hundred years, thanks to the ever-expanding sugarcane industry in the New World, sugar extracted from cane became available to and adored by all classes in much of the Old World.

In the mid-1700s, a German scientist named Andreas Marggraf discovered that sucrose could be extracted from the sugar beet, a vegetable grown in a more temperate climate than sugarcane. One of his students, Franz Achard, then expanded on this research and created a process to extract the sucrose,

a method that spread across Europe, encouraged by, among others, Napoleon Bonaparte, who did not want to be dependent on the English for sugar. Later on, scientists created an inexpensive method for all Europeans to get their sugar fix. In 1853, a Jewish industrialist and landowner in Moravia named Rudolf Auspitz founded a company to produce sugar from beets, becoming one of the first people to spearhead the modern sugar beet industry.

Sugar production today takes place all over the world, with Brazil as the largest producer. But in recent years, sugar and its derivatives have often come to be seen as an evil and something to be avoided (especially products like high-fructose corn syrup).

Still, we need something to satisfy our collective sweet tooth, and so we are turning to less refined products like muscovado (unrefined sugar), agave (a Mexican succulent), maple sugar, stevia (a South American plant in the sunflower family), and one of the oldest sweeteners of all, honey. And who knows? Perhaps someday soon we will realize, as the ancients probably did, that everything in moderation is good for you—even sugar.

Tahina Cookies

One day when I was looking for a cup of coffee on Twenty-Third Street in Manhattan, I stopped by an Israeli coffee shop selling tiny balls of tahina cookies that literally melted in my mouth. Their texture reminded me of Russian tea cakes, *kourambiedes* (Greek Easter cookies), and *polvorones* (Mexican wedding cookies). These addictive cookies, made with ground sesame seeds, butter, and flour, are giving halvah, the ancient sesame candy, a run for its money.

———————

1. Preheat the oven to 350 degrees and line two baking sheets with parchment paper.

2. In the bowl of a standing mixer with a paddle attachment, cream the butter or oil and sugar. Mix in the flour, salt, and baking powder, then the vanilla and the tahina.

3. Roll the dough into balls about the size of a large marble and put on the parchment-lined baking sheets. Press an almond in the center of each, slightly flattening the cookies.

4. Bake for about 15 to 20 minutes, rotating sheets halfway through, until lightly golden and beginning to crisp.

Note I like Soom Foods tahina, made from Ethiopian white humera sesame seeds.

yield: about 3 dozen cookies

8 tablespoons (1 stick/ 113 grams) unsalted butter, at room temperature, or ½ cup (120 ml) vegetable oil

½ cup (100 grams) sugar

1 cup (135 grams) plus 2 tablespoons flour, sifted

¼ teaspoon salt

½ teaspoon baking powder

1 teaspoon vanilla

½ cup (120 ml) tahina

¼ cup (20 grams) blanched and peeled almonds

Rugelach with Spicy Chocolate-Nut Filling

Until fairly recently, a family's iconic recipes were mostly carried down from generation to generation, from mother to daughters. Today, with written recipes, the Internet, and television, you would think that cooks have more knowledge of recipes past and present. But do they?

Fany Gerson is one person who questions this. Mexican-born of Jewish great-grandparents who came from Ukraine in 1929, this Culinary Institute of America graduate now lives in New York City, where she runs La Newyorkina, a group of tiny shops specializing in Mexican ices and sweets.

"My great-grandmother Lena, who we called Babi, made buttery and flaky rugelach," she told me recently. "I didn't know how to make all the sweet things she did. In Mexico, my grandmother taught the cook, who cooked them a little differently so as not to give away her secret. When I moved to New York, inspired by my new surroundings, I tried to develop a recipe for rugelach the way I imagined my great-grandmother made them. The dough was what she used for everything and she wouldn't give the recipe to me." So Fany worked with the rugelach she found everywhere in New York, but it didn't taste the same as her memory of it. First of all, the cream cheese in the States was different. "I wanted to make one inspired by the flavors I knew. I was trying to imagine a dialogue with my great-grandmother that never existed. I wish I knew what she felt when she came to Mexico, so far away, with different things in the market. Now I am in New York, with new surroundings. It is a continuation of the immigration."

Here is one result of Fany's experimenting: Mexican-inspired rugelach that she makes in New York, from a recipe that originated in Ukraine, via Mexico City.

————————

1. **make the dough** Mix the flour and salt in the bowl of a food processor fitted with a steel blade and pulse a few times. Add the cubes of butter and cream cheese, then pulse a few times until the mixture resembles coarse crumbs.

2. Whisk together the vanilla and 2 of the yolks in a small bowl, then pour them over the butter-flour mixture. Run the processor continuously until the dough starts to clump together and turn into a ball.

3. Divide the dough into 3 portions and flatten. Wrap in plastic wrap and refrigerate for a couple of hours or overnight.

4. **meanwhile, make the filling** Grind the hazelnuts or pecans and the chili until finely chopped in a food processor fitted with a steel blade. Set aside.

yield: about 36 rugelach

2 cups (270 grams) unbleached all-purpose flour

½ teaspoon sea salt

1 cup (2 sticks/226 grams) unsalted butter, cut into small cubes and chilled

4 ounces (113 grams) cream cheese, cut into small cubes and chilled

½ teaspoon vanilla extract

4 large egg yolks, divided

Spicy Chocolate-Nut Filling (see below) or Apricot Jam (page 9)

¾ cup confectioners' sugar for rolling out

2 tablespoons sugar

SPICY CHOCOLATE-NUT FILLING

½ cup (60 grams) hazelnuts or pecans, lightly toasted

1½ teaspoons dry, ground árbol or pequin chili pepper, with or without the seeds, depending on how hot you want it

8 ounces (226 grams) good-quality bittersweet chocolate

1 tablespoon unsalted butter

¼ cup (50 grams) sugar

½ teaspoon sea salt

1 teaspoon vanilla extract

5. Melt the chocolate, butter, and sugar in a double boiler, stirring until the sugar dissolves. Remove from the heat, then stir in the nuts and chilies, salt, and vanilla.

6. When ready to bake the rugelach, preheat the oven to 350 degrees and line a 10-by-15-inch baking sheet with parchment paper.

7. Unwrap the dough, dust the board with ¼ cup of confectioners' sugar, then roll out one portion of dough into a circle about 10 or 11 inches diameter, about ⅛ inch thick. Spread one-third of the chocolate-nut filling (about ½ cup) on top, leaving a 1-inch border. Using a sharp knife, cut the circle into 12 wedges. Roll each wedge up from the wide side to the center, then arrange the cookies 2 inches apart on the baking sheets. Repeat with the other two portions of dough.

8. Whisk the remaining 2 egg yolks in a small bowl and brush over the rugelach, then sprinkle with the granulated sugar. Bake about 30 minutes, or until golden and crispy, rotating the baking sheets halfway through cooking. Let cool for a few minutes, then transfer the rugelach to a wire rack to cool completely.

Note You can freeze the dough after forming into a ball or into the individual cookies. Then just bake them whenever you have a craving!

Walnut-Almond Macaroons with Raspberry Jam Thumbprint

In London, as I watched Eileen Dangoor Khalastchy (see page 249) make macaroons, I noticed that as she mixed the batter, she used only her right hand, not a spoon or spatula. "I have to use my hand," she said. "It mixes better and you can feel the consistency."

Eileen has been making these macaroons, called *hadgi badam* in Arabic, all her life, first in Baghdad and for the last forty years in London. A must for both Purim and Passover for Iraqi and Iranian Jews, these cookies were something Eileen helped her mother bake as a child. However, she learned this recipe from her sister-in-law, also her cousin, Renée Dangoor, who was the beauty queen of Baghdad in 1947. "In Baghdad we didn't have sweets ready-made, so we had to do everything at home," Eileen told me. "Today, macaroons remind us of our life in Iraq." The only difference in her recipe now is that she adds one egg yolk, which makes the macaroon chewier and helps hold the dough together. I have also tampered with tradition here. Where Eileen presses a pistachio into her cookies, I add a tiny dab of good raspberry jam.

---

yield: about 30 cookies

1¾ cups (140 grams) blanched almonds

1½ cups (150 grams) walnuts

1 cup (200 grams) sugar, or a little less if you like

1 teaspoon ground cardamom

3 large egg whites and 1 egg yolk

1 cup of rose water or water to dampen your hands

½ cup (63 grams) peeled pistachios or ½ cup (163 grams) good-quality raspberry jam made with sugar, like Bonne Maman

---

1. Put the almonds in a food processor fitted with a steel blade and pulse until mostly powdered but with a few crunchy bits remaining, about 15 to 20 pulses. Remove the almonds to a large bowl, then put the walnuts in the food processor and, again, pulse until mostly powdered. Add the walnuts to the bowl with the almonds.

2. Add the sugar, cardamom, egg whites, and the egg yolk to the bowl and mix with one hand. Cover with a towel and let the mixture sit an hour or so or overnight in the refrigerator to dry out a little.

3. The next day, preheat the oven to 325 degrees and line two baking sheets with parchment paper.

4. Pour the rose water in a small shallow bowl. Dampen your hands with the rose water, shake off any excess, and scoop up about a tablespoon of the dough at a time, pressing it into walnut-size balls. Put the macaroons about 2 inches apart on the baking sheets, flattening the cookies slightly. Use your thumb to make a small indentation in the middle of each.

5. Bake for 15 minutes, then remove and either put a pistachio or dab ¼ teaspoon of raspberry jam in each thumbprint. Rotate the pans and continue baking for 10 more minutes, or until golden and firm. Cool to room temperature on the baking sheets and serve. You can also make these ahead and freeze them.

Note Substituting pine nuts (see my *Quiches, Kugels, and Couscous*) in these cookies makes them similar to the thirteenth-century cookies of Michel de Nostredame—called Nostradamus by most—a physician and astrologer best known for his prophecies, not his recipes. Nostradamus, whose family converted to Catholicism in 1504, came from a long line of men skilled in mathematics and medicine. As a healer, he often used foods and herbs as treatments for various illnesses.

Schokoladenwurst, Chocolate Sausage

In isolated Jewish communities like that of El Salvador (see page 210), a kind of culinary lag exists with regard to holiday foods. There we can often find delicious recipes not found elsewhere anymore.

When I visited El Salvador, Daniel Guttfreund, a local psychologist, organized a Sabbath dinner with Jewish dishes that his family has eaten every Friday night and for holidays since his grandfather came to the country in the 1920s. Whereas communities elsewhere may try trendier recipes, it is clear that pierogi from Chernowitz (now Chernivtsi) in Ukraine and desserts from Berlin define this family.

That evening at Daniel's mother's apartment, the dishes included challah, mushroom and onion pierogi, stuffed cabbage, stuffed chayote, and other Salvadoran dishes. The desserts, especially this *Schokoladenwurst* (chocolate sausage), were favorite recipes from Daniel's Berlin family.

From my time in Israel in the early 1970s, I knew this addictive no-cook chocolate "sausage" as *knackknick* (Hebrew for "sausage"), but it was made with cookies and cocoa powder. It goes by *salami di ciocolate* in Italy and *shokoladnaya kolbasa* in Russia, and was probably invented before or during the First World War, when processed cocoa and chocolate were available and people wanted to conserve gas by not cooking.

Gerda, Daniel's mother, now ninety-four, was born in Chernowitz, raised in Berlin, moved in 1934 to Brazil, where she met her husband, and then moved to San Salvador in 1945. She learned the recipe from her aunt Erma in Brazil. Gerda has been making it for every Sabbath and holiday—even Passover—for the last seventy-plus years.

My favorite part is the instruction to make three cylinders of cookies: one to eat now, then two to freeze, ready for the next time you crave them.

———

yield: 54 slices

9 ounces (255 grams) good-quality 70 percent bittersweet chocolate

3 tablespoons brewed coffee

2 large eggs (see note below)

2 cups (240 grams) whole almonds, coarsely ground

2 tablespoons rum

¾ cup (150 grams) sugar

1 bar (198 grams) marzipan

Note If you are concerned about the raw eggs, use pasteurized, available in most grocery stores.

1. Stir the chocolate with the coffee in a saucepan, heating until the chocolate melts. Pour into a bowl and stir in the eggs, ground almonds, rum, and sugar. Then refrigerate for about a half hour, until it hardens like a soft dough.

2. While it cools, divide the marzipan into 3 pieces and form into logs about 5¾ inches long and ½ inch in diameter.

3. When the chocolate is cool enough to mold, roll it out onto a lightly greased surface until thin. Score the surface into 3 sections and carefully roll and press the chocolate around the marzipan and form into 3 long cylinders. Cover with plastic wrap and refrigerate a few hours or overnight.

4. When ready to eat, slice one cylinder into about 18 pieces. Freeze the others for whenever the craving strikes.

Hamantashen with Poppy Seed, Chocolate, or Apricot Filling

When I was asked to speak to the student body at Phillips Exeter Academy, I thought about the irony of the situation. When I was young, Exeter had very few Jewish students, all male, and those who were open about their Judaism felt isolated.

That is no longer the case. During my two days at Exeter, I cooked with not only Jewish students, but a diverse group of teenagers from around the world.

That night about sixty students attended a Shabbat dinner that a dozen students cooked with me, all organized by Rabbi Jennifer Marx Asch, the advisor to the Exeter Jewish Community. The rabbi bakes *hamantashen* each year from a recipe from her late grandmother, Ruth Cohen Marx, whom everyone called Oma. Born in Berlin, she fled to Tel Aviv in the late 1930s and finally settled in Birmingham, Alabama, in the 1950s.

Until her death, each year, just before Purim, Oma sent her grandchildren *hamantashen,* wrapped individually in plastic wrap, then packed carefully in a recycled butter cookie tin. Although Oma is gone, her granddaughter still has the recipe, lovingly typed out on a manual typewriter.

---

yield: about 60 cookies

¼ cup (50 grams) sugar

1 cup (2 sticks/226 grams) unsalted butter, at room temperature, or coconut oil cut into ½-inch squares

2 large eggs, separated

1 tablespoon (15 ml) distilled white vinegar

2½ cups (345 grams) unbleached all-purpose flour

½ teaspoon sea salt

2 cups Apricot Jam (see page 9), Poppy Seed Filling (see page 313), or Chocolate Chip Pastry Cream (see page 313)

---

1. Using a food processor equipped with a steel blade, cream the sugar and the butter or coconut oil. Then add the egg yolks, vinegar, 3 tablespoons of water, flour, and salt. Process until the dough comes together in a ball.

2. Divide the dough in half, wrap in plastic wrap, and refrigerate, along with the reserved egg whites, for a few hours or overnight.

3. Preheat the oven to 375 degrees and line two baking sheets with parchment paper. Remove the dough from the refrigerator and let sit at room temperature for about 10 minutes.

4. Roll one disc of dough on a lightly floured work surface to a thickness of ⅛ inch. Cut the dough into 2½-inch circles, rerolling and cutting the scraps to use all the dough. Put ½ teaspoon of filling in the center of each circle. To shape the *hamantashen*, first brush a little reserved egg white around the rim of the circle with your finger. Then lift the edges of the dough up to form a triangle around the filling, leaving a little filling exposed.

5. Transfer the *hamantashen* to the prepared baking sheets. Repeat with the remaining dough. Brush the unbaked *hamantashen* with a little egg white and bake for 15 to 20 minutes, or until golden.

Poppy Seed Filling

yield: 2½ cups filling

½ cup (65 grams) poppy seeds

½ cup (110 ml) milk or soy milk

½ cup (100 grams) sugar

10 pitted dates or dried figs (84 grams), chopped

¼ cup (35 grams) raisins

¼ cup (35 grams) walnuts, roughly chopped

¾ cup (85 grams) ground almonds

Grated zest and juice of 1 lemon

1 egg yolk

1. Put the poppy seeds in a small saucepan. Cover with the milk and simmer for a few minutes, stirring occasionally. Turn off the heat and cool.

2. Transfer the poppy seeds and milk to a food processor fitted with a steel blade. Add the sugar, dates or figs, raisins, walnuts, almonds, lemon zest, lemon juice, and egg yolk. Pulse until just combined. Refrigerate until ready to use, or up to 2 days. You may also freeze the filling for up to 6 months.

Chocolate Chip Pastry Cream

Yield: about 1 cup filling

This is a delicious chocolate filling recipe that Uri Scheft, the baker-owner of Lehamim in Tel Aviv and Breads Bakery in New York, shared with me.

3 large egg yolks

¼ cup (50 grams) sugar

1 tablespoon cornstarch

2 teaspoons unsweetened cocoa powder

¾ cup (175 ml) milk or soy milk

½ vanilla bean, split lengthwise

1 cup (160 grams) semisweet chocolate chips

1. In a medium bowl, whisk the egg yolks, sugar, cornstarch, and cocoa powder until smooth.

2. Pour the milk into a small saucepan with the vanilla bean. Over medium heat, bring to a simmer, then remove from the heat and remove the vanilla bean. Scrape the inside of the bean into the milk, discarding the pod.

3. While whisking vigorously, pour one-third of the milk into the yolk mixture, then whisk this mixture into the remaining milk in the saucepan. Simmer over low heat, whisking constantly, until the mixture bubbles and thickens into a creamy pudding consistency, about 5 minutes.

4. Remove from heat and stir in about half of the chocolate chips, whisking until smooth. Let sit at room temperature until cool, then stir in the remaining chocolate chips. Refrigerate for up to 5 days.

Chocolate: From the Drink of the Gods to Dessert Bars

I first fully realized the legacy of Sephardic Jews, especially those called *marchands portugais* in French, when traveling in Bayonne, France. It was here that King Henri IV welcomed those fleeing from the Inquisition in the sixteenth century. They came to France to save their culture, their religion, and even their lives, and brought with them spices, textiles, tobacco, leather, and cocoa beans.

Most important, these refugee Jews, also called Marranos, or New Christians, brought the tradition of chocolate making to Bayonne with them, and over the years making chocolate became a central part of the Jewish livelihood in southwest France.

Cacao beans originated from Central America, where they were used to make a drink of the gods. Christopher Columbus came across them on his fourth voyage and brought some back with him, but at the time no one paid any attention. Later, in 1519, so the story goes, Hernán Cortés became the first European to encounter chocolate (the term comes from the Aztec word *xocoatl*), when he watched Emperor Montezuma drinking a sort of hot cocoa concoction.

Back in Europe, cacao beans were first used only for medicinal purposes. An early cookbook describes the formula: "The principal base [of the remedy] is cacao; the other drugs which are in the composition are vanilla, sugar, cinnamon, Mexican pepper, and cloves; some add orange flower, nutmeg, or ambergris [a waxy substance produced in the digestive system of sperm whales]. Chocolate, warmed, fortifies the stomach and the chest, supports and regulates natural warmth of the body; it nourishes, changes bad moods, fortifies and repairs the voice."

Jews were integral in satisfying the growing demand for chocolate as something that was not just medicinal but also delicious. They were the most revered makers of the drink and the largest exporters of the raw materials to make it. A network of Jews who fled the Inquisition for the Caribbean were active in the early sugar and cacao markets, and also developed refineries for vanilla.

They did this despite the 1684 Code Noir, which banned Jews from living on the French islands because they were "enemies of the Christian faith." *Marchands portugais* of Bordeaux, Bayonne, and Marseille imported the spices and cacao from their connections in the Caribbean and rose to even greater prominence.

The reputation of Bayonnais chocolate spread because of the quality of the cacao beans and the Portuguese Jews' expertise in blending chocolate, sugar, and other spices according to the formulas brought from nearby Spain. But little by little, other Bayonnais learned how to make chocolate, and their numbers increased so much that in 1691 Christian chocolate makers banned the Jews from the trade.

From the south of France, cacao beans traveled throughout Europe and eventually back to the colonized Americas. Aaron Lopez, from a family who had been New Christians for two generations before returning to Judaism, immigrated to Newport, Rhode Island, in 1752, where he became the largest taxpayer in the city. He was one of the few American Jews active in the slave trade and also a distiller of rum and manufacturer of clothing, barrels, ships, and foods. From the West Indies, he brought commodities like sugar, molasses, cacao, coffee, pimento, ginger, nutmeg, allspice, pepper, and cloves to satisfy the colonists. In the archives of the city of Newport, I discovered that he was the first chocolate maker in the colonies, employing local workmen to grind cacao into cocoa powder that turned into a drink of hot chocolate.

We've come a long way in our obsession with chocolate. It has gone from a drink of the gods, to Hershey's bars available to the masses, to a worldwide craving with dessert cafés selling chocolate delicacies, like Israeli chef Max Brenner's. How surprised Aaron Lopez and the chocolate makers of Bayonne would be with our newfound knowledge that chocolate can be good for you.

Kamishbroit with Guava

Gisela Sencherman Savdie is one of those very smart, creative people who can do anything. Born in Venezuela to a Colombian Jewish mother whose parents came from Lithuania, she grew up in Colombia but came to Miami to raise her family with her husband, Raymond Savdie, an Egyptian Jew whom she met in Colombia. Gisela first became a dentist, and her book is the definitive dental textbook throughout Latin America. Now, switching from saving teeth to creating avant-garde still lifes, she has changed professions, becoming an artist.

Probably her most popular artistry—at least with her family and friends—are these guava cookies, which she learned from her mother, who made them filled with plum jam and cocoa. Years ago, Gisela started using guava paste, which she buys in Latin grocery stores in North Miami. I love guava and have added even more to the cookie.

Kamishbroit (the Yiddish word from Ukraine means "funny bread") is usually sprinkled with cinnamon and has neither almonds nor a filling (unlike *mandelbrot*), but for some reason in Colombia this treat has both.

———

1. Preheat the oven to 350 degrees; line a baking sheet with parchment paper.

2. In a medium mixing bowl, whisk together the flour, baking powder, and salt. In the bowl of a standing mixer, cream the butter or the oil with the sugar, using a paddle attachment. Stir in the 2 eggs and vanilla, then gradually stir in the flour mixture to form dough.

3. On a floured work surface, shape half the dough into a narrow rectangle about 12 inches long, 4 inches wide, and ¼ inch thick. Press half of the walnuts gently on top of the dough.

4. Arrange half of the guava on top of the nuts down the length of the dough. Starting from the short end, carefully roll the dough up like a jelly roll so that the guava pieces stay tucked in. You will have a stubby 4-inch fat roll. Then gently roll and form the dough into an 11-by-2-inch cylinder, sealing the ends together so none of the guava spills out. Repeat with the remaining dough.

5. Arrange the cylinders, seam side up, about 2 inches apart on the prepared baking sheet. Mix the egg yolk in a small bowl and paint the rolls well. Bake for 25 minutes or until golden. Don't be alarmed if some of the guava paste seeps out.

6. Remove from the oven and let cool for a few minutes, then cut into ½-inch-thick slices on the diagonal, separating them as you cut. Lay them on their sides and return to the oven and bake for 10 more minutes, or until mostly crisp (the cookies will continue crisping once out of the oven).

yield: about 24 cookies

2 cups (270 grams) unbleached all-purpose flour

1 teaspoon baking powder

½ teaspoon salt

5 tablespoons plus 1 teaspoon (75 grams) unsalted butter, or ⅓ cup vegetable oil

¼ cup (50 grams) sugar

2 large eggs plus 1 egg yolk

1 teaspoon vanilla

¾ cup walnuts (65 grams), chopped

8 ounces (about ¾ cup/ 226 grams) guava paste, diced into ½-inch cubes

Note You can substitute 4 tablespoons diced dates or prunes for the guava filling.

Orange-Almond *Mandelbrot*

Annette Lerner is known for her baked goods, especially her *mandelbrot* (meaning "almond bread"). "These foods are 'Grandma love,' she told me, adding that she has been making these cookies for years, and always brings them to the Washington Nationals' opening day.

What I like about this recipe is Annette's trick of freezing the dough after baking, then cutting it into slices when still frozen before baking a second time. This makes for a thinner cut, fewer crumbs when cutting, and a crisper texture. Through the centuries, especially this last one, *mandelbrot* have morphed from something biscotti-like into proper cookies, with the addition of baking powder, chocolate chips, walnuts, or dried fruits. They are sometimes even stuffed like a jelly roll, or converted into a Passover cookie like this delicious, crispy variation.

———————

1. In a large bowl, mix the matzo cake meal or flour, potato starch, almond flour, ½ teaspoon of the cinnamon, and the salt. Set aside.

2. Cream 1 cup (100 grams) of the sugar and the butter or coconut oil in the bowl of a standing mixer using a paddle attachment. Then add the eggs, one at a time, mixing well after each addition.

3. Mix in the matzo or flour mixture, almonds, vanilla, and orange zest.

4. Place half the dough on a piece of parchment paper about 20 inches long. Use the parchment paper to help mold the dough into a log about 10 inches long and 2½ inches in diameter. Twist the ends of the parchment paper to seal. Repeat with the other half of the dough. Refrigerate both logs for at least 1 hour.

5. Preheat the oven to 350 degrees and line a baking sheet with parchment paper. Unwrap the dough logs and put on the prepared baking sheet, side by side. Bake the logs for 35 to 45 minutes, until just beginning to brown. The dough should not be too cracked on the top. It is better to underbake than overbake.

6. Cool the logs, wrap in plastic, and freeze until you are ready to finish them, or for at least 1 hour.

7. Preheat the oven to 350 degrees and line two baking sheets with parchment paper. Mix the remaining 1 teaspoon cinnamon and ¼ cup (50 grams) sugar in a small bowl and set aside.

8. Remove the logs from the freezer. With a sharp, serrated knife, cut the dough into ⅓-inch-thick slices. Dip both sides of each slice into the cinnamon sugar mixture and put flat on the prepared baking sheets. Bake for 10 to 15 minutes, carefully turn the slices over, then bake another 10 minutes, or until golden brown and starting to crisp.

yield: about 2 dozen cookies

1½ cups (170 grams) matzo cake meal or 2 cups plus 1 tablespoon all-purpose flour

½ cup (85 grams) potato starch

½ cup (55 grams) almond flour

½ teaspoon plus 1 teaspoon cinnamon, preferably Ceylon, divided

½ teaspoon sea salt

1 cup (100 grams) plus ¼ cup (50 grams) sugar, divided

12 tablespoons (1½ sticks/ 169 grams) unsalted butter or coconut oil, at room temperature

3 large eggs

1 cup (100 grams) slivered almonds

½ teaspoon vanilla

Zest of 2 oranges

Pizza Ebraica, Biscotti-Like Cookies with Dried Fruit and Wine

Paola Fano (see page 276) makes *pizza ebraica* by the hundreds to give as gifts during the holidays. She studs the dough with pine nuts, almonds, and hazelnuts and leaves out the dried or candied fruits often called for in other recipes. I like her combination of a mix of nuts with dried cherries and raisins, first plumped in sweet wine. You can add chocolate chips, but do so sparingly, as they can overwhelm. The traditional shape is a large, rectangular loaf, but I prefer them rolled out and shaped in small ovals as Paola makes them. These *pizzas* are supposed to be a little burnt (think of it as "caramelizing" if you prefer!) and stay nicely crisp for several weeks, making them perfect gifts for the holidays.

Paola, a daughter of Rome, insists that this is a traditional dessert for every happy occasion, usually given to guests in a little bag to take home, called a *kavod,* a term that comes from the Hebrew word for "respect."

---

yield: about 20 cookies

½ cup (120 ml) Marsala wine, or another sweet wine

½ cup (60 grams) dried cherries

½ cup (60 grams) raisins

4 tablespoons (½ stick/ 56 grams) unsalted butter or coconut oil, at room temperature

¾ cup (150 grams) sugar

½ teaspoon salt

⅓ cup (80 ml) vegetable oil

½ teaspoon vanilla

2 to 2½ cups (270 to 340 grams) flour

½ cup (60 grams) pine nuts

½ cup (60 grams) peeled hazelnuts or blanched almonds

1. Pour the wine over the cherries and raisins in a small bowl. Cover and allow to soak for at least an hour but ideally overnight.

2. Preheat the oven to 350 degrees and line two baking sheets with parchment paper.

3. Cream the butter or coconut oil, sugar, and salt in a standing mixer with the paddle attachment. Add the oil, vanilla, and ¼ cup (60 ml) of the wine from the cherries and raisins. Gradually add the flour, mixing until a soft dough forms. You might not need all the flour. Remove the paddle attachment and stir in the cherries, raisins, pine nuts, and hazelnuts or almonds with a spoon or your hands.

4. Using your hands, shape about 4-tablespoon portions of the dough into egg shapes about 3 inches long. Put the cookies on the baking sheet about ½ inch apart. They will not spread very much when baking. Bake for about 20 minutes, until golden brown and burning slightly around the edges.

Salty Anise Butter Cookies

Your limbs are an orchard of pomegranates
and of all luscious fruits,
of henna and nard—
nard and saffron,
fragrant reed and cinnamon,
with all aromatic woods,
myrrh and aloes—
all the choice perfumes.
                    —Song of Songs 4:13–14

One day I followed Lior Lev Sercarz, "spiceologist to the stars," as he glided down an escalator and entered the back door of Le Bernardin, Eric Ripert's Michelin three-star restaurant in midtown Manhattan. Carrying a black backpack and pulling a small wheeled suitcase, Lior looked like a kindly, modern-day peddler, with striking blue eyes and a speckled beard. Pulling his wares, Lior twisted and turned through the warren of corridors until he reached the kitchen. It was 5 p.m. on a Friday, and he was two hours late. No one minded.

An Israeli transplant now based in New York, he is one of the city's experts on and distributors of spices and spice blends.

Lior was raised in a culinary culture where spices were central. "My Transylvanian grandmother married a Tunisian," he told me. His father's parents came from Germany and Belgium. *Paprikash* and poppy seeds met peppers and preserved lemons in his childhood kitchen.

Lior is following in the footsteps of ancient Jewish spice traders. "From day one, the Bible mentioned scents in cosmetics and food, the clove and the nutmeg," he said. "But they were reserved for the higher class, the average person didn't have access to them."

Like his French chef mentor, Lior travels to India, China, Indonesia, and elsewhere to procure his goods. He toasts his spices in the oven and then grinds different combinations of them into blends, each one offering a unique story.

As we sniffed his Sri Lankan blend, I imagined Lior in the fourteenth century, bringing Taillevent, the famous French chef, his spices—galangal, ginger, mace, cinnamon, and more. Lior would not have been a chef in those days, rather a Jewish peddler who brought spices back from China or India or Ceylon or bought them from another peddler who had made the journey. Back then, Lior would have courted the great chef and kept a few spices for his wife to cook at home for the Sabbath.

yield: about 3 dozen cookies

6 tablespoons (¾ cup/ 84 grams) unsalted butter (preferably high-fat, European-style), softened

2 tablespoons extra-virgin olive oil

6 tablespoons sugar

1 large egg

½ teaspoon vanilla

1½ cups to 1¾ cups (202 to 236 grams) unbleached all-purpose flour

2 teaspoons anise seed

1 teaspoon coarse sea salt

½ teaspoon fennel pollen (optional)

2 tablespoons Pernod or other licorice liqueur

1 tablespoon orange blossom water (or 3 tablespoons orange liqueur, such as triple sec)

Today, Lior is more like Nostradamus, the sixteenth-century Jewish-born but converted doctor, seer, and pastry baker who knew that the best spices enhance our health and our lives.

Lior bakes these cookies early in the morning and sells them at his spice shop, La Boîte, in New York City, the same place he grinds the spice mixes he provides to superstar chefs across the city. I have dusted the tops with fennel pollen, flourish that is lovely but not required. The cookies are basically a traditional Central European butter cookie, something I grew up with as a child.

———

1. In a stand mixer equipped with a paddle, cream the butter, olive oil, and sugar for about 3 minutes, then add the egg and vanilla. Gradually add 1½ cups of the flour, working in ¼ cup more if the dough is too soft. Then sprinkle in the anise and sea salt. Do not overmix—the salt should not dissolve or break apart.

2. Pat the dough into a ball, flatten into a 1-inch-thick round disc, and wrap in plastic. Let the dough rest for at least an hour in the refrigerator.

3. Preheat the oven to 350 degrees and line two baking sheets with parchment paper or a Silpat.

4. Lightly flour your work surface, then roll out the dough to ¼ inch thick. Cut into 1½-inch rounds using a cookie or biscuit cutter, then gently arrange on the prepared baking sheets. Dust the tops of the cookies with the fennel pollen, if using, pressing lightly with your fingertips to make it adhere.

5. Bake for about 12 to 14 minutes, or until the cookie bottoms are golden brown.

6. Stir together the Pernod and orange blossom water or orange liqueur. Using a pastry brush, brush the mixture on each cookie and let cool on the pan. Use a metal spatula to remove each cookie to a cooling rack, then brush the cookies again with the Pernod mixture. (You can even brush them a third time if you like—the cookies will not become soggy, but rather absorb more of the liqueur flavor.)

Note For a Ginger-Cardamom Butter Cookie, substitute 2 tablespoons chopped candied ginger and ¼ teaspoon ground cardamom for the anise and salt. Substitute Canton, or other ginger liqueur, for the Pernod.

Soufganiyot, Israeli Jelly Doughnuts

Today every baker in Israel makes jelly doughnuts, or *soufganiyot,* probably the quintessential modern Israeli recipe, for the eight days of Hanukkah. According to Gil Marks's *Encyclopedia of Jewish Food,* it was the Histadrut, now the Israeli Labor Federation, which in the 1920s encouraged the spread of jelly doughnuts, which are difficult to prepare at home and therefore generated jobs for workers in bakeries.

Once when visiting my old friends Rafi Magnes and his wife, Liz, who were living in Jaffa at the time, I decided to try making some of these doughnuts myself. After one bite, Rafi was reminded of the doughnuts he enjoyed while growing up in Jerusalem in the 1950s.

"The best *soufganiyot* were at Café Allenby near the center of the city," he said. "Near the window was a huge bath of oil that was bubbling, and a machine that would drop the doughnuts into the oil. There was a lady who would turn them over when they were golden. Then she would fish them out and they would dry out on paper. Then another machine would inject them with red jam. What was good was they were so light with a lot of sugar and so big. Everybody in Jerusalem used to buy these *soufganiyot* for Hanukkah. They were unreal."

———————

yield: about 2 dozen doughnuts

2¼ teaspoons active dry yeast

3 tablespoons sugar, divided

¾ cup (175 ml) lukewarm milk

3½ cups (450 grams) unbleached all-purpose flour (about)

1 large egg plus 1 large egg yolk

Pinch of salt

Grated zest of 1 lemon

3½ tablespoons (50 grams) butter, at room temperature

Vegetable oil for deep-frying

1 cup, about, of apricot, strawberry, or any flavorful jam, *dulce de leche,* Nutella, or lemon curd

Confectioners' or granulated sugar for rolling

1. Dissolve the yeast and 1 tablespoon of the sugar in the milk.

2. Put the flour in the bowl of a food processor equipped with a steel blade. Add the dissolved yeast, whole egg and yolk, salt, lemon zest, and the remaining 2 tablespoons sugar. Process until blended, then pulse until a dough almost forms. Add the butter and process until the dough becomes sticky yet elastic.

3. Remove the dough to a bowl, cover, and let rise in a warm place for at least an hour. If you want to prepare it ahead, as I often do, place the dough in the refrigerator overnight, then let it warm to room temperature before rolling and cutting.

4. Dust a pastry board with flour. Roll the dough out to a ½-inch thickness. Using the top of a glass, cut into rounds about 2 inches in diameter, then roll into balls. Cover and let rise 30 minutes more.

5. Pour at least 2 inches of oil into a heavy pot and heat to 375 degrees.

6. Drop the doughnuts into the oil, 4 or 5 at a time. Cook about 3 minutes on each side, turning when brown. Drain on paper towels. Using a pastry or cupcake injector (available at cooking stores and online), insert a teaspoon of jam into each doughnut. Roll the *soufganiyot* in confectioners' or granulated sugar and serve immediately.

Croquante, Almond Brittle

Croquante is a typical almond brittle that centuries ago was made by the Jews who lived in Spain; it has since traveled with them to the far reaches of the earth. Originally calling for honey, the recipe eventually evolved to use sugar.

This particular recipe came to me from Sandy Amariglio, a ceramist who lives in Athens and whose father's family came from the picturesque island of Rhodes, where about nineteen hundred Jews lived before the Holocaust.

According to Sandy, her family felt relatively safe during the Second World War because they were on an island. But as soon as they learned that the Germans were coming, a cousin rented them a yacht and they fled to Crete. Once there, they had to walk across the island to find the British admiral who had arranged to put them on the boat on which they sailed to safe haven in Alexandria, where they spent the rest of the war. In 1945 they returned to Athens, where her father started a textile factory.

Sandy still feels a real connection to her grandmother, who taught her how to cook, always speaking in a mixture of French, Greek, and Ladino. "She always said to use your hands in cooking. I can still remember her making these *croquantes*, melting the sugar, putting in the almonds, throwing the hot mixture on a marble slab and then quickly taking a lemon in each hand and flattening the candy with the lemons, thus imparting the flavor of the lemon into the candy."

I have used Sandy's grandmother's basic recipe and method, but added a whimsical touch of ginger, mace, and rose petals. You can make this recipe your own by adding other flavorings and spices. This may be one of the world's oldest candies, but it's also one of the most adaptable.

yield: 6 servings (if you are not too hungry!)

Nonstick spray

2 whole lemons

1 cup (200 grams) sugar

1 cup (80 grams) blanched almonds, toasted

½ teaspoon ground ginger

¼ teaspoon ground mace

1½ teaspoons dry rose petals, lightly crushed between your fingers (optional)

---

1. Spray or grease a marble or other stone surface as well as the outside of the 2 lemons.

2. Heat the sugar in a heavy medium nonstick frying pan over medium heat. As soon as the sugar starts to melt around the perimeter of the pan (this will take about 5 minutes), take a wooden spoon and stir, trying to break up any lumps that might form.

3. When the sugar turns to the color of caramel, quickly add the almonds, ginger, mace, and rose petals (if using), continuing to stir until they are all evenly coated with the caramel. Immediately remove from the heat and pour onto the greased surface, spreading and flattening the mixture with the lemons (use the lemons like rolling pins).

4. When the *croquante* is cool and hard, about 5 to 10 minutes, crack it into bite-size pieces.

Natillas, Spanish Custard

Another toreador appears on the scene, earnestly trying to keep composed. He wavers as to how best to secure a profit, chews his nails, pulls his fingers, closes his eyes, takes four paces and four times talks to himself, raises his hand to his cheek as if he has a toothache, puts on a thoughtful countenance, sticks out a finger, rubs his brow, and all this accompanied by a mysterious coughing as though he could force the hand of fortune. Suddenly he rushes with violent gestures into the crowd, snaps with the fingers of one hand while with the other he makes a contemptuous gesture, and begins to deal in shares as though they were *natillas* [custard].
—Joseph Penso de la Vega, *Confusions of Confusions,* 1688

In this earliest known description of the operations of the Amsterdam Bourse, the first stock exchange in history, we see all the charged and chaotic movement that we still do on Wall Street—but in descriptive terms we wouldn't expect from stockbrokers today.

Joseph de la Vega's father, Isaac, was a Marrano who was imprisoned in a dungeon during the Inquisition. While there he made a solemn vow that within a year of regaining his liberty he would openly profess Judaism. He fled with his family first to Hamburg, then to Amsterdam, where he brought up his son Joseph, who became a merchant, poet, and philanthropist writing about the Dutch stock market.

Trading on the Amsterdam stock market was one of the few occupations open to Jews in the city. In those days, food was a big commodity. The Dutch called the practice of dealing in the future, what later became the futures exchange, *windhandel,* meaning "trading of the wind." Essentially, buyers could set the price of a food product, then plan their distribution and shipment, while the seller would account for uncertainties faced from weather or business conditions. Herring, for example, could be bought before they were caught, and cocoa, coffee, grains, and sugar purchased before they were grown. This was a benefit to both buyers and sellers, similar to our CSA (community supported agriculture) shares today.

Natillas is a very creamy and traditional custard that originated in Spain and has different iterations in Latin America, having been brought there with the conquistadores. Only recently at my bed-and-breakfast in Cuba, I was served *natillas,* which were possibly introduced to the island by the first Jews fleeing from Spain in 1492 and other Spaniards who came with Christopher Columbus.

yield: 6 servings

4 cups (1 liter) milk or soy milk, divided

2 sticks cinnamon

½ cup (100 grams) sugar

⅓ cup (40 grams) flour, sifted

¼ teaspoon salt

7 large egg yolks

1 teaspoon vanilla

½ teaspoon cinnamon

1. Put 3 cups (750 ml) of the milk and the cinnamon sticks in the top of a double boiler over boiling water and heat the milk. In a separate bowl, mix the sugar, flour, and salt, then stir in the remaining cup of cold milk and slowly add the egg yolks.

2. Remove the cinnamon sticks from the scalded milk and carefully stir the sugar-egg mixture into the hot milk. Continue cooking over boiling water, stirring constantly until thick. Remove from the heat, let stand a few minutes, then add the vanilla. Pour into a shallow baking dish or 6 individual ones.

3. Refrigerate and sprinkle with cinnamon before serving.

Dates in Brown Butter with Vanilla Ice Cream, Date Syrup, and Halvah Crumble

And did you not love Ishullanu, the gardener of your father's palm grove? He brought you baskets filled with dates without end; every day he loaded your table.
—John Harris, *The Epic of Gilgamesh: An Annotated Prose Rendition Based upon the Original Akkadian, Babylonian, Hittite, and Sumerian Tablets,* 2001

Plump dates, one of the seven foods mentioned in the book of Deuteronomy, are still used as a sign of welcome throughout the Middle East. According to Nawal Nasrallah, dried dates have long been eaten by everyone there, no matter their status or income, while those with means also added other ingredients such as clarified butter, toasted flour, sesame seeds, or nuts.

Heated, pressed, and cooked-down dates were the honey mentioned in the Bible and eaten by Babylonian Jews as *haroset* at Passover. To this day, date honey, also called date jam or molasses, and pressed sesame seeds (tahina) are eaten smeared on bread in Israel like peanut butter and jelly in the United States.

Dates traveled with explorers and conquerors, including Alexander the Great, making their way to India, the African coasts, and Spain. By the 1900s, dates had made the jump to the "Sahara" of America, the Coachella Valley in California. The desert climate and sandy soil proved prosperous for the date palms, and they have been growing there ever since.

After tasting a date cooked in brown butter and drizzled with honey at Sir and Star, a restaurant in Olema, California, I decided to gild the lily at home and serve them with vanilla ice cream, drizzled with date syrup, and topped with crumbled halvah. Halvah was one of the first candies with a long shelf life, if not the first. It traveled everywhere and became popular in America when it was introduced there by Nathan Radutzky, an immigrant from Kiev who started a company on the Lower East Side called Joyva. Halvah, dates, and date jam make an easy yet exotic dessert. And, as an added bonus, this is a perfect dessert to serve your gluten-free guests.

yield: 8 servings

3 tablespoons unsalted butter, divided

8 plump dates, like Barhi or Medjool

A splash of lemon juice

A splash of Pedro Ximénez or other good sherry or dark rum

A splash of honey

1 pint good vanilla ice cream

¼ cup (81 grams) date jam

¼ cup (55 grams) halvah, crumbled

---

1. Using a small frying pan, heat 2 tablespoons of the butter over medium heat until it browns. Cook the dates in the butter for just a few minutes, stirring often so they don't burn, then deglaze with lemon juice, the sherry or rum, honey, and a splash of water. Cook a few minutes longer until the liquid mostly evaporates, then finish off with the remaining butter. You can do this a few hours in advance.

2. Before serving, warm the dates again and put them on 8 plates. Then put a scoop of ice cream on each plate, drizzle with the date jam, and sprinkle the halvah on top.

Note You can freeze dates when they are fresh and then defrost them in the fridge for a few hours or overnight.

There are several date jams on the market. Either make your own—check out my recipe in *Jewish Cooking in America*—or buy the Lebanese brand Al Wadi al Akhdar or the Israeli brand Galil Silan, which is kosher. Sesame halvah is sold in Middle Eastern stores and comes in blocks.

Apple Kuchen

American-born and -bred Daniel Rose is one of the most successful chefs in Paris today. I met him years ago and since then have delighted in his food as I watch his restaurant, his talent, and his fame grow.

One of the things I like best about Daniel is that he has not forgotten his Chicago roots and what he learned from his grandmother. The first time I visited him in his kitchen, he baked his grandmother's apple cake, which I call here apple kuchen. In place of the apples, though, he used yellow plums he had found at the market, cutting them into quarters because some were sweeter than others, and he did not want anyone to get an inferior bite. As he added a pinch of anise instead of the cinnamon her recipe called for, he said, "I don't want to make it too different. I want it to taste like my grandmother's." I serve this for Rosh Hashanah with the first apples of the season.

---

1. Preheat the oven to 350 degrees. Grease a 9-inch springform pan with butter or oil, and set aside.

2. In the bowl of an electric mixer fitted with a paddle attachment, combine the remaining 8 ounces butter or oil, 1⅓ cups sugar, and the salt. Mix until blended. Add the eggs and mix until smooth. Using a rubber spatula, gently fold in the flour and baking powder until thoroughly mixed. Fold in about a cup of the apples, and spread batter evenly in the pan.

3. In a large bowl, toss the remaining apples with the Calvados or other apple brandy, ginger, and cinnamon or anise seeds. Arrange the apple slices in closely fitting concentric circles on top of the dough; you may not need all the slices. Sprinkle the remaining 1 tablespoon sugar over the apples.

4. Bake until a toothpick inserted into the center of the cake dough comes out clean and apples are golden and tender, about 50 minutes. Serve warm or at room temperature.

Note This cake, when it is made with vegetable oil instead of butter, is similar to the "Jewish Apple Cake" found in many church cookbooks throughout America, and was brought to this country by Polish immigrants, like my mother-in-law.

yield: 8 to 10 servings

1 cup (2 sticks/226 grams) unsalted butter or 1 cup (235 ml) vegetable or melted coconut oil, more for greasing pan

1⅓ cups (175 grams) plus 1 tablespoon sugar

⅛ teaspoon salt

2 large eggs

2 cups (270 grams) unbleached all-purpose flour

2 teaspoons baking powder

4 Gala or other flavorful apples, peeled, cored, and each cut into 8 crescent slices, about 3 cups, divided

½ teaspoon Calvados or other apple brandy

1 teaspoon freshly grated ginger

½ teaspoon ground cinnamon or anise seeds

Upside-Down Fruit Cobbler

Ever since I can remember, I have loved fruit tarts in the summer with fresh berries, peaches, plums, or a combination of everything. My mother showed me how to make a German butter crust, called a *Muerbeteig* (which means "crumbly crust"). I used to roll out and prebake the crust like a *crostata*, so that it got crisp, put a little jam on it à la Julia Child, and then carefully arrange the fruit slices into beautiful circles on top.

Since so many people are afraid of soggy crusts, my son David—who used to be a personal chef when he was not acting—suggested that I crumble the dough on top. That way you taste the sweet butter crust but you don't have to have a lot of it. It's also easy and delicious. Sometimes I roll it into circles instead of crumbling the dough. I've given a few of my suggestions below, but you should experiment with whatever fresh, local fruit you have available.

---

1. To make the crust using a food processor fitted with a metal blade, pulse the flour, salt, and ½ cup of the sugar together. Cut the butter or coconut oil into small pieces, add to the bowl, and process until crumbly. Add the egg yolk and process until a ball is formed, adding a tablespoon or two of cold water if necessary.

2. To make the dough by hand, use your fingers or a pastry blender to work the butter into the flour, salt, and ½ cup sugar until the mixture resembles coarse breadcrumbs. Add the egg yolk and work the dough into a ball, adding a tablespoon or two of cold water if necessary.

3. Cover the dough in plastic wrap and refrigerate for at least 30 minutes.

4. Preheat the oven to 375 degrees and put the fruit in a 9-by-13-inch baking dish. Sprinkle the lemon zest, preserved ginger, and the remaining cup sugar over all, stirring gently to combine.

5. On a lightly floured surface, roll the dough to be slightly thicker than ¼ inch, then cut into circles about 2½ inches in diameter using a biscuit or cookie cutter and arrange the dough over the fruit or merely crumble over the fruit. Don't worry about any cracks in the dough—you want it to be like a cobbler.

6. Bake for about 45 minutes, or until the crust is golden brown and the fruit is bubbling. Remove from the oven and serve warm or at room temperature, topped with vanilla ice cream or whipped cream.

yield: 10 to 12 servings

1½ cups (203 grams) unbleached all-purpose flour, plus more for rolling

¼ teaspoon salt

1 to 1½ cups (200 grams) sugar, divided

8 tablespoons (1 stick/ 113 grams) unsalted butter or coconut oil

1 large egg yolk

10 cups (2.85 kilos) mixed diced fruit such as rhubarb, peaches, blueberries, raspberries, and/or strawberries (see note below for more ideas)

1 teaspoon grated lemon zest

¼ cup (55 grams) crystallized ginger, diced

Vanilla ice cream or whipped cream

Note You can make different variations of this dessert all year round—with 9 cups (about 3 pounds/1.35 kg) apples, peeled and cored, 1 cup (225 grams) fresh or frozen cranberries, and fresh ginger in the fall and winter; or 10 cups apples (about 3½ pounds/1.5 kg), peeled and cored, spread with a thick layer of apricot jam (about ½ cup/115 grams) in the winter; and of course rhubarb and strawberries in the summer. For the Fourth of July, a combination of blueberries and strawberries or raspberries, topped with vanilla ice cream, is a way to make it red, white, and blue.

Free-Form Quince Babka

In Matat, way up in the north of Israel, right on the border with Lebanon, lives Erez Komarovsky, the man who brought European breads to the country (he is the former owner of the Lehem Erez [Erez's Bread] chain of bakeries). His house, in an almost biblical garden in Upper Galilee overlooking the Zefat Mountains, is full of charm—decorated with his grandmother's meat grinders, furniture made of distressed wood, and lots and lots of old pots. When I last visited, he was in a bread-baking frenzy, making falafel bread, lamb bread, and what he called a quince freehand babka.

Quinces grow in the fields near where Erez lives—he has a tree in his garden—and are harvested in the fall, at about the time I was visiting. Many people think that quince was the "apple" in the Garden of Eden, forbidden to eat because of its bitter outer skin.

For this babka, the quinces are cut into large chunks, then poached in wine spiked with star anise, cinnamon sticks, cardamom pods, and a vanilla bean. (The poached quinces even make a fine dessert on their own, served over ice cream or with pound cake.) Erez likes to roll out his dough and bake it on a baking sheet, in contrast to most babkas, which are baked in Bundt or loaf pans. This free-form presentation makes for a stunning dessert or brunch item drizzled with leftover poaching syrup.

If you cannot find quinces, you can substitute Bosc pears. Proceed with the recipe as directed, but only cook the pears for about 1 hour, until soft but not falling apart, and reduce the amount of sugar to ½ cup or to your taste.

———————

1. **make the dough** In the bowl of a standing mixer, stir the yeast into ⅓ cup (80 ml) of warm water along with 2 of the tablespoons of sugar. Add 1 whole egg, the butter, heavy cream, and salt, mixing with the paddle attachment until well blended.

2. Switch to a dough hook and gradually add the flour, kneading until a soft dough forms. The dough will be very soft and somewhat sticky; add more flour if necessary so the dough is sticky but not wet. Put the dough in a greased bowl, cover with plastic, and let rest in the refrigerator for at least 8 hours or overnight.

3. **meanwhile, make the quince filling** Peel and core the quinces, making sure to remove their hard inner cores. Cut each quince into 8 slices and put them into a large, heavy-bottomed pot.

yield: 6 to 8 servings

DOUGH

1 tablespoon active dry yeast

3 tablespoons sugar, divided

1 whole large egg, plus 1 large egg yolk for brushing

12 tablespoons (1½ sticks/ 169 grams) unsalted butter, at room temperature and cut into cubes

¼ cup (60 ml) heavy cream, plus 1 tablespoon for brushing

¼ teaspoon salt

1¾ to 2¼ cups (235 to 305 grams) unbleached all-purpose flour

QUINCE FILLING

2 pounds (675 to 900 grams) quinces (about 3 large quinces)

1 lemon, cut in half and seeds removed

1½ cups (355 ml) heavy red wine, such as Cabernet

¾ cup (150 grams) sugar or to taste

2 whole star anise

1 stick cinnamon

1 vanilla bean, split and seeds removed

3 whole pods green cardamom

4. Add the lemon, wine, sugar, star anise, cinnamon, scraped vanilla and the pod, and the cardamom. Bring to a boil, then simmer uncovered, stirring occasionally at first to dissolve the sugar, then continue simmering for about 1½ hours, or until the quinces are very soft but not falling apart. The wine may not completely cover the quinces at first, but the fruit will shrink as it cooks down. Taste, adjust the sugar if the filling is too bitter, and allow to cool. (The quinces may be cooked a few days in advance and kept in the poaching liquid in the refrigerator, which will infuse them with more flavor.)

5. When the quinces are cool, strain and set aside in a bowl. Reserve the poaching liquid and discard the spices.

6. Reduce the poaching liquid in a small saucepan over medium-high heat, until the liquid is thick and syrupy, about 15 to 20 minutes.

7. **to continue making the babka** Line a baking sheet with parchment paper. On a well-floured work surface, roll out the dough to a rectangle about 16 by 14 inches and gently move to the parchment-lined baking sheet. Arrange the poached quince chunks on the dough, leaving a 2-inch border.

8. **to shape the babka** First bring the short sides about 2 inches over the filling, then roll the babka lengthwise like a jelly roll. Position the babka to be seam side up. Brush the dough with the remaining egg yolk diluted with the remaining 1 tablespoon cream, reserving the remaining egg wash. Cover with a kitchen towel and let rise about an hour, until soft and fluffy.

9. Preheat the oven to 350 degrees and brush the dough once more with the egg wash and sprinkle the top with the remaining tablespoon of sugar. Bake for about 45 minutes, until golden. Remove from the oven and brush the babka with some of the reduced poaching liquid. Serve alone or with vanilla ice cream and any remaining poaching liquid on the side.

Roman Ricotta Cheese *Crostata* with Cherries or Chocolate

Estimate the amount of milk necessary for this dish and sweeten it with honey to taste; to a pint of fluid take 5 eggs; for half a pint dissolve 3 eggs in milk and beat well to incorporate thoroughly, strain through a colander into an earthen dish and cook on a slow fire. When congealed sprinkle with pepper and serve.
—Apicius, *De re Coquinaria* (Cookery and Dining in Imperial Rome), first century C.E.

When in Rome, do as the Romans do: Head straight to the tiny nondescript Pasticceria Boccione (also known as the "Burnt Bakery" or the "Jewish bakery") in the *ghetto ebraico* ("Jewish Ghetto") near the Tiber. There, four sisters make the same slightly burnt baked goods until they run out each day. Whether composed of tourists or locals, there is always a line outside.

One of the popular staples is a rich ricotta cake wrapped in a *crostata* crust, called *Cassola,* a Christmas must in Rome. According to Clifford Wright, the Jews of Rome learned to make whey cheese in Sicily and brought the technique with them to Rome.

I have added a delicious Italian *crostata* that I learned from an Italian Jew in place of the heavier crust that Boccione uses. I love the hint of cinnamon with sour cherry jam made from Amaro cherries—or any jam that has a slightly sweet, slightly sour flavor—mixed with the rich ricotta cheese. You can also use chunks of chocolate in place of the jam.

————————

1. **for the crust** Put the sugar, butter, egg yolks, flour, and salt in a large bowl and either rub everything together with your fingers, or quickly pulse the ingredients in a food processor fitted with a steel blade until the dough forms a ball. Either way, do not overwork the dough. Cover in plastic wrap and chill in the refrigerator for a half hour.

2. Preheat the oven to 375 degrees, place the rack in the top third of the oven, and grease a 10-inch tart pan with a removable bottom.

3. On a lightly floured surface roll out the dough into a 13-inch diameter quasi-circle. Fold the dough gently and press into the pan. Trim and flatten the edges with a knife. You want this to be quite rustic. Prick with a fork and bake for 15 minutes, then remove from the oven and set aside.

4. **to make the filling** Stir together the ricotta, egg yolks, sugar, flour, lemon zest, vanilla, and cinnamon with a spoon in a medium mixing bowl.

yield: about 12 servings

CRUST

½ cup (100 grams) sugar

12 tablespoons (1½ sticks/ 169 grams) unsalted butter, at room temperature

2 large egg yolks

1½ cups (200 grams) unbleached all-purpose flour

Pinch of salt

FILLING

2½ cups (560 grams) whole milk ricotta

4 large eggs, separated

¾ cup (150 grams) sugar

1 tablespoon unbleached all-purpose flour

Grated zest of 1 lemon

1 teaspoon vanilla

½ to 1 teaspoon cinnamon

½ cup (130 grams) fresh, frozen, or dried cherries (defrosted and drained if using frozen)

½ cup (170 grams) dark chocolate broken into small pieces or chocolate chips

½ cup (126 grams) sour cherry preserves

5. In the bowl of a standing mixer with a whisk attachment, beat the egg whites until almost stiff peaks form and fold gently into the ricotta mixture with all the cherries and/or the chocolate.

6. Spread the cherry preserves over the entire crust, then spoon on the ricotta mixture, smoothing over the top with the back of a spoon. Bake in the top third of the oven for 40 to 50 minutes, or until the center is set and golden brown; or do as the Romans do, and let it get slightly burnt on the top.

Note I like mixing the chocolate and the cherries, but if you prefer, use just one or the other.

Fluden de Pasach, Cashew Nut Strudel with Guava and Lime

When I visited her home in Recife, Brazil, Mathilde Steinberg's deft hands shaped a *fluden* (called *fladen* or *floden* in some Yiddish dialects), a fruit-layered sweet resembling baklava that is seldom seen in the United States. It is usually made with a paper-thin crust, but at Passover Mathilde uses a thick cashew-nut–matzo-meal batter with a guava-paste filling. It is a recipe she learned from a Jewish friend whose parents came from Belarus to Brazil, where they switched grape jam for guava.

Mathilde and her friends, the tradition-bearers of this community, make signature dishes with a Brazilian twist, like the *fluden,* by the hundreds for *brises,* bar mitzvahs, and weddings.

―――――――

1. Preheat the oven to 350 degrees and grease a 9-by-9-inch baking dish. In a food processor fitted with a steel blade, coarsely grind the cashews but do not pulverize into a powder—you want some crunch. Set aside ¼ cup (55 grams) of the ground cashews.

2. In a medium bowl, mix together the larger portion of the ground cashews, the matzo meal, sugar, and salt. Stir in the lime zest and juice, oil, and 2 whole eggs. Put half the cake-like dough in the pan and pat it down with your hands.

3. Cut the guava paste into long, ½-inch-thick strips and arrange on top of the dough in the pan. You should have a single packed layer of guava paste. Add the remaining batter, patting it down gently with your hand.

4. Beat the egg yolk with a teaspoon of water and paint the top of the dough with it. Sprinkle the remaining ¼ cup (55 grams) ground cashews on top. Bake for 45 minutes, or until it is golden and the sides begin to pull away from the pan. Cool, then slice into roughly 2-inch squares and serve.

yield: about 16 pieces

Nonstick spray for greasing pan

2 cups (305 grams) unsalted roasted cashews

1 cup (115 grams) matzo meal

1½ cups (300 grams) sugar

¼ teaspoon salt

2 limes, zest grated finely and ¼ cup (60 ml) juice reserved

½ cup (120 ml) vegetable oil

2 large eggs plus 1 yolk

10½ ounces (298 grams) guava paste

Classic American Cheesecake
with a European Twist

A few years ago, my husband, Allan, and I stayed at the home of Elisabeth Bourgeois, the chef of Le Mas Tourteron in Gordes, France. The last night of her season—the restaurant closes from November through February—we ate our way through her wonderful menu.

Toward the end of the meal, the buffet cart was rolled out, and among the very traditional French desserts, I saw what looked like a creamy American cheesecake with a graham cracker crust. When I asked Elisabeth what it was, she said, "Oh, that is a new dessert that our guests really like. It is made with Philadelphia. We learned it from a Japanese intern."

Allan and I laughed and then we confirmed that this was indeed an example of the classic American cheesecake born when James L. Kraft, who already owned the Philadelphia cream cheese company, bought a graham cracker company. (When I asked Elisabeth how the Japanese intern found the recipe, she said that she got it off the Internet and made it for the staff.) Today the dessert, less sweet and more lemony than its American counterpart, is a regular on her menu.

On another trip to Europe, I visited Jordan Greenwood, an American cousin living in Belgium. Jordan and his ex-wife ran a cheese store in the Sainte-Catherine area in Brussels, the gourmet ghetto of the city. When I visited the store, I saw on top of the counter, attractively displayed between all the cheeses imported from France, Jordan's grandmother's cheesecake from Galveston, Texas, almost identical to the one I tasted in Provence. Now Jordan, who has moved on to creating a Jewish delicatessen nearby called Delicatessen, also serves the same Philadelphia cheesecake but with a crust made from speculoos cookies made with allspice and cinnamon instead of graham crackers.

The cake, which started in Europe with farmer cheeses, came to America, where it was touched by local processed products, and returned to Europe with Philadelphia cream cheese and found a Belgian speculoos crust. Now Philadelphia cream cheese, exported to France and Belgium, is making what we all think of as a "New York" cheesecake European again.

---

yield: 10 to 12 servings

22 square graham crackers or 40 speculoos cookies

8 tablespoons (1 stick/ 113 grams) unsalted butter, melted

1½ pounds (three 8-ounce/ 113-gram packages) cream cheese, preferably Philadelphia, at room temperature

1 cup (200 grams) sugar

Juice and zest of 2 lemons (about ⅓ cups juice)

4 large eggs

Seasonal berries for garnish

1. Preheat the oven to 350 degrees and line the bottom of a 10-inch springform pan with parchment paper. Tightly wrap the bottom half of the springform pan in aluminum foil to prevent leaks.

2. Put the graham crackers or speculoos cookies in a food processor with a steel blade and process until crumb-like. You will get about 2 cups of crumbs.

3. Grease the bottom and sides of the springform pan with some of the melted butter. Pour the rest over the graham cracker or speculoos crumbs and process until well blended. Press the crumb mixture into the bottom and about 1 inch up the sides of the prepared pan. Bake until lightly browned, 12 to 15 minutes. Let cool on a wire rack.

4. While the crust is baking, bring a kettle of water to a boil.

5. In the bowl of a standing mixer fitted with the paddle attachment, beat the cream cheese on medium until fluffy, making sure there are no lumps. Gradually add the sugar, then stir in the lemon juice and zest. Beat in the eggs, one at a time, scraping down the sides of the bowl after each addition.

6. Slowly pour the cheese filling over the crust, then put the pan in the center of a large roasting dish. Pour the boiling water into the dish, being careful not to splash any water on the cake, until it comes halfway up the side of the springform.

7. Bake the cake until just set in the center, about 35 minutes. Then turn off the oven and open the oven door at least 4 inches. To help prevent cracks, leave the cheesecake in the oven 30 minutes longer.

8. Remove the cake from the oven and let it cool in the pan on a rack for 20 minutes. Then run a small knife around the edge and let it cool completely. Remove the cake from the water and cover; chill overnight and remove the sides just before serving. Serve chilled, decorated with fresh berries.

Aranygaluska, Hungarian Golden Pull-Apart Cake with Walnuts and Apricot Jam

Aranygaluska, also called golden dumpling cake, butter puffs, and monkey bread, has been extolled by Jewish immigrants from Hungary for years. I first noticed a recipe for the cake in George Lang's *The Cuisine of Hungary* from 1971. *Aranygaluska* probably started as a rich cake, like the German *Dampfnudeln* (see my *Jewish Cooking in America*) served with fish or soup on Fridays, when no meat was allowed for Catholics. Jews who separated meat from dairy in their diet would serve it with a fish or nonmeat soup.

Agnes Sanders, who grew up under Communism in Miskolc, Hungary, kindly showed me how she makes *aranygaluska* in her kitchen on New York's Upper West Side. "It wasn't bad growing up during the Communist [period] in Hungary," she told me. "Everyone was equally poor but we could go anywhere." When her mother died, her father, fearful that she would not marry a Jew, sent her to Detroit to live with an uncle in 1965. Everyone else in her family had died in the Nazi concentration camps.

Agnes's version of *aranygaluska,* learned in this country, was not as rich as I remembered it. I have tweaked her recipe here and there, adding ingredients like vanilla to the cake. I also add a chocolate alternative to the nuts, called *kuchembuchem* (one of those marvelous made-up Yiddish rhyming names), often made with leftover babka dough. Try one or both versions.

———————

yield: about 8 to 10 servings

1 tablespoon active dry yeast

1 cup (235 ml) warm milk

½ cup (100 grams) sugar, plus 2 tablespoons

4 large eggs

Zest of 1 orange

1 teaspoon vanilla

1 cup plus 4 tablespoons (2½ sticks/282 grams) unsalted butter, at room temperature, divided

4½ cups (600 grams) unbleached all-purpose flour (about)

1 teaspoon salt

1½ cups (180 grams) ground walnuts

6 tablespoons (83 grams) brown sugar

¾ teaspoon cinnamon

3 tablespoons cake or butter cookie crumbs

¾ cup (150 grams) apricot or plum jam

1. Dissolve the yeast in the warm milk in the bowl of a standing mixer equipped with a paddle attachment. Add ¼ cup of the sugar, the eggs, orange zest, vanilla, and 1 stick of butter. Gradually add the flour and salt, beating until mixed. Cover the bowl and leave for an hour, or until the dough has about doubled in size.

2. Preheat the oven to 350 degrees and butter a 10-inch round pan with some of the second stick of butter.

3. Melt what is left of the second stick of butter plus the remaining half stick and put it in a small bowl. In a separate bowl, mix the walnuts, brown sugar, remaining white sugar, cinnamon, and the cake or cookie crumbs.

4. Roll the dough into a ½-inch-thick circle. Using a 1-inch cookie or biscuit cutter, cut circles of dough. Dip the circles first in the butter, then in the nut mixture and set in the pan, almost touching each other. After a layer is completed, spoon on dollops of jam. Make a second layer, filling in the holes with dough, then jam, continuing and rerolling until the dough is used

up, ending with the walnut topping but not the jam. Bake in the oven for 35 to 40 minutes, or until golden brown and set. Leave in the pan for a few minutes, then turn onto a plate and serve warm. You can either cut the cake or pull the sections apart. Serve for a sweet breakfast treat, or as a dessert, served with good vanilla or rum raisin ice cream.

Note You can substitute ¼ cup good-quality unsweetened cocoa and ¾ cup sugar for the nut topping. Then, after dipping the rounds in butter, dip them in the chocolate-sugar mixture and proceed as above. Substitute the jam with Nutella or another chocolate spread.

Sometimes if serving *aranygaluska* for breakfast for a family gathering, I mold the cake and refrigerate it overnight. The next morning, while my guests are still sleeping, I bake it for them to pull apart when they wake up. Yum!

Ginger Almond Sponge Cake with Cardamom and Pistachios

Soraya Nazarian, the matriarch of the Iranian Nazarian clan in Los Angeles, uses a hefty amount of cardamom in the moist almond sponge cake with pistachios she bakes for Passover. I like its silky texture, the unexpected kick from the cardamom, and its easy preparation. Separating and whipping the whites of the eggs until they are stiff is a technique learned in Spain and exported by Sephardic Jews, who used it in making what they called *pan d'Espagna,* or Spanish bread, basically a sponge cake.

---

1. Preheat the oven to 350 degrees and grease a 9-inch Bundt pan or a 9-inch square pan. Whisk the egg whites in a mixer until they are stiff but not dry, and set aside.

2. With a food processor, pulse the almonds until very finely ground but still textured, stirring once or twice to prevent them from turning into a paste. Add the almond meal, salt, egg yolks, and sugar, and pulse to blend. Then gradually add the cardamom, the ginger, the almond extract, and ½ cup of the oil. Gently fold in the egg whites.

3. Pour the batter into the prepared pan. Bake in the middle of the oven for about 50 minutes, or until a toothpick inserted in the center comes out clean. Allow to cool for 10 minutes, then remove from the pan and finish cooling on a rack. To decorate, dust with confectioners' sugar and chopped pistachios.

yield: one 9-inch cake (10 to 12 servings)

½ cup (120 ml) vegetable oil, plus additional for pan

7 large eggs, separated

2 cups (240 grams) ground almonds (about 1½ cups whole almonds)

2 cups (220 grams) almond meal

Dash of salt

¾ cup (150 grams) sugar

2 teaspoons ground cardamom

2 tablespooons grated fresh ginger and/or 2 tablespoons coarsely ground candied ginger

1 tablespoon almond extract

Confectioners' sugar (kosher for Passover), for dusting

Finely chopped roasted pistachios, for garnish

Flourless Chocolate Cake

I know many good cooks but none who entertains as joyously and effortlessly as Injy Farat-Lew. More often than not, when Injy and her husband, Jason, invite friends for lunch or dinner at their sprawling home on Martha's Vineyard, she will serve this elegant flourless chocolate cake for dessert.

Injy was born into an Egyptian-Jewish family. Her grandfather Emmanuel Mizrahy Pasha was one of the few Jews to serve as Pasha, or financial counselor, to King Fuad I, the father of King Farouk. In 1961, when Injy was twelve and five years after Gamal Abdel Nasser's 1956 revolution, the family fled to Paris from Cairo, leaving this regal life forever.

After studying medicine in Paris, Injy met Jason, also a doctor, on a trip cruising down the Nile. Cairo and Paris are far cries from Martha's Vineyard where Jason is an obstetrician, but Injy has made this island her home and uses nearby farms as sources for ingredients. Because she likes to make food that is easy and delicious for her ever-appearing guests, this flourless chocolate cake—a cake that has been around since Europeans started using chocolate and has wandered as much as Injy's family—is a favorite dessert. It was a big hit the year that Injy brought the cake to our Passover Seder. I like to serve it covered with colorful berries.

---

yield: 8 to 10 servings

8 ounces (226 grams) good bittersweet chocolate such as Caillebaut or Guittard

8 tablespoons (1 stick/ 113 grams) unsalted butter or coconut oil

6 large eggs, separated

¾ cup (150 grams) sugar

Pinch of salt

1 teaspoon vanilla

Unsweetened cocoa for dusting

Raspberries and blueberries for topping

Whipped cream or ice cream (optional)

---

1. Preheat the oven to 350 degrees and butter a 9- or 10-inch spring-form pan with spray or a little of the butter or coconut oil.

2. Melt the chocolate and the butter or coconut oil in a double boiler or in a bowl in the microwave for a little more than a minute. Let cool.

3. In the bowl of an electric stand mixer using the whip attachment, beat the egg whites with ½ cup (100 grams) of the sugar and the salt until soft peaks form. In a separate bowl, whip the yolks with the remaining ¼ cup (50 grams) sugar and vanilla. Using a spatula, slowly stir the chocolate in with the egg yolk mixture. Then carefully fold in the egg whites. Don't over-mix or it will deflate.

4. Bake for 28 to 35 minutes, or until the cake is fully set around the edges. You want it to be slightly gooey in the center.

5. Let cool in the pan for a few minutes, then remove from pan to cool completely, and dust with cocoa.

6. Serve topped with berries and, if you like, with whipped cream or ice cream.

Libyan *Saefra,* King Solomon's Cake

Many families in Libya used to squeeze oranges and bottle the juice to be used all year round. According to Claudia Roden, in her magnificent *Book of Jewish Food,* using oranges in cakes was a particularly Jewish practice. These cakes, usually prepared with the tart Seville oranges that had to be boiled for hours to tame their bitterness, have been enjoyed for centuries. With sweeter oranges and commercial juice available today, we don't have to boil them.

King Solomon's Cake, popular in Libya and attributed to King Solomon himself, is also called *saefra* (yellow) cake—the yellow comes from saffron—and is an appropriate recipe with which to end this book. Many versions are studded with raisins but I prefer this spiced date filling instead. This delicious dairy-free cake was a must for the Sabbath and special occasions. I assume it predates the more elaborate baklava we know today. It was also, according to the late cookbook author Copeland Marks, an aphrodisiac—and, as such, it was served on the eve of the Sabbath to husbands needing help in their conjugal duties.

————

1. Preheat the oven to 350 degrees and grease a 9- or 10-inch springform pan.

2. **to make the filling** Pulse the oil, dates, cinnamon, cardamom, and cloves in a food processor with a steel blade until a thick paste has formed.

3. **to make the cake** In a medium bowl, mix together the cream of wheat, semolina, sugar, baking powder, vegetable oil, orange juice, and orange zest to create a thick batter.

4. Spread half the batter into the prepared pan, then top with the date filling, spreading the mixture with a spatula to the edges of the pan. Pour the remaining batter over the top, smooth the surface, and score the top of the cake into 2-inch diamond shapes. Gently push one whole almond vertically into the center of each diamond, then scatter the sesame seeds over all. Bake for 30 to 45 minutes, or until golden on the top.

5. Fifteen minutes before the cake is done, make the syrup. In a small saucepan, bring the sugar, honey (if using), ½ cup (120 ml) of water, and lemon juice to a simmer and cook for 10 minutes, stirring frequently. Remove from the heat, add the saffron, and let steep for 5 minutes. Pour the warm syrup over the cake when it is done. Let stand for at least 6 hours or more, so the cake completely absorbs the syrup.

yield: 8 to 10 servings

DATE FILLING

2 tablespoons vegetable oil

1 pound pitted dates, chopped

1 teaspoon ground cinnamon

¼ teaspoon ground cardamom

⅛ teaspoon ground cloves

CAKE

2 cups (440 grams) cream of wheat

1 cup (225 grams) coarse semolina

½ cup (100 grams) sugar

1½ teaspoons baking powder

1 cup (235 ml) vegetable oil

1 cup (235 ml) orange juice

Grated zest from 1 orange

½ cup blanched whole almonds for garnish

1 tablespoon sesame seeds for garnish

SYRUP

1½ cups (300 grams) sugar, or ¾ cup (150 grams) sugar and ¾ cup (175 ml) honey

Juice of 1 lemon

¼ teaspoon saffron threads

Acknowledgments

Working on this book took me on an extraordinary journey to the roots and evolution of Jewish cooking. I traveled to five continents and more than fifteen countries in search of recipes and their stories. Along the way I asked questions of countless people, among them archaeologists, cinnamon growers, chicken farmers, diplomats, rickshaw drivers, Talmudic scholars, and, of course, myriad home cooks.

It was Lexy Bloom, my inspirational editor at Alfred A. Knopf, who thought of the perfect title: *King Solomon's Table*. Her presence and enthusiasm have infused this journey. During the process, she not only birthed this book, but also baby Clio.

One of my favorite parts of writing cookbooks is the privilege of learning. Many people have helped translate articles for me and educated me on ancient sources such as the cuneiform tablets and the Cairo Genizah. Others have provided priceless tips such as introducing me to great Iraqi Jewish cooks in London and giving me the tip that I had to go to El Salvador for a no-cook German Jewish chocolate treat. I am so appreciative of the time and generosity of knowledge they shared with me. Among them: Diana Altman, Najmieh Batmanglij, Geraldine Brooks, Eric H. Cline (professor of Classics and Anthropology at George Washington University), Braeden Eastman, Elia Garfunkiel, Vered Guttman, Sharon Horowitz at the Library of Congress, Rabbi Avrohom Keller, Rebecca Lehrer, the late Gilbert Marks, Serge and Suzanne Modigliani, Ruth Naher, Moisés Naím, Irene Kronhill Pletka, Kenneth Robbins, Trina Rubenstein, Robbie Sabel, Tannaz Sassooni, Andrew Smith, Marian Sofaer, and Susan Weingarten.

I love weaving all this material together, but it can be an agonizing process. I want to thank Elisheva Baumgarten, professor of Jewish Studies at the Hebrew University of Jerusalem; Marc Z. Brettler, the Bernice and Morton Lerner Professor in Judaic Studies at Duke University; Ulla Kasten, curator at Sterling Memorial Library at Yale University; Jodi Magness, Department of Religious Studies, University of North Carolina; Pamela Nadel, chair, the Department of History at American University; Nawal Nasrallah, author of *Delights from the Garden of Eden*; Ben Outhwaite, archivist of the Genizah at Cambridge University; Peggy Pearlstein, the former head of the Judaic Section at the Library of Congress; and Jonathan Sarna, the Joseph H. and Belle R. Braun Professor of American Jewish History at Brandeis University, all of whom read parts of this manuscript.

This book required extensive travel. Luckily I could count on generosity around the globe: Mari Carmen Aponte in San Salvador; Leila and Mohamed Benaissa in Asila, Morocco; Constance and Dominique Borde in Paris; Raquel and Riccardo Capua in Miami; Iris Carulli and Kathy Doherty in Rome; Jane Friedman in New York City; Dorothy and David Harman in Jerusalem; Nathan Hevroni in Tel Aviv; Aglaia Kremezi in Kea, Greece; Mathias Laurent and Sandrine Weil in Geneva; Debbie and Michael Lesser in Berkeley; Shelley Nathans and Sam Gerson in Berkeley; Geoffrey and Rachel Paul in London; Peter Poulos in Athens; and Alice Waters in Berkeley.

James Alefantis, Amy Bartscherer, Mark Furstenberg, Carol Brown Goldberg, Marilyn Nissenson, and Cathy Sulzberger gave me good counsel and emotional support on this long journey. Olive Garcia, Aaron Hamburger, Jessie Leiken, and Emelyn Rude assisted me in research and editing.

Through the years the ideas for some of the topics I covered in this book developed in other publications. The *New York Times* has been a regular outlet, starting with an article that I wrote in 1980 on Yemenite Jewish cooking. (But in those pre-Internet days, that first article never actually made it to readers because there was a newspaper delivery strike on the day it came out; later articles, fortunately, were published with no trouble.) Thank you to my extraordinary and supportive editors at the *Times:* Susan Edgerley, Nick Fox, Sam Sifton, Emily Weinstein, and Pete Wells. In the past few years, my monthly cooking column and videos in *Tablet* magazine have allowed me to expand my Jewish food horizons thanks to Wayne Hoffman and Alana Newhouse. Nadine Epstein at *Moment Magazine* and Hanna Rosin, then at *Slate,* have also encouraged me to write additional food stories with a cultural and historical twist.

It takes so many people to produce a book. My agent, David Black, does what a good agent should: he is right there cheering me on. The team at Alfred A. Knopf has once again shown their excellence. My thanks go to Sonny Mehta, Paul Bogaards, Sara Eagle, and Jordan Rodman. Thanks also to Tom Pold, Lexy's assistant, who was unflappable and helpful in so many ways; as was the design and production team: Kathy Hourigan, Kathleen Fridella, Cassandra Pappas, and Kelly Blair. Gabriela Herman, photographer, and Ryan Reinick, food stylist, were a great team to work with to produce the breathtaking photos that adorn this book.

The late *New York Times* editorial writer William Safire once told me that a good assistant will learn from you for the first two months and you will learn from him or her thereafter. Kara Elder is such an assistant.

But most of all I want to thank my husband Allan and my children, Daniela, David, Merissa, and my daughter-in-law Talia, who all made great suggestions about cooks and recipes during the many years I was working on this book. They have put up with my obsessions about Jewish cooking, its origins, and its routes. And, as he knows, I am forever indebted to Allan for his patience and good humor during the exhilarating and challenging periods writing this book.

Bibliography

Here is a list of books and articles that were exceptionally helpful in researching this book. Works cited at the end of each quotation and in their text are, for the most part, not included here.

Abramowicz, Hirsz. *Profiles of a Lost World: Memoirs of East European Jewish Life Before World War II.* Translated by Eva Seitlin Dobkin. New York: YIVO Institute for Jewish Research, 1999.

Acosta, José de. *Historia Natural y Moral de las Indias.* Published in 1590. Seville, Spain: Casa de Juan de Leon, 1590.

Adler, Jerry and Andrew Lawler. "How the Chicken Conquered the World." *Smithsonian Magazine,* June 2012.

Apicius. *Apicius—Cookery and Dining in Imperial Rome.* Edited and translated by Joseph Dommers Vehling. New York: Dover Publications, 1977.

Arciniegas, German. *Latin America: A Cultural History.* New York: Alfred A. Knopf, 1967.

Artusi, Pellegrino. *The Art of Eating Well, 1820–1911.* Translated by Kyle M. Phillips III. New York: Random House, 1996.

Batmanglij, Najmieh. *Food of Life: Ancient Persian and Modern Iranian Cooking and Ceremonies.* Washington, D.C.: Mage Publishers, 2011.

Berlin, Adele, and Marc Zvi Brettler. *The Jewish Study Bible.* New York: Oxford University Press, 2004.

Berliner, Adolf. *Geschichte der Juden in Rom—von der aeltesten Zeit bis zur Gegenwart (2050 Jahre).* Frankfurt a.M.: J. Kauffmann, 1893. Two volumes.

Black, J. A., G. Cunningham, E. Fluckiger-Hawker, E. Robson, and G. Zólyomi. *The Electronic Text Corpus of Sumerian Literature.* Oxford, U.K.: 1998. etcsl.orient.ox.ac.uk

Brenner, Michael. *A Short History of the Jews.* Princeton, N.J.: Princeton University Press, 2010.

Brooks, Andrée Aelion. *The Woman Who Defied Kings: The Life and Times of Doña Gracia Nasi—A Jewish Leader During the Renaissance.* St. Paul, Minn.: Paragon House, 2002.

Bottéro, Jean. *The Oldest Cuisine in the World: Cooking in Mesopotamia.* Translated by Teresa Lavender Fagan. Chicago: University of Chicago Press, 2011.

Candolle, A. *Origin of Cultivated Plants.* New York: Appleton and Company, 1890.

Cato, M. Porcius, and M. Terentius Varro. *On Agriculture.* Translated by W. D. Hooper. Cambridge, Mass.: Harvard University Press, 1934.

Cohen, A. *The Five Megilloth: Hebrew Text and English Translation with Introductions and Commentary.* London: The Soncino Press, 1977.

Cooper, John. *Eat and Be Satisfied: A Social History of Jewish Food.* Northvale, N.J.: Jason Aronson, Inc., 1993.

David, Elizabeth. *Elizabeth David Classics: Mediterranean Food. French Country Cooking. Summer Cooking.* New York: Alfred A. Knopf, 1980.

Davidson, Alan. *The Oxford Companion to Food*. Oxford, U.K.: Oxford University Press, 1999.

Dawidowicz, Lucy S. *From That Place and Time: A Memoir, 1938–1947*. New York: W. W. Norton & Co., 1989.

DeWitt, Dave. *Precious Cargo: How Foods from the Americas Changed the World*. Berkeley, Calif.: Counterpoint, 2014.

Dweck, Poopa. *Aromas of Aleppo: The Legendary Cuisine of Syrian Jews*. New York: Ecco, 2007.

Ezratty, Harry A. *500 Years in the Jewish Caribbean: The Spanish and Portuguese Jews in the West Indies*. Baltimore: Omni Arts, 1997.

Freedman, Paul. *Out of the East: Spices and the Medieval Imagination*. New Haven, Conn.: Yale University Press, 2008.

Fussell, Betty. *The Story of Corn: The Myths and History, the Culture and Science of America's Quintessential Crop*. New York: Alfred A. Knopf, 1992.

Goitein, S. D. *A Mediterranean Society: The Jewish Communities of the Arab World as Portrayed in the Documents of the Cairo Geniza*. Six volumes. Berkeley, Calif.: University of California Press, 1967.

Goitein, S. D., and Mordechai Askiva Friedman. *India Traders of the Middle Ages: Documents from the Cairo Geniza* "India Book." Leiden, Netherlands: Brill Publishers, 2007.

Gosh, Amitav. *In an Antique Land: History in the Guise of a Traveler's Tale*. New York: Vintage Books, 1994.

Harris, John. *The Epic of Gilgamesh: An Annotated Prose Rendition Based upon the Original Sumerian, Akkadian, Babylonian, and Hittite Tablets with Supplementary Texts of Related Sumerian Lore and Selected Sumerian Proverbs*. Bloomington, Ind.: iUniverse, 2001.

Hassan, Linda Guetta. *La Cucina Ebraica Tripolina*. Rome: Gallucci, 2006.

Held, Paul. "The Confusion of Confusions: Between Speculation and Eschatology." Concentric: Literary Cultural Studies, 2006.

Herbst, Sharon Tyler, and Ron Herbst. *The Food Lover's Companion*. Third edition. Hauppauge, N.Y.: Barron's Educational Series, 2001.

Herman, Zvi. *The River and the Grain*. Tel Aviv: Zmora-Bitan, 1988.

Heschel, Abraham J. *Maimonides: A Biography*. New York: Fararr, Straus &Giroux, 1983.

Hoffman, Adina, and Peter Cole. *Sacred Trash: The Lost and Found World of the Cairo Geniza*. New York: Schocken, 2011.

Jurafsky, Dan. *The Language of Food: A Linguist Reads the Menu*. New York: W. W. Norton & Company, 2014.

Katz, Nathan, and Ellen S. Goldberg. *The Last Jews of Cochin: Jewish Identity in Hindu India*. Columbia, S.C.: University of South Carolina Press, 1993.

Katz, Nathan. *Who Are the Jews of India?* Berkeley, Calif.: University of California Press, 2000.

Kraemer, David. *Jewish Eating and Identity through the Ages*. New York: Routledge, 2007.

Kritzler, Edward. *Jewish Pirates of the Caribbean*. New York: Anchor Books, 2008.

Kriwaczek, Paul. *Yiddish Civilisation: The Rise and Fall of a Forgotten Nation*. New York: Vintage Books, 2005.

Kupovetsky, Mark, "Population and Migration: Population and Migration before World War I." *YIVO Encyclopedia of Jews in Eastern Europe*, October 2010.

Lang, George. *Cuisine of Hungary*. New York: Scribner, 1982.

Leon, Sciaky. *Farewell to Salonica: City at the Crossroads*. Philadelphia: Paul Dry Books, 2003.

Lev, Efrayim, and Zohar 'Amar. *Practical Materia Medica of the Medieval Eastern Mediterranean According to the Cairo Genizah*. Leiden, Netherlands: Brill Publishers, 2008.

Löw, Immanuel. *Die Flora der Juden*. Vienna: Loewit, 1924.

Lunde, Paul. "The Fable of the Rat." "Monsoons, Mude and Gold." "The Leek-Green Sea." "The Seas of Sinbad." *Saudi Aramco World: The Indian Ocean and Global Trade*, July/August 2005.

Machlin, Edda Servi. *The Classic Cuisine of the Italian Jews*. New York: Everest House, 1981.

Madariaga, Salvador de. *Christopher Columbus: Being the Life of the Very Magnificent Lord Don Cristóbal Colón.* New York: The Macmillan Company, 1940.

Maimonides, Moses. *On the Causes of Symptoms.* Edited by J. G. Leibowitz and S. Marcus. Berkeley, Calif.: University of California Press, 1974.

Mann, Charles C. "How the Potato Changed the World." *Smithsonian Magazine,* November 2011.

Marks, Gil. *Encyclopedia of Jewish Food.* Boston: Houghton Mifflin Harcourt, 2010.

Marton, Renee. *Rice: A Global History.* London: Reaktion Books, 2014.

Matthioli, Pietro Andrea. *Di pedanio Dioscoride anazarbeo libri cinque della historia.* Translated by George A. McCue."The History of the Use of the Tomato: An Annotated Bibliography." *Annals of the Missouri Botanical Garden* 39, November 1952.

Menocal, Maria Rosa. *The Ornament of the World.* Boston: Back Bay Books, 2002.

Miller, James Innes. *The Spice Trade of the Roman Empire.* New York: Oxford at the Clarendon Press, 1969.

Minkin, Jacob S. *The World of Moses Maimonides—With Selections from His Writings.* New York: Thomas Yoseloff, 1957.

Mintz, Sidney W. *Sweetness and Power: The Place of Sugar in Modern History.* New York: Viking Penguin, 1985.

Morton, Julia F. *Fruits of Warm Climates.* Miami, Fl.: J. F. Morton, 1987.

Motzkin, A. L. "A Thirteenth-Century Jewish Teacher in Cairo." *Journal of Jewish Studies,* University of Haifa, 1970.

Nabhan, Gary. *Cumin, Camels, and Caravans: A Spice Odyssey.* Oakland, Calif.: University of California Press, 2014.

Nasrallah, Nawal. *Dates: A Global History.* London: Reaktion Books, 2011.

———*Delights from the Garden of Eden: A Cookbook and History of the Iraqi Cuisine.* Sheffield, U.K.: Equinox Publishing, 2013.

Ohry, Abraham, and Jenni Tsafrir. "Is Chicken Soup an Essential Drug?" *Canadian Medical Association Journal,* December 14, 1999.

Panayi, Panikos. *Fish & Chips: A History.* London: Reaktion Books, 2014.

Pavoncello, Donatella Limentani. *Dal 1880 ad oggi la cucina ebraica della mia famiglia.* Rome: Carucci Editore, 1982.

Perera, Victor. *The Cross and the Pear Tree: A Sephardic Journey.* New York: Alfred A. Knopf, 1995.

Perry, Charles, A. J. Arberry, and Maxime Rodinson. *Medieval Arab Cookery: Papers by Maxime Rodinson and Charles Perry with a Reprint of a Baghdad Cookery Book.* London: Prospect Books, 1998.

Prinz, Deborah R. *On the Chocolate Trail: A Delicious Adventure Connecting Jews, Religions, History, Travel, Rituals and Recipes to the Magic of Cacao.* Woodstock, Vt.: Jewish Lights, 2012.

Reissner, H. G. "Jews in Medieval Ceylon." *The Ceylon Historical Journal,* 1953.

Rennard, Barbara, Ronald F. Ertl, Gail L. Gossman, Richard A. Robbins, and Stephen I. Rennard. "Chicken Soup Inhibits Neutrophil Chemotaxis In Vitro." *Chest,* 2000.

Roden, Claudia. *The Book of Jewish Food: An Odyssey from Samarkand to New York.* New York: Alfred A. Knopf, 1996.

Rosner, Fred. "Therapeutic Efficacy of Chicken Soup." *Chest,* 1980.

———*The Medical Aphorisms of Moses Maimonides.* Haifa: Maimonides Research Institute, 1989.

———*Moses Maimonides' Treatise on Asthma.* Haifa: Maimonides Research Institute, 1994.

———*Medical Encyclopedia of Moses Maimonides.* Lanham, Md.: Jason Aronson, 1998.

Sachar, Howard M. *Farewell España: The World of the Sephardim Remembered.* New York: Alfred A. Knopf, 1994.

Salaman, Redcliffe N. "Why 'Jerusalem' Artichoke?" *Royal Horticultural Society,* 1940.

———*The History and Social Influence of the Potato.* Cambridge, U.K.: Cambridge University Press, 1985.

Smith, Andrew. *The Tomato in America: Early History, Culture, and Cookery.* Columbia, S.C.: University of South Carolina Press, 1994.

Smith, Page, and Charles Daniel. *The Chicken Book.* San Francisco: North Point Press, 1982.

Sternberg, Robert. *Yiddish Cuisine: A Gourmet's Approach to Jewish Cooking.* Lanham, Md.: Jason Aronson, 1993.

Schneider, Elizabeth. *Vegetables from Amaranth to Zucchini: The Essential Reference: 500 Recipes, 275 Photographs.* New York: William Morrow Cookbooks, 2001.

Toaff, Ariel. *Love, Work, and Death: Jewish Life in Medieval Umbria.* Oxford, U.K.: Littman Library of Jewish Civilization, 1996.

Tudela, Benjamin of. *The Itinerary of Benjamin of Tudela: Travels in the Middle Ages.* London: A. Asher & Co., 1841.

Turner, Jack. *Spice: The History of a Temptation.* New York: Alfred A. Knopf, 2004.

Vester, Katharina. "'The American Table': Tourism, Empire, and Anti-Immigration Sentiment in American Cookbooks in the Nineteenth Century." *Transnational American Studies,* June 2012.

Watson, Andrew M. *Agricultural Innovation in the Early Islamic World.* Cambridge, U.K.: Cambridge University Press, 1983.

Woolfe, Jennifer A. *Sweet Potato: An Untapped Food Resource.* Cambridge, U.K.: Cambridge University Press, 1992.

Index

(Page references in *italics* refer to illustrations.)

apricot(s) *(continued)*:

 Sweet and Sour Persian Stuffed Grape
  Leaves, 76–7

 Syrian-Mexican Chicken with Tamarind,
  Chipotle Sauce and, 261

Arabs, transmission of recipes between Jews
 and, xix–xx, 197

Aranygaluska, Hungarian Golden Pull-Apart
 Cake with Walnuts and Apricot Jam, *340*,
 341–2

Arazi, Ron and Leetal, 170, 292, 293

arctic char:

 with Fennel, Onions, Currants, and Pine
  Nuts over Couscous, 235

 in Spicy Tomato Sauce (*Aharaimi*), *220*,
  221–2

Argan Oil Dressing with Shallots, 93

Arkansas *Schnecken* with Pecans, 42–3

Aronov, Aron and Ella, 282

artichokes:

 Double-Lemon Roast Chicken with,
  266

 Fried, Jewish-Style (*Carciofi alla Giudia*),
  71–4, *72*

Artusi, Pellegrino, 60

Ashe, Tom and Joanne, 205

Ashkenazic food, rise of, xx–xxi

Asilah, Morocco, *ferane* (brick public oven)
 in, 197

Asnkow, Avi, 151

Auspitz, Rudolf, 303

Azerbaijan, Azerbaijani cooking, 107

 Kukusa with Swiss Chard and Herbs,
  14, 15

babkas:

 Chocolate, *44*, 45–6

 Quince, Free-Form, 332–3

Babylon, Babylonian cooking, xv–xvii, xviii,
 257, 277, 282, 302, 327

 Butternut Squash and Leek Soup with
  Kurdish *Kubbeh* (Meat Dumplings),
  140–1

 haroset, 85, 327

 kuku and *kukusa* (egg dishes), 15

 mahshi (stuffed leaves), 76

 origin of word "matzo" and, 154

 taste for sweet and sour in, 76

T'Beet, Baghdadi Sabbath Overnight Spiced
 Chicken with Rice and Coconut Chutney,
 246, *248*, 249–51

tuh'u (beet soup), 120

Babylonian Talmud, xviii, 6, 112, 225

baccalà, 237, 238

bagels, xxvi, 159

 New Old-Fashioned, 27–8

 origin and history of, 29, 159

 topped with onions or seeds, 28

Baghdad, Baghdadi cooking, xviii, xix, xxi,
 4, 68

 Amba, Pickled Mango Sauce, 68–9

 date honey, 85

 Jewish community of, 249, 272

 Sambousak bel Tawa, Chickpea Pillows with
  Onions, 75

 T'Beet, Sabbath Overnight Spiced Chicken
  with Rice and Coconut Chutney, 246,
  248, 249–51

 Walnut-Almond Macaroons with
  Raspberry Jam Thumbprint, 308–9

baharat, 4–5

Bapt, Sophia Young, 57

Baranes, Michal, 125

barberries, in Sweet and Sour Persian Stuffed
 Grape Leaves, 76–7

Barhum, Yakub, 125

barley:

 flour for Passover, 154

 Hamim-Cholent Hybrid, a Wandering
  Sabbath Stew, 277–9

 Seven Sacred Species Salad with Wheat
  Berries, Olives, Figs, Dates, Grapes,
  Pomegranate and, *114*, 115

Basil, Brooklyn, 127

Bassani, Giorgio, 86

Basson, Esperanza and Moshe, 280–1

Bayonne, France, chocolate production in,
 314–15

Bazargan, Bulgur and Tamarind Dip with
 Nuts, 53

bean(s):

 Hamim-Cholent Hybrid, a Wandering
  Sabbath Stew, 277–9

 White, Lamb or Beef Stew with Spinach and
  (*Lubia bel-Saeilk*), 272–3

 White, Soup (*Minestra di Fagioli*), 121

 see also chickpea(s); fava beans

chickpea(s) (garbanzo beans), 10
    and Chicken Dumplings (*Gundi*), *136*, 137–8
    Falafel with Cilantro, Tahina Sauce, and
        Amba (Pickled Mango Sauce), 66–7
    Hamim-Cholent Hybrid, a Wandering
        Sabbath Stew, 277–9
    Hummus with Preserved Lemon and
        Cumin, *50*, 51–2
    Orecchiette with Rosemary Oil, Broccolini
        and, 176–7
    Pancakes with Fennel, Onion, and
        Rosemary (*Socca*), *54*, 55–6
    Pillows with Onions (*Sambousak bel
        Tawa*), 75
    Spiced Moroccan Vegetable Soup with
        Cilantro, Lemon and (*Harira*), 122, *123*
    Spinach and, Slow-Cooked Silky, 188–9
Chilaquiles, Mexican "Matzo" *Brei*, 20
Child, Julia, 124, 266, 268, 330
Chile Relleno, Green, Latkes, *204*, 205–6
chili peppers, 254–5
Chipotle Sauce, Syrian-Mexican Chicken with
    Apricot, Tamarind and, 261
chocolate, 314–15
    Babka, *44*, 45–6
    Cake, Flourless, 344, *345*
    Chip Pastry Cream, 313
    Filling, *Hamantashen* with, 311–13, *312*
    Hungarian Golden Pull-Apart Cake with
        Apricot Jam and (*kuchem-buchem*), 341,
        342
    Nut Filling, Spicy, Rugelach with, 306–7
    Roman Ricotta Cheese *Crostata* with, 335–6
    Sausage (*Schokoladenwurst*), 310
cholent:
    Hamim-Cholent Hybrid, a Wandering
        Sabbath Stew, 277–9
    modern, in slow cooker, 279
chorizo, in Smoky *Shakshuka* with Tomatoes,
    Peppers, and Eggplant, 16–18, *17*
Chremsel, Siberian Matzo Pancake Casserole,
    37–8
Chutney, Coconut, with Cilantro and Green
    Pepper, 251
cilantro:
    Coconut Chutney with Green Pepper and,
        251
    Cream, 210–11
    Ginger Butter, 244
    Pesto, 63

    Spinach Salad with Walnuts and, Racha's
        (*Spanakit*), *104*, 105
cinnamon, 5
    -Spiked Tomato Sauce, 173
    Sri Lankan, 40, 41
    sugar, 6
Claiborne, Craig, 182
Cobbler, Upside-Down Fruit, 330, *331*
coconut:
    Chutney with Cilantro and Green Pepper,
        251
    Milk, Winter Squash Soup with Hot Pepper
        and, *126*, 127–8
    Rickshaw Rebbetzin's *Thatte Idli*, Indian
        Steamed Rice Dumplings with Nuts and
        Raisins, 30–1
cod:
    baccalà, 237, 238
    with Tomatoes, Dried Plums, Onions, and
        Pine Nuts, *236*, 237–8
Code Noir (1684), 314–15
Cold Moon Farms, Jamaica, Vt., 161
Colombia, Colombian cooking:
    Jewish communities in, 169, 317
    Kamishbroit with Guava, *316*, 317
Columbian Exchange, xxiii, 121, 207, 212, 252,
    254–5, 303, 314
Columbus, Christopher, xxiii, 199, 218, 221,
    314, 324
Concia, Crispy Fried Zucchini with Garlic,
    Basil, and Balsamic Vinegar, 191
"cookbook," earliest known, xv–xvi
cookies:
    Biscotti-Like, with Dried Fruit and Wine
        (*Pizza Ebraica*), 319
    Ginger-Cardamom Butter, 321
    Hamantashen with Poppy Seed, Chocolate,
        or Apricot Filling, 311–13, *312*
    Kamishbroit with Guava, *316*, 317
    Rugelach with Spicy Chocolate-Nut Filling,
        306–7
    Salty Anise Butter Cookies, 320–1
    Tahina, 304, *305*
    Walnut-Almond Macaroons with
        Raspberry Jam Thumbprint,
        308–9
Cooperman, Eva Weiss, 213
Corned Beef, Home-Cured, 298–9
Cornmeal Ricotta Breakfast Pudding,
    Romanian (*Malai*), 47

corn tortillas, in Mexican "Matzo" *Brei*
  (*Chilaquiles*), 20
Cortés, Hernán, 314
Court Bouillon, 244
couscous:
  Hand-Rolled, 170–1
  Sardines with Fennel, Onions, Currants,
    and Pine Nuts over (*Couscous con le
    Sarde*), *234*, 235
Craigie on Main, Cambridge, Mass.,
  297
cranberry(ies):
  Challah-Chestnut-, Stuffing, 270
  Maine *Haroset* with Blueberries, Ginger
    and, 89
  Siberian *Chremsel*, Matzo Pancake
    Casserole, 37–8
cream cheese, in Classic American
    Cheesecake, with European Twist,
    338–9
crêpes, 32
croissant, 23, 156
Croquante, Almond Brittle, 323
Crostata, Ricotta Cheese, with Cherries or
    Chocolate, Roman, *334*, 335–6
Crumble Cake, Butter (*Putterkuchen*), 48
Csúsztatott Palacsinta, Hungarian Apple
    Pancakes, 32–3
cubeb, 6
Cucumber and Radish Salad, Persian, with
    Hungarian Paprika, 100
Cuisine de Nos Grand-mères, La (The Cooking
    of Our Polish Jewish Grandmothers), 48
Cukier, Delia R., 210
cumin, 6
curry(ied):
  Beet Borscht with Apples and Ginger, 120
  Fish, Bene Israel, with Fresh Ginger,
    Tamarind, and Cilantro, 231
Custard, Spanish (*Natillas*), 324–5

dafina (overnight Sabbath dish), 197
Dangoor, Linda, 75
Dangoor, Renée, 308
Danish Pastries, Cheese (*Delkelekh*), 39
Darna, Jerusalem, 242
date(s), 302, 327
  Brazilian *Haroset* with Apples, Cashews
    and, 88

in Brown Butter with Vanilla Ice Cream,
    Date Syrup, and Halvah Crumble, *326*,
    327–8
Filling, in Libyan *Saefra*, King Solomon's
    Cake, *300*, 346
honey, *haroset* origins and, 85, 327
Kamishbroit with, 317
Persian *Haroset* with Apples, Pistachios,
    Pomegranate Juice and (*Halleq*), 85
Seven Sacred Species Salad with Wheat
    Berries, Barley, Olives, Figs, Grapes,
    Pomegranate and, *114*, 115
David, Elizabeth, 120
Davidson, Linda, 59
Davis, Mitchell, 35
Dawidowicz, Lucy S., 92
Defo Dabo, Ethiopian Sabbath Bread, 151–2,
    153
Deitsch, Cyrel, 127
de la Vega, Isaac, 324
de la Vega, Joseph Penso, 324
Delicatessen, Brussels, 338
Delkelekh, Cheese Danish Pastries, 39
Denti di Pirajno, Alberto, 120
Derma, Stuffed, with Matzo Meal, Spices, and
    Onions (*Kishke*), 175
de Sequeyra, Dr. John, 16
de Silva, Chaminda, 40
de Soto, José, 127
desserts, *see* sweets
Deuteronomy, xvi, xxvii, xxviii
  seven sacred foods mentioned in, 115, 327
Di Capua, Sandra, 169
dietary laws, Jewish, xiv, xxvii–xxviii
Dill and Caper Dipping Sauce, 230
dips:
  Bazargan, Bulgur and Tamarind, with
    Nuts, 53
  Cilantro Pesto, 63
  Feta and Goat Cheese, Whipped, *202*,
    203
  Hummus with Preserved Lemon and
    Cumin, *50*, 51–2
Discorides, 132
Doughnuts, Jelly, Israeli (*Soufganiyot*), 322
dressings, 115
  Aioli, 108
  Argan Oil, with Shallots, 93
  Lemon, 102
  My Favorite Vinaigrette, 92

Ferrara, Italy, 62
    Haroset with Chestnuts, Pine Nuts, Pears, and Dried Fruits, 86–7
    Minestra di Fagioli, White Bean Soup, 121
Fessenjan, Persian Walnut and Pomegranate Chicken Stew, 257
feta:
    Bulgarian Eggplant and Cheese *Pashtida*, 192–3
    and Goat Cheese, Whipped, *202*, 203
    Quinoa Salad with Squash, Pecans and, 98
    Spinach *Burekas*, *22*, 23–6
feuilles de brik, 21
Fideos Tostados, Toasted Pasta in Cinnamon-Spiked Tomato Sauce, 172, *173*–4
figs:
    Moroccan Sauce of of Dried Plums, Apricots, Raisins and (*Tanzeya*), 293
    Seven Sacred Species Salad with Wheat Berries, Barley, Olives, Dates, Grapes, Pomegranate and, *114*, 115
filo dough, 243
first courses, *see* starters
First Temple, destruction of, xvii, 81, 249, 257, 277
Fischer, Helen Starkman, 35
fish, xviii, 215–44
    Arctic Char in Spicy Tomato Sauce (*Aharaimi*), *220*, 221–2
    balls, 223
    B'Stilla with Rice Noodles and Vegetables, 242–3
    Cod with Tomatoes, Dried Plums, Onions, and Pine Nuts, *236*, 237–8
    Curry, Bene Israel, with Fresh Ginger, Tamarind, and Cilantro, 231
    Escoveitch with Salmon and Scotch Bonnet Peppers, 218–19
    Gravlaks with Mustard Sauce, 227–8
    Grouper, Brazilian-Belarusian, with Wine, Cilantro, and Oregano, 240–1
    Haddie Paddies, Nova Scotian Fried Haddock Cakes, 232–3
    Herring, Pickled, Spread, 229
    Herring and Apple Bites with Dill and Caper Dipping Sauce, 230
    Salmon, Poached, with Ginger-Cilantro Butter and Spinach, 244

Salmon Gefilte Fish Mold with Horseradish and Beet Sauce, 223–6, *224*
Sardines, Sweet and Sour, with Pine Nuts and Raisins (*Sarde in Saor*), 217
Sardines with Fennel, Onions, Currants, and Pine Nuts over Couscous (*Couscous con le Sarde*), *234*, 235
Snapper with Preserved Lemon and Capers, 239
flatbreads:
    Bukharan Dome-Shaped Crisp (*Noni Toki*), 158
    Matzo, Spiced and Fried, 154–5
    Onion and Poppy Seed (*Pletzel*), *160*, 161–2
    Pita, 144–5
Florence Kahn Bakery and Delicatessan, Paris, 161
Flourless Chocolate Cake, 344, *345*
Fluden de Pasach, Cashew Nut Strudel with Guava and Lime, 337
France, French cooking:
    Bayonnais chocolate production, 314–15
    Caramelized Shallots and Goat Cheese *Tarte Tatin*, 57–8
    Jewish communities of, 110
    Pâte Brisée (Butter Pie Crust), 57
    Scourtins, Buttery Olive Biscuits, 64, *65*
Free-Form Quince Babka, 332–3
Frieda's Inc., 124
Friede, Dror and Sarah, 94
Friedman, Mike, 177
frisensal (crusty pasta with sausage of Venice), 291
Fritters, Zucchini (*Kolokuthokeftedes*), *208*, 209
frosted flake cereal, in Sweet and Crunchy Kugel, 182
Fruit Cobbler, Upside-Down, 330, *331*
frying, fried foods, 70
    Artichokes Jewish-Style (*Carciofi alla Giudia*), 71–4, *72*
    Escoveitch with Salmon and Scotch Bonnet Peppers, 218–19
    Haddock Cakes, Nova Scotian (Haddie Paddies), 232–3
    Jelly Doughnuts, Israeli (*Soufganiyot*), 322
    Matzo, Spiced, 154–5
    Zucchini, Crispy, with Garlic, Basil, and Balsamic Vinegar (*Concia*), 191

Guetta, Hamos, 272–3
Gundi, Chicken and Chickpea Dumplings, *136*, 137–8
Guttfreund, Daniel, 310

Haddie Paddies, Nova Scotian Fried Haddock Cakes, 232–3
Hadgi Badam, Walnut-Almond Macaroons with Raspberry Jam Thumbprint, 308–9
Hallegua, Queenie, 259
Halleq, Persian *Haroset* with Dates, Apples, Pistachios, and Pomegranate Juice, 85
halvah, 302
    Crumble, Dates in Brown Butter with Vanilla Ice Cream, Date Syrup and, *326*, 327–8
Hamantashen, Savory Pumpernickel Caraway, with Caramelized Olive and Dried Plum Filling, 83–4
Hamantashen with Poppy Seed, Chocolate, or Apricot Filling, 311–13, *312*
Hamim-Cholent Hybrid, a Wandering Sabbath Stew, 277–9
Hanau, Naftali, 268
Hanukkah:
    Chopped Chicken Liver, 78–9
    Green *Chile Relleno* Latkes, *204*, 205–6
    Slow-Cooked Brisket with Red Wine, Vinegar, and Mustard, 294–6
    Soufganiyot, Israeli Jelly Doughnuts, 322
    see also frying, fried foods; latkes
Harira, Spiced Moroccan Vegetable Soup with Chickpeas, Cilantro, and Lemon, 122, *123*
harissa, 10–11
haroset, 327
    Brazilian, with Apples, Dates, and Cashews, 88
    brought into Passover Seder, 85
    Ferrara, with Chestnuts, Pine Nuts, Pears, and Dried Fruits, 86–7
    Maine, with Blueberries, Cranberries, and Ginger, 89
    Nutless, with Apples, Dried Fruit, and Wine, 90
    Persian, with Dates, Apples, Pistachios, and Pomegranate Juice (*Halleq*), 85
Harris, John, 327

Hawayij, 133
hazelnuts, in Rugelach with Spicy Chocolate-Nut Filling, 306–7
Health Bread Bakery, Toronto, 35
Henri IV, King, 314
Henriques, Anna Ruth, 218
Henriques, Moses Cohen, 218
Herbert Samuel, Tel Aviv, 102
herring, 230
    and Apple Bites with Dill and Caper Dipping Sauce, 230
    Pickled, Spread, 229
Hilbe, 134
Holland, Shmil, 165
Holocaust, xxiv, 100, 341
    Greece's Jewish communities and, 106, 188
    Italy's Jewish communities and, 71, 86–7
honey, 302, 303
    date, 85, 327
Horseradish and Beet Sauce, *224*, 225–6
hot dogs, in *Hamim-Cholent* Hybrid, a Wandering Sabbath Stew, 277–9
hot sauces:
    harissa, 10–11
    zhug, 12
Huevos Haminados con Spinaci, Long-Cooked Hard-Boiled Eggs with Spinach, *80*, 81–2
Hummus with Preserved Lemon and Cumin, *50*, 51–2
Hungarian Kosher Catering, Brooklyn, 180
Hungary, Hungarian cooking:
    Aranygaluska, Golden Pull-Apart Cake with Walnuts and Apricot Jam, *340*, 341–2
    chicken *paprikash*, xiv
    Chicken *Paprikash* with Dumplings, 256
    Csúsztatott Palacsinta, Apple Pancakes, 32–3
    Delkelekh, Cheese Danish Pastries, 39
    paprika cultivation in, 109, 255
    Paprikás Krumpli, Roasted Potatoes with Onions, 213
    Stuffed Chicken, 265

Ice Cream, Vanilla, Dates in Brown Butter with Date Syrup, Halvah Crumble and, *326*, 327–8
India, Indian cooking, xiii
    Bene Israel Fish Curry with Fresh Ginger, Tamarind, and Cilantro, 231

A Note About the Author

JOAN NATHAN is the author of numerous cookbooks, including *Jewish Cooking in America* and *The New American Cooking,* both of which won the James Beard Award and the IACP Award. She was the host of the nationally syndicated PBS television series *Jewish Cooking in America with Joan Nathan,* based on the book. A frequent contributor to *The New York Times, Tablet* magazine, and other publications, Nathan is the recipient of numerous awards, including James Beard's Who's Who of Food and Beverage in America, Les Dames d'Escoffier's Grande Dame Award, and *Food Arts* magazine's Silver Spoon Award, and she received an honorary doctorate from the Spertus Institute of Jewish Culture in Chicago. She was Guest Curator of Food Culture USA for the 2005 Smithsonian Folklife Festival, and a founding member of Les Dames d'Escoffier, and was appointed to the Kitchen Cabinet of the National Museum of American History. Born in Providence, Rhode Island, Nathan graduated from the University of Michigan with a master's degree in French literature and earned a master's in public administration from Harvard University. For three years she lived in Israel, where she worked for Major Teddy Kollek of Jerusalem. In 1974, working for Mayor Abraham Beame in New York, she cofounded the Ninth Avenue Food Festival. The mother of three grown children, Nathan lives in Washington, D.C., and on Martha's Vineyard with her husband, Allan Gerson.